S0-AIR-321

LANGUAGE AND POLITICS

Contributions to the Sociology of Language

10

Edited by

JOSHUA A. FISHMAN

MOUTON · THE HAGUE · PARIS

Language and Politics

Edited by

WILLIAM M. O'BARR and JEAN F. O'BARR

MOUTON · THE HAGUE · PARIS

ISBN: 90 279 7761 5
Jacket design by Jurriaan Schrofer

Printed in the Netherlands

Foreword

The sociology of language has, of late, been subject to the microsociolinguistic pressures of variational linguistics, on the one hand, and of ethnomethodology, on the other. Both of these pressures have contributed mightily to the growing empirical, methodological, and theoretical rigor of the sociology of language, but they have both exacted a great price in so doing. The price has not only been that of learning 'more and more about less and less' but of doing so under 'self-destruct' instructions which foresee and encourage the demise of the field itself.

Sociology per se, basically a many-splendored discipline with a strong macroscopic wing, has, nevertheless, sorely needed an ally in order to withstand the onslaught of microsociolinguistic astigmatism. Certainly the 'sociology of language' cannot long remain restricted by a notion of society as something no greater than 'conversations' or 'face-to-face interactions' or, indeed, the 'routines of everyday life'. This is not to say that all of the foregoing do not exist within a greater social context, but only to stress that it is that very context that needs to be seen.

The volume which the O'Barrs have put together is refreshingly and unabashedly macro-interested, although it is as microtechnical as any rigorist might desire. As an anthropologist and a political scientist working together, they have provided a prospective map of a field that sorely needs to be formulated: the political sociology of language. It is high time that we all returned to social reality in our concern for language in society, and there is nothing more real than the allocation of power in social relationships. This allocation so frequently either follows language lines or invites language demarcations corresponding to it that the many examples attested to in this volume cannot but direct our attention to the larger scene that has so often escaped the attention of sociolinguistic specialists.

Our innocence of nations and other political units and of their impact on language behavior has not merely been tantamount to overlooking the elephants at the zoo. In addition, due to individual biases, it has been 'justified' theoretically, thus finally presenting as a virtue the necessary astigmatism to which all young and volatile disciplines are prone. The O'Barrs have put the 'nation' back into the agenda of serious sociolinguistic researchers and, as a result, it will now be more difficult to forget it or any other societal structure for the control and organization of scarce resources.

It may be, of course, that nations are prominent influences in societally patterned language behavior only when the nations are as young, as raw, as formative as are Tanzania, India, and Papua New Guinea today. Older, more secure, more successfully routinized nations may be far less prominent configurations in the social behavior of their citizens. However, only volumes with the temerity to raise big issues and to view them unflinchingly will bring us closer to understanding such or other macrosociological factors in the lives of men. It is precisely because the O'Barrs did not fear to take a big step into the unknown that they and their associates deserve to be congratulated and that we must acknowledge our vast indebtedness to them.

With the appearance of this volume we may hope that conferences, courses, and careers devoted to an explication of 'language and politics' will begin to multiply. The world of scholarship at large, and sociolinguistic scholarship in particular, would both benefit thereby.

Yeshiva University
New York

Joshua A. Fishman
General Editor

Acknowledgments

A generous conference grant from the Program for the Comparative Study of Legislatures at Duke University provided funds for a symposium held at Quail Roost Conference Center near Durham, North Carolina, January 18–20, 1973, where many of these papers were discussed. All contributors to the volume attended the sessions with the exceptions of Jyotirindra Das Gupta, John Flynn, Barbara Flynn, and Ranier Lang, who, for various reasons, were not able to be present. Supplementary funds from the Programs of African and South Asian Studies at Duke University are gratefully acknowledged.

Without the considerable efforts put into this volume by those who have contributed papers to it, the study of language and politics would be in an even more rudimentary state than it is today. In addition to those who have contributed directly, a number of other persons helped in various ways. Of particular assistance at critical times were the suggestions and comments of Maurice Bloch, Don Brenneis, Paula Brown, Ronald Casson, John Condon, Carol Eastman, Ainslee Embree, Charles Ferguson, Joshua Fishman, Richard Fox, Paul Freidrich, Marc Galanter, Yash Ghai, Joseph Guillotte, John Gumperz, Jay Hakes, Raymond Hopkins, Dell Hymes, Byron Mook, Samuel Mushi, Baldev Raj Nayar, Ralph Nicholas, Karl Reisman, Alan Rew, Michelle Rosaldo, Harvey Sacks, Emanuel Schegloff, Jonathan Silverstone, Richard Sisson, Arthur Sorenson, Franklin Southworth, Marilyn Strathern, Mark Tessler, Vernon van Dyke, and Brian Weinstein.

We also acknowledge the support and encouragement of Allan Kornberg and Joel Smith of the Program for the Comparative Study of Legislatures at Duke. Without their faith in our project from the very beginning, this book might never have been. Two student assistants, Eugene Conti and Susan McDaniel, put innumerable hours and much effort into background research and preparation of the manuscript, and their untiring work behind the scenes helped make the Quail Roost Conference run smoothly. Finally, Jean Bowe, Sylvia Terrell, Dina Smith, Anna Stinson, and Dot Weathers provided great assistance through their persistent care and hard work in the typing of the manuscript.

Duke University,
Durham, N. C.

William M. O'Barr
Jean F. O'Barr

Table of contents

List of Maps and Tables

WILLIAM M. O'BARR

1

The Study of Language and Politics

The study of language and politics is of potential interest to most of the social sciences, to development planners, and to those whose primary interests center on politics or linguistics. Yet, none of these specialists have paid enough attention to the language-politics relationship for its study to achieve subdisciplinary prominence. What concern has been devoted to it has been subsumed under studies of sociolinguistics, sociology of language, political science, anthropology, jurisprudence, and economic development. There are no important theories about how language is different from other political issues (if indeed it is), about how what might be called *politico-linguistics* differs from sociolinguistics, or about how language factors intervene in and thus affect the outcome of political processes. This volume is devoted to a consideration of such issues, but, despite its length, it cannot explore all of them fully. Yet, the broad range of topics which it does cover is more than enough to demonstrate that the study of language and politics is at once timely, socially relevant, and theoretically interesting.

Most former European colonial outposts in the Third World achieved their independence over a decade ago. In the meantime, their political goals and interests have shifted from mobilization to achieve nationhood to a focus on the issues of economic, political, and national cultural development. Almost without exception, the multilingual nature of these countries has brought linguistic concerns into the foreground; and, in many of them, a consideration of the effects of the country's linguistic profile upon development efforts, communication, education, and the nation state itself has entered the national political dialogue. The sorts of practical solutions which have been suggested have not, of course, been the same everywhere, since each nation's linguistic constitution and developmental history is, to a large degree, unique. Yet, for the moment at least, much political attention continues to be devoted to language, while the linguistic complexity of these countries, at the same time, appears to shape and influence – even to limit – the political process itself.

The extraordinary growth of sociolinguistics in the last decade or so has shown convincingly that language is closely linked to its context and that isolating it artificially for study ignores its complex and intricate relation to society. Linguistic studies which depend upon elicitations from only one or a few informants are now recognized as leaving unanswered many significant questions about the relation between language and the social context in which it is always embedded. In some quarters, such studies are even passé. It has become widely accepted as axiomatic by many sociolinguists that much of the heretofore unexplained variation in a speech community reflects both the strata within the community at any given point in time and the lag resulting from different rates of linguistic change in its different sectors. Language is no longer viewed as a closed system, but as one which is in perpetual flux. And linguistic change, once thought to be impossible to describe until it had happened, is being studied in process (see, for example, Labov 1965). Many linguists believe that language is basically neutral and that its variability reflects social differences, making it a particularly sensitive mirror of its context (see Sankoff, Chapter 14). Views such as these, and empirical investigations predicated upon them, are new and revolutionary. It is perhaps much too soon to speculate where they will ultimately lead. Within this new tradition (and the interest it has generated along with the number of practitioners it has attracted suggest that it is not too soon to refer to it as such), relatively little attention has, however, been paid to the political uses of language.

It is not only linguistics which stands to grow from a concern with language and politics. Students of the political process have paid relatively little concern to the myriad ways in which their subject is intertwined with language. All too often, politics and government are explained as self-enclosed systems. Too much attention devoted to the economic or psychological bases of politics is likely to be considered as ventures into unprofitable reductionism. The language of politics and the communications systems which underlie and thus support political systems have received only a very small proportion of the total effort expended by researchers from the many disciplines interested in understanding politics and government. Whether the approach is from political science, anthropology, sociology, or jurisprudence, sharper focus on language portends the distinct possibility of contributing to our greater understanding of political and legal processes by illuminating some aspects which are poorly understood at present. Questions which need answering are: how is language used as a resource by individual politicians and governments? how does multilingualism complicate the political life of a nation? and are monolingual nations somehow immune or less liable to difficulties stemming from language? There are surely other questions as well, which, like these, may shed considerable insight into the nature of politics itself as we begin to have more substantial answers to them.

These, then, are some of the reasons which motivate our study of language and politics. Before attempting to provide a framework for the chapters which follow by looking more deeply into types of language-politics relations, offering a rationale for our choice of case study materials and levels of focus, and drawing together some comparative generalizations based upon our findings, we must attempt to explain what we mean by each of the terms *language* and *politics.* Since this is not the place for a treatise on the nature of either concept in its own right, we shall only attempt to circumscribe the range of our concerns.

We use *language* to encompass the total verbal communication system, spoken and/or written, and aspects of it. Although this usage may be considered by some to be much too imprecise, we feel justified in retaining a broad orientation to the communication system since our objective is to include any aspects of language and speech behavior which may be relevant to the study of political processes. We have taken care not to limit our concerns unnecessarily at this stage. Some of the aspects of language which we consider in relation to politics in this volume are the jargon of politics and law; various forms of esoteric speech (both whole 'languages' and 'styles'[1] or 'registers'[2] within particular codes); dialect (but as we shall see the distinction between language and dialect is not only hard to draw but often pedantic and unnecessary when we focus on its involvement and connections to the political process); various rhetorical and oratorical devices `(such as hyperboles, code-switching,[3] speech-making, and the like); and multilingualism. Thus, our concerns with language are broad enough indeed to make them synonomous with most aspects of spoken and/or written communication systems. In considering their effects upon politics, we have tried to include whatever aspects of language might be relevant and to ignore none by too narrow a definition.

Similarly, in *politics,* we include both formal governmental institutions and non-institutional power relationships. Although we have found it necessary to place some practical limits on the range of political situations which we would consider in this volume, it should be kept in mind that we do not envision the same limits when considering the connections of linguistic phenomena to politics. Much of interest in the study of politics is associated with governmental institutions, and indeed the studies in the chapters which follow demonstrate this well. But all of politics, all power relationships, are not to be contained within such formal institutions. Interpersonal interaction often involves power struggles and it commonly proceeds in a verbal medium; and as more attention is devoted to language phenomena at this level, it will surely prove to be a very fruitful area in the study of language and politics. Thus, when considering its relations to language and the communication system, we believe that our understanding of the political should not exclude any categories of power relations which might be relevant, whether or not they are to be found associated with formal institutions of government.

LANGUAGE-POLITICS RELATIONSHIPS

One of the most basic ways in which language and politics are related is through the fact that a verbal communication system of some sort is associated with every system which we would call *government.* Brute force and physical coercion are used all too frequently as modes of human interaction; yet we know of no system of government which does not involve the use of language. Those which rely heavily upon force and coercion for support have at their core verbal communication systems, for even colonizers in linguistically alien environments must at some point communicate via language. Language is thus a prerequisite upon which all governmental systems are predicated.

Human political communities are embedded in a vast array of different linguistic systems which range, at one extreme, from those having a relatively homogeneous language known throughout the various levels of the community to those, at the other extreme, having several heterogeneous languages distributed in some complex fashion across the population. What we do not know at this point in our understanding of language-politics relationships is the minimal communication prerequisites for governmental systems to operate. We can conceive, for example, of a hypothetical political community whose members each speak two languages, with each language having only two speakers. Paths of communication from the center to the peripheries and elsewhere in such a community would be so limited that the term *community* would not itself seem appropriate. Putting aside such fabrications, we are left with the question of what relationship exists between the political life of empirical communities and the verbal exchange systems which make interaction, and hence their governments, possible. Besides Deutsch (1953), Fishman, Ferguson, and Das Gupta (1968), Rogers (1969), Kelman (1971), and a few others who have concerned themselves with the problems of building national communications systems in developing countries, few scholars have concerned themselves with variations in verbal communication systems and the kinds of human societies with which different systems are associated.

Beyond the fact that governments are everywhere embedded in verbal communication systems, there are at least three important categories of relations between language and politics: (1) those situations in which governments intervene in and attempt to control the communication system itself; (2) those in which language factors intervene in and thus affect the processes of government and politics; and (3) those in which language and politics are in mutual interaction, feeding back upon one another.

Politics/Government affecting language. When we ordinarily think of language and politics, many of the situations which readily come to mind are those which we might describe as involving language as a dependent variable in the relationship. We refer here to those instances where governments attempt to manipulate or control the linguistic make-up of communities under their jurisdiction. One of the most common of such situations is the setting of language policies by national governments which state in specific terms what languages are to be used, when, by whom, and for what purposes. Related to this is what has come to be known as *language planning* in which governments and/or international bodies consciously attempt to assess linguistic needs, problems, and priorities and to establish guidelines whereby these goals may be met. Throughout recorded history, governments appear to have considered language policies to be within the domain of their jurisdiction and they have legislated and decreed about them, generally attempting to manipulate communication systems to suit political objectives.

A brief but provocative essay entitled 'Language in a Political Situation' (1968) by the linguist Jan Knappert reads like a catalogue of many well-known examples. His summary of the Soviet manipulation of languages in Southern Siberia is representative of the general phenomenon:

'In Southern Siberia, the Turkic dialects, of which the most prominent were Turkmen, Özbek, Kara-Kalpak, and Kirghiz, were not used in literature; one literary language was in use for most of Turkestan: Jaghatay (Djagadai), written with Arabic characters. Soon after the Russian revolution, different orthographies were devised for each of these dialects, based on Roman script. About ten years afterwards, in the middle thirties, these Roman alphabets were abolished, and replaced by newly designed orthographies based on the Cyrillic script. This and the many Russian loanwords give the impression that the purpose of these languages is only to be stepping stones for students whose higher degrees will be all in Russian. In this way the speakers of the Turkic dialects will be tied to Russian as the central language of the country, and will be less conscious of their relations with their neighbors. They are not able to understand them as soon as the conversation turns to a more educated subject: then Russian has to be used (Knappert 1968:64).'

Many new states include language engineering schemes as aspects of their national development programs. The ostensible reason usually given for such programs is facilitating national communication and fostering national identification; yet those involved in the formulation and realization of language policies are quick to recognize the enormous power over people which stems from the ability to manipulate their language. The recent volume *Can Language Be Planned?* (1971) edited by Joan Rubin and Björn Jernudd contains case studies of language planning and its effects in Ireland, Israel, the Philippines, East Africa, Turkey, Indonesia, and Bangladesh. Although primarily concerned with technical and economic problems associated with language planning, the volume contains many insights into the politics of language which is an invariable concomitant of the planning process.

Some instances of governments affecting language may result from grass-roots mobilization, as for example in the case of Canadian bilingualism. During the last decade or so, the mobilization of concern among French-speaking Canadians over the inferior status of their language in both governmental affairs and the private sector led to the appointment of a Royal Commission on Bilingualism. A number of recommendations made by the commission were put into effect through the Official Languages Act of 1967 which made both French and English official languages. The government initiated specific recruitment programs designed to draw French-speakers into many top positions. In addition, the occupants of certain positions in some districts are required to be proficient bilinguals. A number of reforms have been recommended for industry and the non-governmental sector as well; however, changes here are somewhat more difficult to effect. The recent history of Quebec thus shows how French-speaking Canadians who had been systematically denied, through language requirements, access to certain positions of power and prestige mobilized to press for changes in the official status of their languages – changes which are beginning now to open channels once closed to the French-speaking community.

Language affecting the political process. Social scientists have paid less attention to a second category of language-politics relationships. Here, we include all sorts of situations in which language is a resource in the political process, whether in the hands of individual actors or of governments, and in which it is used to control, manipulate, and achieve political ends. Only some of the situations which fall into this category result directly from language policies set by governments. A great many result from the naturally occurring linguistic and communication systems in which the political process is embedded. Either way, there is much evidence that extant communication systems, either in whole or part, play a variety of roles in political processes. Looking at one of the first situations which came to our attention and which stimulated our early thinking about language-politics relations in general will serve as an introduction to this category of concerns.

In a paper in which she examines the political organization of Kuma society at three points in its recent history, Marie Reay (1964) makes some provocative, but not fully exploited, suggestions about the ways in which bilingualism affects the political process in the highlands area of New Guinea which she studied. First, she reports the case of Nopnop, a political entrepreneur who turned the advent of the Australians to his own personal advantage. Unlike most of his fellows, Nopnop went out of his way to learn to speak Tok Pisin[4] at a time when very few highlanders knew it. As a result, he managed to become employed as a government interpreter. He used the cash he earned and his position to rise in the traditional status system. Although he was not the sort of person who would have enjoyed much success in the traditional system, Nopnop's early knowledge of Tok Pisin and his continual efforts at manipulating the political environment eventually won him a nomination for the House of Assembly.

Elsewhere in the same article, Reay reports the replacement of the *luluai-tultul* system of colonial administration by a system of local government councils around 1960. Confused as to whom they should select as representatives to the council, the Kuma 'chose the few men over 30 who spoke [Tok Pisin], irrespective of any other qualifications or disqualifications they may have had for the post' (Reay 1964 : 251).

Reay does not fully analyze in this very brief article the effects of bilingualism on local-level politics in the New Guinea Highlands. But since only some members of the community are bilingual, it is important to ask who the speakers of Tok Pisin are and to know the conditions under which they learned to speak it — for these appear to be critical factors in understanding the access to political power and prestige in comtemporary Kuma society.

Reay's comments about language and politics in a New Guinea society reminded us of a different sort of connection we had observed in Tanzania during 1967 and 1968. In one of the Pare communities where we lived and worked, we observed the operation of a system of double-talk which was used repeatedly by the members of a local council to deceive itinerant government officers. Verbal planning for government initiated projects, which took place during council meetings, was elaborate. Time and again, the government men left happy, thinking that they had witnessed the realistic planning of practical community development projects. The local people, using their sophisticated system of double-talk, actually had no intention of carrying out the projects which they planned so carefully in the meetings. Although communication problems did not seem to be *why* the development projects continued to fail in this particular community, the communication system was certainly a major key to *how* the development plans were impeded time and again.[5]

It was these two cases, Reay's brief but provocative statements about Kuma and our own fieldwork in Tanzania, which started us to thinking about language and politics and gave rise in time to the kernel idea for this volume. While we were also interested in the sorts of situations we have labeled *politics/government affecting language*, we wete more intrigued by the less well described and understood situations which fall into our second category, *language affecting politics.* As we talked among ourselves and with others whom we found to share our interests, we realized that there was indeed a third category representing a synthesis of the first and second.

Language and politics in mutual interaction. The pragmatic necessity of relatively synchronic field studies often precludes our understanding of the diachronic interrelationships between language and politics in which each affects the other in a feedback system. Real world examples of this sort appear to occur in all situations where language policies are set by governments or where language repertoires of communities are consciously manipulated for political purposes. The manipulation of language and communication systems per se qualifies for inclusion in our first category above. But once the policies are effected, once a shift in the communication system has taken place, social life proceeds in an altered sociocultural environment. Such environmental changes may in turn affect the political process in various ways, giving rise to new situations, which, if seen in isolation from their larger context, qualify for inclusion in our second category as instances of *language affecting politics.* The language-politics relationship in the three countries (Tanzania, India, and Papua New Guinea) where we focus most of our attention in later chapters of this book certainly qualify as situations where language and politics are in mutual interaction and feedback upon one another. Yet, the overall process is so large that it is difficult to conceptualize its multifaceted complexity at once. Few specific studies are able to touch on the totality of the language-politics relationship and the complex chain of reactions of *language-affecting-politics-affecting-language-affecting-politics—etc.* We should not, however, fail to reflect upon the larger and more general context as we focus upon various problems of language and politics in particular cases.

THE CONCERNS OF THIS VOLUME

In the fall of 1971 when this volume on language and politics in developing countries was first conceived, we began to think about the sorts of situations which we would include in an initial investigation into language-politics relationships. Within the academic disciplines of the two editors (anthropology for WMO and political science for JFO), we began to find that a great many field researchers had recognized the influence of language upon the political process. Yet, we could find few indeed who had studied such relationships in sufficient detail or given enough concern to them to warrant papers based on their own field studies. As we discussed our ideas with other anthropologists and political scientists, we drew up a list of twenty of thirty persons who might contribute papers at a conference which we intended to host at Duke University during 1972. The list included persons whose interests ranged widely across levels of governmental institutions where language issues were of significant concern, across countries in the Third World, across vastly different linguistic environments, and across the academic disciplines concerned with the study of linguistic and political processes. We were faced with a dilemma of choosing between a set of participants representing the widest possible range of qualified specialists who might illuminate language-politics relationships and restricting our concerns in some ways so as to provide reasonable depth and comparability among a smaller number of case studies. We chose the latter alternative primarily because we had so often been unsatisfied by general collections of papers which were able to do little more than whet our appetites. We wanted more than a mere collection of papers on language and politics in developing countries. After much discussion between ourselves and our colleagues at Duke, particularly Allan Kornberg and Joel Smith, we arrived at a structure which provided the framework for both a symposium held at Quail Roost Conference Center near Duke in January of 1973 and for the present volume.

Our objective was to select three countries which had somewhat different linguistic profiles (such as degrees of societal multilingualism, extent of individual bilingualism, uses of lingua francas and European languages, literacy rates, and the like) but which had basically similar governmental institutions. We wanted to know how different kinds of linguistic environments affect the functioning of formal institutions of government. Our own research had taken us to Tanzania in 1967–68 and we were keen on examining language and politcs in that country. In order to provide some controls, we decided that the other two countries should be based on British models of government rather than further complicating our comparisons by adding nations whose governmental structures were derived from other traditions. This narrowed our choices significantly. We decided upon India next since there are few nations which can rival its linguistic complexity and where language has proved to be so great a political issue. Moreover, a large number of anthropologists, political scientists, and linguists had conducted field studies in India and we felt that it would not be difficult to find a large number of potential participants interested in our undertaking. Papua New Guinea was chosen as the third country because it offered significant parallels and contrasts to the other two. Unlike either, it had not yet achieved its independence[6] and would therefore provide an opportunity to consider language and politics just prior to independence. Its linguistic situation was complex: there were a large number of language communities with relatively small numbers of speakers, and one or two lingua francas in addition to English which were fairly widely known. And, like the other two countries, Papua New Guinea had been studied from many disciplinary vantages.

Once we had settled on the countries, we established some limits on the sorts of political arenas in which we wanted to consider the language-politics relationship. The concerns of the Committee for the Comparative Study of Legislative Institutions which provided generous funds for the support of the Quail Roost Conference shaped our consideration to some extent. Recognizing that all that is of interest in politics is by no means localized within formal governmental institutions, we decided to set our primary focus on legislative institutions, broadly defined, in the three countries and proceed from there. To us, legislative institutions included not only national legislatures but all sorts of sub-national and local-level decision making bodies: state legislatures, district and local councils, and courts. These limitations seemed reasonable ones since we wanted to look across levels of governmental institutions and retain at the same time enough of a base for comparability.

Thus, in deciding whom to invite as participants in the symposium and ultimately as contributors to this book, we hoped to have at least one person who could speak authoritatively about language-politics relations in each of the categories shown in Table 1.1. We by no means expected that single individuals could represent all the institutions and concerns which might fall into each box in the table. But we did feel that anyone who had direct research experience in the area could inform us about the problems which *in his opinion* were of relevance in studying those sorts of institutions in the particular country where he had worked. And, we felt, he could speak in comparative terms about the issues which did or did not arise in similar institutions in the other two countries and throughout the governmental bureaucracy in the country of his expertise. We have indicated in the table the persons whose papers most directly represent these various levels.

In presenting each of the three cases, we have included two general papers which provide the necessary background to the linguistic constitution of each country on the one hand and the range of its contemporary political institutions on the other. Each overview is written by a person thoroughly familiar with the country and reflects his assessment of the current linguistic or political environment in which the more detailed studies are embedded. The linguistic overviews were included among the papers presented at the original conference where they proved to be of tremendous assistance. So many questions arose during our discussions at Quail Roost about the organization and genesis of the governmental institutions mentioned in the case studies that we have felt it appropriate to include institutional overviews in the volume as well. It is our intention, therefore, to help those whose understanding of Tanzania, India, or Papua New Guinea may be limited through providing them with these linguistic and institutional overviews.

Table 1.1 *Levels of analysis across the three cases*[a]

	Tanzania	India	Papua New Guinea
National legislatures	J. O'Barr (4)	J. Das Gupta (10) M. L. Apte (11)	E. Wolfers[b]
Local councils	W. O'Barr (7)	F. G. Bailey (13)	R. F. Salisbury (17)
Courts	M. J. Swartz (6) F. DuBow (5)	R. L. Kidder (12)	R. Lang (16)

[a] Numbers in parentheses refer to chapters in this book. Many persons consider a wide range of topics and levels in their papers and this scheme is meant only to refer to the particular levels of expertise for which we invited the person to participate.

[b] Dr. Edward Wolfers, although unable to attend the Quail Roost Conference, kindly sent a tape recording containing his observations on language in the Papua New Guinea House of Assembly. Since Papua New Guinea became independent in December, 1973, he has served as a consultant in the Chief Minister's Office. The many demands which this consultancy has placed on him have made it impossible to complete his paper in time to meet the production schedule for this volume.

Although we have not been able to include all disciplines for which language and politics may have relevance, we have asked several persons to include assessments of the issues in this volume as they relate to their own disciplines. These persons and their disciplines are:

J. Rubin	Sociolinguistics (18)
W. O'Barr	Political Anthropology (19)
M. Jewell	Legislative Institutions (20)
H. Bretton	Political Science (21)
A. Leibowitz	Law (22)

LEGISLATURES, COUNCILS, AND COURTS

We have already disclaimed any association with the contention that all of interest in the study of politics is to be found in formal governmental institutions. There are, however, important theoretical and practical reasons for limiting our focus to formal institutions at this relatively early point in the development of language and politics studies.

First of all, it has been frequently assumed in the literature on political development that linguistic diversity is an obstacle in the way of efficient government. Language is believed to be connected to the day-to-day difficulties faced by many governments, especially those in ethnically and linguistically complex countries (Almond and Coleman 1960; Pye 1966). Solving their linguistic problems, the argument continues, would result in the development of more viable national political systems. Although such speculations about the probable effects of linguistic diversity on political development have been common, there have been virtually no attempts to demonstrate just how this diversity actually complicates the business of government. Since formal arenas – legislatures, councils, and courts, or some variants of them – are found as parts of most political systems, they provide some quite specific contexts to examine the degree to which different linguistic environments really do affect the workings of government.

The close historic connections of courts, councils, and legislatures both in European and other cultural traditions is a second reason for considering them together. In Europe, the history of formal political institutions reveals a similar process whereby a more generalized court/council/legislature evolved into separate and differentiated institutions serving executive, judicial, and legislative functions (Shepard 1933; Radin 1933). This process of structural elaboration and functional differentiation of formal institutions had been more or less completed in Europe at the start of the age of exploration and colonization of the non-Western world. European administrators of colonial territories, however, typically encountered societies with generalized political institutions which had not undergone the same processes of structural and functional differentiation that had occurred in Europe. The transfer of European models of government went hand in hand with colonialism; and consequently, *differentiated* institutions were introduced to India, the Americas, Africa, and the Pacific Islands as the indigenous forms were found to be inappropriate adjuncts to the colonizers' ideas of efficient government. Richards (1971:9–10) describes the efforts of the British to introduce their models of local government to Africa:

'Colonial administrators . . . were not unnaturally impatient of large meetings which slowed down procedure and held up the type of discussions which they felt to be the proper tasks of local government councils. As time went on they began to try to stream-line the procedure by fixing the personnel of councils, whether by nomination or election. The new activities which local government councils were to undertake also demanded more specialised knowledge and a European-type education. Hence the efforts of colonial administrations during the thirties and forties to introduce new elements into traditional councils such as teachers and members of welfare services, and to set up small specialist sub-committees such as finance and education committees.

'The traditional councils had . . . multiple functions, and this was natural in types of societies in which most authorities, family or lineage heads, village headmen, and chiefs had multiple functions as leaders of kinship groups, judges, economic or military leaders or ritual specialists. British colonial authorities, in contrast, tried to define very carefully the powers of different councils they "recognised" and to assign different duties to each level of council, village, district or tribe, and . . . they also tried in time to separate judicial courts from local government bodies. The allocation of annual budgets and sometimes rate-raising powers to the most important councils in a tribal area or a town, made the definition of each body's powers even more exact.

'The priorities of both types of administration were also different. Colonial officers judged the success of a local council in terms of the welfare activities it undertook, the speed with which it acted, and its skill and probity in handling its budget. The traditional council seems to have put first its duty to settle disputes. . . .'

Jean O'Barr's overview (Chapter 3) of the history of Tanzanian governmental institutions shows a specific instance of the process which Richards describes. Richards' remarks are by no means limited to Africa, however. The papers by the Flynns (Chapter 9) and Staats and Conti (Chapter 15) show the replication of the same basic process in the colonization of India and New Guinea. The fact that all three types of institutions were derived from a common structural antecedent makes their consideration together particularly appropriate.

A third reason for a joint treatment of these institutions lies in their structural similarity, due, at least in part, to their common genesis. From our point of view, the most basic similarity of relevance to language and politics is the fact that all these institutions are verbal exchange systems in which the primary business is conducted through discussion, argumentation, discourse, speech-making, questioning, etc., most usually through the spoken word but at times through writing. Although the use of specialized jargon, formal or institutional language, limitations on appropriate topics, a more restrictive turn-taking system, and the like make the communications systems of formal institutions different from ordinary conversation, all of them are nonetheless verbal exchange systems. From the point of view of sociolinguistics, it is this aspect of formal institutions which draws our attention and which provides the base for considering in the chapters which follow some of the ways in which the particularities of the communications systems operative in courts, councils, and legislatures *affect* the operation of these institutions.

Thus, by focusing on certain of the formal institutions of government in Tanzania, India, and Papua New Guinea, we hope to discover whether the different language situations of these countries result in different problems and obstacles in the way of local and national governments. Related to the academic concerns in our minds is the practical question of the degree to which resources put into engineering linguistic change would actually result in more efficient and effective organs of government, however these might be defined in each of the three particular countries.

ISSUES RAISED BY THE CONTRIBUTORS

The contributors to this volume were asked to focus upon the ways in which language factors affect political processes in formal arenas. Beyond that, they were given carte blanche. We offered only the most rudimentary outline of possible topics and provided synopses of only two cases of language affecting politics (Reay's Kuma materials described on page 8 of this chapter and William O'Barr's materials on *kingua* described in Chapter 7). Without exception, the uses of language in political contexts which are considered in the specific case studies in this volume can all be said to be one or another aspect of the general use of language as a political resource. Individual political actors, groups with political goals, and governments alike were found to employ language in goal-oriented strategies. The papers which the contributors wrote ranged from consideration of the individual's linguistic and oratorical skills, or the lack of them, to the establishment of language policies setting out linguistic requirements for participation in political arenas. Whatever our level of focus (individual, group, or government) and across formal institutional types (legislatures, local councils, and courts), we found language making its way into and becoming intertwined with politics.

Rather than detailing the issues raised in each of the papers at this point, we believe it will be of greater utility to the reader to provide a few introductory comments and suggestions in the form of an editorial preface to each of the three cases. There are, however, a number of different themes which cross-cut the papers in various ways. Readers may wish to study certain chapters in conjunction rather than following the country by country order in which we have presented them. Some of these themes and the relevant chapters are:

National legislatures	Chapters 3, 4, 9, 10, 11, 15, 20
Courts	Chapters 3, 5, 6, 9, 12, 15, 16, 22
Local councils	Chapters 3, 4, 7, 9, 13, 15, 17, 19
Language used to control access to political arenas	Chapters 3, 4, 5, 11, 12, 13, 16, 19, 20, 21, 22
Language used as a political resource	Chapters 6, 7, 12, 13, 14, 16, 17, 19, 21

A word should be said about the level of analysis undertaken by most of the contributors to this volume and its relationship to the total range of phenomena which are ultimately of interest in the study of language and politics. Our concerns in this volume lean toward what we might call the *macro* level of analysis. By this we mean large-scale, national, subnational, or at least community-level problems. There are many issues at the level of interpersonal interaction and of non-govermental power relations which are excluded from our concern. A focus on *micro* level problems of language and politics portends significant possibilities of adding to our understanding of human social relationships on the level of interactional phenomena. Brown and Gliman's classic study (1960) of pronouns of power versus solidarity, several recent studies of verbal dueling (see, for example, Dundes et al. 1972; Labov 1972), and ethnomethodological concerns with conversation and greeting behavior (see, for example, Sacks, Schegloff, and Jefferson 1974) are just some of the kinds of issues which can be studied on this level. Each of them can be seen as involving the working out of status and power relationships among individuals, and in that sense, they are of interest to language and politics. It has not been possible in this volume to handle all the interesting questions which are relevant at what we have termed the macro level of analysis. We have only been able to scratch the surface of power relations at the micro level. The thoughtful reader will discover many potential avenues where the concerns represented in this collection can be followed up and expanded. We believe, however, that there is enough here to serve as a stimulus to his thinking about some of the more interesting research problems.

COMPARATIVE GENERALIZATIONS

At the outset, we had expected to find significant differences among the patterns of language-politics interactions resulting from the different linguistic situations and/or the different colonial and developmental histories of the three countries. The conclusion which has emerged from our comparative study of the three countries, however, points us in the opposite direction. Despite some important differences among the three, we have found that language is used as a political resource *in roughly similar ways* in all three countries.

We are led to the conclusion that the acquisition of a single language or the resolution of conflict between two or more languages will not automatically solve or eliminate the sorts of political difficulties which have been considered in this book. The real issues are political, not linguistic; and their solutions must lie in the resolution of differentials in power relations. Language is a common medium for the expression of political difficulties; it is the *how* of many political struggles and manipulations in political systems, but it is not the *why*. The chapters which follow provide ample documentation of these conclusions.

Our comparison of *courts* across the three cases has revealed that the use of a single language is no guarantee of an open court system to which all segments of a population have more or less equal access. More complex linguistic environments provide a greater range of devices whereby access can be denied, but the decision to provide widespread popular access to courts or to concentrate its power in the hands of a select minority is political. Legal jargon can serve the same functions in a so-called monolingual country as different languages in a multilingual country. Barriers may be erected by entire languages or by specialized styles within particular languages.

Both Kidder (Chapter 12) and Lang (Chapter 16) have shown us how multilingualism is used by linguistic brokers (both lawyers and court interpreters) – whether consciously or not – to manipulate and shape the outcome of cases which lie before the court. Yet, the very sorts of manipulations which they describe are not limited to courts where the language of litigation and of the litigant may be different. Does not the lawyer in an American court act as broker between the esoteric speech requirements of the formal court and his client? And is there not, in the 'monolingual' American court, much the same potential for lawyer acting as linguistic broker as he interprets and 'translates' the court proceedings to his client? We must not be misled into believing that such processes are limited to those situations where the 'language' of the court and of the litigant are different, for the discrepancy between ordinary speech and that of most courts makes all societies to some degree multilingual. In short, the process can operate at the level of whole languages, of dialectical differences, or within what is popularly believed to be the same language. It is perhaps most innocuous in those latter cases where, like America, the litigant is often led to believe the court uses his language. Where court language differs significantly from ordinary speech, the litigant is perhaps more likely to be on guard, although he may be able to do little about what he suspects are incidents in the court which operate against his best interest. Edelman (1964) has argued that one of the functions of legal language in the United States is to allow lawyers to interpret it as broadly as different occasions demand. That legal language is precise is a carefully protected myth. If it were so, we should not have so much need of lawyers to interpret it for us.

DuBow shows us how language is a means of *facilitating* equal access to courts in Tanzania. It would be facile to argue that the use of Swahili per se makes Tanzanian courts egalitarian. The distribution of Swahili across the population in Tanzania, while widespread, is nonetheless unequal. Such inequality – the common state of all or most languages, as sociolinguistics reminds us – can be used easily either to give or to deny access. Which purpose it is actually used for is *not* answerable by looking at language.

In *local councils,* we see again how language is used in the service of politics. Two of the papers show how language can be used to separate councils either from their subordinate constituents (Bailey, Chapter 13) or from the superordinate government (W. O'Barr, Chapter 7). In neither case, however, are the problems linguistic ones. For the people of Mlimani in Tanzania, language is a means of separating themselves from intruders. Why they should wish to separate themselves cannot be understood as an aspect of the communications system but must be seen in the light of the dynamics of local community politics. Using his Orissa materials for inspiration, Bailey shows how councils, under certain conditions, develop esoteric institutional speech. The tendency is greatest, he argues, when a council has both power and legitimacy. When there are shifts in these *political* dimensions, the language policy of the council is likely to reflect the changes. Councils with declining power and legitimacy, for example, are not likely to maintain esoteric institutional speech and will probably move in the direction of using a communication medium close to ordinary speech. In both cases, however, language is a tool, a resource, in the political process, not the source of the council's success or debility. Similarly, Salisbury (Chapter 17) shows how the Tolai of New Britain use their own language in local councils to symbolize ethnic exclusivity, but again this is a political process reflected in and symbolized by language. Tolai ethnic sentiments are not caused by language exclusivity, rather language is a means of demonstrating separatism. Salisbury's paper is especially illuminating since he has managed to show us how language attitudes and usage patterns among the Tolai have changed over time *as political shifts have occurred.*

Similar generalizations apply to *national legislatures.* While it is doubtlessly the case that legislative bodies with a minimum of linguistic complexity have fewer technical problems which stand in the way of communication, it is important to recognize that linguistic homogeneity of the legislators is no guarantee that they *will* communicate with one another. Moreover, when the desire to communicate is great, technical problems can usually mangae to be solved. Whether the linguistic constitution of a particular legislature impedes communication or not is, we suggest, more appropriately considered as a political rather than a linguistic problem.

Apte shows in Chapter 11 how language issues can provide a basis for political argumentation and cleavage within the Indian political context. Language merely symbolizes the regional cultural differences which are present within the nation of India. It is not the sole reason for them. Within the Indian Parliament, language has provided an easy and convenient focus for argumentation. Yet, if language were not available for this purpose, we suspect that another focus for regional politics would be found.

In Tanzania, replacing English with Swahili in the national legislature seems an important symbol of the Africanization of the governmental infrastructure which remains as a legacy of colonial Tanganyika. While a single language facilitates communication among legislators, whatever genuine solidarity exists stems from political loyalties and commitment to the regime. In Tanzania, language may facilitate the national political process but it by no means single-handedly forges Tanzanian unity. At best, it is a catalyst for national political unity, not its cause.

Since the early 1960s, Papua New Guinea's House of Assembly has used simultaneous translations (English, Tok Pisin, and Police Motu) to facilitate interaction among its members. The fact that there is no common language for all members does mean that the communication system of the assembly is complex. Gatekeepers who manage the translation process control the flow of information to some degree and have significant power to manipulate channels of communication. Yet in a monolingual assembly, there is no basis for assuming an even flow or distribution of information across the assembly. Blackouts may exist in any system, since not everyone is likely to talk with everyone else in either monolingual or multilingual assemblies. A single language may reduce certain technical problems of communication and hence facilitate communication and interation among legislators, but it will not make them talk with one another! Similarly, when the communication system of a country is as complex as that of Papua New Guinea, there are nonetheless ways to communicate *if there is a desire to do so.*

The comparative study of the three cases thus reveals many of the intricacies of how language *reflects* political processes. The case studies in the chapters which follow show *how* the complexities of language are used in various political maneuvers and strategies; but they contain ample evidence as well to show that *language is not why* the political process tends to operate as it does. It has been all too common in the past to blame political difficulties and malfunctioning institutions on language problems, whether the unit under consideration has been a local council in a multilingual village community or a large international gathering of representatives of the world's nation states. Advocates of linguistic reform must realize that linguistic changes can, at most, facilitate intercourse and that the real barriers to effective communication are seldom linguistic. Communication problems in political systems should be seen first as political problems. Then and only then is it possible to deal with the technical problems which stand in the way of effective communication.

SUGGESTIONS FOR FURTHER RESEARCH

The majority of the contributors to this volume did not undertake the study of language and politics directly. Most were concerned with other primary research problems and discovered language's role in political processes during the course of their studies. In order to further the understanding of language and politics, we need more studies which undertake the consideration of such relations directly as a major research goal. Many of the arguments and conclusions contained in this volume need refinement of the sort that can come only when language and politics studies move from the shadows into the research spotlight. The extraordinary growth of interest in language and society will inevitably stimulate these developments; but they come none too soon.

The priorities for further research in language and politics will of course differ for the various academic disciplines and applied specialties which share these concerns. We have asked the contributors to Part IV to assess the interests of their various disciplines in language and politics and to suggest priorities for research as they see them, and there is no need to repeat their ideas here. The collaboration of efforts of researchers working from many disciplines and theoretical perspectives in this volume has, however, highlighted a few topics which can be useful as a guide for thinking about further research in language and politics. These areas are:

1. *language as a political issue.* Das Gupta has suggested in Chapter 10 that language is different from other political issues in India. We need to know just how general this proposition is and, precisely, in what ways language differs from other issues.

2. *language as a group of variables affecting political processes.* We need to move beyond language as an issue to explore more fully how language, in its many aspects, affects and reflects social and political processes. The papers in this volume have gone far in setting out some of the dimensions of such relationships, but in terms of

possibilities for research, we have only begun.

3. *differences between language and other political resources.* The contributors to this volume have made us aware of many uses of language as a political resource, but what has not been considered in any detail is just how and in what ways language is like and different from other political resources.

4. *differences among various aspects of language in political processes.* Hyperboles, metaphors, and bilingualism are all linguistic devices, but their forms and range of functions are not the same. We need more research about the actual functions of different aspects of language in politics.

5. *differences among communities related to the political uses of language.* Communities differ from one another in their social and linguistic make up. Consequently, we may expect to find some correlates of differences between communities and the ways in which language is related to politics as an issue, as a resource, and in controlling access to participation.

6. *differences between language-politics relations at national and community levels.* Related to the previous topic, we know that national, regional, and local political processes differ in important ways from each other. What we do not know is how language affects national political processes differently from local ones.

7. *differences between language-politics relations in formal and informal political contexts.* Most of the studies in this volume have focused upon language and politics in formal political institutions. Doubtlessly, many of the processes will be found in non-formal arenas and in interpersonal relations as well. What we need to consider is how language and politics may differ between formal and informal contexts.

These topics will by no means exhaust the range of possibilities for future research, but, coupled with the suggestions contained in the chapters in Part IV of the book, they provide a guide for considering the areas in which we might move next.

A BIBLIOGRAPHIC NOTE FOR NON-LINGUISTS

The field of sociolinguistics has virtually sprung up and developed during the last ten years or so. Like any new and growing discipline, its terminology, methods, and theories are in flux. There are several good overviews of the field for those non-specialists who desire an introduction to its basic concerns. The following select bibliography will provide some assistance. This list by no means does justice to the vast literature of sociolinguistics and of the sociology of language, but it provides a place to begin.

Ardener, Edwin C., ed. 1971. *Social Anthropology and Language.* London: Tavistock (ASA Monograph No. 10).
[Collection of papers, most by social anthropologists, assessing the relevance of linguistic theory to the understanding of society; contains both historical and general overviews and some specific applications of linguistic theory to social analysis.]

Bright, William, ed. 1966. *Sociolinguistics.* The Hague: Mouton.
[One of the first collections to focus specifically upon the relations between language and society; proceedings of a 1964 conference held at the University of California at Los Angeles.]

Burling, Robbins. 1969. *Man's Many Voices.* New York: Holt, Rinehart and Winston.
[Often used as a basic textbook in courses on language and society; useful as an introduction to the field of sociolinguistics.]

Fishman, Joshua A. 1972. *The Sociology of Language.* Rowley, Mass.: Newbury House.
[Explication of the dimensions of the field known as 'sociology of language' as distinct from 'sociolinguistics' by one of its leading proponents.]

Fishman, Joshua A., ed. 1968, 3rd printing. *Readings in the Sociology of Language.* The Hague: Mouton.
[Extensive collection of reprinted articles covering a broad range of topics in sociolinguistics and the sociology of language; useful in understanding the range of concerns of those studying the relations between language and society.]

Fishman, Joshua A., ed. 1972. *Advances in the Sociology of Language.* 2 vols. The Hague: Mouton (Contributions to the Sociology of Language, 1 & 2).
[Collection of papers representing different perspectives in the study of language and society; useful as an introduction to the field, but more advanced than Burling above.]

Fishman, Joshua A., Charles A. Ferguson, and Jyotirindra Das Gupta, eds. 1968. *Language Problems of Developing Nations.* New York: John Wiley.
[Collection of original papers assessing the problems of language in the newly independent nations; a wide spectrum of countries and topics.]

Giglioli, Pier Paoli, ed. 1972. *Language and Social Context.* London: Penguin.
[Collection of reprinted papers, most already classics in their own right, which give a concise introduction to the breath of interests in sociolinguistics and sociology of language.]

Goody, Jack, ed. 1968. *Literacy in Traditional Societies.* Cambridge: Cambridge University Press.
[Original papers by social anthropologists assessing the role and consequence of literacy in traditional societies.]

Gumperz, John J. and Dell Hymes, eds. 1964. 'The Ethnography of Communication.' *American Anthropologist* 66(6), Part 2.
[Original papers by American cultural anthropologists exploring the ethnographic study of communications systems; like Bright above, this is an early but important collection which helped establish modern sociolinguistics.]

Gumperz, John J. and Dell Hymes, eds. 1972. *Directions in Sociolinguistics.* New York: Holt, Rinehart and Winston.
[Well-edited selection of papers, mostly case studies, representing recent research in sociolinguistics.]

Rubin, Joan and B. Jernudd, eds. 1972. *Can Language Be Planned?* Honolulu: The University Press of Hawaii.
[Collection of original papers exploring the problems of language planning; illustrates some practical applications of recent theoretical developments in sociolinguistics.]

Shuy, Roger W., ed. 1973. *Sociolinguistics: Current Trends and Prospects.* Report of the 23rd Annual Round Table Meeting on Linguistics and Language Studies. Washington, D. C.: Georgetown University Press.
[Proceedings of a 1972 conference assessing the state of sociolinguistic research.]

Sudnow, David, ed. 1972. *Studies in Social Interaction.* New York: Free Press.
[Recent studies of conversation in the tradition of ethnomethodology.]

Whiteley, W. H., ed. 1971. *Language Use and Social Change.* London: Oxford University Press.
[Original papers representing theoretical overviews of sociolinguistics and sociology of language and some empirical case studies based on field research in Africa.]

In addition to these books, there are two journals which focus specifically on these fields of inquiry. One, *La Mondo Lingvo Problemo,* is more practical in orientation while the other, *Language in Society,* tends to publish more theoretical papers and reports of field research.

NOTES

1. The term *style* is used in sociolinguistics to refer to the co-occurrent changes at various levels of linguistic structure within one language.
2. The term *register* is similar in meaning to *style.* It refers to the way of speaking in a particular situation.
3. *Code-switching* refers to the shifting of linguistic style in order to conform to the total context of the speech event.
4. Also known in the literature as Neo-Melanesian and New Guinea Pidgin English.
5. See Chapter 7.
6. Papua New Guinea became independent on December 1, 1973.

PART ONE

Tanzania

Introduction to Part One

In the period since national independence in 1961, the Government of Tanzania has undertaken a number of steps to rid the country of many colonial institutions and practices not deemed appropriate to the egalitarian goals of *ujamaa* socialism. A policy elevating Swahili to national language is just one aspect of governmental efforts to extend popular involvement in the political process. The ability to use Swahili, now spoken by almost ninety percent of the population, gives Tanzania an advantage over many other countries which must devote large portions of their resources to the development of national communication media. Swahili, already widely known throughout Tanzania at independence, is now the medium of modernization, of education, of government and politics, of economic development, and of national culture. Using Swahili for these purposes not only facilitates communication among linguistically diverse communities but also has important symbolic consequences. Swahili *is* Tanzania: speaking it symbolizes involvement and participation in national events whether in the capital city of Dar es Salaam or in the rural farming communities where 95 percent of the country's population live.

Chapters 2 and 3 set out the cultural, linguistic, and political parameters of the more specific studies in Chapters 4–7. Chapter 2 provides an overview of the languages spoken in Tanzania, their patterns of distribution and use, and of the national language policies since independence. Chapter 3 traces the evolution of governmental institutions from pre-contact times through the colonial period to contemporary Tanzania. Prior to the nineteenth century, the region which now makes up Tanzania consisted of a large number of small-scale polities and more or less autonomous communities. Stimulated by trade and contact with the coastal region, many of these societies were in the process of expanding when colonial hegemony was established late in the nineteenth century. Under first German, then British control, a series of Western political institutions were introduced. Some of these colonial institutions, often in highly modified form, have been retained while others have been eliminated as the nationalist movement assumed the reins of government in Tanzania.

In Chapter 4, Jean O'Barr evaluates the effects of the language policies of both colonial and independent Tanzania upon the functioning of the formal institutions of government. In the British period, English was the language of higher levels of government while African languages were used to administer local areas. Nowadays the national government encourages Swahili usage throughout the governmental bureaucracy. On the surface, the wider use of Swahili appears to extend the potential for involvement in government and politics, or at least to reduce the degree to which language obstructs the access of many Tanzanians. Yet, closer scrutiny shows that this may not always be the case. The expansion of Swahili from its former colonial role as intermediary language between the highest levels of government and the linguistically diverse local communities of rural Tanzania to a place as the language of the national assembly as well as of the village council may only open access in some situations while restricting the involvement of non-Swahili-speaking Tanzanians (perhaps twenty percent or so) in others. But as the author points out, whatever short-term disadvantages result from current policy must be weighed against the long-term advantages which will accrue from a unification of the language of government throughout Tanzania.

Tanzania's linguistic complexity results in a considerable portion of the efforts put into developing the legal system being focused upon the solution of language problems. In Chapter 5, DuBow examines the relation of the linguistic requirements of the legal institutions to the distribution of linguistic skills in the population. As J. O'Barr does in Chapter 4, he raises the question of just how well the current language policy actually achieves the stated goals of egalitarianism and accessibility of government to people. As in legislative and administrative institutions, Swahili is becoming the language of all of Tanzania's courts. Yet such a move does not always result in greater access and participation of all litigants. In some ways, the former linguistic flexibility of colonial courts may have actually made them more open. Litigants are not the only ones for whom the language requirements of the courts may pose difficulties. Many of Tanzania's lawyers were educated in English and now find the courts operating in Swahili. The legal profession has simply not been able to keep pace with the relatively swift reforms within the courts in the period since independence. One step which was taken in the effort to ease the transition to Swahili and to help unify the national legal system in Tanzania has been the production of a Swahili-English law dictionary which provides a series of Swahili equivalents for many English legal terms. This project has shown that adequate terms can be derived in Swahili to express the ideas and concepts of law, but the problems which arise in its use are more cultural than linguistic.

Legal reforms in Tanzania have left intact the basic system of law which remains as a legacy of the British colonial period. The efforts in the first decade since independence have been directed to making it work more efficiently and with greater equality for all of Tanzania's peoples. There will continue to be for some time to come practical problems relating to the functioning of the courts and the legal system. Apparently desirous both to create a standardized national legal system and to remain sensitive to the local cultural differences among Tanzania's many ethnic traditions, there can be no simple program of legal reform in the next decade or so.

While J. O'Barr and DuBow are concerned with problems of access to governmental and legal institutions, Swartz exemplifies the concerns of many other contributors to this volume by considering language as a political resource. Swartz focuses on the dynamics of the political process within a *baraza,* or dispute settlement session, in southern Tanzania. During his field studies, Swartz was concerned with why the Bena, an otherwise quite literal and straightforward people, so frequently deviate from customary procedure in barazas and use hyperbolic speech. In his paper Swartz puts forward the thesis that the use of hyperbole in Bena barazas may be a strategy employed by those who realize they are arguing lost causes. This is an important paper because it demonstrates how we might analyze the political uses of rhetoric in other situations. The complexities of language use in politics make it virtually impossible to conceive of a complete analysis of all possible uses of language for political ends even within a single cultural tradition such as Bena, and we are still a long way from any statematic treatment of the relationship between rhetorical devices and political strategies. Swartz's paper, however, provides some stimulating ideas for us to think about. Political anthropologists will also find his discussion of whether we are dealing with rules versus regularities (pages 114–115) in situations like the Bena use of hyperbole of relevance to recent theoretical debates in the literature of that discipline.

The communications system in which a political institution is embedded may have significant effects upon the functioning of that body. In Chapter 7, William O'Barr's concern is understanding how a local council in rural Tanzania operates. Both the government and the local people consider this particular council ineffectual. To examine why this is so, O'Barr first employs the conventional modes of analysis in social anthropology. He finds that extant models are adequate to explain why the council takes most of its decisions through consensus rather than majority vote and why as a political body it is largely ineffectual to both the superordinate government and the people it is supposed to represent. Then, he shifts to consider the communication system which provides the verbal medium for the operation of the council and finds that a particular rhetorical device, *kingua* double-talk, which is rife in the council has significant effects upon its functioning. Viewed as a device for limiting the intrusion of outsiders into the business of the local community, *kingua* is quite efficient. But in assessing its impact on the working of the council toward its practical problems, its effects can only be described as crippling. This paper serves to demonstrate what additional things might be learned by extending our traditional concerns with the form and functioning of political institutions to include the communication medium in which they operate. Non-linguistic reasons lie at the base of why the people of Mlimani obstruct the functioning of the local council; but the means whereby this obstruction is accomplished is decidedly linguistic.

WILLIAM M. O'BARR 2

Language Use and Language Policy in Tanzania: An Overview

Joseph Greenberg has called Africa one of the most complex linguistic areas of the world, rivaled perhaps only by the situations in aboriginal South America and New Guinea (Greenberg 1959 : 15). With less than one-tenth of the world's population, Africa accounts for at least one-fifth of the world's languages (Berry 1970 : 80). Most of them are spoken by relatively small groups of people, and there are only a few African languages spoken over wide areas of the continent.

Colonialism added new dimensions to an already complicated linguistic situation. Partitioned among the various European powers whose imperialistic interests took them to Africa in the last several centuries, the Africa of the 1970s consists of no less than forty-two countries, few of which have official languages of African origin. Most countries face no alternative to relying heavily upon the language of the European power which dominated them during the colonial period – usually English, French, or Portuguese. There are at least two important reasons which lie behind this situation: (1) the colonial language is often the most widely known in such countries, and (2) having to choose among the myriad African languages spoken within a country would likely cause serious cleavages in the typically precarious political balance. Thus, it is not a happy situation when Africans find themselves forced to rely upon European rather than African languages to direct their internal affairs and to pursue relations with their neighbors.

By African standards, Tanzania's linguistic problems are small ones. Although its African population, numbering over 13 million according to the most recent census, speaks more than one hundred different languages, Swahili, a genuine African language, is widely known throughout the country. This fact has made Tanzania the only African country of its size able to entertain seriously the possibility of using an African tongue as an alternative national and official language.

THE LANGUAGES OF TANZANIA

There are three categories of languages spoken in contemporary Tanzania. First of all, there are the African vernaculars, usually said to be about 120 in number. Second, there is Swahili, clearly a Bantu language in its structure although it owes substantial lexical debts to Arabic and English. Finally, there is the European colonial language, which in the case of Tanzania has been English since the end of World War I at which time the British assumed responsibility for much of what had been German East Africa. In addition to these, a number of Asian languages are spoken in the overseas Indian communities which grew up as a result of the large scale immigration of these people to East Africa at the instigation of the British during the early decades of this century. The languages which these people speak should be considered in this classification along with the African vernacular languages, for they function similarly.

The general situation which obtains in Tanzania today is a bilingualism among the African majority in a vernacular language as mother tongue plus varying degrees of knowledge of Swahili as a second language. Those Africans who have been educated through the higher levels of the school system also know English. The elevation of Swahili to status of national language after independence in 1961 has resulted in the gradual decline of the importance of English. During the colonial period, however, there was great prestige associated with knowing English, making it much more important than Swahili for those who had facility with both languages. For such people, Harries has argued that Swahili was clearly a third language (Harries 1969 : 277).

The European and Asian minorities of Tanzania frequently relied on English during the colonial period as a language which could symbolically separate them from the Africans. Most of these people

Table 2.1 *Classification of languages of Tanzania*[a]

Language group	Number of units	% of population
Bantu	102	94
Highland Nilotic (e.g. Luo, Masai)	7	3
Eastern Cushitic (e.g. Iraqw)	4	2
Click	1	0.3
Mbugu		0.1
Total	114	99.4

[a] After Whiteley (1971a:247) who based his data on census information which was collected by the Government of Tanganyika in 1957. Whiteley cautions that these data are based upon ethnic rather than linguistic units.

considered Swahili to be the language which one used in speaking with those who could not use English – household servants, office assistants, and the amorphous mass of Africans who lived apart in the 'native quarters' of the urban areas and in the vast rural hinterland of the country. Many Englishmen and Asians made a point of speaking broken Swahili, showing thereby the low esteem in which they held both the language and those who were forced to rely upon it.

Whiteley has estimated that about 94 percent of the African population speak languages of the Bantu family (Whiteley 1971a). These languages share many structural similarities and much basic vocabulary (see Table 2.1). This high degree of similarity for the majority of Tanzania's vernaculars would obviously facilitate secondary language acquisition. The wide use of Swahili, however, makes it unnecessary in most cases for Africans moving outside their home areas to learn other vernaculars. They rely instead upon Swahili, whose acquisition is facilitated along the lines suggested above since it too is a Bantu language. The remaining 6 percent or so of the African population are widely believed to have great difficulty in learning Swahili. To my knowledge, however, there are no detailed studies of the differences in knowledge of Swahili among those whose mother tongues are Bantu and those whose mother tongues belong to other language families. Map 2.1 shows the distribution of the major language families in Tanzania. Map 2.2 shows the relative linguistic homogeneity of Tanzania in comparison to neighboring Kenya and Uganda.

Map 2.1 *Major language families of Tanzania*

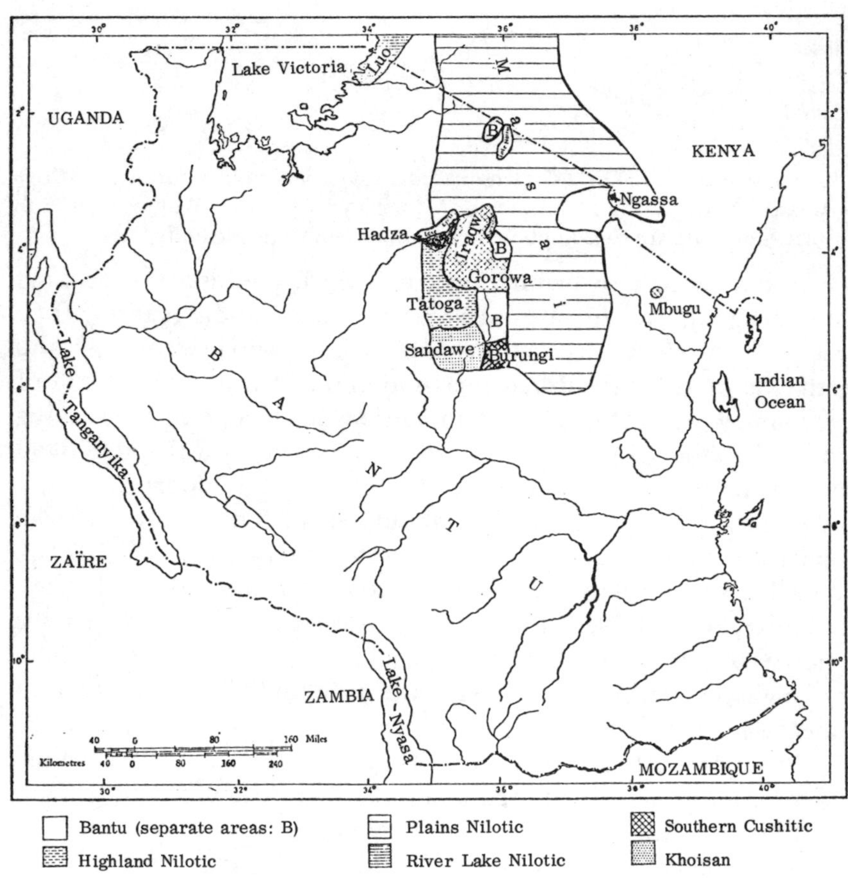

From: John Sutton, 'Languages and Peopling', in L. Berry (ed.), *Tanzania in Maps*, London: University of London Press, Ltd. 1971.

Map 2.2 *Main ethnic groups of East Africa*

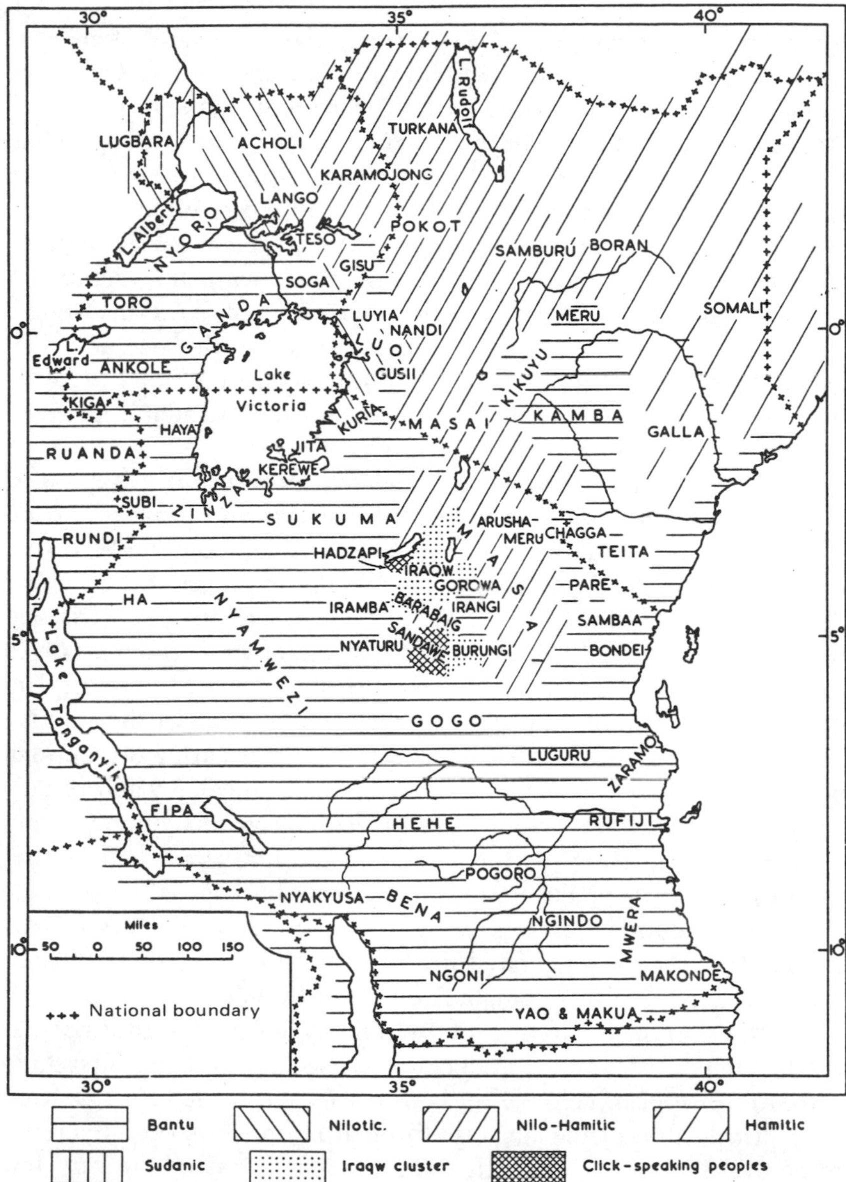

From: J. E. Goldthorpe and F. B. Wilson, *Tribal Maps of East Africa and Zanzibar*, Kampala, Uganda: East African Institute of Social Research (East African Studies No. 13), 1960.

THE EVOLUTION OF SWAHILI

A paucity of written records has left the origin of Swahili somewhat vague. Historians of the language, however, are agreed that dialects of Swahili were spoken along the East African coast by the beginning of the eighteenth century. The movement of Arab traders along Indian Ocean ports encouraged the development of similarities among the various dialects from Somalia to Mozambique and resulted in a heavy influence of Arabic on the language. Coastal traders began developing an interest in the interior of East Africa during the eighteenth century, and it was they who introduced Swahili to the inland communities along their trade routes. Most of the peoples they encountered were Bantu speakers, and the linguistic affinity between their mother tongues and Swahili facilitated the introduction of the latter as a genuine lingua franca (Whiteley 1969).

Later, in the latter half of the nineteenth century, the explorers, missionaries, and German government officials who came to Tanzania used Swahili speakers as guides, assistants, and junior administrators. The German administration in East Africa fostered the further development of Swahili. The assumption of German East Africa by the British at the end of World War I gave even more momentum to its development. Like the Germans, the British used it as the language for administration, but they penetrated sections of the country and parts of life where Swahili had not been used during the German period. Increasing numbers of Africans came to speak Swahili as they made contact with the colonial authorities, engaged in commerce and wage-labor occupations with people who did not speak their mother tongues, and entered European schools and churches. Most of these situations required some knowledge of Swahili. A few of the churches and schools operated in the vernaculars, but these did not reverse the trend of increasing utilization of Swahili.

Strangely enough, the use of Swahili by colonial authorities has not left it tainted today with a colonial bias. The fact that first Arab and later European colonialism is primarily responsible for the very wide distribution of the language throughout modern Tanzania tends to be over-shadowed by another fact: that it is one of the very few African languages known widely enough to serve major mobilizing and communication roles.

The political value of Swahili is enhanced by its not being closely identified with any single ethnic group. Indeed, *Waswahili* ('the Swahili people') tends to be a pejorative term throughout the interior of the country referring to detribalized people or strangers (Arens 1972). The very low esteem in which most inland people hold native speakers of Swahili has indeed made it possible for their language to gain relatively great currency without also furrowing to the top one of the many tribal groups of Tanzania. Whiteley (1968 : 327) has estimated that Swahili is the first language of less than ten percent of Tanzania's people.

In 1930, an interterritorial committee was established to standardize Swahili in British East Africa. Its primary function was to oversee the production of Swahili language textbooks and teaching materials to be used in the schools of the three East African countries. In the late 1920s the Zanzibar dialect was chosen over the Mombasa dialect as the model for standard Swahili. The committee has served over the intervening years in a number of capacities aimed at furthering the development of the language. It has overseen the standardization of written Swahili and its orthography. Shortly after the opening of the University of Dar es Salaam in 1964, the committee was transformed into that university's Institute of Swahili Research.

The evolution of Swahili, however, did not take place in a social vacuum. Whiteley (1971 : 146) has pointed out the tri-focal nature of contemporary language behavior in Tanzania, a situation which owes much to the way in which the colonial administrations, the educational institutions, and the missions responded to the linguistic diversity they encountered in East Africa. The administration used Swahili and fostered its development in many ways. The schools, until very recently, emphasized English as the language of education. Often beginning with the vernacular and shifting later to Swahili, their ultimate objective was the teaching of English, the language of the secondary schools and all higher endeavors during the colonial period. A number of missions emphasized the necessity of utilizing the various mother tongues of East Africans in order to reach them emotionally so as to have greater success in winning them over to the teachings of the Christian religion. These differences in emphasis of colonial institutions helped establish the relationship which existed among the three languages at the beginning of the colonial period.

Elsewhere, I have argued that the domains considered appropriate for each of the three languages today is roughly as follows (O'Barr 1971). The vernaculars are appropriate for all sorts of traditional activities – home life, indigenous religious and ritual activities, traditional subsistence activities, and the like. Swahili is the appropriate language for introduced situations like schools, hospitals, government and party meetings, many of the new religious institutions, reading, interethnic communications, etc. Finally, English is appropriate when dealing with Europeans and other foreigners who do not speak Swahili, in the institutions of higher learning, in certain offices of government and business, etc. My work in rural Tanzania in the late 1960s convinced me that this relationship among the appropriate uses of the three languages is fairly stable. In rural Tanzania, English has never had many uses. It is confined to school teachers, students speaking with one another, reading things written in that language, and working in certain government offices. Many of these functions are slowly being taken over by Swahili. But, in traditional areas of life, Swahili does not appear to be gaining at the expense of the vernaculars. The latter continue to be used where they have always been used while Swahili remains associated with introduced, non-indigenous situations.

WHO SPEAKS SWAHILI?

There are no data yet available which answer this question authoritatively. Edgar Polomé and associates, working with the Language Survey in East Africa in the mid-1960s, conducted extensive surveys of language knowledge and use patterns in Tanzania. When these data are published, we may expect some more conclusive answers to this question. In the meantime, we are forced to rely upon more intuitive generalizations and less ambitious surveys.

In 1968, I surveyed language knowledge and use patterns in a highland Pare community (O'Barr 1971). While the precise findings of that survey may not apply to every Tanzanian community, the trends found there are indicative of what a number of researchers report from other parts of the country. The Pare data revealed three distinct trends in Swahili language knowledge: (1) men almost universally tend to speak Swahili, (2) younger people have greater facility in using it than do older people, and (3) the more literate and educated a person is the more likely he is to be a fluent speaker of Swahili.

This relationship of Swahili language ability to maleness, youth, and education is likely to obtain throughout much of Tanzania, except of course for the coastal fringe where the native speakers of the language tend to be concentrated. These trends can be easily explained historically. Men learned the language working away from home at wage-earning jobs in cities and on plantations, and perhaps while serving in one of the world wars. In general, males have had greater exposure to educational institutions and have operated in more contexts in which Swahili is used. The association of Swahili with youth is due to both the increasing usage of Swahili in general and the greater exposure of young people to formal educational institutions. And the close association of literacy and Swahili results from the fact that Swahili is the medium of instruction in most schools, especially since the beginning of British administration in Tanzania.

Abdulaziz has estimated that bilingualism in Swahili and one of the local vernaculars may be as high as ninety percent (Abdulaziz 1971 : 171). My data from Pare showed about eighty percent of the particular community where I worked to be bilingual. But all such estimates are meaningless without some further consideration of the situations and contexts in which people have language fluency. Tanzania's Asian community, for example, is fluent in Swahili *when speaking about economic matters.* But to my knowledge, nobody has really investigated the limits of their Swahili abilities, nor, for that matter, those of any of Tanzania's other people. About all we can say at this point is that Swahili knowledge is biased toward maleness, youth, and education. It may be biased as well toward coastal peoples, toward those who have associated themselves with the Christian and Islamic religions, and those whose native languages are Bantu – but these contentions have yet to be demonstrated conclusively.

TANZANIA'S LANGUAGE POLICY

The role which Swahili played in mobilizing support for the independence movement in the 1950s set the stage for its elevation to national language following independence. Being the most widely known language among the 13 million or so citizens of Tanzania, it was better suited than English to foster the egalitarian ideals of Nyerere and his political party. Those who emphasize Swahili's anti-elitist character are quick to point out that Nyerere, speaking throughout the country in order to gain support for TANU and its independence platform, almost never had to rely upon a translator (Abdulaziz 1971 : 165). It was not surprising, therefore, that Swahili was declared the national language shortly after Nyerere took office.

Whiteley, in assessing the significance of Swahili's new role in independent Tanzania, has concluded that

'It is not always clear what Tanzanians mean by the term [national language]. One thing is clear, however, that, amongst its many meanings, that of "the language to be used on national occasions and whenever the image of the nation is on display" is very important. This does not mean, however, that Tanzanians are no longer trifocal in their language behavior, but rather that there has been some reallocation of the settings in which specific languages are held to be appropriate. This reallocation has largely been at the expense of English in favor of Swahili and has taken place especially in those public settings most likely to catch the public eye (e.g. street signs, coinage, public notices, etc.), but it has resulted in Swahili being used in the national assembly, town councils, party meetings, the lower courts, and the like. Efforts have also been made to extend the use of Swahili into the civil service (Whiteley 1971a : 150–151).'

In reflecting upon Swahili's altered status in post-independent Tanzania, Lyndon Harries has pointed out that Swahili has been made both the symbol of the new Tanzania and the medium for helping to create it. It seems clear to Harries that the close association which Swahili had with Islam and the cultural tradition of the coastal peoples is giving way to its role in Tanzanian national culture. Whatever the components of this new culture may eventually become, it does not seem to be merely, or even primarily, based in the Islamic coastal culture, formerly so closely associated with Swahili

(Harries 1969 : 276). In order to keep up with its new role, Swahili is undergoing certain changes both in form and use.

'Swahili is constantly having to catch up with developments in the national life, because frequently the developments introduce new terms, new concepts, new styles, which have no immediate equivalent in the national language. But as each new sector, each new development, becomes absorbed into the system, so the language develops – if it is allowed to do so – and becomes a viable means of expression for the relevant sector or development (Harries 1969 : 277).'

Two government ministries are involved in the task of helping Swahili develop and grow to fulfill the new demands placed upon it. First, the Ministry of Community Development and National Culture has a Promoter of Swahili whose role it is to further the extension of Swahili into the lives of Tanzanians. He has particularly been given the task of helping encourage the development of plays, prose, and poetry in the Swahili language – a development not much encouraged during the colonial period when English was considered more appropriate as a medium for such undertakings. This office has been concerned also with vocabulary development and the standardization of orthography and grammar. Regrettably, some of its projects had to be tabled for lack of finances. The other government bureau concerned with the promotion of Swahili is the Ministry of Education. It has given over much effort to the development of a Swahili curriculum and teaching materials. But among the many obstacles it faces in the short run is the limited Swahili ability of many of Tanzania's teachers whose educations were conducted at the higher levels in English. At the upper grades, this problem expresses itself in the facility of teachers themselves with the language. At lower levels, teachers' abilities in dealing with technical subjects, particularly those which they studied themselves in English, is something of a problem. But the last few years have seen the extension of Swahili as the medium of instruction through the primary into the secondary school years. English remains the language of the University of Dar es Salaam, although there are now a few courses given in Swahili and the curriculum designed to study that language is developing.

Despite its official importance, Swahili continues – and will [illegible] continue for some time to come – sharing the stage with [illegible] and the many vernacular languages spoken in Tanzania. As I [illegible] lready argued, there are still many areas of life where the ve[illegible]culars are considered by everyone to be more appropriate than Swahili. I do not believe that it is merely a question of time before Swahili intrudes into these areas of life. If we look carefully at the functional domains of the two sets of languages, I think the evidence suggests that the rather stable diglossic situation is likely to persist over the next several decades.

Swahili's greatest gains in the last decade are at the expense of English, but that language still has a role in contemporary Tanzania. Abdulaziz has this to say about its place in the national linguistic repertoire:

'The importance of English as a language of science, technology, higher learning in general, international trade, and communication is well recognized. In the educational system of Tanzania it still plays a vital role. It is a subject in Primary schools, and the medium of learning in Secondary schools and higher institutions of learning, including the University. It is also the main language of Banking and Commerce. It is used generally as the secondary or supplementary official language, especially in areas in which Swahili may not yet be in a developed enough position to function as efficiently. Division of roles between the two official languages is by no means clear-cut at the moment, and there is a great deal of overlapping of functions. But it would seem that in many areas English will progressively yield its function to Swahili, until such time as the two languages reach a more stable relationship (Abdulaziz 1971 : 174).'

SWAHILI'S ROLE AS NATIONAL LANGUAGE

Since becoming Tanzania's national language, Swahili has undergone a number of significant changes. More than anything else, it has perhaps proved itself very fertile in conveying the political culture of Tanzania. Older terms like *taifa* ('nation') have been extended in characteristic Swahili derivational fashion to produce new terms like *taifisha* ('nationalize') as changing times required them. These developments have made modern Swahili rich in political vocabulary.

Maendeleo ('development') became a national catchword in the 1960s. Nyerere cautioned his countrymen with the metaphor *'Usiwe kupe'* ('don't be a tick', meaning don't subsist on the lifeblood of others). They were instructed instead *kujitegemea* ('to be self reliant'). Terms like *ujamaa* ('familyhood') and *ushirikiana* ('cooperation') became the bases for communicating the concepts of African socialism to the masses. And the massive campaign in the schools to make both spoken and written facility in Swahili of highest priority for the young people of Tanzania has been supplemented by adult education classes, radio programs, and newspaper articles aimed to teach and explain new words and concepts to those not presently in school.

Nyerere set about to explode the popular myth that Swahili was not fit for higher education by his translation of Shakespeare's *Julius Caesar.* Peter Temu (1966) followed this lead with the publication of an economics textbook *Uchumi Bora* written especially for an East African audience. Temu, anxious to show that a technical jargon can be developed for discussing the concepts of economic analysis, provides his readers with an extensive glossary in which he coins the necessary terms and gives their English equivalents. Both these efforts are admirable ones and both have gone far in dispelling the myth that Swahili is unfit for such jobs. However, there are precious few books beyond these. One of Swahili's greatest problems in its role as national language is that there is virtually no national literature (Harries 1968:421). Topan has considered some of the problems which attend such a development of Swahili and concluded that in all its forms – poetry, prose, and drama – the language is playing a major role in expressing Tanzania's new national political consciousness. The constraints placed on this development by fact that local publishers tend to look closely at the classroom market (thereby ignoring much that is not of value for such situations) and the lack of a tradition of prose literature in Swahili have restricted its greater development in these areas (Topan 1971).

One of the largest specific tasks undertaken in developing Swahili has been the compilation of a Swahili dictionary of law (Weston 1965). With a strong base in English law as a legacy of the colonial period, the dictionary necessarily begins with many English legal terms and attempts to develop appropriate Swahili equivalents for them. Harries has criticized this project for its failure to take into account the legal culture of the East African peoples and its heavy reliance instead upon English legal concepts. Many of the terms which have been coined simply have no referents in the legal systems of Swahili speakers (Harries 1968 : 423–425). Nonetheless, the attempt to popularize legal concepts and to break down the esoteric speech barriers which exist between the people and the courts is a further step in developing the Swahili language along lines consonant with Tanzanian political ideology.

In considering Swahili's role as Tanzania's national language, Whiteley (1971 : 151) has cautioned against a confusion of the ideological and the technological aspects of the language policy. There are multitudinous technical problems which need to be overcome before Swahili can serve all the tasks which it has been asked to undertake. It needs to be more widely known among the population, it needs promotion, it needs even more prestige, it needs a literature, it needs teachers, and so on. Solving all these problems will take years and many resources. Yet through all this one thing is clear: Tanzania seems to have made a firm commitment, at least ideologically, to Swahili as a symbol and medium in developing its national culture.

JEAN F. O'BARR

The Evolution of Tanzanian Political Institutions[1]

The 342,170 square miles of mainland Tanzania[2] encompass a wide variety of land forms. Tropical lowlands form the coastal belt along more than 500 miles of the Indian Ocean. In the center of the country, dry savannah and scrub brush predominate. Along the other peripheries of the country which do not border on the ocean, there are both rolling agricultural lands and spectacular mountain ranges, of which Mt. Kilimanjaro in the northeast is the most famous. The bulk of the country's 13 million people live around the 'rim' of the country which encircles the tsetse fly infested center. While the rate of population growth is rapid (two percent per annum), there is little serious over population in most areas as of yet. Urbanization in towns over 100,000 is small (amounting to about six percent of the population). Tanzania is thus a primarily agricultural country and is likely to remain so in the future.

As a result of at least two factors, no single ethnic group dominates the political life of Tanzania: (1) there are, on the one hand, a large number of ethnic groups, and (2) ethnic differences have not, on the other, been reinforced by the religious affiliations and the patterns of economic stratification which have been introduced in Tanzania. The national census recognizes over 120 ethnic groups. In addition to these indigenous groups, Arabs, Asians, and Europeans live in Tanzania. Although their numbers are small, less than one percent of the total population, they have had a prominent role in Tanzania. As the better educated and wealthier of Tanzania's peoples, they have influenced education, the economy, and the civil service. In the last decade, the Tanzanian regime has progressively minimized, although not eliminated, the foreigner's role in Tanzanian national life. Religious identifications – be they Christian or Muslim – do not closely coincide with ethnic differences. In most areas of Tanzania, Christianity was accepted by Africans living near points of mission contact, Islam by those in coastal areas or along trade routes where the Arabs who brought the Muslim faith had passed. Any given ethnic group is likely to have both its Christian and its Islamic subgroups. The overall population breakdown is 26 percent Christian, 25 percent Muslim, with the remainder following traditional religions. In addition, economic differentiation has not followed exclusively ethnic lines. The capital, Dar es Salaam, is on the coast, geographically distant from the largest ethnic groups. Ethnic groups that have prospered in the modern economy – the Chagga with coffee, the Sukuma with cotton, for example – while numerically among the largest, are neither large enough in absolute terms nor close enough to the national center to be viewed as serious threats by other groups.

Economically, Tanzania is one of the poorest countries in the world. Her gross domestic product per capita was $71 in 1965, ranking her 123 out of 135 nations. Tanzania is primarily a rural country – over one half of Tanzania's gross domestic product comes from agriculture. The falling prices on the world market for her primary exports (coffee, sisal, and cotton) have more than offset the substantial gains in productivity which Tanzania has made since independence. Unlike many other developing countries, she has managed to export more than she has imported in the last decade as a result of careful economic planning. Tanzania has also broadened the scope of her trading partners far beyond the British-dominated pattern inherited as a legacy of the colonial period. Since independence, Tanzania has pursued a socialist economic strategy involving the nationalization of formerly foreign-controlled interests, the development of cooperative practices among peasant farmers, and a preference in economic planning for agricultural development rather than industrialization.

Politically, Tanzania has evolved since independence from a Westminster style polity to a *de jure* one-party state under the Tanganyika African National Union (TANU). Tanzania's constitutional forms both reflect its political realities and attempt to safeguard opportunities for popular control. The tendency toward administrative growth at the expense of other parts of government and a national focus on 'development', which are apparent in most African regimes, are also evident in Tanzania. Tanzania differs from other African regimes however in the emphasis it places on the communal aspects of traditional society and in the way it harnesses these cooperative patterns to the contemporary drive for economic and political development. This blend of ideology and realism, referred to as the *ujamaa* policies,[3] is the guiding philosophy of Tanzania. The influence of *ujamaa* on formal political institutions becomes evident in the following pages.

INDIGENOUS POLITICAL INSTITUTIONS

Tanzania possesses a contemporary political system which has cultural, economic, social, and political roots among the amalgam of people who have settled in this portion of East Africa. Tanzania has been peopled for centuries by groups immigrating from various parts of central and north-central Africa and more recently by expatriate populations, all intermingling and being changed as they interacted with one another. The Bantu-speaking peoples form the largest-group among contemporary Tanzanians (see Map 2.1). Migrants to the area since the first centuries of the first millennium A.D., they tended until very recently to be cultivators who lived in discrete localities usually surrounded by unoccupied bush areas which served as a buffer between them and their neighbors. Cushitic speakers, a second group in contemporary Tanzania, arrived in East Africa before the first millennium A.D. Like a third group, Nilotic speakers (who arrived in the sixteenth century and later), Cushitic peoples pursued a pastoral, nomadic way of life. Both Cushitic and Nilotic peoples occasionally conflicted with the Bantu-speaking groups if they vied for the same land. A fourth group, the speakers of Khoisan or click languages, make up the smallest group of indigenes in modern Tanzania. Their precise origin is unknown but these former hunter-gatherers are thought to have been the original occupants of eastern Africa. Arab, Portuguese, German, and British people have also occupied Tanzania as we shall see below.

The nineteenth century is an important date in Tanzanian political history. Prior to extensive contact with the coast in the nineteenth century and the changes stimulated as a result of this increased contact, the region which is now Tanzania was comprised of local, small-scale sociopolitical units which were liable to frequent flux as neighboring groups interacted through trade (both local and long distance), through expansion and migration motivated by the search for new farming and grazing lands, and through other processes resulting in the fissioning or fusioning of already existing groups. By the time Arab caravans penetrated into the interior during the early years of the nineteenth century, a complex trade network was in operation.[4] The societies which they encountered spanned the gamut of political organizational forms known in Africa's ethnographic record. The hunter-gatherers were organized at the band level. Some of the peoples in the interior had complex governmental bureaucracies with the accoutrements which these entail: kings, state rituals, tribute, and the like. The majority of societies fell somewhere in between these two extremes. In these mid-range societies, families resided together; effective authority over people was based on familial and sacred ties and exercised by persons whose status derived from their age. Characterized by consensual decision-making and legitimized by reference to long-standing cultural norms, these family groups governed themselves. Groups of families deferred to recognized individuals and/or lineages with special ritualistic abilities but were in no way part of centralized, territorially based political units.

Prior to the nineteenth century, in most Tanzanian societies, a single body performed both legislative and judicial activities (establishing goals, reconciling differences, insuring prosperity). Such a body was composed of elders whose basis of authority was their status in the community. Those who were regarded as possessing political authority varied with the type of society in question. In acephalous societies, such individuals might be clan elders or others thought to possess special knowledge and/or abilities for the issue at hand. In societies in which the office of 'chief' was well-defined, the membership of the council-court was somewhat more fixed and possibly represented clan or ritual divisions within the society. In the more highly centralized societies there were well established patterns of recruitment to such courts and councils. Nonetheless, in all cases, legislative and judicial functions were generally combined in a single institution. The basis of authority was familial and/or sacred, and the membership of the councils was flexible and defined by ad hoc criteria. Beginning in the nineteenth century changes occurred which substantially altered these aspects of political institutions in Tanzania.

EARLY CONTACTS

The evolution of the societies of the interior was paralleled by and only rarely affected by changes on the coast prior to the nineteenth century. Trading towns had grown up along the Indian Ocean coast from the tenth century on. The most striking feature of these towns was that they were located on offshore islands. They were founded by Arab peoples whose orientation was towards the western Indian Ocean, rather than the African continent, and whose world view was shaped by Islamic teaching. The towns interacted with their immediate hinterland but did not affect to any discernible extent the mode of existence of the interior.

The Portuguese traveled to the coast of Tanzania in the fifteenth century and established hegemony over much of the East African coast throughout most of the sixteenth century. They were able to dominate the Arab coastal towns because of their naval superiority and advanced weapons and because the towns were not politically united. The Portuguese defeated the towns one by one, exploiting existing loyalties and disloyalties for their own purposes. Portuguese authority diminished during the seventeenth century, challenged by the Omani Arabs.

In 1840, the Sultan Seyyeid Said moved from Oman on the Persian Gulf to Zanzibar. Said wanted to expand and control the trade between eastern Africa and the rest of the world. He proposed to do this by collecting duties through his control of the ports along the coast and by trading into the interior as an independent entrepreneur. Said leased the right to collect customs to a governor who paid him a fixed sum in return. The degree of control which Said excerised over these governors or *wali*s varied considerably. Some were able to become almost autonomous rulers in their own right. The Arabs are important to the evolution of the Tanzanian polity because of the commercial contact they initiated and the concomitant social changes this contact brought.

'Each coastal settlement had its own governor, customs officials, a few Baluchi soldiers, its Indian merchants counting their riches by the debts owing to them, and the Arabs, organizing expeditions, setting off, or returning . . . it is clear that Said's Governors, with only a handful of poor soldiers at their call, did little governing. On Said's behalf they may have heard appeals from the judicial decisions of the local Sheikhs; but, in general, though Said was in theory the overlord and the Sheikhs his vassals, they were in practice and in the normal course of events the almost unchecked masters of their own little parcels of the coast. They paid their feudal "tribute" in the shape of the dues on their trade; and that was practically all that Said and his deputies required of them (Friedland n.d.:9).'

In the interior, the Sultan's control was tenuous. Relationships with the societies of the interior were generally characterized by a live-and-let-live policy. Facilitating commerce was the Sultan's prime goal and to that end policies were designed to avoid conflict so long as Arabs were dominant. The impact of the trade in new items, of the introduction of new ideas and languages, of the changing basis of legitimization for the interior societies were the indirect consequences of Said's commercial ventures. Later, in the German and British periods, mercantile trade, the introduction of Western education and the Christian religion, and the institutionalization of European political practices were given priority over commercial affairs.

'Said's attitude to the African chiefs and the tribes inland was much the same as his attitude to the Arab coast towns. He would have no trouble with them if he could help it. Peace, not war, was the condition of good trade . . . he had no appetite for conquest, no desire to impose his rule. He would no more interfere with the affairs of an African chief than with those of a sultan of an Arab seaport – unless his claim to a general and loose, *but exclusive,* overlordship were seriously threatened from within or without (Friedland n.d. : 11).'

In the first half of the nineteenth century, changes emanating from the coast began to penetrate the political systems of inland Tanzania. Long distance trade meant at least two things to the societies of the interior: new opportunities opened up for individuals in these societies to acquire political power; devastation in the form of slaving and disease weakened many societies which had been contacted. If one looks at the societies of the interior during this period of extensive Arab contact, one can see the dramatic changes in the political institutions outlined earlier. In all societies, the basis of authority shifted. For the first time, money, employment, and travel became the criteria by which some men could gain political authority. As such new men emerged, the composition of the traditional political bodies began changing. Bodies of elders serving decision-making functions found it necessary to pay heed to them, often in a non-harmonious manner. Although no external system of administration was actually set up, contact with the Arabs did mean that an alternative source of authority to the traditional ones was available and could be used against traditional leaders if conflict arose. The shift from purely sacred to secular and usually military power as a basis for political authority as well the subsequent development of the territorially-based institution of chieftainship transformed the nature of political institutions in the nineteenth century and provided the basis upon which the colonial and independent governments designed their governmental structures.

GERMAN COLONIAL ADMINISTRATION

European explorers and missionaries began arriving in Tanzania from the 1850s onwards. Their journals and correspondence are filled with commentaries on the changes that the societies they encountered were undergoing: 'increasing trade and warfare, introduction of new goods and ideas, and growing intertribal contract' (Bates 1962 : 399). The period from 1850 to the first world war was characterized by a series of grass-roots revolts against the alien harbingers of commercial and political control who were attempting to dominate the indigenous societies. By the 1880s, the Arabs had lost their tenuous control of the interior trade routes and coastal ports to German agents. In 1890, Germany declared Tanganyika a protectorate to be administered by the German Foreign Office, a move which rectified a decision made in 1885 to let a German commercial company administer the protectorate. While the Arabs and Germans struggled among themselves for control of Tanganyika, a series of revolts initiated by Africans sought to repulse their uninvited overlords. The most vigorous of these, the Maji Maji Rebellion, occurred in 1905.[5]

In retrospect, two streams of German colonial policy are important to the evolution of Tanzanian political institutions. One is the early emphasis on pacification and the consequential military character of colonial administration. The other is a later emphasis on economic development and the creation of colonial infrastructures. The first two decades of German rule are often characterized as the period of the establishment of control. Friedland categorizes German administrative centers with a five part typology which illustrates the multiple aspects of control they sought to establish: trade and communication centers, built mostly on Arab contact points; centers of real or potential rebellion which emerged as territorial control was extended; centers of existing population density; centers for potential economic expansion; and centers for possible protection against British encroachment from the north (n.d.: 17–18).

Throughout these first two decades, German administration was above all thin: in 1896, there were only thirty-seven German administrators in the capital of Dar es Salaam, and another eighty-nine throughout the rest of the country (Friedland n.d. : 20). At the center, the administration was essentially a military command post with a governor as the highest civilian and military authority. No councils existed; what advice the governor got came from his military aides. In the various administrative centers (numbering fifteen in 1896), a German district officer, the *besirksamtmann,* commanded the outpost. He had very wide powers both in terms of the areas of life he claimed to control as well as in terms of whom he recognized as legitimate indigenous leaders. All indigenous leaders within his territory were theoretically responsible to him.

In areas where indigenous leadership was not immediately obvious to the Germans, they relied on a system of administration created by the Arabs during their period of control on the coast. *Akida*s were African or Arab assistants to the German district officer who spoke the local language as well as Swahili, who were literate, and who had some abilities to act as intermediaries between indigenous peoples and the colonizers. *Akida*s rarely came from the area where they worked – hence they had no traditional position in the societies they governed. Originally they were given authority for an area, working with the German district officers to insure law and order and to recruit forced labor. After 1896, they were responsible for the collection of the hut tax. As Bates (1962 : 402) has observed: the *akida* 'was not acceptable to the people whom he had to administer since he had no traditional authority over them, while on the other hand he had little chance of guiding German policy in accordance with his local knowledge'. German administration through *akida*s made no provisions for any local involvement in decision-making at the local levels. Likewise, the judicial setup under the Germans tended to be arbitrary. Offenses which came to the attention of a district officer personally or through his *akida*s were dealt with directly with little reference to local traditions or customs. Thus, the early German administration used little or no popular judiciary nor did it involve the local peoples to any significant degree in decision-making. Government of indigenous societies remained more or less intact except for the incorporation, to varying degrees, of these societies into the colonial infrastructure.

Significant changes did take place during this period, however, in economic networks. The beginnings of a postal, transportation, and telegraph network were set up; a monetary system was created; new crops (primarily coffee, cotton, and sisal) were introduced; missionaries began establishing schools, churches, and hospitals, all of which fed into the continuing series of changes being brought to local groups. The modern structure of the Tanzanian economy and its social system thus dates from the German period.

In 1907, domestic politics in Germany forced the Colonial Office to reexamine its overseas policies. This reexamination led to some fundamental changes in Tanganyika, most importantly to the establishment of a national advisory council and to an administrative restructuring. At the national level, governors were drawn from civilians rather than military men as they had been in the past. They acquired civilian chief secretaries (*referente*) and civilian departmental heads. An advisory council, modeled on the British legislative system, and composed of three official members, all *referente*, and from five to twelve unofficial members,[6] all of whom were German-born residents of the colony, met three times a year to advise on the budget and give opinions on forthcoming legislation. The Governor named his council from a list of nominees drawn up by the German residents of the colony. In terms of local administration, the territory was divided into nineteen districts with district officers (plus two military districts). The system of local governance was extended; *akida*s were given specific territorial assignments; local leaders were recognized as *jumbe*s, certified by district officers, and assigned to work as assistants to *akida*s in maintaining law and order, collecting taxes, and hearing cases within their territorial jurisdictions. Thus, towards the end of the German period reforms were introduced which broadened administration from a military control operation to a set of political institutions which sought a very limited amount of local opinion at the center and capitalized on existing means of governance throughout the colony. The Arab and German attempts to designate indigenous spokesmen and brokers backed by external authority, coupled with the vast social and economic changes that were occurring with local societies as a result of commercial penetration, combined to lay the basis for the development of local and national government during the British period and after.

THE BRITISH LEGACY AND TANZANIAN MODEL

Britain assumed responsibility for Tanzania as a League of Nations mandate on January 10, 1920, when the Treaty of Versailles was ratified. The first few years were spent in rejuvenating the economy and in disposing of German lands and holdings. In looking at the growth of political institutions in Tanzania from World War I onward, several developments are important. One is the evolution of the colonial advisory bodies, the Executive and Legislative Councils, into the contemporary Parliament of Tanzania. The history of the National Assembly is intimately linked to the growth of the nationalist movement and the preeminent role of the party, TANU, in national affairs. While the space limitations placed on this chapter mean that it cannot deal directly with the growth of TANU, it will be important to see how the party's development helped shape the evolution of the National Assembly.

A second development is the establishment of the system of

indirect administration. Tremendous amounts of colonial energies went into the creation of the native authority system. After independence there was a tendency to centralize all administration, ignoring the institutions of indirect rule so laboriously begun under the British. In the last few years, this trend has been reversed somewhat through a revival of interest in creating viable decision-making units at the district and village levels.

A third development is the eventual separation of judicial and legislative activities within the governmental structure. Where the Arab *akida* and the German *besirksamtmann* once held all judicial and executive power, the native authority court system and later the local court system (which now reaches up to the High Court of Tanzania and beyond that under certain circumstances to the East African Court of Appeals) have been established to handle these activities independently.

The Executive and Legislative Councils as forerunners of Parliament. The Tanganyika Order in Council of July 22, 1920, set Great Britain up as the civil authority in Tanzania. A governor, representative of the British Crown appointed by the Crown, was the chief executive – responsible for peace, order, and good government – and the link between the Colonial Office and the territory. The Governor was assisted by an Executive Council which he was bound to consult but whose advice he was not compelled to follow. The first Executive Council consisted of four official members – i.e. members who held their seats by virtue of being heads of departments in the colonial government. Although the number of official members increased as the complexity and variety of tasks the Tanzanian government faced increased, no unofficial members – i.e. members who were not committed to support government proposals and presumably able to voice non-governmental opinion – were appointed until 1939. The four 1939 appointees included one Asian on the previously all European body. The number of official and unofficial members of the Executive Council grew after World War II. In 1957, six assistant ministers were chosen from among the unofficial members as a preliminary step to the creation of a ministerial system of government. In 1960, the Executive Council was abolished when internal self-government was achieved. The Executive Council evolved from an official advisory body, composed originally only of European civil servants, to a more broadly representative body which was ultimately replaced by a cabinet, some members of which are drawn from the popularly elected National Assembly.

The Legislative Council was first set up in Tanzania in 1926 at the suggestion of Sir Donald Cameron, the second governor, who wanted the opinions of other than his ministers. The Order in Council which established the Legislative Council allowed for thirteen official members committed to support the government and a maximum of ten unofficial members. The thirteen official members consisted of the six official members of the Executive Council plus seven other high government officials.

'Both the Executive and the Legislative Councils were created primarily as subsidiary advisory organs. But in practice, because the Governor was physically incapable of dealing with every detail of administration, their opinions carried considerable weight. This applied chiefly to advice given by the official members of the councils, but also to the opinion of unofficial members. Since the colonial officials were often less familiar with the history, geography, and social and economic life of Tanganyika, the unofficial members, as representative of the permanent element of the territory, were depended upon for such information. The Governor, therefore, despite official majorities in each council, would probably reconsider any measure that had the unanimous opposition of the unofficial members (Taylor 1963 : 42–43).'

The Legislative Council steadily grew in size from 1926 until after World War II. The 1950s are an important period in the growth of the Legislative Council because of the growth of the nationalist movement and the impact of TANU on legislative evolution. The first Indians had been appointed to the Legislative Council in 1938, the first Africans in 1945. Africans and Indians had been appointed in the 1950s on a parity scheme whereby one European, one Indian, and one African represented each province. The membership of the council more than doubled between 1955 and 1959 in response to the demands of the nationalist movement. TANU, although diametrically opposed to the multiracial principle then in operation, did participate in the 1958-59 elections (rather than boycott them as some leaders urged). TANU won seventy out of the seventy-one seats being contested; from that time on, TANU members made up the directly elected members of the Legislative Council.

While the present day National Assembly of Tanzania is the institutional descendant of the Legislative Council, it has undergone a number of transformations since its inception in 1961. Its size has steadily increased and its role in policy formation has been progressively specialized. The approximately 200 members of the contemporary Parliament come from several categories. There are 107 from constituencies on the mainland. Members are elected every five years by universal franchise from a two-person ballot which is drawn up through TANU channels. There are fifty-five members representing Zanzibar whose selection procedure is somewhat different. The National Assembly also has fifteen national members, a novel feature of Tanzania's political system since 1965. The President nominates people who are not necessarily politicians but whose background and experience make them potentially valuable members of the National Assembly. The National Executive Committee of the party approves the list; directly elected members of the National Assembly then elect these fifteen in turn. Seven members serve in the National Assembly as nominees of the President. Finally, the seventeen regional commissioners of the mainland, who are the administrative and party heads of regional government, are Members of Parliament. The composition of the National Assembly is thus varied; it is made up of conventional politicians, citizens outside the political arena, and administrators. The basis of authority for such members differs according to the constituency they represent.[7]

The functions the National Assembly performs are best understood in terms of its role vis-à-vis the National Executive Committee (NEC) of TANU. In the more than ten years since Tanzania gained independence, the NEC has emerged as the dominant policy-making institution. It is composed of eighty members, all party professionals, some elected, some appointed, which meets at least once every three months and is answerable to the annual national conference of the party. The division of responsibility between Parliament and the NEC has been spelled out as follows:

'The NEC is concerned with the formulation of the broad lines of policy . . . the National Assembly, on the other hand, is primarily concerned with the more detailed task of giving effect to Government policy through appropriate legislative measures and exercising vigilant control over all aspects of Government expenditure (McAuslan and Ghai 1966 : 497).'

The Parliament of Tanzania by this arrangement tends to be a legitimating forum in which general policy guidelines are translated into plans and projects and in which popular opinion is expressed. Unlike the parliamentary institutions of many other African countries, the Parliament of Tanzania remains vigorous. While Parliament shares its decision-making responsibilities with the NEC, it contributes to national political life through its representative character and its ability to question the priorities set by TANU.

Indirect administration and the local government legacy. The contemporary organization of local government in Tanzania is an intermixture of two quite distinct currents. One is the system of indirect administration nurtured under British colonial auspices. The second is the influence of TANU, especially as it is now expressed in terms of the ideology of *ujamaa.* The interaction of these currents provides the context in which local government operates in modern Tanzania.

Shortly after Tanzania came under British control, a Native Authority Ordinance was enacted. Local leaders were authorized by the colonial government to issue orders and regulations for maintaining peace and preventing crime. 'Local leader' was loosely defined and included a variety of individuals all with some claim to political legitimacy. The governor at the time, Donald Cameron, who had had extensive experience with the system of indirect rule in Nigeria, always reiterated that he had set up a similar system in Tanzania because he believed it to be best suited to the needs of indigenous peoples. Two problems plagued the native authority system from its inception until its abolition after independence. One was the question of who should be recognized as local leaders. The second was how these individuals could simultaneously serve both people and government.

Under the system of indirect administration, the British colonial government sought to find individuals who were popularly viewed as indigenous leaders. In some cases, community opinion was sought. In others, various contestants for the office presented their cases to the colonial government. In still others, those who had served the Germans were simply transferred. In an official list published in 1927, 679 tribal chiefs were named. Some twenty years later, the system of native authorities could be classified into three types: chiefs individually recognized as embodying authority in their own person (numbering 329); councils which exercised authority (34); people appointed by the government with no traditional base (44) (Friedland n.d.: 42). From their original mandate to execute a limited set of directives, native authorities' responsibilities increased through the 1940s. All the amendments to the original ordinance increased the autonomy of local units by broadening the activities native authorities could perform. They collected and dispensed funds, supervised education and other social welfare functions, and passed regulations on agriculture and veterinary programs.

In addition to their executive and financial responsibilities, the native authorities also administered justice. Native courts began operation in 1929; the chiefs, recognized as native authorities, sat as magistrates in these courts[8] which were part of the administrative rather than the judicial system. Appeals from native court went directly to the British officer rather than the national judicial system. The national judicial system, applying British colonial law, using English, and staffed by legal professionals, operated primarily for non-Africans. Cases could be heard on appeal from the native courts by the district officer and his superior, the provincial officer, as administrative officials but not as part of the judicial system.

In the 1950s the native authority system and the developing nationalist movement came into conflict. The native authority system had been built up to teach self-government to the people of Tanzania. The number of activities and the degree of autonomy had been expanded over the years, but colonial control meant that genuine self-government was always absent. The native authorities themselves were beginning to find it difficult to serve as brokers between government and people. On the one hand they were increasingly prohibited from using traditional constraints; hence, they were increasingly isolated from traditional sources of power and authority. On the other hand, they were not responsive to the demands of more modernized individuals who were asking them to challenge the system itself. Recognizing these two sets of conflicting demands, the colonial government proposed the development of tribal councils to provide the native authorities with increased legitimacy as well as to give the emergent groups a legitimate forum within the colonial structure. The offer was too little, too late. Native authorities had lost their indigenous base after years of colonial subservience. New nationalists rejected the proposal to rejuvenate a structure they viewed as meaningless and turned instead to the national arena. Councils at the district level then were the scenes of much activity in the 1950s as this relationship between the native authorities and the nationalist movement was being worked out. The result was that the nationalists opted for the larger arena and local government councils stagnated from the mid-fifties to the mid-sixties.

After independence the native authorities were abolished and a series of experiments in various kinds of district and local councils was adopted. At the district level, the tribal councils were transformed; popularly elected representatives replaced the native authorities. The change in composition, however, did not solve the larger problem of functions for the council. A tendency toward centralization of development efforts and the lack of a financial base, coupled with the usual problems of inefficiency and lack of direction, meant that no meaningful role was carved out for the councils immediately after independence. The announcement in 1967 of the Arusha Declaration, which calls for local initiative in development efforts, led to a reorganization of structures at the district level. This reformation is spelled out in *Decentralisation* (Nyerere 1972), the most recent statement of development goals and strategies. The district council has been replaced by a district development committee, made up of elected representatives, whose primary function is the setting of development priorities for the district and the supervision of their execution. Funds for development activities will be given directly to each committee. Raising monies and supervising education, the two problems which proved the undoing of the district council, have been removed to central ministries. At the sub-district level, councils had had similar negative experiences. The village development committees (VDCs) which were created at independence to replace the native authority system have recently been replaced by ward development committees (WDCs). The ward committees are empowered to formulate development goals which, when authorized by the district development committees, are to be administered by the WDCs. Both the district and the ward development committees are composed of elected members as well as party and government officials and are broadly representative of the areas from which they are drawn.

The separation of courts and councils. The court system of contemporary Tanzania is now a separate entity. Judicial decisions which affected the African population in the Arab and German periods were made by administrative officers without any form of litigation. Under the native authority system, chiefs sat as magistrates in native courts but appeal from their decisions went to the administration, not the judicial hierarchy. Since independence a three-tiered national court system has been set up which completely separates judicial process from administration. Dubow's chapter in this volume discusses some of the rationale for and subsequent workings of the courts in Tanzania.

RECENT INNOVATIONS AND FUTURE DIRECTIONS

Political institutions are continuing to evolve in Tanzania. As this overview of councils and courts has demonstrated, these institutions grew up under both indigenous and colonial auspices. The impact of the contemporary government of Tanzania on these institutions has been extensive. The two innovations most often mentioned where Tanzania is discussed are the *ujamaa* villages and the cell system. Immediately after independence in 1961 the president of Tanzania, Julius Nyerere, began formulating his ideas about the future directions of Tanzanian life in a series of speeches.[9] The theme running through these speeches was that the positive practices of traditional life could be molded to fit the modern situation. The idea of *ujamaa* villages, small-scale cooperative communities where each individual works to the best of his ability and joins in the decision-making which guides his life, has gained increasing popularity over the years. Nyerere has been diligent in his efforts to explain to the peasants who live in such villages that their best hope for government services as well as for self-reliance is in a communal undertaking. In the face of the sometimes frightening pace of social change, the link with the past also undoubtedly has important psychological dimensions for the people of Tanzania. In the summer of 1972, it was estimated that ten percent of the population was now living in some form of *ujamaa* villages.[10]

The cell system is a second innovation which has had an impact on governmental institutions in Tanzania. Created in 1965 as a grass-roots level of party organization, the cell is comprised of approximately ten contiguous households. Each cell has an elected leader who serves as a broker between his constituents and the party and government hierarchies on the local level. Disputes are not accepted in local court until the clerk is satisfied that the cell leaders of those involved in the case have exhausted the channel of arbitration at the cell level. Cell meetings are held in which the neighborhood discusses problems, projects, and aspirations. The results of such meetings often become the agenda items of the WDC. Cell leaders perform a variety of functions: they are agents of control, supervising the law and order of their neigborhoods; they are agents of mobilization, working with party people and bureaucrats to implement the development projects; and they perform a wide variety of mediation tasks for their cell members.

Tanzania places priorities on institutions which directly affect her rural peoples, as this very brief discussion of *ujamaa* villages and cells indicates. That commitment is borne out by the priorities of the most recent development plan in which the rural sector receives the greatest amount of both money and thought. The future direction of Tanzania then is in an active commitment to rural development.

NOTES

1. This paper refers only to the mainland portion of contemporary Tanzania which was known as Tanganyika before the union with Zanzibar in 1964. Although the two countries have formed a political union for over a decade, their internal organization remains separate.
2. These data come from Taylor and Hudson (1972).
3. *Ujamaa,* a Swahili word, is best translated as 'familyhood'.
4. Until recently historians thought that it was not until the coming of the Arabs that an extensive trade complex operated. Recent investigations into nineteenth century trade suggest that indigenous peoples were well organized for the carrying on of long distance trade.
5. This period in Tanzanian history is detailed in Austen (1968) and Iliffe (1969).
6. The distinction between official and unofficial members is explained in the section on Tanzania's British legacy. Germany, as a newcomer to African colonization at the end of the nineteenth century, had virtually no backlog of colonial policies. Often, when confronted with a problem, in this case the demands of German residents for a voice in colonial government, they looked to the experience of the British and French. Britian's development of executive and legislative councils in her colonies was at the time a much discussed political innovation and one which served as a model for the Germans.
7. See Hopkins (1971) for a discussion of the backgrounds of members of Parliament in Tanzania.
8. The Swahili term *baraza* was usually applied to the native courts. *Baraza* however can be used to mean discussion groups of many kinds. See Ch. 6.
9. These are found in Nyerere (1968a and b).
10. This estimate was given in the *East African Standard* (August 2, 1972, p. 5).

JEAN F. O'BARR

4

Language and Politics in Tanzanian Governmental Institutions

This paper examines the impact of the colonial and post-independence language policies of Tanzania on the operation of certain of that country's governmental institutions. In particular, it focuses on the consequences of language policies for popular enfranchisement and involvement in the political process. First, I review both the evolution of Tanzania's language policy and the contemporary patterns of Swahili language knowledge and use. Then, after examining the structure of the Tanzanian government, I explore the interaction of language policy and politics in several legislative bodies, ranging from the national assembly to the lowest level of independent Tanzania's governmental institutions, the ten-house cell. In conclusion, I consider some of the political implications of the contemporary language policy of Tanzania.

SWAHILI IN TANZANIA

The widespread use of Swahili in Tanzania can be traced to at least two primary factors. First, Swahili was the language used before independence for a wide variety of introduced social, economic, and political activities. People who were exposed to Swahili in these situations began to speak and use it with relative facility. Second, in the decade since independence, Swahili has been officially promoted as the national language for all aspects of life from presidential addresses and parliamentary debates to village affairs. Observers frequently praise the use of Swahili in Tanzania, stressing the positive contributions it makes to national integration. While, in general, I agree with their evaluation of Swahili's contribution, I will suggest later in this paper that there are some negative consequences of this policy which have not been given much attention.

Many commentators have noted the close link historically between Swahili and the growth of nationalism in Tanzania. As people grew in political consciousness and became aware of the possibility of independence, Swahili became the mode for expressing that awareness. The Tanganyika African Association, a forerunner of TANU, had a constitution written in Swahili and carried out most of their organizing in it. Abdulaziz reports an episode which illustrates the role Swahili played in furthering national consciousness. The annual meeting of the T.A.A. in 1947 was held in Zanzibar, attended by delegates from all parts of Tanzania. 'The Chairman made his introductory address in English, whereupon a number of delegates protested and demanded that the speech be translated into Swahili. . . . From that incident it was agreed that all future T.A.A. meetings should be conducted wholly in Swahili' (1971 : 165).

TANU, founded in 1954, conducted its mass meetings as well as its strategy sessions in Swahili. Swahili became the medium for developing a political consciousness in the years preceding independence. As Whiteley has pointed out, TANU 'used the language as a means of political communication, and, when this was seen to be effective, it began to stress its role in the political unification of the country' (1971a : 146). Swahili stood – and continues to stand – both as a symbol of national identity and as a means for furthering it.

Swahili is an effective means of communication in Tanzania where somewhere between 80 and 90 percent of the population is bilingual in a vernacular and Swahili. William O'Barr has argued in Chapter 2 that the Swahili speakers tend to be the men, the younger people, and the educated. This relationship of Swahili language ability to certain categories of people appears to have been relatively constant over time. That is, even during the colonial period, these same categories of people spoke Swahili – men because they traveled and engaged in wage labor more than women and were exposed to situations in which they learned and used Swahili; younger people and literates because they attended school where Swahili was taught.

TANZANIAN GOVERNMENT

When the British assumed control over mainland Tanzania under mandate from the League of Nations at the close of World War I, they began setting up a governmental structure which resembled certain of their other colonies. A Governor, appointed in London to represent British authority, was the head of government. He was assisted by Executive and Legislative Councils at the national policy-making level. The country was divided into seven provinces for the purposes of regional administration. Each province was headed by a provincial governor who reported to the territorial governor. Within each province, districts were created whose boundaries followed existing ethnic and linguistic boundaries to some degree. Each district was administered by a British district officer who used local chiefs and their assistants to oversee tax collection and the maintenance of law and order in their chiefdoms. Modeled on the British experience in Nigeria this native authority system precipitated far-reaching changes in traditional politics in Tanzania where the men chosen as chiefs usually did not possess the same degree of indigenous authority as their Nigerian counterparts had.

Table 4.1 *Levels of governmental structure in Tanzania in colonial times and at present*

	Colonial period	Since independence[a]
National	Territorial Governor Legislative Council Executive Council	President National Assembly
Regional	Provincial Governor	Regional Commissioner
District	District Officer Tribal Council (c. 50)	Area Commissioner District Development Committee (60)
Sub-District	Native Authority Chiefs Parish Assemblies	Ward Commissioners Ward Development Committees
Neighborhood	—	Cell Leaders Cells

[a] The institutions listed in this column refer to those in operation in 1973. There have been a number of changes in titles and activities between 1961 and the present which are not included in this discussion.

Legislative institutions grew up during the colonial period at some of these levels of government to provide a degree of popular participation in decision-making (Listowel 1968). At the national level, the Legislative Council expanded throughout the 1930s and 1940s. The 1950s saw the dissolution of the Executive Council and the elevation of the Legislative Council into Parliament. Councils never existed at the provincial level which was an administrative tier and not a policy-making level.

At the district level, native authority chiefs met in 'tribal' council to hear the district officer's plans and to air their grievances. The chiefs' power was more apparent than real. Established as an integral part of the system of indirect rule, to educate the chiefs in the responsibilities of modern government as well as to provide legitimacy for the colonial government, these tribal councils evolved through the 1940s and 1950s into arenas where the conflict over control of local affairs was waged.

By the 1940s, the colonial administration had attempted in some districts to set up sub-district councils or parish assemblies. Like the tribal council at the district level, they were to be forums where villagers would hear of plans, projects, and regulations and where they could voice their concerns. The plans to create parish councils crossed another social current, a current which eventually stifled them. The demand for popular and meaningful access to governmental institutions on the part of the 'new men' – returning military men, traders, laborers, and recent school graduates – was growing. These groups were critical of the whole native authority system as conservative and irrelevant to contemporary needs. Eventually their demands for participation in governmental institutions were granted. By restructuring the district councils to include elected representatives, the basis for parish councils as arenas of support for chiefs was undercut and forgotten.

A year after independence, Tanzania removed the last formal vestiges of British presence by declaring herself a republic with Nyerere as President. In 1965, the Interim Constitution went into effect formalizing the system as a single party one, with the Tanganyika African National Union (TANU), the nationalist movement, as the only political party. The emergence of TANU as the major political force in the country has important consequences for governmental structure. At the national level, the Parliament now more widely known as the National Assembly has taken an increasingly secondary role in the policy-making process. The National Executive Committee (NEC) of TANU has emerged as the prime policy-maker. The NEC debates the general lines of policy, while the National Assembly formally enacts measures into law. Instead of a provincial administration, the country is divided into seventeen regions for development purposes, each headed by a regional commissioner who combines in one office the functions of head of government and head of party. The regional Commissioner is responsible for executing all development projects and overseeing the bureaucracy. He is also the regional secretary of TANU (Tordoff 1967).

At the district level most of the colonially defined districts have remained intact but are now headed by area commissioners, who, like the regional commissioners, combine executive and political functions. The district councils, like their forerunners the tribal councils, retained some importance as the areas for the discussion of local affairs in the years immediately after independence. Within the last year, district councils have been abolished. The central government has taken over responsibility for the collection of taxes and the supervision of education, formerly the two most important activities of the district councils. In their place, district development committees (DDC), composed of elected members, have been instituted. These DDCs are projected to grow into important decision-making bodies under the 1972 decentralization proposals (Nyerere 1972). According to the latest plans, monies will be collected nationally and redistributed to the districts. The DDCs will establish priorities among development projects as well as supervise the implementation of those projects. These proposals have only recently come into effect so that no assessment of the DDCs is possible. However, the potential exists at the district level for a vigorous policymaking body to emerge.

Districts are divided into wards, each headed by a ward commissioner who like the regional and area commissioners above him combines bureaucratic with political functions. The ward development committee (WDC) is the organ of representative government at the subdistrict level in contemporary Tanzania. The chieftaincy system and its councils were abolished shortly after independence in 1961. Village development committees (VDCs) became the new councils at this level. By 1965, virtually every area in Tanzania had a VDC, composed of elected members. Since 1969, the VDCs are being replaced by WDCs whose membership is smaller, whose jurisdiction is wider, and whose responsibilities remain similar.

The WDC is composed of ten cell leaders chosen from among all the cell leaders of a ward, TANU party workers and representatives, the ward's delegate to the district development committee, local government civil servants, and numerous technical personnel who are stationed in the ward. The WDC is empowered by the central government to carry out works, keep the peace, and plan and execute development projects. As its responsibilities make clear, the WDC is designed primarily to deal with development activities within a small area. As a local council it possesses only limited policy-making prerogatives. Its authority is circumscribed by the authority and policies of the central government. The WDC is a creation of the center and did not emerge as an expression of local initiative. In that sense, it resembles the councils of American counties (which are administrative arms of state government with limited jurisdiction) more than the councils of American municipalities (which are granted wider areas of responsibility by their original charters).

Every ward in Tanzania is divided into cells. A cell consist of appproximately ten contiguous households. A leader is elected from among the adult residents of the ten houses. When cells were set up in 1965 by TANU they had only party responsibilities: to serve as a communicator between the people and the party, to strengthen the identification of people with TANU, to encourage participation in development projects, and to assist in the preservation of law and order. In 1966 the cell leaders were made the official members of the VDC. At present, under the ward system, some continue to serve on the WDC. Cell leaders act as the primary conveyors of information from party workers, government officials, and technical experts to the people for a variety of activities which affect their daily lives. Cells can only be considered councils in the most general sense of the term. If anything, the meetings which are held in cells resemble town meetings where everyone enters in and in which the issues of the moment (particularly local disputes, but also farming conditions, development projects, and forthcoming events) are discussed and dealt with.

OFFICIAL LANGUAGE POLICIES

Table 4.2 shows the languages in use at the various levels of government during colonial and contemporary times in Tanzania. A comparison of the two periods shows that Swahili has been given an increasing role at both the higher and lower levels of the government since independence. As a consequence of this shift, the roles assigned to English and local vernaculars have decreased concomitantly.

The political impact of the greater use of Swahili in Tanzanian governmental institutions is hard to overestimate. Generally speaking, its effect has been overwhelmingly positive for the regime whose major efforts have been directed toward mass involvement in party and government institutions. Swahili has a number of characteristics which make it appropriate in fostering national identification and in contributing significantly to mass involvement. First, it carries no stigma of European colonialism.[1] Second, it is not clearly identified with any single ethnic group.[2] Third, despite certain exceptions which we have considered, it is widely spoken throughout the country.

Table 4.2 *Language use in legislative bodies in Tanzania*

	Language used	
Level	Colonial period	Since independence
National	English	Swahili and English
District	Swahili	Swahili
Village	Vernacular	Swahili
Neighborhood	–	Vernacular

Most observers of Tanzania are enthusiastic about the contribution that the use of Swahili makes to political consciousness, the effect it has on stimulating popular participation in politics, and its role as an egalitarian force. The prolific critic of East African politics Ali Mazrui has explored the symbolic aspects of Swahili for a regime committed to creating a socialist state. I think it would do well to quote him at length:

'Another point of contact between socialism and the choice of a national language lies in class-formation. There is no doubt that the English language has been a stratifying agent in countries formerly ruled by Britain. Benjamin Disraeli once demonstrated imaginatively how economic factors had divided England into "two nations", the rich and the poor. English has had much the same tendency in many parts of Africa. Where the national language is English, the choice of national leaders is inevitably restricted.

'In a country such as Tanzania, national leadership can be recruited from a wider sector of the society. First Vice-President Abeid Karume has no command of English, and there are many important TANU figures who hold high office without the credentials of fluency in the English language. It used to be said that "every American is a potential millionaire". This was always a gross exaggeration, but it was a useful way of portraying the United States as a land of capitalistic opportunity. Today it can be rhetorically claimed that "every Tanzanian is a potential TANU leader". This too is a gross exaggeration, but it indicates the range of egalitarian opportunities in Tanzania. And the sector of political recruitment is larger and more varied than in the neighboring states partly because the national language, Swahili, is not an elite language (Mazrui 1967:61).'

While there is little doubt that Tanzania is more fortunate than most other African nations with regard to its language situation, its continued multilingualism produces certain problems for its governmental institutions. In the next few pages, I want to consider the way in which the distribution of language knowledge across the population and the official language policy interact to improve popular access to politics in certain contexts while restricting it in others. In particular, I will examine the effects of the language policies in operation during the colonial and contemporary periods on popular participation in the legislative institutions of government at the various levels of the political hierarchy.

THE NATIONAL LEGISLATURE

The language policy of the Legislative Council, the precursor of the modern Tanzanian Parliament, limited discussion and debates to the English language. This colonial policy severely restricted the participation of Tanganyika's African majority. In 1926, when Sir Donald Cameron, newly appointed governor of the territory, established the Legislative Council to enact bills and debate the annual budget, he wanted an elected council. The Colonial Office in London refused to go along with his 'democratic ideal' and he was forced to settle for a 'mere talking shop' which he appointed himself. The first council consisted of thirteen senior government officials and seven nominated members of whom five were European and two Asian. According to Cameron, 'no African could be found with a sufficient command of the English language to take part in the debates of the council' (Listowel 1968:79).

The council remained a legislative body whose business was transacted in English until independence. The addition of the first four African members in 1945 did not alter its linguistic makeup. The four were knowledgeable in English; they could participate in council deliberations. Many who might have challenged them were unable to act in English and hence had their political participation restricted in the formative days of the nationalist movement.

The Legislative Council was significantly expanded in 1958, 1959, and 1960 with the election of members in preparation for independence. Moreover, the English language requirements in operation during the colonial period were incorporated into the independence constitution. Candidates and hence Members of Parliament had to be 'able to read and understand Legislative Council documents and be sufficiently fluent in English to follow Council debates' (Tordoff 1967:192). The independence constitution and the restrictions on membership which were continued in it from the colonial period were put aside with the establishment of the republic and its constitution, in effect from December of 1962 through 1965 (Cole and Denison 1964:273). The interim constitution came into effect in 1965. It does not mention language as a basis for selection. There are, however, stipulations that the electoral campaign meetings be held in Swahili, which in effect insures that all Members of Parliament are fluent in Swahili.

A comparison of the language requirements for the contemporary National Assembly of Tanzania with that of Kenya illustrates the degree to which the former reflects the egalitarian ideals so often associated with Nyerere and his philosophy. In Kenya, candidates in the 1969 national election had to comply with the regulations governing eligibility for membership in Parliament. They were required to pass an English proficiency test. Hydén and Leys (1972:396) report that although no overall figures on the results of these test are available, press reports suggest that in three districts the rate of failure was at least half. The result of the English language restriction, according to Hydén and Leys, is that the election perpetuated those in power – so much so that the Kenyan government's supervisor of elections felt obliged to publicly announce that the candidates were 'not being sorted out by KANU officials in some smoke-filled back room'.[3] The Tanzanian stituation stands in stark contrast to this. The lack of English language restrictions on running for Parliament means that the system is relatively more open to larger numbers of the population.

Informal arrangements have been made to accommodate the differing language abilities of Tanzanian MPs. Tordoff (1967:8) noted that even before Swahili became the official language of Parliament, members spoke informally to each other in Swahili and only used English when necessary, i.e. in formal debates. From the early 1960s the Hansard Reports published speeches in the language in which the person spoke. In the mid-1960s, the title pages of the Hansard Reports started to be printed in Swahili – a further indicator of the direction in which the government was moving.[4] By the 1970s the proportion of members who use English has further declined. There are no longer any European members of Parliament; the last elected one (Derek Bryceson) left in 1971 to head the National Tourist Board.

The contemporary situation in the national legislature of Tanzania with reference to language is that Swahili is almost exclusively the medium of communication. With estimates of up to ninety percent of the Tanzanian population speaking Swahili, very few people who might wish to run for office in the national legislature are blocked by language restrictions. This egalitarian aspect of the national legislature stands in contrast to the situation that existed during Tanzania's colonial period and continues to exist in the neighboring country of Kenya. Although language policy in the national legislature is but one indicator, it does demonstrate a significant degree of openness in the Tanzanian political system.

DISTRICT COUNCILS

While the shift from English to Swahili in the national legislature increased the potential for participation of Tanzania's African majority in that body, the use of Swahili tends, at least for specific categories of people, to restrict popular participation in district affairs.

Throughout the colonial period and up to the present day in independent Tanzania, Swahili has been the language of communication and debate in district affairs. The Germans used Swahili as their administrative language and deposed some chiefs when they could not speak it (Abdulaziz 1971:162–163). The British colonial administration continued to use Swahili. Whiteley says that 'when administrative districts were set up by the British, they commonly comprised two or more language units'. He goes on to specify that:

'Of the fifty-two districts listed in the 1957 census, only in 21 per cent did the dominant language constitute 75 per cent or more of the population of that district. In 33 per cent of the cases, it constituted between 50 to 74 per cent of the population; and in 46 per cent, it constituted between 17 and 49 per cent. This type of situation, where the units were numerically small, clearly favored the use of Swahili for administrative purposes. There were isolated occasions during the later years of the colonial period when separatist movements, with concomitant language loyalties, sought to split districts along ethnic lines, but these proved to be abortive (1971a:143).'

During the early British period, the native authority chiefs were the members of the district council. And while these men were not necessarily the most fluent speakers of the Swahili language, the use of Swahili did give them a common tongue in which to conduct their affairs. The use of Swahili at this time had at least two effect on district councils. Swahili usage allowed the British colonial officers to participate in as well as oversee the council's actions since they tended to know some Swahili (or were able to hire interpreters) and were much less often fluent in the local vernaculars. Secondly, using Swahili was a way to avoid potential rivalry within the district over which language or dialect should be spoken.[5]

After World War II, when elected members were added to the district councils formerly composed of only chiefs, those who spoke Swahili tended to have an advantage in being selected. Not only were women and older men (who tenden to be less fluent than younger men in Swahili, if indeed they knew it at all) excluded from consideration, but it seems that on some occasions at least knowledge of Swahili appears to have been a virtual prerequisite for election. Gulliver pointed out that the Arusha believed they should elect Swahili speakers to the tribal council in 1948 because this ability would give their representatives greater clout in dealing with the British government (1963:193).

Thus, the use of Swahili in district councils during the colonial period tended to facilitate interaction among the representatives as well as with the British, avoided allowing language choice to become a political issue, and furthered national awareness (especially after 1954). Nonetheless, it did restrict the full participation of all people in such political arenas. The continuation of this same policy in the era since independence has not altered the favoritism which it shows toward youth, maleness, and the educated.

VILLAGE COUNCILS

The parish assemblies of the colonial period conducted their discussions in the local vernaculars. This made them, at least as far as language was concerned, open in theory to all people including the old, the women, and the uneducated. The village level councils of post-independence Tanzania, at first the VDCs and now the WDCs, utilize Swahili instead of vernaculars. This is the case even though members and constituents tend to have a common mother tongue, unlike the situation in the district councils. And this policy, like that in district councils, restricts potential participation to the Swahili speakers in the villages. And as we have seen elsewhere, the consequence of this is a tendency to disenfranchise the women, the old, and the less educated.[6]

The Tanzanian government, in requiring that Swahili be used as the medium of communication in village council meetings, intends to foster among the members of the council an identification with the nation of Tanzania. No doubt this purpose is being accomplished as I argued in the section on national language policy – but only at the price of excluding important categories of people in the village, at least in the short term. My study of Pare District VDCs in 1968 showed that while people nearly always used Swahili in such councils, Swahili was perhaps not the easiest medium of communication for them.[7] Except for the few non-Pare government officers who attended the meetings occasionally, all members of the VDCs were bilingual in the Pare language and Swahili. Meetings were usually scheduled for 10 a.m. or noon, depending on the particular village, but they typically began some time later, a delay which was perhaps as much a carry-over from the customary long wait for the colonial officers who never seemed to be on time as it was a cultural norm to be unconcerned about precise times. The lengthy gathering period of the councilors was characterized by palaver in the vernacular during which time the members of the council discussed and even settled many of the matters to be brought before them in the official meeting. When the meeting actually began, there was a shift to Swahili. Business was transacted in a matter-of-fact fashion, usually following the lines decided upon during the premeeting discussion which had taken place informally in the vernacular.

The requirement to use Swahili, which is often evoked by the presiding officer, places a constraint on the operation of village councils. While the use of Swahili does reinforce a national awareness and allow some officials and technical experts linguistic access, speakers are at a disadvantage in the discussions. In Pare, I often witnessed old people who came to the council with a request or complaint and who found they could not follow the debates. Likewise, some of the women, representatives of the *Umoja wa Wanawake wa Tanganyika*, the woman's branch of TANU, whose Swahili was limited, often spoke in the vernacular before the meetings but were reluctant to address the council once in session in Swahili. The lack of Swahili language ability exacerbates the problems these people face when they appear before the council.

NEIGHBORHOOD POLITICS

The policy of using Swahili does not apply to the most recent extension of the local government hierarchy, the ten-house cell. The cell serves many functions which are not handled at other levels of the governmental hierarchy. It is the forum for adjudicating local disputes; it is the basis for self-help development projects; and, through the leader, it is the primary medium of communication between government and people. And it is important to recognize that these functions operate without interference from language. Cells almost always are culturally and linguistically homogeneous, except in urban areas. As a result of this homogeneity, and lacking any directions as to which language should be used, the business of cells tends to be conducted in the most convenient medium, which in rural Tanzania is likely to be the vernacular. The consequence of this is the full potential participation of every member of the cell, making the cell unique among the governmental institutions of multilingual Tanzania in the degree to which language is simply not an issue or a factor which is likely to become entwined in the political process.

CONCLUSION

This paper has examined the interaction of language policy and political access in Tanzanian legislative institutions, from national to neighborhood levels. The results of this survey reveal that the languages used in such arenas result in wide enfranchisement of the population in some cases while restricting access for certain categories of persons in other cases.

In concluding, the question of just what functions these various legislative bodies serve in the overall political process of Tanzania warrants at least brief discussion. The criticism is often heard that formal legislative institutions are not the most critical ones in the governments of developing countries. It is certainly the case that the most important policy decisions in the Tanzanian government appear not to be reached in the national legislature but in the National Executive Committee of TANU. The National Assembly functions to second or legitimate these decisions and to serve as a forum where individual members question the ramifications of policies for their own constituencies. This process is largely a symbolic rather than an integral part of the decision-making process. However, the shift from English to Swahili as the language of the Tanzanian Parliament has played an important part in the *symbolic* involvement of Tanzania's African majority in the questioning and seconding process of the Parliament. The use of Swahili rather than English has had the sort of democratizing effect which Nyerere is working so hard to bring about throughout the country.

The more critical question comes with reference to local councils (district and ward) because it is in such local governmental bodies that Nyerere believes the heretofore uninvolved African masses, the rural peasants as he calls them, must take the initiative to decide collectively what should be done in their local communities to carry out the general goals of socialistic development in Tanzania. Nyerere's most recent political change is the new policy of decentralization which is aimed at helping a local community spend government money on its immediate needs without going through a lengthy process of channeling their requests through innumerable levels of the bureaucracy (Nyerere 1972). Since local councils are the bodies in which such decisions should be made, it is critical to ask whether the language policy in effect in such councils opens the access of the citizenry to participation as widely as possible, or alternatively restricts certain sectors of the society from serious involvement in the process. By requiring Swahili in such councils, the government intends to further the language's role as symbol of the nation. But, given the distribution of Swahili language knowledge in the society, it is having a restrictive effect on those categories of people in the society whose knowledge of Swahili is likely to be limited. These people, as we have seen, are likely to be the old, the women, and the uneducated. Restricting the access of these people, particularly the women and the uneducated, is familiar in other political systems. Most students of Tanzanian politics argue that Nyerere has gone much further than most other African leaders in involving the citizens of his country in the national political process. But it is critical to recognize that even though this democratization has been relatively successful in Tanzania when we look comparatively at the problems of political development in other third world countries, there are dangers of retaining some of the same old inequities which are familiar to students of comparative politics. The positive effects of Swahili's use as symbol of national involvement in local council arenas must be weighed in the balance against the negative, restrictive effects that this language policy has upon participation of certain categories of citizens. We must not be deceived by symbolic involvement of some while real involvement of others is precluded by the very same policy.

Thus, the use of Swahili in the national legislature of Tanzania serves important democratizing functions and extends participation both symbolically and potentially to the large majority of Tanzania's people who do not speak English. And at the most local level of the political hierarchy, the cell in the neighborhood, language plays no significant role in the political process. However, in the mid-range, at the levels of district and ward councils – where increasingly the power to effect the development goals of Tanzania is being placed – the language policies governing the operation of these bodies do disenfranchise certain segments of the population.

NOTES

1. It is sometimes said that Swahili is the language of Arab domination because of the way in which it was brought into Tanzania. However, the Bantu elements of Swahili are many and it is similar to the mother tongues of many non-Arabs. Swahili's connection with earlier Arab domination has not become a contemporary political issue.
2. For a discussion of this point see Eastman (1971) and Arens (1972).
3. Quoted in Hydén and Leys (1972:396).
4. Personal communication with Professor Jay Hakes.
5. This was a problem for many districts as Whiteley suggests. For example, in Pare District, the 'Pare tribe' is really made up of two language communities – Asu and Gweno speakers. Asu, spoken by the larger proportion of the population, has a number of distinct dialects. Using Swahili in the Pare Council avoided any decision about whether Asu or Gweno should be used, and, if Asu, which dialect.
6. Language ability is not of course the only factor which limits political activity for these people. Kidder makes a similar point in his paper for this volume when he says that English is only one of the devices by which the elitism of legal specialization and differentiation is perpetuated.
7. See also Chapter 7.

FRED DUBOW 5

Language, Law, and Change: Problems in the Development of a National Legal System in Tanzania

Like so many other new states in Africa and Asia, Tanzania has sought in the period since its independence to develop and strengthen its national institutions, including its legal system. The process of building a national legal system involves establishing the authority of the court system in at least two ways. First, the legal order must become a part of the plurality of communities within the state. The local courts, the furthest extension of the legal system into the community, must compete with other local institutions for legitimacy. Once established, a nation-wide network of courts provides a mechanism to implement standards and policies with a degree of uniformity. Second, control over legal decisions and the content of the law must be centered in the state rather than in the political and legal institutions of an external power. Creating a Tanzanian legal system thus entails challenges to local authorities and influence as well as to the colonial legacy.

In this paper, I analyze some of the problems that have arisen in developing a national court system in which factors of language have played significant roles. Most of the discussion of law and language in Tanzania thus far has focused primarily upon the use of the national language, Swahili, as the language of the law. Much consideration has already been given to the problems and strategies of transferring legal conceptions in the process of translation into Swahili (Weston 1965, 1969; Harries 1966). In this paper, such questions receive little attention. Instead, I concentrate upon relating the linguistic requirements of various legal institutions to the existing distribution of linguistic skills. I emphasize the ways in which language knowledge affects the ability of law and legal institutions to change and to be accessible to various groups within the society.

In all but the earliest years of British colonial rule in Tanganyika, there were two types of court systems. One set of courts was patterned on English courts and used, for the most part, British law or – more accurately – the law that Britain used in her colonies. The official language of these courts was English. These courts were presided over and addressed by persons with formal legal training. Appeals from the lower level district court were heard by the High Court of Tanganyika. I will refer to these courts as the 'regular courts' for they were part of the judicial administrative structure and were operated, at least in theory, in accord with formal legal procedures.

Under Governor Cameron, a staunch advocate of indirect rule, a second set of courts known as 'local' or 'native' courts was established outside the judicial system of the government (Cameron 1939). These courts were a part of the administrative rather than judicial apparatus of government. They were staffed at the lowest levels by indigenous Africans who were employed by the local Native Authority. Appeals from such courts were subject to review by administrative rather than judicial officers and the procedural standards used to evaluate cases were far less elaborate than those used in the 'regular' courts. In the local courts, proceedings could be conducted in local languages or in Swahili, but official records were to be kept in Swahili. Only Africans could appear before these courts; cases involving non-Africans were heard by the 'regular' courts.

With only minor changes, this pattern of language usage in the two sets of courts persisted until the courts were integrated into a single legal system in 1964. At that time, local courts were replaced by primary courts and became the lowest-level courts in a new three-tiered national court system. Unlike the local courts of the colonial period, the new primary courts were staffed by full-time magistrates who were employees of the national judicial administration. Appeals from lower courts were no longer subject to review by such administrative officers, as the native courts had been, but were heard instead by magistrates in higher level courts. There were no longer any courts that were part of the administrative apparatus (DuBow 1973).

Changes were made with regard to the substantive and procedural rules of law as well. The primary courts are now empowered to hear a wide range of cases involving criminal offenses and ordinance violations. Only the more serious offenses such as murder and armed robbery must go directly to a district level court which is the next level of the judicial hierarchy above the primary courts. The practice of hearing criminal offenses against native law and custom was abolished. Only the national penal code is now used in criminal cases. Customary law, however, continues to play a role in civil cases. All cases involving customary law, no matter what is at issue, must first be heard before a primary court. Most other civil suits, however, go directly to district level courts.

The highest tier of the present judicial hierarchy is the High Court of Tanzania.[1] This court has jurisdiction over appeals from cases originating in the district level courts as well as primary court cases which are further appealed after having been reviewed by the district level courts. The High Court in addition has a limited amount of original jurisdiction over the most serious criminal offenses.

In designing the codes of civil and criminal procedure for the primary courts, an effort was made to provide a simplified and realistic version of the procedures used in the higher courts. The divergence between procedures used in the primary and higher courts was expected to be greater with regard to civil than criminal cases. These changes demonstrated the commitment of the government to providing greater uniformity in the standards of justice among the various courts than was found during the colonial period, but preserving at the same time a sensitivity to local cultural differences as expressed in customary law. The need for assured standards of court proceedings was balanced by an effort to make the courts accessible to the mass of the people. Language requirements for the various courts represent an important aspect of this strategy of bringing about change without destroying continuity and popular participation.

From independence, the government's policy has been to establish Swahili as the language of the law at all levels. In 1964, Swahili was made the official language of the primary courts. All testimony is to be given in or translated into Swahili. The primary court magistrate writes summaries of the testimony as well as the text of his judgement in Swahili in the case file. In the district level courts and in the

High Court, testimony could be given in either English or Swahili but the official case record is kept in English. Cases on appeal from the primary courts must have their records translated into English before they are heard by the higher courts.

It should be noted that the distribution of linguistic skills among the judiciary at that time was probably the major determinant of the official languages of the various courts. The primary court magistrates and their litigants were almost all Africans; few had a proficiency beyond one or more African vernaculars and Swahili. The district level courts were staffed by a mixture of British, Asians, and Africans[2] while the High Court began in the post-independence period without any Tanzanian African Judges. The personnel of both of the higher level courts had only one common language, English. For any legal professional trained in British law, English language ability was, of course, a prerequisite.

LANGUAGE SKILLS AND LEGAL INTERACTION

In the early years after the primary courts were created in 1964, they were faced with two different kinds of communications problems: first, problems arising from communication between litigants and court personnel, and second, problems of communication between the primary courts and the higher levels of the judiciary.

The widespread use of Swahili in all parts of Tanzania is a major asset in the government's effort to create a sense of national unity and to develop truly national political institutions. It has been estimated that Swahili may be a second language for up to ninety percent of the population (Whiteley 1969). Swahili was made the official language of the primary courts for both practical and political reasons. The policy of the judicial administration, similar to that of many other parts of the Tanzanian administrative structure, is to rotate the assignments of personnel frequently. As a result, most primary court magistrates work outside their home districts and consequently are likely to be unfamiliar with both local customary law and local languages. Beyond this practical necessity, there is a strong commitment within the party and government to the use of Swahili as part of the effort to promote national identification.

Within the amorphous group who may be labeled Swahili speakers are persons of widely varying language ability in Swahili. Their knowledge may range from those who can move with ease from their first language into Swahili to those who have great difficulty in conversing in Swahili. For the former, Swahili usage is a matter of choice, whereas for the latter, Swahili is used only when there is no alternative. Tanzanians who grow up along the coast or in the inland cities generally possess greater fluency in Swahili, and for some it may even be a first language. Those who live in ethnically homogeneous communities carry on everyday conversations primarily in a vernacular language. Swahili is reserved for instances in which the common knowledge of a tribal language does not exist.

These variations in the ability to use Swahili are one of the factors which influence the willingness of potential litigants to use the primary courts. Speakers who do not use Swahili with facility will have greater difficulty in presenting their case in the courtroom in Swahili than if they speak in their first language. On the other hand, if they speak in their tribal language and a translation is required for the magistrate to understand the testimony, then they lose a degree of control over the case. There do not appear to be any general standards by which translators are picked for the primary courts. Frequently, court personnel such as messengers or court assessors serve as translators when needed. When litigants who have trouble speaking Swahili come to court without their own translators, they must rely on a translator who is not a partisan in their cause. Such a situation gives rise to the possibility of biased translations, but the more typical problem is that the translations have a neutral tone. Law and legal argument are largely a matter of words in which connotation and tone may be critical. Adversaries choose their words carefully to put their own case in the best light. Statements of fact may involve interpretations of motive which require judgments of degree that are difficult to differentiate. A translator may miss the emphasis in a qualification or fail to emphasize a key word in a statement. Faced with such possibilities in translation, litigants have reason to feel less legally efficacious.

LANGUAGE SKILLS IN LOCAL COURTS: A CASE FROM THE ARUSHA DISTRICT

Further situations in which language usage influences the character of court interactions can be seen in materials based on my observations of the primary courts in the Arusha District of northern Tanzania. The western half of the district is inhabited primarily by the Arusha people. The Arusha closely resemble the Masai people with respect to language, dress, and cultural values except the Arusha have now become agriculturalists (Gulliver 1963). The Arusha speak the Masai language which, unlike most Tanzanian vernacular languages which are part of the Bantu language family, belongs to the Nilo-Hamitic language group. The Arusha, like the Masai, have continued to demonstrate a higher commitment to preserving traditional cultural practices than most other Tanzanian peoples (Gulliver 1969). The strength of this commitment is evident in their insistence on wearing traditional patterns of dress despite the occasionally harsh efforts of the government to make them abandon it. These Masai-speaking people assert their cultural distinctiveness with pride.

One primary court in the part of the district inhabited primarily by the Arusha people contained a linguistic situation which is likely to develop wherever the magistrate and the majority of the litigants in the court share a common vernacular language. In the Enaiboishu court, the magistrate was a former assistant chief of the area. Although he was able to converse with ease in Swahili, he conducted most of his court cases in the Masai language. A non-Masai present in his court had little chance to follow the proceedings. When the parties and witnesses were all Arusha people, Swahili would not be heard at all during the proceedings. If the case involved persons of another language group, however, a Masai to Swahili translation would be made.

Strictly speaking, the law establishing the primary courts required all court statements made by magistrates to be in Swahili and all testimony to be translated into it. The deviation from this requirement in courts like Enaiboishu would be unlikely to receive administrative attention since the case records were always kept in Swahili with no mention that the proceedings were carried on in a vernacular language.

Magistrates sitting in such courts are aware of the conflict between their practice and the proper procedures, but decide in favor of the vernacular for both practical and political reasons. To use Swahili would mean adding an additional step in the proceedings which are already slowed down by the magistrate's job of keeping a hand-written account of the testimony. More importantly, the magistrates believe that the use of translations when all concerned parties speak in a common vernacular language and know that they are understood by the magistrate would be interpreted as a mindless formality, insulting to the people. The incidence of this situation is decreasing as magistrates are transferred more frequently to areas away from their homes.

The choice of language by litigants may represent cultural attitudes as well as convenience. In using a particular language, the speaker associates himself with the culture with which the language is associated. The loaded nature of such linguistic choices is well understood by the Arusha. The Arusha assert their cultural distinctiveness by using Masai in the courtroom. This attitude more than their abilities in speaking Swahili explains their courtroom behavior. In another court in the Arusha district, Emaoi, neither of the primary court magistrates spoke Masai. The majority of litigants in the court were Arusha. Many of them used Swahili, while other chose to use Masai even though they might have been able to use Swahili with facility. Evidence that the Arusha were using Masai out of choice rather than necessity was available in several forms. It was not uncommon for the magistrate to ask questions in Swahili which the litigant or witness would answer in Masai without the need for the questions to be translated into Masai. Even more striking was the ability of some Masai-speaking litigants to read the Swahili court record. In these interactions the magistrates often became agitated for they interpreted the responses in Masai as unnecessary obstructions that challenged the legitimacy of the court.

This perception of the Arusha attitudes was quite correct. They have traditionally been hostile to courts which speak in the name of an external authority even when they are staffed by members of the Arusha tribe (Gulliver 1963). However, the Arusha are becoming increasingly involved in disputes in which traditional mechanisms of dispute settlement prove ineffectual. Reluctantly, they come to the primary court with growing frequency. Despite efforts by the government to minimize the courts' alien quality, they remain arenas in which the Arusha continue to demonstrate their tempered defiance of national authority.

In this court, not all resistance to using Swahili could be explained by lack of skill in Swahili or by political motivation. Some Arusha used language choice as a trial tactic. When Arusha claim not to understand questions asked in Swahili, they may be seeking to avoid answering an embarrassing question or they may be gaining time to compose a reply. This tactic also made it more difficult for the magistrate to pressure a person with a series of rapid questions.

LANGUAGE COMPETENCE AND DISPUTE SETTLEMENT

When disputes arise in Tanzania the disputants may have their disputes settled in any one of three different legal contexts. These three contexts differ in terms of personnel, formality of the proceedings, authority of the decisions, and substantive law used. Despite a degree of uncertainty in the relationships among the three contexts, disputants generally recognize that they represent a set of alternatives.[3]

Most interpersonal disputes are settled out of court. They are settled by informal means, guided by local customary law and generally accepted local standards. While these out-of-court settlements are informal by comparison with the procedures of the courts, they are for the most part not merely ad hoc arrangements. The same forums and persons may be used to attempt settlements. There are two principal types of informal dispute settling mechanisms. First are those prescribed by custom. These include hearings before members of such groups as the clan, age group, or village (Gulliver 1963). These traditional forums are primarily effective in handling disputes among persons for whom some formal social relationship exists. The other type of informal dispute settlement forum is conducted by members of non-traditional local institutions such as the ten-house cell, the political party, the government, and the church. In both kinds of informal contexts, the local language is generally used. The only important exception to this general use of the vernacular occurs when disputes are brought before non-indigenous government officials such as area or regional commissioners.

A second dispute-settling mechanism is the primary court. The proceedings in such a court follow, in varying degrees, procedures which are considerably more formal than those forums in the first category. In addition to more formal proceedings, there is often a written law that must be followed and, in all cases, a written record must be kept of the trial. Despite this added formality, disputants usually have the competence to handle their own cases. The proscription on professional legal representation and the lay character of the magistrates result in proceedings that are free of most legal jargon and are generally intelligible to popular audiences. Since most primary court magistrates are not indigenous to the areas in which they are working, the requirement that the courts be conducted in Swahili is followed.

A third legal context is that of the district and high courts. These are the courts of the legal professionals involving magistrates with formal legal training, private attorneys, and public prosecutors. The language of the courts is replete with the rhetoric and references of the law and the proceedings are often only partially understandable to unschooled persons. Until 1971, the records in both the district and the high courts were kept in English. By that year almost all of the district level magistrates were Tanzanian Africans, a situation which made Swahili an acceptable court language for the first time. The High Court continues today to function in English as it still includes non-Tanzanians.

Language skill is a significant factor in a person's deciding where among these three contexts to present his case. Each of the three legal contexts varies both in the degree of formality and the predominant language. Those who lack a high competency in Swahili may feel handicapped in the primary court. In the primary court, unlike the informal settings, the disputants must speak for themselves without the assistance of a legal representative. Lack of skill in Swahili is not one of the grounds under which the prohibition on representation in court is waived by magistrates.[4]

When the district level courts were staffed primarily by non-Tanzanians and the courts were conducted in English, even fluency in Swahili could place a disputant at a disadvantage if his opponent spoke English. In the higher courts one way to overcome such a handicap was to hire an attorney. Besides having knowledge of the law, an attorney could literally speak the language of the court. Of course, few Africans could afford the services of a professional advocate. An alternate means to compensate in part for a lack of linguistic skills was to hire a public writer. Although these men could not appear in court they were asked to draft letters of appeal.

THE CHANGING REQUIREMENTS OF LEGAL COMPETENCE

Sometime in the early 1970s the entire body of Tanzanian judges and magistrates will be of Tanzanian origin. When this transformation is completed, the potential will exist for personnel at all levels of the judiciary to communicate with each other and to conduct court proceedings in Swahili. It is likely that Swahili will soon become an acceptable alternative official language for all court proceedings as it already has for parliamentary debate and record keeping. This transformation will have implications for the skills required of legal professionals. Previously, attorneys argued in English, the language which was a prerequisite for their legal training. When Swahili becomes the preferred – if not the required – language of the courts, Swahili competency will be needed to employ the legal knowledge acquired through English.

Such a requirement will have a differential impact on the private bar. For the Tanzanian African attorneys the use of Swahili in court does not pose problems of linguistic ability beyond the general problems faced in translating English legal terminology into Swahili. However, in 1971 there were only six Tanzanian Africans in private legal practice.[5] The rest of the private bar were Asians and Caucasians from English-speaking countries. While many of the Asian attorneys have fluency in Swahili,[6] a large number of the non-Africans are not competent to conduct trials and argue legal points in Swahili nor are they likely to gain this competency.

In the longer run, it is possible that English competency may become unnecessary in the acquisition of a legal education. However, the absence of any law school texts in Swahili, the need for expatriot law professors in the immediate future, and the continuing influence of English tradition on Tanzanian law make this development unlikely.

In the short run, the changing linguistic requirements are likely to encourage the flourishing of a private Tanzanian African bar. The new pattern of requirements will have shifted sufficiently to make clients think twice before hiring an English-speaking firm. Only government intervention would prevent this development when law school graduates complete their required terms of service with the government.

LANGUAGE AND INTER-COURT RELATIONS

Thus far, I have concentrated on the factor of linguistic knowledge as it affects the willingness and ability of disputants to use the courts. I would now like to shift focus and consider how variations in language skills influence relations within the judicial hierarchy. In particular, I will suggest two instances in which the differences in language usage in the primary and higher courts have reduced the awareness of judicial policy-makers of problems influencing the effectiveness of the primary courts.

The Tanzanian courts follow the English tradition of being guided by judicial precedent. In such a system, lower courts should take cognizance of decisions in the higher courts. The present character of inter-court communications makes this almost impossible for the primary court magistrate. All of the High Court decisions are presently delivered in English without an accompanying Swahili translation. Even the English version of a High Court decision is sent only to the primary court from which a particular appeal originated. More importantly, the general reference source for decisions of the High Court, the *High Court Digest,* is written by members of the Faculty of Law at the University and is available only in English. For the non-English speaking primary court magistrate, there is simply no source from which he can routinely become aware of the precendents that he is expected to follow. As a result, the practices of the primary courts are mostly uninformed by higher court interpretations. At long intervals the judicial administration may send out a new set of guidelines which are influenced by High Court opinions, but communications in this form make the operation of the primary courts more akin to a code law than common law. Theoretically, judges in a common law legal system find much of the law which they shall use in previous decisions, especially in opinions of higher courts. By contrast, the primary court magistrate uses codes and high court circulars without teasing legal doctrines from cases.

Second, the legal professionals have given attention to the problems of translating highly technical legal terms from English into Swahili, but they have given almost no consideration to dealing with the imperfect knowledge of simple Swahili legal terms by court users. The language of the primary courts may be untechnical in comparison to the higher courts, but for those who do not command a deep knowledge of Swahili, there are significant opportunities for misunderstanding. To illustrate this point, I will once again draw upon my observations of courts in the Arusha District. Most Swahili speakers in the district have significantly less knowledge of Swahili than would be found among the peoples living along the Tanzanian coast. Few household heads questioned in a sample survey conducted in 1970[7] could answer the Swahili version of the question, 'What is the difference between a civil and a criminal case?' This was not because they did not understand that there were two types of court cases, but because they did not recognize the Swahili word for criminal case, *jinai.* Few respondents in Arusha knew what a *jinai* was, although they knew that in some cases you could be punished and sent to prision while in others you could not.[8] More impressionistic observations along the coast suggest that the word *jinai* was widely recognized as the term to contrast with *madai,* the Swahili term for a civil case. This difference in terminology is introduced not for its intrinsic interest but because it has consequences for the operation of the primary courts in Arusha. Before these implications can be understood, a bit of further background information is needed. In the rural courts, citizens may initiate criminal or civil cases by coming to court directly. In the cities they are expected to take their criminal cases to the police before coming to court. In rural areas where there is no proximate police post, people bring all types of cases directly to the court. The court clerk listens to the story of the dispute and then fills out the papers to initiate a case. In rural Arusha, many people coming to court to open a case, begin by saying *ninamstaki,* 'I accuse him' of having done something. By this, they mean that someone has violated their rights in some way. The dispute in legal terms is often, by Western and Tanzanian criteria, civil in nature. However, the verb *kustaka* from which this expression is derived is used in the court to mean 'to charge or accuse' in a criminal case. The proper Swahili meaning 'to sue' is *kudai.*

Clerks who open a case without listening carefully to a complete version of a dispute occasionally open a criminal case by mistake. The disputants do not realize the error if they are told that their case is '*jinai* number ———' because of their unfamiliarity with the term. This confusion leads to mistrials and delays when magistrates later realize the true nature of the dispute after the trial is underway.

CONCLUSION

This discussion has centered on the relation between language knowledge and the operation of the present court system. The central focus has been on the manner in which participation in the lower, primary courts is affected by language skills. To understand this process it was necessary to locate the primary court, both institutionally and linguistically, in relation to alternative forums of dispute settlement whether informal or a higher court. Because of this emphasis on the primary court, less attention was given to a second set of language problems relating to the law. This second set of issues relates to the use of a special, esoteric form of discourse so common in legal systems dominated by legal professionals.

The introduction of a special legal language has at the present time been kept to a minimum in the primary courts. It is true that terminology dealing with legal concepts may still prove a barrier to the legal participation of some members of the society. The example of the troubles in Arusha with the term for a criminal case is one such instance. However, through various policies the government has implemented its commitment to keeping the primary courts accessible to and usable by the general population. The foundation of such a policy is the prohibition of the practice of law by attorneys in the primary courts and the use of non-professionals as primary court magistrates. The magistrates are non-professionals in the sense that they lack formal legal educations. They are, however, full-time magistrates with career commitments to their jobs.

The absence of legal professionals has inhibited the introduction of special legal language in the primary courts which would almost inevitably result were legal professionals to be present. Without legal professionals procedures are kept relatively simple and can be followed by the majority of the litigants. In contrast to courts in Tanzania and in other societies dominated by lawyers, Tanzanian litigants in the primary courts are for the most part able to handle their own cases with facility. This participatory character of the primary courts is a marked contrast to the bewilderment and powerlessness which clients represented by lawyers so typically experience.

Language skills do play a role in the development of a national legal system. Tanzania, considered lucky by many because it has a widely-known lingua franca and now national language, still has language problems in developing its legal system. It can be argued that most of the interactions discussed will diminish in importance as the knowledge of Swahili becomes universal. The closer this situation comes to fruition the greater attention will be given to the problems that the use of esoteric language can play for lay participation. By not compounding these problems in the lower courts, Tanzania has avoided most of the distortions of the legal process which are so characteristic of attorney-dominated lower courts in such countries as India (Kidder 1971), Ghana (Lowy 1972), or the United States (Blumberg 1967, Ross 1970, Lobenthal 1971). Nevertheless, greater attention is yet required to the ways in which language and legal skills may affect the possibility and the experience of court participation in the future.

NOTES

1. An unusual legacy from the colonial period was the ability to appeal cases from the High Court to the East African Court of Appeals. This court is composed of judges selected by the three East African governments, Kenya, Uganda, and Tanganyika.
2. In the 1960s, a number of professionally trained Nigerians worked as Resident Magistrates in Tanzania.
3. Tanner (1970) describes these three legal cultures but says little about the role of non-traditional, informal dispute settlers.
4. This is set out in Magistrates Courts Act of 1963, 12 (1) and The Primary Court Manual.
5. All graduates of the law school of the University of Dar es Salaam are presently employed by the government and are not available for private practice until after a period of required national service. Many English-speaking lawyers are leaving Tanzania as the prospects for a business law practice have declined with the increasing role of the government in the economy.
6. I am indebted to Professor Yash Ghai for this point.
7. Further elaboration on the methodology and content of the survey is found in DuBow (1973).
8. The distinction between civil and criminal as understood in Anglo-Saxon countries is generally accepted to exist in African customary legal formulations but is of less importance than it is in Western legal systems (Elias 1956). The difference identified by the respondents in the survey emphasized the variation in the way courts treated civil and criminal cases rather than a difference in the type of wrong committed.

MARC J. SWARTZ

Hyperbole, Politics, and Potent Specification: The Political Uses of a Figure of Speech

Political speeches are, at least stereotypically, often characterized as having a good deal of exaggeration and extravagant statement. In other words they are hyperbolous. In this paper I am going to examine the idea that hyperbole is a special sort of political resource and that its use is not restricted to speeches. That is, that it is used to gain particular ends and to win or retain support for special procedures or states. The basis of this argument is that hyperbole provides a means for focusing attention on specific aspects of reality (whether social or physical) in such a way as to bring about awareness of values and norms associated with those aspects in an emotionally charged way. In focusing attention on some aspects of reality rather than others, it structures that reality in ways open to manipulation by users.

Stated abstractly and divorced from actual occurrences the putative working of hyperbole in politics is not easy to assess, much less to accept or reject. In an attempt to remedy this I propose to consider two Bena baraza cases in some slight detail. Bailey's paper in this volume (Chapter 13) argues covincingly that dispute settlement (and barazas are dispute settlement sessions) is a political activity and I will not repeat his convincing position since it is available to all of you. I will note in further support of his general position that among the Bena of Tanzania the baraza has been a feature of Bena village politics for a long time (Swartz 1965) and that it provides a fundamental source of support for Bena political officials at all levels (Swartz 1966). I will not be totally limited to Bena barazas in that I will refer a time or two to Bena political speeches as heard in a Bena village and, *mirabile dictu,* I will undertake an excursion beyond the Bena into the political significance of hyperbole in general.

But first, the Bena dispute settlement sessions. Very briefly, these sessions are made up of any group of people which assembles to hear one party present a grievance against another and the accused offer a defense. The two disputants stand with their hands behind them and, when they speak, choose their language so as not to give the impression they lack respect for the assembled company. The parties (almost always individuals but occasionally small groups) stand in the midst of a rough circle of seated fellow villagers. The seated people serve as questioners and judges, but it must be understood that no decision is enforced. A disputant who utterly rejects what the members of the baraza suggest will be thought a 'stubborn' person (*mkatagi* in Swahili; *mnyangng'ani* in Kibena). Usually nothing will be done about his refusal. Despite this, the baraza has an enormous majority of its 'decisions' carried out. I have tried to explain why this is so in another paper (Swartz 1966) and I will not recapitulate that discussion here.

In all barazas the procedure is for the seated persons to ask the disputants questions. These questions concern the facts of the matter at issue and typically the two parties to the dispute are taken in great detail through their account of what happened. The close questioning is done by anyone who wishes to do it but, usually, a few senior men do more than anyone else. These men are often seated on chairs or stools (others sit on the ground) and the disputants stand facing them directly. These same men are typically the ones who are most active in the last phase of a baraza. This phase follows the minute dissection of each disputant's story and is made up of suggested settlements. After the questions on what happened are ended – sometimes before they are really finished – some individual will propose a settlement. This settlement may be altered by others present through simply suggesting a variation on it or by proposing a quite different one. This can go on for some time and is ended when some seated baraza participant offers a suggested settlement which is not followed by further changes or alternatives and is accepted (often tacitly) by both parties to the dispute. The suggestions for settlements typically come from the senior men who sit facing the disputants, but anyone else who wishes to suggest a settlement may, and not infrequently does, do it.

Barazas are either under the general charge of a political official or of a senior man who is acceptable to both disputants. This person always sits with the senior men. All three cases to be considered here come from sessions under the charge of the Village Executive Officer. This string of words is the title held by the highest village level official as things were arranged in Tanzania 1963. Henceforth this status will be referred to as 'VEO'. To say that something happened in the VEO's baraza is not to say that the VEO was instrumental in its happening or, even, that he was necessarily present when it happened. The official who is said to be in charge of a baraza has no necessary duties at that baraza other than to attend it from time to time. If he wishes to be silent, he may do so and this will not alter the fact that the baraza's ability to settle quarrels will redound to his credit and its failures to his diminution and disgrace. Again, I will not tax anyone with the details of how this works since that is available elsewhere (Swartz 1966).

Now to the cases of hyperbole use in the barazas. I was led to consider this figure of speech because of its contrast with the way Bena individuals concern themselves with accuracy, or at least the appearance of accuracy. It is tempting, but hyperbolous, to say that many Bena are obsessed with accuracy in ordinary speech. Some idea of how far this concern with accuracy goes can be had from considering the following quote lifted from the life history of a Bena man.

'There were seven of us in the truck – no, forgive me a little, there were eight. We travelled until morning and then we arrived in Tanga [a large coastal city where many Bena men worked on sisal plantations]. They put us in a house with twelve others. No, forgive me a little, I think there were prehaps more than twelve'.

[MJS: 'When did this happen?']

'This was in 1957 on April 26th. No, it was April 27th. Yes, the 27th exactly.'

It might be thought that this deep concern with accurate reporting is as much the result of my being present and using a tape recorder as of any pervasive interest in getting across the facts 'as they are'. However, any prolonged association with the members of this group shows that a large number of them – especially a large number of men – produce a great deal of everyday speech filled with details and corrections of details. Not every Bena man and woman does this and none does it unceasingly, but a large proportion of them do do it and do it frequently. Compared to what one hears from the members of various social groups in this country the Bena exhibit a notable attention to being accurate or, at least, to sounding accurate.

Given this concern with accuracy in many contexts the hyperbole sometimes heard in barazas and in village speeches is particularly striking. The sort of speaking I am referring to as hyperbole can be seen in the first baraza case we will consider. It is between two men who till neighboring fields. One of the men, named Majuli, had borrowed the field he was using from the other man, Biroos. Biroos was, Majuli claimed, destroying the cassava plants Majuli was growing in the field he had borrowed by hoeing over the dividing line between the fields and by letting the fire Biroos set to clear his field spread into Majuli's. Under the usual close questioning by the people who attended the baraza it came out that the damage to Majuli's field was limited to a very small part of it rather than the whole field as Majuli implied in the beginning. Further questioning brought out that nothing had been damaged by the fire and that precisely six cassava plants had been deracinated by the errant hoeing. The Bena are poor people and their food supply is exiguous, but cassava is not a valuable crop and six tubers cannot have figured significantly in Majuli's household economy. Early in the session some of those present began to believe (they told me later) that Majuli was less concerned with specific damage to his crops on the borrowed field than he was with Biroos trying to drive him from that field. This concern did not become explicit until nearly the end of the case when the VEO, not Majuli, mentioned it (see quote below).

With this background the following dialogue between Majuli and the VEO can be understood. The quoted material is intended to illustrate the sort of hyperbole found in some Bena barazas as well as to add to this specific case.

VEO: 'Although things [in the field] are only a little harmed you should think about your loss. But mostly you should think about this man [Biroos, the defendant] using force and not coming to you in a friendly way to take his field back. The thing about destroying the plants is only minor since he destroyed only a little.'

Majuli: 'It is not just a little. He has not ruined me only a little [*Asiniangameza kidogo tu*]. He has killed me. He's taken all my food.'

Villagers who knew of the case agreed in discussion after it was over that the VEO had been correct in saying that the damaged property was of only minor significance and that what really mattered was the obvious attempt by the defendant to drive Majuli off the field that had been lent him. Majuli, however, would not accept this recognition as sufficient and, in fact, he took the case for further hearing to a baraza outside the village at the area's administrative center. Majuli's explicit complaint was that the defendant had 'taken all my food' but this is difficult to take seriously as his real concern not only because all but a very small part of the roughly half acre in the field in question was unharmed but also because the man had a number of other fields in other areas. How, then, can we interpret his assertion that he had been 'killed'?

In accord with the hypothesis at the beginning of this paper Majuli's claim that he 'had been killed' and that all his food had been destroyed by Biroos' uprooting of his six plants will be looked at as a political resource in action. The end Majuli is trying to gain is safety from Biroos' attempt to reclaim his field and, more powerfully, protection from the use of force. The Bena are extremely concerned about the use of force and Majuli made it very clear in our discussion subsequent to the case cited here that he feared what Biroos might do to him. To protect himself from the source of his fear he took Biroos before the baraza and told of his plants being destroyed.

An examination of some meanings and their communication is in order. Majuli's position as a disputant was communicated by his standing before the assembled baraza (and, earlier, by his notifying the VEO he wanted to bring a dispute to the baraza). The specific damages he had suffered were made clear to the baraza by his account of what had happened. However, Biroos did not threaten him most by what he had already done. His real threat came from the meaning Majuli attached to what he had done: that Biroos would use force against him when he wished to.

Bena barazas, like Bena daily speech, are very closely tied to specific occurrences, and cases proceed on the basis of more or less clearly established fact. The idea that someone might be enjoined from doing something in the future is uncongenial to Bena – and many others. The baraza deals with events and the events in this case were not very dramatic. Majuli had the satisfaction of hearing Biroos told that it was wrong to use force to get a field back instead of asking for it 'in a friendly way'. That, however, did not satisfy him. To him the threat was so great that only Biroos' punishment could protect him from further assaults.

Majuli's saying he had been killed and his food all destroyed followed the VEO's issuing a reproof to Biroos. This reproof had been indirect since it was said to Majuli and that weakened it in Majuli's eyes. Even a stronger reproof would not have satisfied Majuli, he told me. He thought Biroos' actions so threatening that extreme measures had to be taken to protect himself and the community. Majuli tried to make the force of Biroos' threat to the values against force poignant by exaggerating the effect of Biroos' actions against him. He wanted to overcome some, to him, unimportant aspects to reality (that is, the minor damage done) and bring into focus the salient part of reality: that Biroos had damaged his crops and might do that, or worse things, in the future. He failed from his point of view and the seriousness with which he viewed the situation can be seen in his taking the unusual step of going to a baraza above the village level. He had used hyperbole to communicate the meaning of what had happened as he experienced it. He tried to remove the ambiguity from a complex situation and to make the important part of that situation emotionally potent. By saying he had been killed, he tried to overcome the fact that one part of the reality, the actual damage, did nothing to help him get the end he sought: Biroos' punishment by the baraza. At the same time he tried to emphasize that another aspect of reality was present. An important value concerning the use of force had been flaunted, and he tried to show this in a dramatic way. He failed in his attempt because the meaning he attached to what Biroos had done was partly rejected by those to whom he addressed his hyperbole. That is, they agreed that the use of force was deplorable, but they did not agree with the further extension of this that led Majuli to believe that having used force in a mild way Biroos was very likely to use it again and with less restraint unless punished. The ambiguity was that there was damage on the one hand, but that on the other hand it was not very consequential.

His attempt to simplify this by asserting that the damage was great did not overcome the baraza members' view that both aspects of reality were to be considered roughly equally.

The six cassava case shows hyperbole as an attempt at manipulation through focusing on one fact ('there was damage') and ignoring another ('it wasn't much') while appealing to a shared value ('force is bad in many circumstances'). The next case shows hyperbole being used to focus on a very limited aspect of social reality to the exclusion of another aspect while demonstrating the consequences of how a shared understanding about social relations works.

In a dispute over two hundred shillings, two brothers (men having the same father and the same mother) appeared before a baraza. The elder brother said his younger brother owed him the sum in question. After stating that the younger brother was in his debt the older brother was led by questioners to describe the circumstances under which he lent the money, the use to which the money was put, and the way in which the younger brother was going to get the money to repay his debt (he was going to sell a cow). The questioning then turned to the younger brother. What about the debt, he was asked; was it as the elder brother had said? His answer to this was to say: 'I don't know this man.'

This seems a rather startling reply. No one present (and there were perhaps fifty people there) was ignorant of the fact that the two men were brothers. Yet one of these men said of the other *simjui* ('I don't know him'). Equally notably no one present explicitly questioned the disavowal. This is notable because those who attend barazas often greet the unacceptable statements of litigants with vigorous signs of disbelief and disapproval. Someone demanding an outrageous bridewealth from a son-in-law or excessive damages from a defendant may well be greeted with the Kibena derisive sound *tsss* or, even, the sound of disgust and repugnance, *kaa.* Users of hyperbole rarely receive this treatment and the man who said he didn't know his brother had that statement accepted without audible demur. In the cassava destruction case the accuser's statement that the loss of six plants had killed him was also accepted without manifest rejection.

An obvious question which can be considered before looking at the brother-debtor case more closely is why hyperbole is more acceptable than at least some other kinds of distortion of reality. It seems to me that this question is not limited to the Bena. In American society politicians are allowed to be hyperbolous in speeches without generating much – or any – correction to what they have said. An official can say something like 'I have devoted my entire life to public service' or 'I did not enter into a political career for gain' without being subject to contradiction. This may be despite the fact that the man did not really devote his whole life to public service (he was a used car salesman until he was thirty) and even after taking office he continued to read novels, go to the theater, and make love to his wife. He may not have entered into politics for gain (seeing into the hearts of men is sometimes difficult) but, in fact, he makes more money as a senator than he did as a salesman and has power besides. Imagine the reaction if he said 'I entered politics at the urging of the Pope' when in fact that was false. It would be branded a lie as his two 'exaggerations' are not likely to be.

Going back to the Bena, if Majuli had said Biroos had burned down his house, I am sure that there would have been many *tsss* sounds and *kaa*s. Majuli hadn't lied when he said he had been killed. He had simply structured reality by focusing on one part of it and stating it in an extravagant way. This is allowable in Bena barazas. It is much less allowable in ordinary conversation among Bena. Hyperbole is allowable in American political speeches under some circumstances at least. It is certainly more allowable there than in claiming deductible expenses on an income tax form. The kinds of things about which hyperbole can be tolerated almost surely reveal some kind of pattern in many sorts of groups, too, but I am less clear about this – for the Bena and in this country – than I am about the two 'regularities' I have mentioned. The point of all this is that as with other political and, more broadly, social resources the use of hyperbole is subject to rules and its effectiveness depends upon at least some adherence to those rules when using it.

To return to the brother-debtor case. In discussing this case with the younger brother, I asked him why he said he didn't know his older brother. He said that what he meant was that *as a creditor* he didn't know him. He also said the man was unquestionably his older brother because 'blood has strength', but – and here is a separate but crucial point – if his older brother didn't act like an older brother that was a thing of consequence. In his view bringing him before the baraza and claiming two hundred shillings from him was not the way an older brother should treat his younger brother. If he owed him the money, he said, his brother should have had pity on him and given him more time to find it. As it was, his brother wasn't acting in a way he considered brotherly.

There are two explanations in the younger brother's remarks to me for his denial of his older brother. First, he wanted to make clear that a relationship of debtor to creditor was being proposed and he was not a party to such a relationship. He exaggerated by saying he had no relation at all to a man with whom he had an undeniable relation based on kinship in order to emphasize the absence of a relationship based on debt. This is similar to part of what Majuli did when he said he had been killed. It takes one aspect of reality and inflates it so another disappears. Majuli so hyperbolously stressed the fact that there had been damage that the minor character of that damage was put in the shadows. The younger brother stressed the absence of one sort of relation so vigorously that the presence of another was lost from his statement. In both cases conflicting aspects of reality are brought into accord or structured by emphasizing one at the expense of another.

In the brother-debtor case, however, part of the potency of the figure of speech clearly derives from its extremeity. To deny one's relationship with one's brother altogether makes the denial of a debtor relationship with him even more potent. It may be that the same thing is at work in claiming that the trivial loss of a bit of cassava is fatal. In both cases, perhaps, the extent of the exaggeration may be part of the effectiveness of the figure of speech. It certainly seems so in the brother case. Whether it is equally true in the six cassava case is unclear, but the sort of rules for using hyperbole surely also apply to how much exaggeration of what kind is possible and what sorts of exaggerations are most effective. The younger brother did not claim there was no such thing as two hundred shillings in the world or that he had never borrowed anything in his life.

He tailored his statement to his view of how to use language to help him gain his end at the baraza and, perhaps, to help him gain other ends. To him the most effective exaggeration was the denial of a blood relationship as part of denying the debtor-creditor relationship. In doing so he calls attention to the fact that his brother is not acting as brothers should. In saying that it was of consequence to note that his brother was acting toward him in an unbrotherly way he suggests that his denial was related to the values governing brotherly relations. In effect he is saying that brothers are brothers only so long as they act like brothers. Here, then, the two explanations come together. His brother charges him with an unpaid debt. He (the younger brother) views this as a way no brother could treat another. It is a way a creditor could treat a debtor. His accuser is not acting like a brother and he himself denies there is a debt. Therefore, he does not know the man. That is, the younger brother has no creditor since he owes no money and he has no brother since a brother would not accuse him falsely before a baraza.

In the two cases discussed the use of hyperbole played an important role in individuals' attempts to gain desired ends. In neither case did they actually gain their main end. Majuli did not see Biroos punished by the local baraza and the younger brother was told to 'find' the money for his older brother. I cannot help noting that the hyperboles probably did bring the values involved to the fore; that Majuli's hyperbole reminded the people who heard them how 'bad' force is and that the younger brother's denial emphasized that there are ways brothers should and should not act. This, however, is both beyond the scope of this paper and beyond the scope of my data since I did not talk to people about this. The fact that the two hyperbolous disputants lost does not affect the main argument. It may, however, point to a rule which governs hyperbole in Bena barazas and perhaps elsewhere. The main concern of this paper is to suggest what can be learned from this sort of examination of how language is used.

In order to do this it must be noted that hyperbole does not occur in all Bena barazas. Litigants quite often make charges and describe damages without the sort of extravagance and exaggeration Majuli used. Some barazas are totally without anything that can clearly be identified as hyperbole. In fact, of the roughly 250 barazas I recorded I can find clear hyperbole in only about ten percent. The error in this would be in the direction of failing to discover hyperbole when it was really present rather than claiming it was present when, in fact, it was absent.[2] Taking a rough estimate, then, hyperbole occurs in between ten and twenty percent of all barazas so that probably eighty percent or more of all of them are without this figure of speech.

What may account for this relatively rare appearance of hyperbole is that it is best suited (or most pressingly suggested to its users) to situations in which there are several aspects of reality all bearing on the same value but affecting differently that value's implications in the situation. That is, that people in Bena society at least are more likely to use hyperbole if there are 'facts' in a case which seem to them to point in different directions. There is crop damage, but it is minor damage. There is a relation of kinship, but no relationship based on debt. What is suggested is that hyperbole is likely to be chosen as a resource when the user feels a need to structure reality so that some aspects overshadow others.

But surely, speakers almost always feel that they must structure reality for their listeners if they are to gain their ends and they do not always do this by exaggeration or extravagant statements. The particular type of situation in which the attempt to restructure is by hyperbole seems to be one in which the speaker recognizes that there is a strong basis for a different structuring from the one he feels is necessary to gaining the end he seeks. Thus, in a speech the chairman of the Village Development Committee urged the citizens of his village to increase the size of the fields they worked. He said: 'It is better to die of overwork than of hunger.' This hyperbole was directed at his perception of the resistance to his proposal. He knew (and told me) that people felt they already worked very hard and that making their fields more extensive would be a very serious burden. The chairman himself felt the weight of that feeling and this, I propose, is something which increases the likelihood of the occurrence of hyperbole. Speakers who not only want to restructure reality but who feel that the resistance to this restructuring is strong and, possibly, well founded will be more likely to use hyperbole than speakers who do not feel such resistance. Putting this somewhat differently, I would expect that hyperbole will be the resource used where the speaker feels most concerned or uneasy about his ability to get his audience to see the world as he wants them to see it.

This last is specifically proposed for the Bena, but I suspect that it applies elsewhere as well. If it does, and this brings us to the beginning of my foray into politics beyond Benaland, an examination of speeches might illuminate not only what the speaker thought he needed to say but also what he was most anxious about in the issue at hand. Clinically it is well established that individuals exaggerate most in the areas of their greatest weaknesses as they perceive them and this appears true, *mutatis mutandis,* as regards public statements intended to gain chosen ends.

Further, it seems that hyperbole is likelier yet to occur if the speaker believes the audience has a value which can be activated and applied to the issue at hand in a way that would strengthen his case. Hyperbole might be seen as an attempt to induce hearers to experience a fantasy which shows what consequences the issue has regarding a valued thing or state. The VDC chairman is obviously doing something of this sort by reminding people that although work can be unpleasant, hunger is also bad. Hunger is a very real thing to the Bena and the values clustering around its avoidance are powerfully held. The chairman tried with his hyperbole to make people come to see the government's desire that they cultivate larger fields in the light of those values. He offered them the fantasy choice of more hoeing, even unto death, or no cultivation and consequent starvation. Similarly, the younger brother's denial of his older brother can be seen as an attempt to get the audience – including the older brother – to see that the values attached to kinship relations, especially those that hold that 'blood is strong', are seriously threatened by the kind of thing the older brother did. Majuli held up the fantasy of extreme violence, murder, to show the force of his view of what Biroos had done.

If any of this is true in other societies, and I think it probably is, it would be expected that hyperbole would occur concerning things about which the speaker believed the audience held common and compelling values. Should this be so, an examination of hyperbolous speech should indicate to us not only the areas of the speaker's greatest concern but also areas where he believes the audience to hold particular values.

FIGURES OF SPEECH AND POLITICAL ACTIVITY: SUGGESTIONS AND QUESTIONS

All of the foregoing has been an attempt to establish the conditions under which speakers are likely to employ hyperbole in the course of what can broadly be considered political activities. It was suggested that speakers use hyperbole as a device to bring the audience to see the facts at issue in the way the speakers want them to see these facts. However, hyperbole is not the only means to do this and it is further suggested that a speaker's perception that there is a strong possibility the audience will see the facts in a way different from his way increases the likelihood that hyperbole will be used. When the speaker senses the possibility that the members of the audience have a value which will work to his advantage if he can stimulate them to experience a fantasy concerning the consequences of the facts as he wants them seen, the probability of hyperbole being used increases even more.

The three suggestions just noted concern the speaker's views of his audience and the way these views might affect his speech to them. If they proved to be correct, we would have a useful tool for making inferences about the understandings speakers have of the audiences they address and of the speakers' beliefs concerning what the members of those audiences think about the issues at hand. A fourth suggestion concerned the speaker himself and how his own state of mind affects the use of hyperbole. Here it was suggested that hyperbole is likelier to occur when speakers are unsure about their ability to gain the audience's acceptance of the speakers' construction of reality. If this were shown to be so generally, we would have an interesting lead for investigating the speaker's areas of insecurity, at least as concerned the issue or issues he was speaking about.

It is important to note that in all of the above attention has been directed to what the speaker was doing or perceiving and not what the members of the audience did or perceived. Nothing has been said about audience reactions to hyperbole. This is not because I think that an unimportant issue. On the contrary, it is a vital one. I neglect it because I do not have the data which permit me to discuss it. I would speculate that what I have said about speakers' attempts has a good deal of bearing on audience reactions. Unfortunately, I do not have a case where hyperbole clearly worked. In the last example cited the villagers did ultimately come to accept government's directive that each person cultivate more; but whatever may have brought this about, the chairman's speech had only a small role at best. This seems to be so because a year after the 'hoe-or-die' speech the government order was still unimplemented. It may be that hyperbole is a resource of lost causes and that the speaker's perception that there is formidable opposition to his view of things is usually correct. If this is so, it would be a most interesting finding.

As a final issue, it would be extremely important from a theoretical point of view to determine whether what I referred to earlier in this paper as 'rules' really are rules in the sense that actors consciously and knowingly tailor their behavior to act in accord with them. Nicholas (1968:302ff.) distinguishes a number of different sorts of rules of political activity and all of them have as a key element the fact that actors consciously know about them and behave in the light of that knowledge. Nicholas also discusses regularities (1968:306–307) which are influences on political activity not recognized by the central participants in that activity. The rules for succession to office, for example, are usually known to all those concerned with succession and although some or all may attempt to change, subvert, or circumvent those rules, the rules are known and this knowledge affects behavior. Regularities, on the other hand, are not known to participants and their effect on behavior comes in ways other than through their knowing manipulation by actors. Nicholas uses the relationship between population pressure and land shortage in Indian villages as an example:

'. . . they do not perceive a large number of children as a threat to agricultural livelihood and to the relative power of a family in village society. They know the immediate effects of local clinics, dispensaries, and DDT spraying, but they do not see how the operation of these factors lengthens the average lifespan and adds to the strain on their meager resources. Knowledge of regularities like rates of population increase, the absolute poverty of Indian villages (which do not produce enough food for all their residents), and declining soil fertility, belongs exclusively to the observer's model (Nicholas 1968:306).'

I think the propositions I have suggested regarding the use of hyperbole are to some extent rules in Nicholas' sense in that actors are at least partly aware that conflicting aspects of reality and one or more common values regarding that reality are a prerequisite for the effective use of hyperbole. It is less clear, however, that actors know they exaggerate in areas where they are insecure. Taking this together with whatever lack of consciousness may be discovered regarding the sort of issues they exaggerate about and the aspects of reality most and least subject to exaggeration, there is a strong possibility that the use of hyperbole is not wholly governed by calculation. To the extent that political activity is not carried out according to rules in the above sense but is, rather, to be understood according to regulatities unknown to those most directly affected by them, to that extent we have to view political activity as something other than a rather purely rational maximizing of advantage by calculated means. Some anthropologists, recently and notably Fredrik Barth (1966) in, for example, his influential *Models of Social Organization,* have stressed rationality as the key and virtually exclusive element in determining political behavior. The empirical basis for this emphasis, however, is not a very extensive one. This paper suggest that, in the examination of even so small a thing as the use of a type of metaphor, it might be possible to make progress toward establishing the extent of conscious calculation and the extent of influence of non-conscious forces. The slim evidence offered here suggests that in at least one aspect of political activity in at least one social group there are influences on behavior in addition to rules.

NOTES

1. I am grateful to my colleague David K. Jordan for discussing the material covered by this paper with me. He is not responsible for the final formulation presented here, but his comments were extremely valuable to me. My comment about hyperbole occurring in areas where speakers feel insecure or concerned is the result of a discussion with Saul H. Karlen.
2. The failure to identify hyperbole when it was present can come from two main sources. First, my notes of many barazas do not contain all the statements of all the main parties and this incomplete reporting cuts down on my ability to determine the presence of hyperbole much more than the

reverse determination. Second, my ignorance of 'real' situations can lead me to see some statements as accurate when, in fact, they are exaggerations. The opposite also happened, I am sure, but I checked more extreme-seeming statements for accuracy more than I did accurate-seeming statements. Both sorts of errors undoubtedly occurred, but I believe the overall result is an underestimation of hyperbole.

WILLIAM M. O'BARR

7

Language and Politics in a Rural Tanzanian Council

In this paper, I attempt to explicate the operation of a local council in rural Tanzania by focusing on its structural characteristics and on the system of communication which underlies it. First, I shall rely upon the conventions of social anthropology to explain why the council takes most of its decisions through consensus rather than majority vote and why as a political body it appears largely ineffectual both to the superordinate Tanzanian government and to those people whom it is intended to represent. Then, I shall move to a consideration of certain aspects of the communication system at work in the council and their effects on the political process which it embodies. Finally, I raise questions about the implications of this study for the gamut of political structures being examined by the contributors to this volume.

THE VILLAGE DEVELOPMENT COMMITTEE

Village Development Committees (VDCs) were instituted as part of the reforms in local government undertaken by Nyerere shortly after Tanganyikan independence in 1961. Throughout the country, the system of local government by indirect rule utilizing either indigenous chiefs or those who had been established for such convenience during the colonial era was abolished. Representative councils, the VDCs, were intended to take the place of chiefs in many local government functions. The specific nature of the VDCs varied somewhat throughout the country and underwent a number of changes between their inception and the time of my first field trip to Pare in 1967–68.

Throughout Pare District in 1968, the VDCs theoretically were made up of one representative from every ten houses in a ward, which in practice usually ranged between 30 and 60 such councilors. These people met together periodically in council with the civil servants assigned by the government to oversee the ward in question and were joined from time to time by any technical experts who were either stationed in the area or happened to be passing through. (The presence of such visitors was often a reason for calling a VDC meeting.)

The VDC was empowered by the central government to handle certain functions of local government. It was given the responsibility for planning and overseeing the execution of local development projects like road building, encouraging the local people to take interest in improved farming methods, construction of schools and government or party buildings, etc. In addition, this council was responsible for carrying out certain directives issued from above, which in addition to development projects included such things as planning for the reception of visiting officials and for the celebration of national days. The council, in 1968, at least, was the body which recommended excusing tax responsibilities for hardship cases. Litigation as such did not come under the purview of the VDC. The local court was the formal governmental institution given judicial powers by the government. This organization of local government structures thus represented basically a continuation of the separation of executive, judicial, and legislative functions laid down in the transfer of British governmental models to Tanganyika during the colonial period. Thus, the VDC was primarily the local government body charged with the responsibility of administering the directives sent down from the higher levels of the governmental bureaucracy.

In this paper, I shall limit my concern to the VDC in one of the villages where I worked during 1968. For convenience, I call this community Mlimani, although this is a fictitious name. Typical meetings of the VDC were held out of doors under an old tree where the now deposed chief used to sit with the elders of the community. Although the chief in council as a native authority was in existence throughout the British colonial period in Tanganyika, this group of men (chief plus elders) was the remnant of the village moot or chief's court which had existed in this area prior to the advent of the Arabs,

Germans, and British during the last one hundred years. The people continued to prefer this location for the VDC meetings, except in inclement weather, when they met in the nearby community center which had been built by these people through the instigation of the government.

Meetings, supposed to occur on a monthly basis, were actually called at intervals of one to two months by the TANU chairman, the elected head of the VDC who had been selected by the members of TANU in the local community. A few days prior to a meeting, the secretary sent messages by letter or word of mouth to the members of the council, announcing a date and time for the meeting. He usually called it for any weekday except Friday since a few councilors were Muslims. On the appointed day, the members of the council would begin arriving around ten o'clock, the time for which the meeting was usually called. But others came some time later, often up to a couple of hours after the scheduled opening. This period of slow gathering of the councilors was marked by informality, by gossip, and by sharing news from various parts of the ward. The topics which had been announced for discussion during the meeting would probably be discussed as well during this preliminary period, giving opportunity for the members of the council to form opinions and air grievances among themselves outside the context of the formal meeting. The language used during this period was almost invariably Pare rather than Swahili although the government had already begun to require the latter for all official meetings. Once the meeting was called to order, say around noon, the informal conversation ceased, the language shifted to Swahili, and the councilors spoke one at a time as they were recognized by the chairman who presided over the meeting.[1] To the outside observers like myself and the itinerant government officials, some of whom were not Pares themselves, the verbal exchanges which constituted the program of the council's meetings through two to four hours appeared orderly and straightforward. I propose to show shortly that this overt appearance was only a façade behind which operated a covert system of communication known as *kingua* and which had important consequences for the operation of the Mlimani council and for the very nature of the political process encompassed within it.

THE DECISION-MAKING PROCESS WITHIN THE VDC

The VDC reached most of the few decisions it actually made through consensus rather than through majority vote. In the observation of about a dozen such meetings in two Pare wards, neither Jean O'Barr nor I ever observed a decision reached by majority vote. The discussion which took place preliminary to the actual meeting facilitated the consensual procedure. In fact, decisions almost invariably appeared to have been reached by the time the meeting was finally called to order, and this in itself made it easy to give the impression that consensus was always present. But this is in reality a weak argument for explaining consensus, for although it says something about the process whereby consensus was reached it says nothing about why consensus rather than majority voting was the basis for decision-making in the Mlimani VDC.

I am convinced that majority voting as a decision-making procedure was really quite foreign to the people of Mlimani. It had no apparent precedent in Pare traditional culture; its genesis seemed to have been a clear derivation from Europe during the colonial period. Thus, I would extend my argument to say that majority vote had simply never 'caught on' as a decision-making procedure in Pare. This is doubtlessly part of the reason, but I think Bailey's paper on decisions by consensus in councils and committees, with special reference to village and local government in India, is really more incisive (Bailey 1965). In that paper, he points out that certain structural characteristics of committees/councils are correlated with the consensual decision-making process while others are associated with majority voting. Bailey has suggested that the alternative of consensus really applies only to small councils, usually less than fifteen active persons, since larger groups usually find it impossible to reach consensus.[2] Withing councils which fall within this size range, any of the following characteristics of the council may favor the consensual process:

1. an administrative function, especially when the council lacks sanctions; or
2. an elite[3] position in opposition to their public; or
3. concern with external relationships (1965 : 13).

Councils favoring majority vote tend to have one or more of the opposite characteristics: policy-making functions, operation as an arena council, or concern with internal relationships. By focusing on which of these characteristics best describe the Mlimani VDC, we discover that Bailey's model is adequate to describe the structural characteristics of the council which tended to favor consensus. The VDC was charged with administrative functions by the superordinate government; it took few, if any, policy decisions on its own. It lacked sanctions to enforce the directives it issued.[4] Finally, its greatest concern was with its relationship to the outside, in which regard the members of the council went to great lengths *to give the impression* that they were agreed on what should be done and how they should do it.[5]

THE EFFECTIVENESS OF THE MLIMANI VDC

As an organ of local government, the VDC was considered by both the district government and the local community of Mlimani to be ineffectual despite the fact that it gave the appearance of attempting to administer government requests. Yet, it was obvious to almost everyone that the VDC was failing to mediate between the local community and the development plans and directives of the central government. Why was this?

Probably the most important reason was the inappropriateness of a single national development plan for the entire country. Despite the diffuseness of governmental directives in 1968 and the emphasis on each community's concentration on local problems, development projects were almost invariably suggested by the superordinate governmental structure and did not originate with the members of the local community themselves. The underused community center building was a good example of a development project suggested by the central government but carried out by the local people. Other projects suggested to them from time to time included such things as road building and the use of improved, hybrid corn seed – all of which, like the community center, were externally suggested projects. The members of Mlimani community did not want or need a community center. They had built it under pressure from the government and only used it when bad weather made it necessary to hold the VDC meetings inside. The members of the local community did want a good road, motor vehicles, and easier transportation to the outside. But they had worked on the road many times in the past. Lacking any means to acquire motor vehicles themselves, the only cars which the people of Mlimani ever saw passing over their roads belonged to government officers and missionaries. A number of people had tried hybrid corn and liked it, but many found that the cash outlay required for new seeds each year was excessive. Over and over again the people of Mlimani had been urged to undertake certain projects. Yet much of the time, the concomitant changes required to make these projects successful were not undertaken simultaneously.

I cannot emphasize too strongly that problems like these play a very significant role in why the VDC in Mlimani was not more successful. The projects were externally inspired, and while they responded to local problems, they did not attack them in enough depth to be successful. The people of Mlimani were experiencing the partial, and thereby almost totally inadequate, solution to many of their problems through the development projects undertaken by the VDC at the instigation of the superordinate government.

A second reason which helps explain the ineffectualness of the VDC is the fact that there was at work in the council meetings a linguistic device which gave one sort of meaning on the overt level and another on the covert. This device was a long-standing tradition in the community of Mlimani. Called *kingua* in the vernacular, it is perhaps best translated into English by the term 'double-talk'. *Kingua* was used by the members of the VDC to trick and deceive the government officials by giving them one impression of what was going on in the VDC meetings, while many understood a covert meaning of the proceedings. To understand how this 'double-talk' operated in the VDC, we must first understand *kingua,* its history and its uses in the communication repetoire of Mlimani.

EXCURSUS: KINGUA DOUBLE-TALK

Mlimani is located in the remote highlands of the South Pare Mountains, about 100 miles from the Indian Ocean. The Arab traders who first contacted the area in the nineteenth century spent little time in Pare since they were more interested in the riches of Kilimanjaro and the interior of East Africa. Nevertheless, the passing of the caravans through the Pare foothills resulted in certain not insignificant changes in the organization of the mountain communities as the highlanders mobilized to exchange foodstuffs for trade goods (see Tessler, O'Barr, and Spain 1973).

Linguistically, the early colonial period brought changes as well. The language spoken by the traders was Swahili (Whiteley 1969), and it was they who introduced it to the interior of Tanganyika at this time. The advent of German explorers and missionaries during the final years of the nineteenth century resulted in further changes. Despite significant intrusions into Pare communities, German policy did not call upon Africans to speak the language of the colonists. In fact, early German missionaries attempted to teach the skills of literacy in the local vernaculars, a trend which the British later reversed. The increasing pressures to learn Swahili during the twentieth century (such things as education in schools using Swahili, temporary labor migration, increased interethnic communication, and the like) have resulted in a widespread knowledge of Swahili in the Pare highlands. Elsewhere I have estimated that about eighty percent of one highland community is fluent in both the Pare language and Swahili (O'Barr 1971). Those who lack the ability to speak Swahili today are primarily the old people, especially the women. Trends broken down by age groups show that young people tend to be fluent in both languages. These figures in point of fact describe the linguistic situation in Usangi Division in northern Pare District. The Mlimani community is located in the southern part of the district, and, while I do not have such precise figures from Mlimani, I am confident that detailed investigation would reveal a similar profile, showing, if anything, an even higher percentage of the population as bilingual. This would be due primarily to the fact that Mlimani has a higher proportion of Christians whose education has been attended to by the missionaries. Contemporary societal trends, should they continue, indicate that virtually the entire population can be expected to be bilingual within a couple of decades.

Along with this widespread bilingualism has come a relatively stable diglossic relationship between Swahili and the vernacular. The

Pare language remains the language of home, of mother and her children, and of farming and herding activities. Swahili is the language of education and, hence, of literacy, of many of the churches, of Islam, and of government and TANU meetings. Most highlanders tend to accept these roles for each language as right and proper. English is not used much by the people of Mlimani and only a few of them have any real facility with it.

The already complex communication system of Mlimani is further complicated by the use of *kingua* double-talk. The nature of this system of double-talk, as we shall see, does not restrict its use to any particular language. Considerations of time, place, topic, and relation between speakers are the primary determinants of code choice between Swahili and the Pare language (see O'Barr 1971). *Kingua* takes many different forms, but its function is always to communicate messages on two levels. As an example of how it operates, consider the following conversation, which in its phonological and syntactic character, does not differ from ordinary speech.[6]

1. Where is *Mapombe?*
2. He is with a friend, but the elder *Nzano* is looking for him. If *Nzano* meets up with him, he'll call *Mapombe* away.

Overtly, this conversation appears to be about two men, Mapombe and Nzano. But to understand another meaning which it may have, we must consider the system of naming in this community. In addition to family names derived from kinsmen in one's grandparent's generation, a Pare child is typically given another name which refers to an event surrounding the child's birth. Such a name might be *Senzia* ('on the path', perhaps referring to the fact that the child was born on a path) or *Navwasi* ('illness', perhaps referring to the child's or the mother's bad health at the time of the birth). In the verbal exchange above, the conversation could refer to the natural events which these personal names also represent. The personal name *Mapombe* means 'water' while *Nzano* is 'sunshine'. Thus, the conversation instead might be understood as follows:

1. Where is the *water?*
2. It's with a friend [in this case, the earth or the fields], but when the *sun* catches up with it, it will take the *water* away.

A person overhearing this exchange may not comprehend its real meaning, for even this simple example contains much room for manipulation. One possibility is that the speakers really wish to talk about the two men instead of water and sunshine. In such case, the speakers might elaborate their discussion of the rain, the dampness of the field, the weather, etc. On the other hand, attempting to communicate covertly about the elements of nature, for whatever reasons they might have, they could carry on a protacted, carefully fabricated, but overtly false exchange about certain people either using their names given to describe the birth events or perhaps, to conceal their real intentions even further, using any of the other names which people are called. The possibilities here are many. Given the emphasis which the people Mlimani place upon the ability to communicate in this fashion, quite a few people in the community are adept at the verbal art of *kingua* double-talk.

The example I have given is only one way in which *kingua* works. Across its many forms, it need only have the characteristic that the overt meaning is not the real meaning to be called *kingua* by the people of Mlimani. Let me go through some of its social uses in the community, and in the process I shall be able to illustrate some of the other forms it takes.

One common use of *kingua* is simple euphemism. A pregnant woman who realizes that her labor is beginning might say, for example, to a female companion, 'Let's go eat some porridge.' The companion, knowing that delivery is imminent, understands that the speaker is asking for help. Male informants told me that women have their own *kingua* (read *euphemisms*) which they employ in the company of men to speak about those things which are considered to be the exclusive domain of women. Childbirth is such a feminine domain.

Kingua is used by anyone who does not wish, for whatever reason, to speak openly. For example, a man, wishing to confirm beer drinking plans with a friend without also informing others who might overhear the conversation of the specific plans, might speak as follows:

'I say, do you recall that I told you I might brew some beer to drink tomorrow? Well, I had so much work that I didn't get around to brewing it at the time I planned. You'd better come the day after tomorrow instead.'

When understood as *kingua,* this means to the friend that he should come ahead at the originally appointed time. For any others, it serves to throw them off base as to when the beer will actually be ready. This particular form of *kingua* is appropriate for confirming already discussed plans in public places or, as is more common in the terrain of Pare country, by shouting from a hillside across a valley to a friend.

Because *kingua* is so common in the communication system of Mlimani, most people are suspicious of what they hear and tend to be reluctant to take anything at its face value. The shrewd person learns to be constantly on the lookout for the real meaning of what is said. It is not really necessary to point out that the implications of this situations for interpersonal relations are great. A continual suspicion of deceit, an extreme caution in dealing with others, and the generally atomistic orientation which obtains in Mlimani result in a community whose daily fare is more divisiveness than solidarity.

The power of this covert communication system has many uses in the political life of Mlimani. Consider, for example, the following statement which one man makes to a group which has assembled in one of the local shops:

'Say, do you think Abdullah is a witch? I really believe he is. You know, he came to visit me some time ago. He looked at my banana grove and remarked about how well it was doing. Now it has almost dried up.'

The speaker's intent in making this statement is to accuse one of those present of the kind of witchcraft known as *uchawi wa mdomoni* ('witchcraft of the mouth' or verbal cursing). He actually believes that one of those present, not the Abdullah whose name he mentioned, did such a thing to him. One of the hearers might think he is the real referent of the remarks about Abdullah, but he dare not say so, for to challenge the speaker's intent would surely elicit the claim to have meant only the overt meaning of the remarks. Moreover, launching an accusation against the speaker would be considered tantamount to an admission of guilt.

It is easy to see the political value of using *kingua* in such contexts. It allows a person who believes himself to have been wronged to accuse a suspect indirectly, outside the process of formal litigation, while at the same time, leaving the suspect with few alternatives. To speak out denying the accusation is likely to result in one's being considered guilty by virtue of his reading a personal referent into the remarks. This situation affords great leeway and protection to the accuser, but it hardly gives the accused any rights at all.

About the only channel open to mediate such a situation is for the accused to go to a mutual friend explaining what he believes the speaker really meant. The mutual friend may act as an intermediary by relaying to the speaker the fact that his *kingua* message has been understood. But even in this situation, the accuser must bear no direct liability for his remarks, since in point of fact he has never made a public accusation. Left in this situation, the accused may attempt to return the insult in another way, such as through witchcraft. Here again we see the divisiveness which *kingua* precipitates in Mlimani.

Uses of language similar to the ones I have described here are surely common in many languages. If anything distinguishes *kingua* from similar uses in other languages, it is perhaps the degree to which it operates as an institutionalized part of the communication system of Mlimani.

Although double-talk is common throughout Africa, what evidence I have points to a fairly recent origin, or at least elaboration, of the system of double-talk which operates in contemporary Mlimani. The term *kingua*[7] appears to have emerged during the German colonial period when double-talk was an important means of helping resist European incursion into Mlimani. It was the practice of the Germans to call the highland residents to meetings, often at considerable distances from their homes. At these meetings, the officials would announce plans for public work projects and taxation. To gain compliance, the Germans directed the chiefs and headmen to order their people to do as told. The chief of *Ngua,* a sector of Mlimani, reached an understanding with his people that they would do the opposite of whatever he told them in the meetings which the Germans called. Thus, standing before his people, the chief would say, 'Come, let's work on the road.' As he spoke, the people would run away as quickly as possible. Oral traditions recalling the early colonial period tell of the reputation of this chief in speaking in a way only he and his people could understand. The name *kingua* literally means 'the language of *Ngua*', but it has come to signify any kind of double-talk in which people hear one thing but understand another.

During the colonial period, *kingua* expanded to include non-verbal forms of communication. The traditional *baragumu* ram's horn which had served to call the community together came to signal just the opposite. And gestures, an aspect of the culture which Europeans tended to neglect even when they attempted to learn the local language, became an additional base for indicating intended versus the overt meanings.

KINGUA – MODERN POLITICAL USES IN THE VDC

Kingua continues to have important political uses in the post-colonial period. From the vantage of the local community, many directives of the national government are unpopular. To combat adverse and unwanted projects, members of the local community often employ *kingua*. During the late 1960s, government officials in district headquarters continually asked the people to give over one day a week to such nation building activities as road construction. Having no motor vehicles themselves, no government vehicles stationed in the area, and no apparent prospects of having any, the local people found unpalatable the government's insistence that the road be widened, improved, and kept up through communal work. As a result, the VDC whose job it was to plan the execution of such development projects was rife with *kingua*. In the early months of my field work in Mlimani, I sat unknowingly through hours of VDC meetings listening to the intricate planning for road building activities. The plans were always elaborate, naming individuals, their responsibilities, and the areas where they would work. The government men left the meeting happy to see that plans had been made. But on each appointed day, I would wait to no avail for the plans to become action. When I was finally clued into the secret of *kingua*, I realized that what I had been witnessing was the formulation, for official consumption, of a plan for road building. The planners had known all along that they had no intention of building the road.

Kingua double-talk is confusing even to the initiated. One can never be quite sure what is intended by a particular statement: the overt meaning, some hidden meaning, or an even deeper, more subtle meaning. As a consequence, it has been an effective rhetorical device time and again for dealing with outsiders. The itinerant government officials usually do not understand the conventions of *kingua.* Even if they did, they would likely be impotent in dealing with them.

DEGREE OF COGNITIVE SHARING AND SYSTEM UNDERSTANDING – A DIMENSION OF VARIATION IN COURTS, COUNCILS, AND LEGISLATURES?

In an often cited paper, A. F. C. Wallace has suggested that many social institutions characteristically require the non-sharing of certain cognitive maps among participants for their very operation. He has gone on to suggest that 'many a social sub-system simply will not "work" if all the participants share common knowledge of the system' (1961:40). What is required on the parts of the various participants in such systems, according to Wallace, are 'partial equivalence structures' or learning to predict the behavior of other actors in the system without necessarily knowing their motives or their own views of how the system operates.

'The equivalence structure model should be congenial to that tradition in social anthropology which interests itself in the relations between organized groups. Thus reciprocal interactions between the representatives of geographically separate groups as alien as American Indian tribes and colonial or state governments have proceeded for centuries, with only minimal sharing of motives or understanding, on a basis of carefully patterned equivalences. Similar observation might be made of the relations between castes, social classes, professional groups, kin groups, factions, parties, and so forth. In no case is it *necessary* that a basic personality or a basic cognitive framework be shared, but it is necessary that behaviors be mutually predictable or equivalent (1961:40–41).'

Wallace does not go on in his discussion to analyze such institutions that depend upon cognitive non-sharing for their very operation, although he does give us enough leads to see how this might work in particular situations. I should like to propose that an analysis of the Mlimani VDC in terms of cognitive non-sharing and its political consequences adds a further dimension to our understanding of the operation of this council.

Kingua double-talk is understood only by members of the local community and not by the itinerant government officials whom it is intended to deceive. This immediately means that outsiders and insiders have vastly different impressions of what transpires in a meeting. In this case, the outsiders, the government men, know least about the system's operation. Those with greater knowledge, understanding both overt and covert meanings of what is said, are able to manipulate the system to their greater political advantage. The outsiders, with less understanding, must be satisfied with power struggles within the overt system. The insiders can play both overt and covert systems to their advantage and win at politics every time through their greater knowledge (read *power*) of how the system operates.

But the system is more complex than this. While factionalism between insiders and outsiders is surely a part of the Mlimani VDC, the very ambiguities contained in *kingua* double-talk are such that even those insiders who are aware that it is being used are often at a loss to explain what a person's 'real' meaning is. Since it is only generally agreed among the representatives to the VDC that outside intervention in local affairs should be kept to a minimum, there is much room for individual participants to speculate about the true intentions of any one of them who speaks during the meeting. It can even happen, and sometimes does, that some people want to effect a particular project while others do not. Since the members of the VDC will proceed to discuss until they come to consensus as to a decision, those who really want the thing cannot be certain that other members of the VDC are not speaking *kingua.* This insidious characteristic of the communication system gives participants only fragmentary knowledge of what is really happening. It gives them, to use Wallace's terminology, only a limited cognitive map of the system and its operation, sufficient to utilize in operating within the council but inadequate to really explain what is happening.

The primary implication of the use of double-talk in the Mlimani council is that those insiders with the greater knowledge of the system are more powerful in operating it. But since *kingua* is always ambiguous to some degree, it means that participants may have only very limited knowledge of the system and its operation. Bailey has suggested in a paper written for another symposium that there are as many political cultures as there are cognitive systems (Bailey 1972a). I believe that he meant this with regard to local language and cultural communities. But the implications of his statement also apply to individual differences as well. In the VDC of Mlimani, there sometimes seem to be almost as many political cultures as there are individuals operating within the sytem.

Bailey's paper in this volume (Chapter 13) has asked the question of why some courts, councils, and legislatures rely upon esoteric language whereas others do not, rightly pointing out that its use is a dimension of variation in these bodies. In a similar vein, searching for the dimensions of variation and their correlates, I think we might well ask to what degree all such bodies depend upon cognitive non-sharing as we see in the Mlimani VDC or whether there are some in which a high degree of cognitive sharing underlies the system's operation.

POSTSCRIPT: PROSPECTS FOR THE MLIMANI VDC

In the summer of 1972, I returned for a few weeks to the community of Mlimani which I had studied in 1968, and found that the institutions of local government had continued to evolve. The system of VDCs had been replaced by WDCs (Ward Development Committees). The basic organizational differences between the two lie in the fact that in 1972, instead of all ten-house cell leaders being representatives to the WDC, only ten of these leaders were chosen to participate in the newly established WDCs. The precise selection process was unclear to the members of the local community of Mlimani and there was discussion around this subject during the time I was there. In delegated functions, the WDC was supposed to have more jurisdiction over the spending of certain governmental funds given to the local community, which were intended to assist in its community development projects. The tax system had been changed during the interim, with a sales tax having replaced the standard local rate. The increased power of the WDC in policy-making decisions revolving around the funds allocated to the community was part of the decentralization policy of the central government (Nyerere 1972). But there had been no significant changes in the operation of the council. Decision-making was still consensual rather than by majority vote. Whether by inertia of tradition or the fact that the policy-making functions had not been the subject of divided opinions in the council making majority vote a way to bridge these differences, there had been no significant changes in the decision-making process. Similarly, *kingua* double-talk was still in use in the 1972 WDC. I attribute this to both its long-standing use as a political device in such local councils in Mlimani and the fact that the ideas of decentralization reforms had not had much of an impact on Mlimani. The use of *kingua* double-talk was a fundamental problem in the WDC as it was in the VDC which proceeded it. I am hesitant to speculate about what sorts of factors might bring about a change in the operation of the WDC in Mlimani, but I am certain that until there is a shift in the patterns of cognitive sharing, that is, in the political culture of the community and its councils, the WDC is not likely to become an effective council in furthering local development projects. Its effectiveness continues to be limited to resisting outside incursion, and in this regard it is a masterful system.

ACKNOWLEDGEMENTS

The fieldwork on which this research is based was supported by an NIMH fellowship (5-F01-MH 37229–03) in 1967–68 and by the Duke University Research Council and Committee for African Studies in 1972.

Don Brenneis, Gillian Sankoff, and Karl Reisman offered especially helpful insights and suggested general additional research questions which I hope to follow up at a later date.

NOTES

1. See Jean O'Barr's analysis of the political effects of using Swahili in VDC meetings in Chapter 4.
2. Consensus, or what appears to be consensus, in larger groupings is in reality little more than acclamation or legitimation of decisions taken elsewhere (Bailey 1965:2).
3. The distinction between elite and arena councils is explained in his paper in this volume (Chapter 13) as well as in Bailey (1965).
4. Although VDCs were empowered by the central government to levy fines for non-compliance with its directives, the Mlimani VDC never utilized this prerogative as did VDCs in some other parts of Pare District and Tanzania. The VDC in Mlimani, because it never utilized this power, operated as though it had no sanctions.
5. The evidence which supports this statement is presented later in the paper.
6. This dialogue was given to me as an example of how *kingua* operates. The informant had in mind two men, of similar age, speaking to one another as they worked in adjacent fields. The time, place, topic, and relation of speakers would mean that such a conversation should take place in the vernacular.
7. When speaking Swahili, the people of Mlimani often employ the term *kinyume* as a translation for *kingua.* The Johnson dictionary translates *kinyume* as 'the back part, the rear, behind, the contrary, backwards, after time, late, in a contrary way' and gives the phrase *maneno ya kinyume* (i.e. *kinyume* words) as 'a kind of puzzle-language, the last syllable of each word being made the first'. Steere (1964:144–145) contains a brief discussion of a *kinyume* word game in a coastal dialect of Swahili. Such verbal games are also common in Mlimani. The connotations of *kinyume* are broader than *kingua.* These published sources do not suggest that the Swahili term *kinyume* really includes the sort of two-level double-talk I have described here, although the Swahili term is used in that way by the people of Mlimani.

PART TWO

India

Introduction to Part Two

In contrast to Tanzania, India has more languages and a lower incidence of bilingualism. Apte's overview of the sociopolitical implications of Indian multilingualism in Chapter 8 surveys the languages used in India and examines the domains of each. At the national level, Hindi and English continue to vie with each other for predominance or, at least, a stable relationship. Hindi (including closely allied languages which are sometimes enumerated separately) is spoken by over thirty percent of the Indian population, making it the most widely known indigenous language. Yet, the vast majority of these speakers reside in North India. English, the language of administration for 150 years of British rule, is more widely accepted as a lingua franca in Southern India. At the regional level, a large number of official state languages are used, making these a second important category of languages in India. There are many other languages, spoken over wide regions of the subcontinent with large numbers of speakers and extensive written literary traditions, which lack this status of official language at either national or state levels. Beyond these are localized, 'minor' languages lacking large numbers of speakers and written traditions. Bilingualism in India is greatest among those whose mother tongues fall into this latter category, unlike Tanzania where bilingualism in Swahili and a vernacular may run as high as 80 to 90 percent across the entire population. Most bilingual Tanzanians, moreover, are monolingual in written language as most of those who are literate were formally educated in Swahili only. In India, a large number of languages have distinctive scripts and extensive literary traditions. In addition to providing us with facts and figures on the nature of Indian multilingualism, Apte's paper in Chapter 8 reviews constitutional provisions in post-independence India for the protection of linguistic minorities, assesses the roles of English and Hindi in contemporary India and the quest for a common all-India language, and reviews the factors leading to the reorganization of India into linguistic states beginning in 1953.

The historical overview of the evolution of courts, councils, and legislatures in India by Barbara and John Flynn in Chapter 9 complements Apte's linguistic overview. The political institutions of contemporary India are products of centuries of complex influences. Traditional governmental procedures and institutions were influenced by Middle Eastern invaders during the Mughal period (1526–1757). The British East India Company set out to establish economic links between England and India and became eventually more important as an agent of political change and foreign hegemony than a mercantile force. With inextricable ties between England and India firmly established by the middle of the nineteenth century, the British Government assumed control of India for nearly a century, during which time the seeds of Indian nationalism flourished. In 1947, the subcontinent was partitioned into India and Pakistan, with governmental institutions modeled in large part after British prototypes. As the Flynns points out, a great deal of British imperial policy owes its origins to the British experiences in India. Thus, when examining British colonialism in Tanzania and, by extension through Australia, in Papua New Guinea, we see many reflections of tactics and policies stemming from the British experience in India.

In the first of two papers dealing with language and politics in the national legislature of India, Das Gupta (Chapter 10) argues that language planning appears to function differently from economic planning. It is less a matter of scarce resources to be allocated among many contending claimants and more a question of changing political priorities to which the Indian Parliament has been responsive. Das Gupta suggests that language policy planning has not been merely the implementation of prior goals. Rather, he shows that the language goals of the early nationalist period were modified by political events in the nation at large and that Parliament was instrumental in working out a series of compromises to conciliate the contending language groups. Thus, Das Gupta puts forward the proposition that language is different from many other kinds of political issues, and consequently that the political process is altered somewhat when language rather than another issue like economic development is at hand. The fact that language as a political issue may shape the nature of the political process must be seen as one of the ways in which language affects politics. Only Das Gupta considers this aspect of the language-politics relationship to any significant degree in this volume, yet it is a topic deserving of further consideration.

Apte's analysis of language controversies in the Indian Parliament during its first eight years (Chapter 11) reveals a great deal both about language as a political issue in India and about the uses of language as a political tactic within the Parliament itself. During its early years, the Indian legislature was preoccupied with linguistic issues. The most significant of these were the creation of linguistic states and the implementation of Hindi as the official language of India as had been designated in the constitution. Through a careful study of the Hansard reports for the period 1952–1960, Apte is able to reconstruct many of the techniques which were used by MPs to draw attention to linguistic issues in the Parliament. Apte concludes that the creation of linguistic states in the 1950s and the resolution of the official language issue in the 1960s have quieted down the controversies over language which raged in the Indian Parliament during its first decade.

Kidder's focus in Chapter 12 is on local courts in Bangalore. Although English is the court language, few litigants have facility in the language and must depend instead on their lawyers' knowledge and abilities in it. Kidder argues that courts are not viewed as legitimate dispute settlement arenas by most litigants. While language is not the source of the difficulties in the legal process, English is 'an additional weapon in the arsenal of elitism'. Kidder's sensitive analysis of language in Bangalore courts ranges from a concern with the oratorical style of lawyers and the functions of English in the mystification of the courts to a consideration of whether using vernaculars rather than English would alter the situation significantly. He concludes that the roots of the problem are political and legal. Language is a tool, a resource, a support in the system maintenance – but it is not the cause of the problems. This study is one of the most direct examples in the volume of language supporting and reflecting the power relations of the sociopolitical system.

Bailey argues in Chapter 13 that courts, councils, and committees bear a number of resemblances to one another. Not the least of these is the fact that the political contests which take place within them are primarily verbal – contests of 'jaw' not 'war'. Inspired by his study of local councils in Orissa, Bailey's paper is a theoretical exploration of the correlates and functions of esoteric or institutional speech codes in formal institutions. Why, Bailey asks, do some councils develop specialized speech codes that differ from the ordinary speech of the coummunity while others do not? The key to these differences lies in the variations in the power and legitimacy of councils. Bailey is not content with a mere consideration of the structural correlates of institutional speech. He explores the processes of change which may occur in the speech codes of councils as shifts in power and legitimacy occur. Bailey makes no pretense to have answered all the questions he has raised. His provocative paper leaves much room for further research about the correlates and functions of institutional speech codes.

MAHADEV L. APTE

8

Multilingualism in India and Its Socio-political Implications: An Overview

The main objectives of this paper are to provide some factual information to illustrate the multilingual nature of India, to discuss the various consequences of such multilingualism, and to suggest some possibilities for research in certain areas of language and politics.

GENERAL INFORMATION

The data from the 1951, 1961, and 1971 censuses provide the basic facts about linguistic diversity in India. (The 1971 census figures are provisional and all relevant statistical data are not yet available.) The number of languages and dialects as listed in 1951 and 1961 are 782 and 1652 respectively. The languages spoken in India belong to four language families: Indo-Aryan, Dravidian, Austro-Asiatic, and Tibeto-Burman or Tibeto-Chinese. Indo-Aryan languages are spoken by approximately 73 percent and Dravidian by approximately 24 percent of the Indian population. Although there are many languages which belong to the remaining two families, in terms of numbers of speakers they constitute a small percentage. For example, Austro-Asiatic languages are spoken by only 1.5 percent of the population and Tibeto-Burman by 0.70 percent (see Map 8.1).

The fact that the number of mother tongues enumerated in the 1961 census is very high is due to a number of factors. For several hundred of these mother tongues there are very few speakers. For example, there are altogether 64,432 speakers for 527 languages. As many as 210 of these have no more than one or two speakers each.

Another category of 400 languages has a total of 426,076 speakers. Quite often a single mother tongue gets enumerated under several slightly different names. People often give names of their castes, localities, or occupations when asked about their mother tongues. The census authorities themselves have to classify and aggregate the various mother tongues under a much smaller number of languages, as has been done for the 1961 census. Thus, the 1652 languages can be reduced to a considerably smaller number.

Among the languages of India, thirty-three have over a million speakers each. Out of these, fourteen are listed in the Constitution of India. These fourteen languages account for almost ninety percent of the population. In addition, another forty-nine languages have over one hundred thousand speakers each. Of these, ten are spoken by over half a million speakers each. (See Appendix I, pages 159–160.)

Sanskrit, which is claimed to be the mother tongue of only 2544 persons, is included in the Constitution because of its importance as the language of the religious and cultural tradition of the majority Hindu population. With the exception of Urdu and Sindhi, which are spoken by scattered groups all over India, the other languages listed in the Constitution are concentrated in various geographical regions which have been recognized as linguistic states.

Within each of the major languages there are speech variations based on such factors as geographical location, age, sex, education, caste, religion, and occupation. Despite such variations, a certain variety in each language is recognized as 'standard' and is used for literary and journalistic writings and for official communication and broadcasting.

English, though not listed in the VIIIth Schedule of the Indian Constitution, continues to be an important language. It was the language of administration for over 150 years during the British rule and continues to be an official language along with Hindi. English is the mother tongue of 191,579 persons, and, in addition, approximately twenty to twenty-five million people have some knowledge of it.

Most of the major languages have their own separate scripts. There are eleven different scripts in India. Three languages (Sanskrit, Hindi, and Marathi) use the same script called Devanagari, and many languages use scripts which are variations of Devanagari. The four major

Map 8.1 *Linguistic divisions of India*

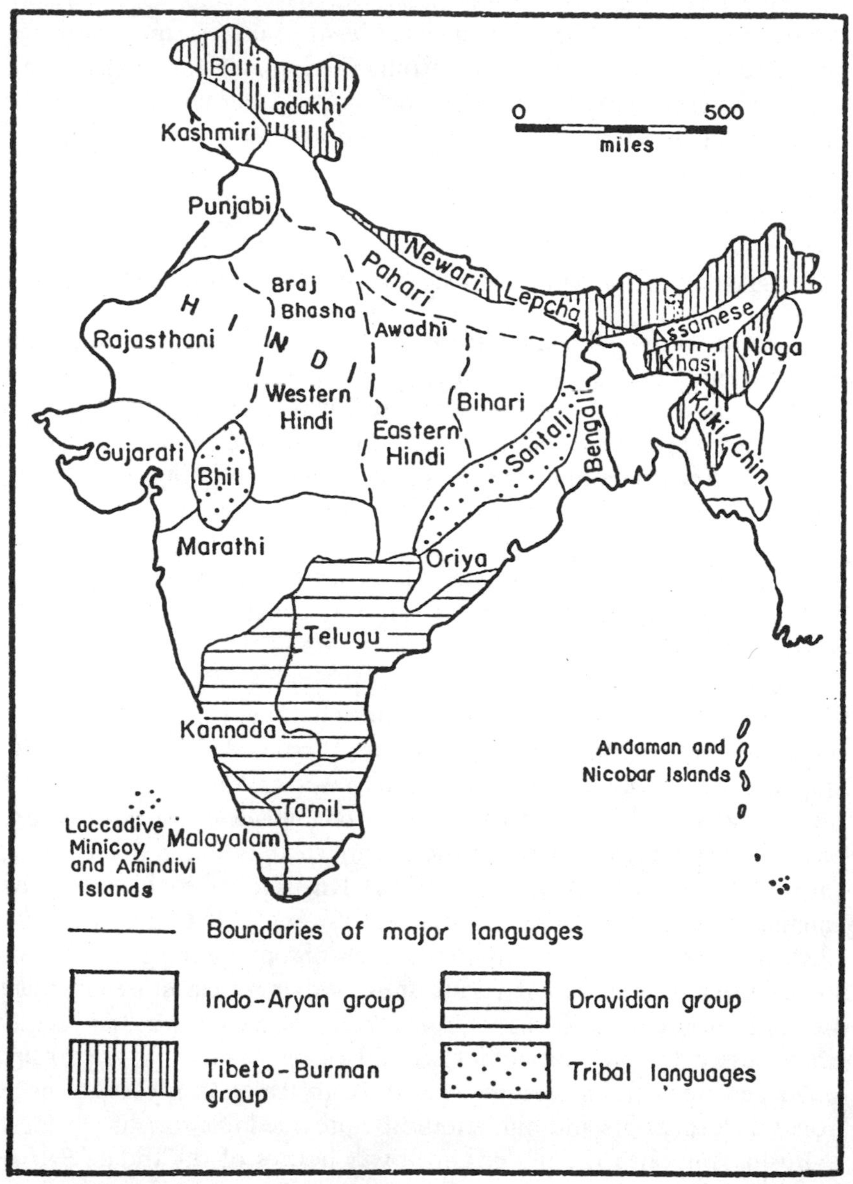

From: Baldev Raj Nayar, *National Communication and Language Policy in India*, New York: Praeger Publishers, excerpted and reprinted by permission.

Dravidian languages have their own scripts. The various scripts can be classified into four major categories: Devanagari and its variations; the scripts of Dravidian languages; Perso-Arabic scripts used for Urdu, Sindhi, and Kashmiri; and Roman script used for English. This variety of scripts is noticeable on the Indian paper currency. On the back of rupee notes are found the words 'one rupee' written in eleven scripts.

CONSTITUTIONAL RECOGNITION OF LINGUISTIC DIVERSITY

Because of the multilingual nature of India, the makers of the Indian constitution paid special attention to specifying which languages were to be used for official purposes, which were to be regional languages, which were to be used for education and for general administration (including legislative, executive, and judicial domains), how the rights of linguistic minorities were to be safeguarded, etc. The whole of Part XVII of the Constitution is devoted to language and, in addition, various other articles in it refer to language. The following is a brief summary of all the constitutional provisions relating to linguistic issues.

The official language of the Union is Hindi in Devanagari script. However, provision is also made to continue English. Numerals to be used, however, are in international form. Hindi or English is to be the language of communication between states and the union government. States are free to adopt one or more languages for internal use or to use Hindi for official purposes. Until such a time as this is done, English is to continue as the official language of each state. The language of the Supreme Court and of the High Courts is to be English. However, states can (with the consent of the President of India) authorize the use of Hindi or any other official state language for legal proceedings in High Courts. Allibills, acts, rules, and regulations passed by the Parliament should be in English. If any other languages are used in a state legislature for these purposes, translations of all such acts and bills should be provided in English.

Business in both the upper and lower houses of the Indian Parliament is to be conducted in Hindi or English. But with the permission of the speaker or the chairman, a member may be allowed to address the house in his mother tongue. Similarly, business in the state legislatures is to be transacted in either the official language(s) of that state or in Hindi or English. However, with the permission of the speaker, a member who cannot adequately express himself in any of these languages may be permitted to speak in his mother tongue.

Any citizen or group of citizens having a distinct language, script, and culture has the right to conserve the same. No citizen is to be discriminated against because of his language. An individual is entitled to submit a representation for the redress of any grievance to any state or union authority in any of the languages used in the country. Adequate facilities for instruction through the primary level of education in the mother tongue are to be provided by the states to various linguistic minorities within their jurisdiction. Special officers to investigate all matters regarding safeguards for linguistic minorities are to be appointed.

The government of India has been keenly aware of the considerable importance of linguistic matters. Although initially the central government concentrated on the development of Hindi, it has recently taken steps to develop all other Indian languages. In addition to the Central Hindi Institute at Agra in North India, which is primarily for the advanced training of Hindi teachers, the government established in 1969 the Central Institute of Indian languages. The headquarters of this institute are located in Mysore city in South India, and currently there are over seventy scholars affiliated with the Institute who are engaged in various activities connected with language development and other matters of linguistic interest. The Institute also has four regional centers, one each in the East, West, North, and South zones where training is offered in the major languages of the respective regional zones. Several activities have been undertaken by the Institute. The various functions of the Institute as specified in the first issue of its bulletin are listed in Appendix II (pages 160–161). The government has also taken over the financing and administration of the Central Institute of English at Hyderabad in South India. This institute was originally established by the British Council. Its main functions are to train teachers of English and to conduct research on various aspects of Indian English and English linguistics.

HISTORICAL BACKGROUND OF LINGUISTIC STATES IN INDIA

One of the major tasks accomplished by the Congress government in India after independence was the reorganization of the country into linguistic states. Today there are eighteen states and eleven union territories. Out of the eighteen states, only Himachal Pradesh and Nagaland are not fairly homogenous linguistically. The rest of the states have more than fifty percent of the population speaking a single language.

Although the actual process of reorganizing India into linguistic states started in 1953, the principle of linguistic homogeneity and autonomy has its roots in the pre-independence period, going as far back as the beginning of the twentieth century. For example, in 1908 the Indian National Congress began to argue for making linguistic homogeneity the basis of forming provincial units by treating Bihar as a separate Congress province. In 1928, the principle of linguistic homogeneity was again reiterated by the Congress party. There was already an example of how powerful the sentiments of the masses were, as in the case of Bengal, which the British had tried to divide into two separate administrative units in 1912. The protest was so forceful that the government felt inclined to reunify the province of Bengal. All these factors were thus in favor of the linguistic reorganization of the country.

Accordingly, a commission was appointed in 1948 exclusively for the purpose of considering the whole question of linguistic organization. The commission was lukewarm to the idea although it recognized the importance of the development of major regional languages, and the possibility that such development could be accomplished through the creation of linguistic states. Because of the inherent dangers and tendencies of separatism which the Congress leaders felt might accompany the creation of linguistic states the Congress government tried to stall the process of reorganization until events in the province of Andhra forced its hand. In Andhra, a man by the name of Potti Shriramulu died after fasting for fifty-six days because he wanted a separate linguistic state for the speakers of Telugu. Soon after, the state of Andhra Pradesh came into existence on October 1, 1953.

Another commission was appointed to look into the territorial boundaries of the various states to be created and to examine the views of linguistic minorities in all regions. The commission interviewed people from all walks of life in all parts of India and submitted its report in 1955. The Congress government accepted most of the recommendations and began the stupendous task of reorganization of the country. This in turn created several problems about the boundaries between contiguous states and the inclusion of major cities in one state or another. Disputes regarding boundaries between contiguous states still survive in the form of political agitations. For example, the border dispute between the Kannada-speaking state of Mysore and the Marathi-speaking state of Maharashtra is still not settled. A second problem, particularly with regard to the city of Bombay, was solved only after considerable agitation and the political defeat of the Congress party in western India during the period from 1956 to 1960. Similar problems have since arisen because the division of regions into linguistic states has continued even in the sixties. For example, the state of Punjab was sub-divided into the Hindi-speaking state of Harayana and the Punjabi-speaking state of Punjab as late as 1966. The solution which has evolved for dealing with any disputed territories is to govern them centrally. Such has been the fate of the city of Chandigarh which was a disputed territory in the creation of the two states just mentioned. Similarly, Goa has remained a separate union territory because of a dispute over its merger with the neighboring state of Maharashtra.

QUESTION OF A LINGUA FRANCA AND THE PROJECTED ROLES OF HINDI AND ENGLISH

The problem which has most occupied the attention of political leaders, scholars, administrators, educators, and other experts from many disciplines is that of a common language for India. A large body of literature is already available on this subject and more is being added every year. The primary concern in the matter has been the position of Hindi as an official language vis-à-vis English. English was used during the British rule for administration and became the language of the elites. It still continues today as one of the two official languages. Indians are aware of the international importance of English. Yet at the time of independence it was felt that an indigenous language should be the lingua franca, and Hindi seemed to be the most suitable because of its numerical strength. There is no question that Hindi speakers constitute the largest single linguistic group in the country. The 1951 census figure of Hindi speakers is about 150 million constituting about 42 percent of the total population. However, this number also included speakers of Punjabi, Urdu, and Hindustani. In the 1961 census the percentage of Hindi speakers dropped to about thirty because Punjabi, Urdu, and Hindustani were listed separately; and a number of speakers who stated Hindi as their mother tongue in 1951 gave the names of their so-called dialects in 1961, thus increasing phenomenally the number of speakers for such mother tongues as Bhojpuri, Khari Boli, Maithili, Maghai, and Braj.

Despite such ups and downs in the census enumeration of Hindi, the fact remains that varieties of Hindi are used for communication not only within the large Hindi region of North India, but also outside this region. There are substantial numbers of speakers throughout India who understand Hindi even if they are not actually able to communicate in it. As compared to this situation, English is spoken by a much smaller percentage of the Indian population, including even those who have only a smattering knowledge of English and also those who probably only understand English, but do not speak, read, or write it. Yet the fact remains that those who speak English constitute the elites of Indian society, and it is they who are responsible for running the government machinery, for operating the educational system, and for efficient management of the technological progress in the country.

The major opposition to Hindi comes from South Indians who prefer continuation of English as the official language. There also has been a fear of political and economic domination of the non-Hindi speakers by the Hindi region (Gopal 1966:231–232; Nayar 1969: 116–117, 123; Tambiah 1967: 232). In addition, it is claimed that Hindi is not as well developed a language as some other Indian languages, especially Tamil and Bengali which have long literary histories. Hindi is therefore considered inferior in this respect and it is argued that it should not therefore be the official language (Government of India 1956:288–289, 296–297, 322; John n.d.: 46–48; Yadav 1966:56–57). There is, moreover, a question of terminology. Why should Hindi alone be called the 'national' language when other languages are spoken in India and could rightfully be called national languages (Contractor n.d.:42–47; Shah 1968:53–54; Yadav 1966:39–40)? The terms most in vogue now are 'link' or 'common' language (Chagla 1967:4).

A plan commonly known as the *Three Language Formula* has been discussed frequently and is considered to be the answer for teaching Hindi and English in all regions and for developing socio-cultural and political cohesion. Under this scheme, in all non-Hindi-speaking regions three languages would be compulsorily taught at the secondary school level: a regional language, Hindi, and English. For Hindi-speaking areas, another Indian language would be substituted for Hindi. However, numerous variations have been suggested, and at no stage has there been a complete agreement between the union and the states about the exact nature and implementation. With the political power structure changing after each election, new commissions have been appointed periodically to review this formula. As late as 1967, a committee appointed by the union education minister even ventured to recommend a *Two Language Formula* whereby a student, up to the high school stage, would be required to study his mother tongue and only one other language (which could be any language). The primary reason for this new formula was the feeling that students were being required to study too many languages in their early years of schooling. The aim of this formula was then to reduce the number of languages a student would have to learn in secondary school (Nayar 1969: 159–160).

Since the effect of the *Two Language Formula* would have been to dispense with the compulsory teaching of Hindi at the secondary school level, the central government was not very receptive to it and instead decided to pursue the *Three Language Formula.* However, no uniformity exists in the manner in which various states have implemented the original scheme. Also worthy of note is the fact that, for linguistic minorities, the original formula becomes a *Four Language Formula,* requiring the study of mother tongue, a major regional language, Hindi, and English. The non-Hindi regions have also accused the Hindi regions of taking the easy way out in the implementation of the original scheme, i.e. allowing the students to study Sanskrit from which Hindi evolved instead of a modern, preferably a non-Indo-Aryan language.

The constitution of India specified that Hindi would replace English as the official language of India within a period of fifteen years. However, the strong-arm tactics and impatience of the Hindi protagonists created an atmosphere of considerable suspicion. Despite tremendous efforts by the supporters of Hindi to develop technical vocabularies in Hindi and to develop Hindi as the official language, when the actual date for the transition arrived, there was strong agitation in South India, and the Congress party, acutely sensitive to the political repercussions of such a change-over, reached a compromise position by passing the Official Languages (Amendment) Act in 1967. This act specifies that Hindi *and* English may be used as official languages for all official purposes and for communications between the union and the states. Thus, it can be said that, for all practical purposes, the change-over from English to Hindi has been postoned indefinitely.

LINGUISTIC DEVELOPMENTS IN THE STATES

With the creation of linguistic states, the development of various major regional languages gained considerable momentum. The Constitution of India has given complete freedom to the states to determine their offical languages and many states have taken decisions to use the major regional language as the state official language. However, there are some other interesting developments.[1] Six states in Northern India (Bihar, Harayana, Himachal Pradesh, Madhya Pradesh, Rajasthan, and Uttar Pradesh) have adopted Hindi as their official language. Six other states use their respective major regional languages as official languages (Telugu in Andhra Pradesh, Assamese in Assam, Marathi in Maharasthtra, Punjabi in Punjab, Tamil in Tamilnad, and Bengali in West Bengal). One state (Gujarat) uses both a major regional language (Gujarati) and Hindi as official languages. Three states (Mysore[2] and Kerala in the south and Nagaland in the northeast) use only English as the official language. One state (Orissa) uses both English and its major regional language (Oriya) as official languages. The most interesting situation exists in the State of Jammu and Kashmir where Urdu is the official language, although it is the mother tongue of only a very small percentage of the population. The majority of the state speaks Kashmiri.

The situation in the union territories is equally interesting. Five (Chandigarh; Dadra and Hagar Haveli; Goa, Daman, and Diu; Laccadive and Minicoy Islands; Manipur) use English as their official language. Two (Andaman and Nicobar Islands, Delhi) use English and Hindi. One (Tripura) uses a major regional language, while another (Pondicherry) uses English and French as the official languages. In the case of Pondicherry the majority of the population speaks Tamil, yet French has been continued as one of the official languages because of the legacy of French colonial rule!

Despite such variation, the states have given considerable attention to the development of their respcctive major regional languages. Almost all states have appointed special committees for developing technical, legal, administrative, and legislative vocabularies. Shorthand systems are being developed for the state languages and typewriters are being manufactured in different scripts for the individual regional languages. There are special schools for training administrative personnel in the use of the state languages. Translations of all acts, laws, rules, and regulations passed by the state and central governments have been undertaken. These translations are usually from English or Hindi into the official language(s) of states. The Constitution of India, which incidentally was first written in English, has now been translated into various state languages. The many forms and documents needed in the state administrative bureaucracies are now available in the regional languages. All such forms were previously in English.

Similar developments have also taken place in the field of education. New textbooks have been written in regional languages, while others have been translated from English. Many states have adopted the policy of using the state language as the medium of instruction at all levels, including universities. A great deal of discussion and controversy has gone into the merits and disadvantages of using regional languages as the media of instruction at the university level. Arguments have been made against using such languages at the university level since it could deprive linguistic minorities of higher education unless they are also proficient in a major regional language. It is also claimed that such a step would limit the mobility of educated persons, especially the university teachers and students (Chagla 1967: 21). It has been argued that attempts by state governments to implement pilot projects for introducing the regional languages as the media of instructions at the university level have not been successful. For example, although Tamil was introduced as the medium of instruction at the university level by the State of Tamilnad, the attempt failed for lack of student participation and also because of other factors, such as lack of textbooks, inability of professors to teach the subjects in the regional language, etc. (Kumaramangalam 1965:66–70; Nayar 1969:264–265). It has been advocated that English should be retained as the medium of instruction in major universities and other all-India institutions of higher learning (Chagla 1967:21). Thus, the whole question of using regional languages at the university level is related to the development of such languages by way of the availability of textbooks in all subjects, the ability of teachers to teach various subjects in these languages, and also the future of English in free India. Since English has been accepted as the official language along with Hindi, its high status will not be affected. Consequently, the replacement of English at the university level by instruction in regional languages may not take place in the immediate future. What is most likely to happen is that students will be given the option of receiving university education either through English or through a major regional language. There is an extensive literature, including several government reports, which explores various aspects of the linguistic controversy in the field of education.

In spite of what may appear to be a great deal of effort put into developing regional languages, it must be remembered that this is a fairly recent phenomenon. Even after the creation of linguistic states, the primary focus still remained on Hindi and English. But since that question has at least temporarily been solved through postponing a final decision, the efforts for the development of state languages have accelerated during the last five years or so.

PROBLEMS OF LINGUISTIC MINORITIES

One of the major problems which both the union and state governments have to tackle is that of linguistic minorities. It is important to note that none of the states is totally monolingual. The percentage of population which speaks the major regional language in a given state varies anywhere from 57 percent to 95 percent. In some states no single linguistic group constitutes a majority. For example, in the state of Assam. Assamese is spoken by only 57 percent of the population. On the other hand, in the state of Kerala, 95 percent of the population speaks Malayalam. In the state of Himachal Pradesh the largest linguistic group constitutes only 38 percent of the total population. Appendix III (pages 161–163) provides information about the major language group and other minority language groups in each state and union territory.

When we consider linguistic minorities, we ought to think of them as falling into two major categories. The first category consists of linguistic minorities which speak one of the languages listed in the constitution. For example, in Assam the Bengali speakers constitute a linguistic minority because they are 18 percent of the population. However, Bengali is also the state language of West Bengal. In such cases, there is always the possibility for members of minority groups to move to the state(s) where their language is an official one if they feel that they are being discriminated against. The second category consists of minorities who speak one of the many languages which fall into the category of 'tribal' or other languages which are indigenous to the region but whose speakers are numerically small. Members of such groups have no alternative because no matter where they go, their languages will always be minority languages. They also are at a disadvantage because their mother tongues are not being given the same attention as major regional languages are. Speakers of all such languages of necessity have to be bilingual in their mother tongue and the official language of the state in which they are domiciled, if they want to gain socio-economic benefits.

There are various safeguards for linguistic minorities outlined in the Constitution of India. In addition, a scheme was developed in consequence of Constitutional provisions, primarily in the domains of education, the use of minority languages for official purposes, and recruitment to state services. For our purpose, the most relevant of these is the use of minority languages for official purposes.

The specifications in this respect are the following:

1. At district level and below, like Municipality, Tehsil [adminis-

trative unit], etc. where a linguistic minority constitutes 15–20 percent of population, important government notices, rules, and other publications are to be published in minority languages also.

2(a). District level – Where 60 percent of the population in a district use a language other than official, that language may be recognized as an additional official language for that district. Recognition for this purpose is to be given ordinarily to the major languages mentioned in the Eighth Schedule.

2(b). At the State headquarters, a Translation Bureau may be set up where arrangements may be made for translation of the substance of important laws, rules, regulations, etc. into minority languages for publication.

3. In correspondence with the public, petitions and representations received in other languages are to be replied to, wherever possible, in the language of the petition representation.

(From: Eleventh Report of the Commissioner for Linguistic Minorities, 1968/69.)

As specified in the Constitution, a position called the Commissioner for Linguistic Minorities was created. The primary function of this officer is to take note of any and all complaints by linguistic minorities and advise the state governments on solutions to such problems. It is also his responsibility to see that proper steps are taken by proper authorities to implement policies to safeguard the interests of the linguistic minorities. The Commissioner has submitted annual reports beginning from 1957 on the developments relatinng to linguistic minorities in all parts of India. These reports include suggestions made by the Commissioner to various states to answer complaints and the degree to which they have complied with his suggestions.

According to the specifications stated earlier, all states have been urged to prepare lists of districts in which there are linguistic minorities constituting fifteen percent or more of the total population. The Tenth Report of the Commissioner for Linguistic Minorities includes such a list for many of the states. However, the reports of the commissioner are discouraging regarding the implementation of the safeguards by various states. In many cases the states have done precious little beyond preparing the list.

The Commissioner, however, has no authority to implement any decisions. He acts only in an advisory capacity, and it appears from his reports that the states often ignore his recommendations. Sometimes the state government at the highest levels may make provisions for the benefit of linguistic minorities; however, these are often not implemented at the lower levels. More often than not, the state governments are either disinterested in responding to the complaints, or are clearly opposed to the suggestions made by the Commissioner. Sometimes the state governments, despite previous agreements, continue to pursue policies which force the linguistic minorities to learn the state language. For example, although it was agreed in the Chief Ministers' Conference in 1961 that knowledge of the state official language should not be a prerequisite for recruitment to state services, and option for using English or Hindi as a medium of examination should be allowed, many states continue to insist that the candidates show proficiency in the official state language to be eligible for state services.

FUNCTIONAL IMPORTANCE OF VARIOUS INDIAN LANGUAGES

From the discussion above, it should be clear that although there are numerous languages and dialects in India, they do not all have the same standing. Considering such factors as functional value and prestige, it is obvious that some languages are more important than others. At the top of the hierarchy in terms of importance are English and Hindi. Both are 'link' languages and are used for official and unofficial communication in much of the country. Hindi has the all-out support of the central government for its development. In terms of prestige, however, English appears to have a higher value primarily because of its international position and its extensive scientific and literary contributions.

Next in the hierarchy are the official state languages. These are all spoken by over a million persons, and have a written literary tradition. Because they have been adopted as the official languages by various states, they have a high functional value and prestige. They serve as the media of legislative, executive, and educational bodies plus a score of other official and unofficial activities. They enjoy a privileged position. Any resident of a state who desires to achieve social, economic, and political gains needs to know its official language.

The state official languages are followed by other major languages. They too have written literary traditions and millions of speakers. But due to lack of official status they have lost some of their prestige. Some of these major languages are concentrated in certain regions while others have speakers scattered in all parts of India. Some of those that are concentrated in certain regions have the potential of increased status since they can, and probably will, be adopted as the official languages of the states in which they are spoken. For example, Kannada, a major language, will most likely be adopted as the official language of the state of Mysore. On the other hand, Sindhi is less likely to achieve such a status because it does not have a home base.

At the bottom of the hierarchy are languages spoken by a tribal population or by a small number of people. These can be considered minor languages. They have no written tradition, little functional value and much less prestige than those mentioned above. Most speakers of these languages will have to learn at least one of the major languages, preferably those which are either official state languages or link languages. It is not surprising, then, that the highest percentage of bilingualism occurs among the speakers of these minor languages.

SUGGESTIONS FOR FUTURE RESEARCH POSSIBILITIES

To anyone familiar with the available literature on the various aspects of linguistic diversity in India, it is obvious that a great deal has been written on the question of a national language. The problem has been analyzed from the social, political, and economic as well as from the linguistic points of view. In India, a considerable amount of information is available about the teaching of English and Hindi and the divergent views about using either one or the other of these languages. In short, the problem has been over-analyzed. However, when we turn to certain other areas such as language and politics at the state and local levels, there is almost no literature to be found.

Let us look at some of these problems and the availability of data concerning them.

Although the language of the Supreme Court and that of the High Courts has been – and will probably continue to be – English, provision has been made for the use of Hindi in the High Courts of some Hindi-speaking states. As for the lower courts, the legal proceedings in them are often in the regional languages. Again, no studies have been made of problems of translations of documents; the nature of actual court procedures when an indigenous language is used; the kinds of disputes which are primarily conducted in the indigenous languages; language options available to the linguistic minorities in a region in court proceedings, especially in the districts where the minority groups constitute a substantial percentage of the local populations; and frequency of the appointments of judges who are bilingual, in both the state languages and the language(s) of the minorities, to courts in such areas.

Another area worth investigating is the selection of candidates by political parties for winning elective positions in areas which are linguistically heterogenous. Questions such as the following need to be answered: Are candidates from minority groups selected by political parties; how often is this done; what are the results of elections in such cases; what are the consequences if members of the linguistic minorities are elected; what role do language issues play in the patterns of voting in linguistically heterogenous areas. Similar studies can be undertaken in big cities like Bombay, Madras, or Bangalore where significant percentages of linguistic minority groups exist side by side with speakers of the major regional languages. Such studies could investigate the workings of political and administrative bodies such as the municipal corporations.

It is possible to list many other areas where little or nothing has been done, but the questions raised above should give some idea of the type of research which needs to be undertaken in India. Linguists and political scientists have excellent opportunities to collaborate with each other in investigating problems of the kinds discussed. India is indeed a fertile area for such research.

NOTES

1. The information presented in this context is based on sources published in 1971. Since policies relating to state official languages are still in a flux, it is quite possible that a few states and union territories will have changed their official languages by the time this paper is published. Therefore such information should be updated, if necessary.
2. When this paper was originally presented at the conference in January 1973, this state was still known as Mysore. Since then however, it has been renamed 'Karnataka'. However, the old name has been used throughout this paper.

APPENDIX I: LANGUAGES OF INDIA[a]

A. Languages listed in the VIIIth Schedule of the Indian Constitution

Name	*Number of speakers in millions*	
1. Assamese	8.95	
2. Bengali	44.52	
3. Gujarati	25.65	
4. Hindi	153.72	
5. Kannada	21.57	
6. Kashmiri	2.42	
7. Malayalam	21.91	
8. Marathi	41.72	
9. Oriya	19.72	
10. Punjabi	13.90	
11. Sanskrit		(2544)[b]
12. Sindhi	1.20	
13. Tamil	37.59	
14. Telugu	44.70	
15. Urdu	28.60	

B. Languages not included in the Indian Constitution, but spoken by over one million speakers

Name	*Number of speakers in millions*
1. Bagri	1.05
2. Bhili/Bhilodi	1.25
3. Bhojpuri	14.34
4. Chattisgarhi	6.69
5. Dogri	1.29
6. Garhwali	1.27
7. Gondi	1.54
8. Konkani	1.52
9. Kumauni	1.23
10. Kurukh/Oraon	1.24
11. Lamani/Lambadi	1.20
12. Maghai/Magadhi	6.63

[a] From: R. C. Nigam, *Language Handbook on Mother Tongues in Census.* Census of India, 1971. Census Centenary Monograph No. 10. Delhi, 1972.
[b] The figure given for speakers of Sanskrit is based on the 1961 census. Information from the 1971 census is not yet available.

Name	*Number of speakers in millions*
13. Maithili	6.12
14. Marwari	4.71
15. Nepali/Gorkhali	1.28
16. Pahari	1.26
17. Rajasthani	2.09
18. Santhali	3.69
19. Tulu	1.15

C. Ten other languages have between one half million and one million speakers each. Another thirty-nine languages have between one hundred thousand and five hundred thousand speakers each.
D. English is the mother tongue of 191,579 persons. In addition, about 20–25 million persons have some knowledge of English.
E. Among the languages listed in sections A and B above, Santhali belongs to Austro-Asiatic family and Lamani/Lambadi belongs to Tibeto-Burman family. This later affiliation is not universally accepted. Gondi, Kannada, Kurukh/Oraon, Malayalam, Tamil, Telugu, and Tulu belong to Dravidian family. The rest are Indo-Aryan languages.

APPENDIX II: CENTRAL INSTITUTE OF INDIAN LANGUAGES[a]

Functions

1. To co-ordinate the work of State Language Institutes; Tribal Research Institutes and Bureaus; University Departments of Languages and Linguistics; Central Institute of English, Hyderabad; Kendriya Hindi Sansthan, Agra; the Anthropological Survey of India; Language Division of the Registrar General's Office; and other academic bodies or organizations.
2. To serve as a clearing house of information on all matters relating to the development of Indian languages in this country and abroad.
3. To promote the development of languages of Scheduled Tribes.
4. To promote the development of Sindhi and Urdu.
5. Formulation and execution of important co-operative projects which will highlight the inherent unity among the languages of India.
6. Development of suitable interdisciplinary courses for giving linguistic orientation to social scientists and social sciences orientation to linguists.

---

[a] From: *Vartavaha,* Bulletin of the Central Institute of Indian Languages, Manasagangotri, Mysore 6, No. 1, December 1969.

Functions

7. Development of methods, material and aids for teaching Indian languages, and conducting language courses. This would be designed either for specific level or specific needs of learners so that they can equip themselves with minimum knowledge of the languages for the purpose desired.
8. Development of suitable translation techniques and conduct of courses for translators.
9. Holding of seminars, workshops, summer institutes and short-term courses for special groups like language teachers, telephonists, radio announcers, etc.
10. Application of language technology to Indian languages with a view to promoting their effective use in modern media of recording and communication.
11. To collaborate with other organizations and institutions working for the development of Indian languages.
12. To undertake such other activities as are found necessary for achieving the objectives of the Sansthan.

APPENDIX III: LANGUAGES OF STATES AND UNION TERRITORIES[a]

Name of State or Union Territory	Official language	Major regional language and percentage of speakers		Some minority languages and percentage of speakers	
States					
1. Andhra Pradesh	Telugu	Telugu	85.9	Urdu	7.1
				Lambadi	1.62
				Tamil	1.55
2. Assam	Assamese	Assamese	57.14	Bengali	17.6
				Hindi	4.4
				Bodo	2.9
3. Bihar	Hindi	Hindi	44.3	Bihari	35.39
				Urdu	8.93
				Santali	3.57
4. Gujarat	Gujarati and Hindi	Gujarati	90.5	Urdu	2.8
				Sindhi	2.42
				Bhili	1.34

[a] From: Eleventh Report of the Commissioner for Linguistic Minorities, 1968/69. Figures, which may not add up to one hundred in many cases, are quoted as given in the original source.

Name of State or Union Territory	Official language	Major regional language and percentage of speakers		Some minority languages and percentage of speakers	
5. Haryana	Hindi	Hindi	88.6	Punjabi	8.1
				Urdu	2.77
6. Himachal Pradesh	Hindi	None	––	Pahadi	38.4
				Mardeali	16.7
				Hindi	10.6
7. Jammu and Kashmir	Urdu	Kashmiri	54.4	Dogri	24.4
				Pahari	6.84
8. Kerala	English	Malayalam	95.04	Tamil	3.12
9. Madhya Pradesh	Hindi	Hindi	78.07	Rajastani	4.9
				Marathi	3.8
				Gondi	3.2
10. Maharashtra	Marathi	Marathi	76.5	Urdu	6.8
				Hindi	3.1
				Gujarati	2.7
11. Mysore	English	Kannada	65.1	Telugu	8.6
				Urdu	8.6
				Marathi	4.5
12. Nagaland	English	None	––	Konyak Ao	15.4
				Sema	12.8
				Angami	11.4
13. Orissa	Oriya and English	Oriya	82.3	Kui	2.9
				Telugu	2.2
				Santhali	2.1
14. Punjab	Punjabi in Gurumukhi script	Punjabi	67.2	Hindi	35.2
15. Rajasthan	Hindi	Rajasthani	56.49	Hindi	33.32
				Bhili	4.13
				Urdu	2.5
16. Tamil Nadu	Tamil	Tamil	83.1	Telugu	9.9
				Kannada	2.8
				Urdu	1.8
17. Uttar Pradesh	Hindi	Hindi	85.3	Urdu	10.7
				Kumauni	1.3
				Garhwali	1.0
18. West Bengal	Bengali	Bengali	84.28	Hindi	5.4
				Santhali	3.27
				Urdu	2.3

Name of State or Union Territory	Official language	Major regional language and percentage of speakers		Some minority languages and percentage of speakers	
Union Territories					
1. Andaman and Nicobar Islands	English and Hindi	None	––	Nicobarese Bengali Malayalam	21.9 21.8 10.5
2. Chandigarh	English	(Figures not available)			
3. Dadra and Nagar Haveli	English	Varli	51.47	Gujarati Konkani Dhodia	19.5 12.9 6.9
4. Delhi	Hindi and English	Hindi	77.3	Punjabi Urdu Bengali	11.9 5.7 1.3
5. Goa, Daman and Diu	English	Konkani	88.8	Gujarati Marathi Urdu	5.5 1.8 1.5
6. Laccadive, Minicoy Islands	English	Malayalam	83	Mahl	16.7
7. Manipur	English	Manipuri	64.46	Tangkhul Thado Mao	5.6 3.6 3.6
8. N.E.F.A.	(Figures not available)				
9. Pondicherry	English and French	Tamil	88.2	Malayalam Telugu	5.6 4.4
10. Tripura	Bengali	Bengali	65.2	Tripuri Manipuri	24.8 2.4

BIBLIOGRAPHICAL NOTE

The principal sources for statistical language data are the Census of India publications (1951, 1961, and 1971). The following sources, in addition to those mentioned in the paper, discuss various sociocultural aspects of linguistic diversity: Emeneau (1956); Ferguson and Gumperz (1960); Grierson (1928); Gumperz (1957, 1961); Poddar (1961).

The Government of India publications of 1928, 1948, 1953–54, and 1956 are useful for discerning the various policy trends and public opinions leading to the linguistic organization of states.

A number of sources, in addition to those mentioned specifically in the paper, provide numerous discussions on the following topics: selection of the lingua franca, development of Hindi in non-Hindi-speaking areas before and after independence, pros and cons for continuation of English, development of regional languages, changes which occurred in the language planning policies at the national level during the last twenty-four years, and various extra-linguistic factors which have played an important role in the language controversy. Some of the most important of these are Apte (1971); Das Gupta (1970); Desai (1956); Friedrich (1962); Gandhi (1956); Gokak (1964); Harrison (1960); Kelly (1966); Morris-Jones (1967). Nayar (1969) has the most exhaustive discussion of the planing and implementation at the national and state levels regarding instruction of Hindi and English at all levels of education. Das Gupta discusses the political implications of language controversy in the context of overall national development.

The reports of the Commissioner for Linguistic Minorities from 1957–1968 constitute the single most important source for the problems of linguistic minorities. Srivastava (1970) also discusses these problems extensively.

BARBARA W. FLYNN and JOHN M. FLYNN

The Evolution of Courts, Councils, and Legislatures in India

India's diversity and complexity make a simple and straightforward presentation of the development of courts, councils and legislatures a difficult task. India is a large geographical area exhibiting wide physical diversities – the plains of North India, the plateaus of the central regions, and the rain forests of the South and East. Before contemporary times geographical distinctions frequently demarcated different empires and kingdoms, precluding the political unification of the subcontinent. Continuous culture contact with the West began at the turn of the seventeenth century; British hegemony existed by 1800. Thus India was in contact with Britain and the West while revolutions in Western political ideas and practices were occurring. This has meant that modern Indian political institutions evolved over a much greater time period than those of other colonial countries. In addition, there are widely divergent cultural traditions on the subcontinent. For example, there are two major language families – the Indo-European in the North and the Dravidian in the South. Several major religious systems coexist, the two most often in serious conflict being Islam and Hinduism. The stratified nature of the society (resulting from the Hindu caste system) means that what is true for one segment of society may not be true for another. Finally, the large number of political systems that existed until Indian independence meant that a wide variety of institutions and arenas of power coexisted.

Given these complexities, this chapter will present a brief overview of the evolution of Indian institutions. Our goal is not to give the entire history of political and institutional development but rather to present some factors which have shaped and continue to influence contemporary Indian political life. Even today because of local and state differences India does not have a homogeneous political system. For the purposes of this overview, it is useful to discuss the formal political institutions in five periods – 'traditional' India, Mughal rule, East India Company supremacy, Crown rule, and independent India. These discussions should viewed as archetypes rather than as accurate descriptions of reality at any given point of time. They will attempt to extricate the essence of institutions which have gradually evolved over considerable time spans. Also, we will briefly examine the major political and social events as well as the important ideological developments which influenced the evolution of these formal institutions.

TRADITIONAL POLITICAL INSTITUTIONS

During the long history of the Indian subcontinent, there have been many indigenous political systems. For the purpose of this paper the term 'traditional' refers to all these systems, regardless of time period or region in which they existed. Only with independence in 1947 did all of India come under a single modern political system. The common element in all these traditional political systems is that they share the Hindu concepts of society, law, and ethics. These ideological elements (rather than the particularized institutions) are what are important to modern political development. Certain basic patterns of economic organization also play a major role in structuring political institutions.

The structure of 'traditional' government whether of large empires or small states was generally pyramidal, with the king at the apex, revenue-producing villages at the base, and one or more layers of intermediary authorities in between.[1] The few systems that were not monarchies are not relevant to institutional development. The way in which each monarchy operated was similar on each layer although the substantive concerns of each may have differed. The king collected revenue, kept order, protected the kingdom, and made war. His power was limited only by the theoretical controls imposed by Hinduism – that the priestly function took precedence over the ruler's. The priests and the king jointly kept the social order intact.

Other institutions existed at the center to facilitate governing. The king headed an administrative system whose primary task was to collect revenue. It included police and internal spies to keep order within the kingdom. Further, the king commanded an army. Although the king made ultimate governmental decisions, he was assisted by a council composed of wise, learned men. Perhaps the most characteristic institution at the center was the *durbar,* in which the king in council held a public audience to hear the petitions of his subjects. In the *durbar,* the king often acted as the final authority of the legal system.

The legal system was based on the cosmic order of the sacred law (*Dharma*). Other bases for the law were kingly edict, custom, and contract. Generally, a pronouncement of the king on a legal question was taken to be the application of the divine law. Brahmin scholars were important in defining and elaborating the law. There were courts presided over by magistrates or panels of magistrates. On the royal level, the judge, if not the king himself, was likely to be a specialist, whereas at lower levels the magistrate tended to be an administrative official. No single body of law and punishments existed. Caste and status determined what law would be applied to any given individual (Basham 1959: 100–121). For purpose of contrast with the system imposed by the British it is important to note how the courts operated. Evidence was not restricted to the precise charge under consideration. Instead all evidence bearing on those involved was admitted. Decisions were seldom absolute. They tended to be more of a compromise, especially in civil suits. This procedure and decision type applied at all levels.

The importance and scope of regional government varied in each kingdom. There were always one or more layers between the village and the king. Administrators on the regional level competed with the king for power. A strong king would determine the number of intermediate authorities according to principles of administrative convenience and he would closely supervise them. A weak king could not control the number, and the regional authorities could often become nearly autonomous. The institutions, especially in the more autonomous situations, paralleled those of the center.

The lowest administrative unit was the village. The village headman dealt with outside authorities and had power to rule within the village. He usually controlled more land than anyone else and was a member of the dominant caste. In many villages there were councils which helped govern. Referred to as *panchayats*, these were of two types – village councils made up of respected elders without reference to caste and caste councils made up of elders of a single caste. All castes had caste councils which decided intra-caste disputes. Sometimes the caste council of the dominant caste would also serve as the village council. In both types of councils decisions were made by consensus. Councils performed all governing functions, including legal ones.

Early Islamic invaders and internal dynamics continuously modified the traditional system described above, but we will ignore these changes and go on to consider the governmental system imposed by the Mughals. This is justified because the Mughals were the main power that the early British conquerors dealt with, and their system was the one the British took over and, with modifications, spread throughout the subcontinent. Moreover, a discussion of the Mughal system allows more specificity than was possible under the general rubric 'traditional'.

MUGHAL RULE

The Mughals were of Islamic and Turkish extraction. From 1526 until 1757 they ruled in fact, and until 1858 they ruled nominally in large areas of North India. At the height of its power, the Mughal Empire stretched from modern Afghanistan in the West to Bengal in the East, from Kashmir in the North to the Deccan in the South. Politically, the most important period was under Akbar, from 1556 until 1605, whose institutions and political ideas were the basis of all Mughal rule.

Before setting forth the structure of Mughal government, it is necessary to note at least two important cultural changes brought by the Mughals which had far reaching implications for Indian politics. One was the Mughal introduction of Persian as the official language of the empire and the language of all governmental records. Officials in the Mughal Empire were both Muslims and the native Hindus. The latter group needed to learn the new language as facility in Persian was a prerequisite for participation in the government. A second cultural change concerned religion. Akbar himself believed in religious toleration and attempted to form a syncretic religion. Later Mughal rulers were not as tolerant and their rule was characterized by a pronounced Islamic bias. This second cultural change put the two major religious systems – Hinduism and Islam – in conflict. The cleavages created led to the differential development of the two great religious groups which was only resolved with the partition of the subcontinent in 1947 into India and Pakistan.

The Mughal Empire was an autocracy with the emperor holding absolute power. Theoretically he controlled all appointments and promotions, and was the final dispenser of justice, the chief legislator, the commander of military forces, and the head of government. Akbar attempted to translate this theory into practice and was to a large degree successful. Although Akbar's system was based on the traditional one, he refined this system in such a way as to make possible efffective centralized control of a large empire. The two keys to improvements were the public service structure and the reorganization of the land revenue system.

In staffing his administrative structure, Akbar tried to ensure the personal loyalty of his servants. He attempted to keep out all subordinates who had local power bases in the land and could therefore counter his wishes. In order to do this, he abolished hereditary rights to collect land revenue and in their place established the *mansabdari* system, a ranking system of personnel based on military lines. The Emperor appointed the *mansabdar*s. A high proportion of them were foreigners, giving Akbar added control. *Mansabdar*s were all-purpose public servants who could serve in any military or civilian bureaucratic post. To prevent creation of local power bases they were transferred every four or five years. Akbar established two methods of remuneration: salary, which was preferred, and *jagir*s, or land grants. Payment of salaries in cash from the Emperor's treasury was a revolutionary concept because of the implications this had for ensuring loyalty to the Emperor. In practice, salaries were never extended to the whole bureaucratic system due to the economic realities of the time. The less preferred method, the grant of a *jagir,* conferred the right to collect revenue from a piece of land calculated to yield the salary appropriate to the given *mansabdar*'s rank. These rights were not permanent and hereditary but in later practice they tended to become so.[2]

The other reform which buttressed Akbar's power was revamping the land revenue system in three significant ways. All land was measured. After this it was classified according to fertility and to the value of the crops raised on it. On the basis of this the government provided inducements for growing profitable crops. Finally the rate of taxation owed to the government was fixed, based on ten year averages (Edwardes and Garrett 1956:201). Previously, the government had taken a fixed percentage of any given year's crop, a practice that resulted in yearly revenue fluctuations which hurt long-term planning. Under Akbar's system the government received a steady, set income. Even in famine years the peasant had to pay. The government accepted payments in both cash and kind, cash being preferred because it provided a more flexible tool for central control, but total monetization was not possible in practice.

Akbar's administrative units were the center, the provinces or *suba*s, the *sarkar*s or districts, and the *pargana*s or sub-districts. At the center, there were regular departments with specific functions, written rules to delineate the functions and departmental interrelationships, and control of all departments through the keeping of detailed written records. This specific delineation of powers and this record keeping allowed centralized control and marked a major change from the traditional system. The Emperor had personal advisors and ministers, but they did not constitute a legislature. As in the traditional system, the *durbar* served as a forum to air grievances and opinions, the Emperor making final judgments. Thus, the *durbar* was the final court of appeal in legal as well as policy decisions. The administration of justice was not conducted through an independent judiciary. Rather, administrative officers or traditional leaders dispensed justice, the final petition being to the Emperor. Both Hindu and Islamic law were used. Speed characterized all judicial decisions. Complicated procedures to preserve 'civil rights' were non-existent. As in the traditional system, law was not codified. Justice had a decidedly ad hoc character. At the provincial level, the administrative officials replicated the system at the center. On the village level, there was little institutional change from the traditional system.

Akbar's system combined elements of tradition and of more modern political ideology. Certainly the most important feature was the centralization of power through a hand picked and theoretically non-hereditary public service. The effectiveness of this system steadily declined after Akbar's reign. In the first place it ultimately depended upon the personal skill of the emperor. None of Akbar's descendants had the administrative ability he possessed. In the second place the size of the bureaucracy greatly increased to the point where there were not enough *jagirs* for payment. Finally, as the size of the empire was extended through military conquests it became more difficult to control the periphery. The outlying provinces became a drain on the treasury instead of contributing to it.

THE EAST INDIA COMPANY

Shortly after Akbar's reign the Europeans discovered India and were impressed by the wealth and civilization they encountered. Thus, as Mughal power declined a new force entered the Indian political arena. Trading companies from France, Britain, and Holland saw the immediate advantages of gaining privileged status to trade in certain areas to ensure themselves a market. Unlike other 'exploiters' or conquerors of India who had traditionally come overland from the northwest, the Europeans came by sea and their influence was first felt in the coastal areas. While the Europeans competed for supremacy in trading rights, other native powers like the Marathas and the Sikhs arose to challenge the Mughal hegemony, weakening the Mughal system. This gave the European traders the opportunity to assist one side against the other and win favorable trading rights. Political involvement proved to be commercially advantageous.

Intra-European struggles for economic supremacy in India ended in 1761 when the French surrendered to the British East India Company at Pondicherry. During the following one hundred years the East India Company secured not only trading monopolies but also became the *de facto* and later the *de jure* rulers of a large portion of the subcontinent. The period of Company rule represents a third major stage in the institutional development of India.

Unlike the cases of Tanzania and New Guinea, the establishment of imperial rule in India was not the result of direct governmental intervention with the intent of establishing an imperial domain.

Rather, the British East India Company, a commercial trading organization, slowly took on more and more ruling functions. The Company did not go to India with the idea of conquest nor did the British government of the eighteenth century see this as the Company's role or its own. This is significant for Indian political development. Neither the Company nor the Crown (when it took over the  rule of India in 1858) had a system of imperial rule. In fact, the British evolved their ideas of imperial government in India. The structures that emerged were a curious blend of the native Indian institutions, the exigencies of the situation, the changing ideas of governance held by the Company's Board of Directors, and the changing political climate in England. It is important to realize that the evolution of the imperial institutions in India reflected changes in England as much as changes in India. The late eighteenth century and the nineteenth century were periods of dynamic changes in the social, political, and economic make up of England. Only at the end of this period did imperial rule become fully articulated.

From 1650 onwards, the East India Company had been *de facto* rulers of the English trading establishments of Calcutta, Madras, and Bombay where they had built their own forts. Slowly they were granted privileged trading rights. To protect these, the Company servants became more and more involved in local and regional politics. Company men fought not only European competitors but also Indian challengers who threatened regional stability. Institutionally, the major step occurred when the Emperor, Shah Alam, gave Lord Clive, the Governor General, the *diwani* of Bengal in 1765. The grant of the *diwani* meant the company could collect revenue and dispense civil justice in the province. In so doing Shah Alam officially recognized the Company's military and administrative power. Theoretically, the *nawab*, as the deputy of the Emperor, had the *nizamat,* the power of commanding troops and dispensing criminal justice, but in fact this was also under Company control since it was exercised by a Company nominee. This was the first step toward direct Company administration of the Province of Bengal from whence Company power spread. Once the Company's permanence was assured, the Emperor and *nawab* became little more than puppets maintained for legitimacy and to preclude Parliamentary interference. The system of dual control quickly resulted in anarchy and in 1772 Parliament intervened. The Company assumed direct control of Bengal rather than operating through puppets. Until 1858, a series of Parliamentary acts increasingly ensured the Company's accountability to the British government for its actions in India. Within the limits of this overview, the details of the relationship of the Company to Parliament, the various military and political battles by which the Company spread its power, and all the stages of institutional development cannot be discussed. Instead, we will attempt to analyze the effects of culture contact and changing ideologies on the development of policies and institutions and to discuss these institutions when fully formed.

The Company's shift from a trading to a ruling role was accompanied by a major change in its perceptions. After 1800, the servants' viewpoint shifted until by the end of the period they were denigrating their predecessors as rapacious exploiters. They saw themselves as Platonic rulers bringing enlightenment, order, and good rule to replace the anarchy and darkness that had engulfed the subcontinent. This shift in the perceptions of Company servants was reflecting changes in English society wrought by the industrial revolution which gave the West supreme confidence in its superiority. The rise of the middle classes, their participation in the political system, and the Protestant ethic led to a change in the type of men who served in India and to the type of institutions they fostered. These changing notions of government were as important for Indian institutional development as they were for English politics.

The key administrative task in India as always was the collection of revenue. To begin with, the Company conducted revenue collecting operations in the traditional manner. The governmental share of village produce passed up through layers of intermediaries until it entered Company coffers rather than those of the Emperor. All personnel were Indians. This system of indirect rule proved unworkable. Searching for a better system, the Company introduced two major reforms which completely altered the existing system. First, it devised new land settlements for the areas it governed. Whether these settlements were permanent or were subject to review differed in each area, but all were characterized by a contractual relationship between the Company and the landlords in which the Company vested ownership rights in the landlords in return for an annual fixed amount of revenue. The Company believed that it was merely clarifying and regularizing a somewhat confused system. But, in reality, the Company was introducing a concept novel to the Indians: the ownership rights in land which included the right of free disposal of the land. In investing these rights in Indians holding large tracts of land, the British hoped to create a gentry class comparable to that which existed in England. The expectation that this class of gentlemen farmers would invest in the land and raise productivity never materialized. Instead, the successful landholders became the new urban elite. Land was sold and subdivided, creating havoc as well as thousands of court cases. The peasant, rather than being better off as the British predicted, became the victim and his poverty increased.

The second major reform was the creation of a British civil service. The Company discovered it could not maintain effective control relying on Indian intermediaries. Indians were replaced by Company servants at the upper levels. Gradually, the principles which govern the Indian bureaucracy today evolved. This, in Weberian terms, was the beginning of a modern, legal-rational bureaucracy. The characteristics of this service included remuneration by salary rather than by trading profits, power adhering to the office rather than to the individual, and formal training in specialized institutions rather than on the job training. This last point raised the question of what kind of training would best equip men for service. Initially the recruits received formal training at Fort William College in India. There the views of the Orientalist school predominated – that civil servants should understand and be sympathetic to Indian culture and that they should speak the native language. Later, formal training shifted to Haileybury, England, and its content changed significantly. Company servants were seen as the transmitters of British culture and values; therefore, learning about British institutions took precedence over learning native customs and languages. This had important implications for the widespread use of the English language in India and for the introduction of English political institutions. In the end a civil service was developed with an ethos of honesty, fairness, and disinterestedness which was something new on the subcontinent and which made a deep impression on all Indians.

Company rule had a significant impact on the legal system and the administration of justice. The British perceived the existing system as both unfair and imprecise and sought to transform it into a system reflecting British ideas of property and justice. As mentioned above, ownership rights were vested in the landlord class. The cultivators, who previously enjoyed traditional rights to work the land and share in its produce, became tenants under the control of the landlords. Attempts were made to codify the laws. In theory, British law was not to be imposed but the difficulties involved in codifying the welter of customary and sacred laws meant that, in practice, British legal concepts and categories were employed. The Company established courts along British lines which utilized the adversary system and British rules of procedure and which followed the principle of equality before the law – a very strange concept in a society structured by caste. The Indians found these institutions esoteric. A class of legal intermediaries, the Indian lawyers, developed. Of necessity, these men became educated in Western ideas and stood at the forefront of the Westernized elite who later emerged as the new political leaders.

Culture contact also transformed the educational process and influenced certain social practices which in turn affected contemporary governmental institutions as well as Indians' response to those institutions. Long before the Company had begun to rule India, many Indian traders had seen the immense advantages to be gained by learning English. The necessity of speaking English became increasingly important with Company hegemony. After Orientalist ideas went out of fashion around 1830, English became the official government language. In order to serve as a clerk to the British one had to speak English. Hindu clerks and scribes who had served the Mughals were quick to learn the new language, giving themselves the greatest opportunities for advancement in the new system. On the other hand, the Muslims clung to Persian education which meant they could not fill government posts. This had important implications for later developments.

As the English language became an important tool for advancement, so too did Western education. The growth of Western education had two aspects. First was the demand for this type of learning from natives who wished to enter the legal profession or to serve the new government. Second was the British attitude. With the rise of the Utilitarians in England, Lord Macaulay wrote his famous 'Education Minute' in 1835. Macaulay and Lord Bentinck, then Governor General, believed that Indian learning and literature were useless and that one of the great objects of British rule was to promote European literature and science. Henceforward all funds were to be spent on Western education in English. Although this was later modified to allow some financial aid to native institutions, a major reorientation resulted. English medium schools and colleges teaching Western subjects spread. This change, coupled with the use of English, meant that any Indian who aspired to a role in public life or private business had to imbibe of Western knowledge. Traditional learning lost its prestige and was often cast aside. The educational system and the English language were the salient points at which culture contact between the two nations occurred. In this period Western ideas took root in the consciousness of Indians where they have remained to shape their ideas up to the present.

The institutions as they existed at their maturity under Company rule were important for later political developments. After 1833, the Company was forbidden to trade in India and was solely an administrative body. Its major function was to appoint those who governed. The Governor General was the head of the governmental structure in India. He exercised his official policy making role in concert with a council composed of a small number of government officials who had served in India for at least ten years. The Governor General could act without his council, giving him almost unlimited powers. During the last phase of Company rule an articulation was made between the executive and legislative function. The Legislative Council included all members of the Executive Council plus one member for legislation. In the 1850s it was expanded to include representatives of the provincial governments. Final authority remained with the 'Governor General in [Executive] Council' which had the power to make all laws. The Governor General implemented these policies through the civil service and the army.

The administration of justice was a thorny problem, a fact which is reflected in the great number of judicial structures built and dismantled during the Company period. The source of difficulties was the conflict between native and European concepts of the law. The British attitude of non-interference with native laws complicated the picture. In general the highest level courts in the provinces were the final forums of appeal, but exceptionally important cases could be appealed as high as the Crown in England. Each community – European, Hindi, and Muslim – had its own set of courts on both the civil and the criminal side. Each province had a supreme court which originally dealt with cases involving Company servants but which later became prototypes of the high courts created under Crown rule. There were various types of intermediate courts applying a welter of uncodified law. During the Company period the entire legal system was in flux.

The British were attached to their legal system and generally attempted to extend it to the district level and below. They encountered real problems in doing this. For example, the ideal was to separate revenue functions from the administration of justice. In Bengal these were first separated under Cornwallis in 1793 when a collector and a magistrate were posted to each district. The problem with this and with other British concepts was that complications in procedure allowed manipulation of the institutions by insiders and led to the ultimate frustration of justice. Furthermore, litigation multiplied and litigation was expensive for the common man. In sum, the common man could not perceive justice emanating from this system. Therefore, later the functions were again unified in one man. Still later there was another cycle of separation and unification of functions. The most satisfactory results appear to have been achieved by the un-British tradition of all-purpose district officers dispensing speedy, ad hoc justice.

The three British provinces were Bombay, Madras, and Bengal. The Governor General governed Bengal as well as the central government until 1854 when a lieutenant governor was appointed to govern this huge province stretching from Calcutta to Delhi and beyond. The structures of the central government were replicated at the provincial level. The governors had councils to advise them. Ultimately they were responsible to the Governor General but in fact they had great independent power because of poor communication and the right of direct appeal to the Board in England.

For administrative purposes the provinces were divided into divisions, headed by commissioners, and districts, headed by an officer variously designated deputy commissioner, collector, or district magistrate. There were no formal councils on these levels. The key unit in the Company administrative system was the district. A European always filled the post of chief district officer, the lowest level at which this is consistently true. Just as the districts were based on similar Mughal units, so the style of the district officer contained many elements of the Mughal style. The district officer was an autocrat in his district. An important institution was the tour in which he would survey the condition of his domain, hold a *durbar*-like session under canvas in which he heard the petitions of the people, handed down decisions and dispensed justice on the spot. The resemblance to the Mughal practices was striking. Although important variation occurred in different times and in different areas, the dominant pattern was that all functions – revenue, justice, magisterial – were combined in one man. District officers took great pride in their paternalistic style of rule. The major differences from Mughal rule at this level derived from the efficiencies of a modern bureaucracy and the ethos of the Company civil service. The British presence was strong, persistent, and did not wildly fluctuate with changes in the person of the district officer. The ethos instilled a pattern of fairness and disinterestedness in his conduct. Under the district officer was a bureaucracy staffed primarily by Indians which reached into the villages. The main functions of the district government remained with the collection of revenue and the maintenance of law and order.

Villages generally had a headman who dealt with outside authorities and who made decisions affecting the village. Depending on the power distribution, he might or might not have advice from others. There was also a village accountant who was charged with keeping land and revenue records straight. The strength of the district government appears to have sapped some of the strength of the traditional village institutions. Appeal could always be made to a powerful outside authority. In general, the *panchayats* or councils were not very strong during this period.

CROWN RULE

The Indian Mutiny of 1857 marked a watershed in British-Indian relations and in the governance of India. The nature and causes of the Mutiny have been widely debated, but all agree it represented a challenge to British authority and to Westernization and the changes it wrought in the Indian system. Basically, the mutineers came from two groups in the society: Indian members of the army who believed certain military practices caused them to break religious customs and large landowners and the rulers of some princely states who felt Western ideas and advances threatened the traditional system of beliefs and their personal power positions. The Mutiny raged for almost a year. That such a small number of Britons could emerge victorious in this widespread revolt highlighted Western superiority in the minds of the newly educated elites.

The shock of the Mutiny produced important changes in the organization of the government and the psychology of the British in India. Most obviously, the British government assumed direct rule of the subcontinent. The Company increasingly had become an anomaly – a trading corporation forbidden to trade and mandated to govern. Besides, a duplication of institutions had occurred since before 1858 in that both the Company and the Crown had armies in India. With the assumption of direct control, London had a greater voice in Indian affairs. A Secretary of State for India headed the new structure. He was a political appointee of the party in power and was directly responsible to the Cabinet. He had a council of advisors, the Council of India. Technically he had to ratify all policy decisions and legislation passed in India. Together with the Council, the Secretary controlled expenditures and appointment of all Europeans, civilian and military, in the Indian services except for the Governor General, the law member of the council, provincial governors, and the advocate generals who were appointed by the Crown.

Under the new structure, the Governor General had the added apellation of Viceroy, making him the personal representative of the British Sovereign in India. He was appointed by the Crown on the advice of the Prime Minister. The post of Viceroy of India was a tremendously prestigious post. In most cases the Viceroy had not served in India before his appointment. Most Britons and Indians believed his previous non-involvement made the Viceroy a wise and benevolent ruler.

More important for government policy than administrative changes were the psychological consequences of the Mutiny. The major concern became how to avoid mistakes which might lead to another catastrophe. The bond of trust the British had assumed existed between themselves and the Indians was broken (Smith 1961: 675). India was viewed as a large, inhospitable, rather barbaric country where death and defeat were always close at hand. Out of this perception emerged the idea of the 'white man's burden' – that the British must spread the glories, institutions, and beliefs of their society to the degraded, feudalistic Indians. The belief that there was an unbridgeable gap between the East and the West became axiomatic. This shift in perception changed British goals in India: the new view of India was that the British would exercise parental care without any hope for real development rather than the idea of earlier years that a Westernized India would eventually attain self-government (Smith 1961: 681).

The altered British attitudes changed their policies concerning the princely states, social reform, and the traditional aristocracy. The Company had a policy of territorial expansion and annexation, but at the time of Crown ascendance, Britain did not control all of India. Large areas under indigenous political systems remained independent. The rulers of some of these states, fearing extinction, were involved in the Mutiny, but others remained loyal to the British. The new government rewarded these loyal rulers with titles and gifts of land. Moreover, the British realized that they had to seek some accommodation with these independent rulers to prevent future uprisings. They adopted the doctrine of paramountcy under which the Crown assumed sovereignty over the princely states. This implied that the states were part of the Empire and the British had the right to interfere in their governments but would not conquer them. Thus, India was divided into two governmental systems which persisted until independence.

Besides appeasing the princes, the British sought to ensure the loyalty of other traditional elements of society like the wealthy landowners. The British viewed the Indian system as being feudal in nature. They felt that the aristocracy should have a stake in any society which was formed through modernization. Ideas for Indian participation were geared toward this group and its members were the ones who received British appointments and honors. The new, Western-educated elite were displeased with such a policy since they believed they should hold these positions.

The British now placed their faith in the traditional leaders of Indian society while failing to recognize that the Mutiny was a challenge by old rulers who no longer were the men of consequence. The Western-educated elite, Britain's own creation, were slowly emerging as the most important political sector among the Indians. The British encouraged their rise to prominence by the post-Mutiny policy of having more Indian participation in the government. The British seemed to believe that the elite would be content with what the British saw as their place in government – the lowest posts. But education led to higher aspirations. In the early 1860s, Indians began to compete for jobs in the Indian Civil Service (ICS), the top cadre in the civil service structure. British policy generally frustrated these attempts. Since 1853, entry into the ICS had been based on competitive examination in England. Up until the twentieth century the British tightened regulations making it more and more difficult for Indians to gain admittance. During the same period, Indians increasingly went to England for education and then discovered they could fill only the lower positions.

The difficulties Indians encountered when trying to enter the ICS were symptomatic of the general frustrations facing the Western-educated elite. While studying the West, they had learned about Western political ideologies, institutions, and processes. They saw themselves as the leaders of India and wanted their fair share in the government. Thus in 1885, they formed the first nationwide political movement, the Indian National Congress, to voice their hopes and aspirations. The early Congress members were mainly Westernized Hindus from the cities.

Until the 1880s, British government in India was autocratic and predominantly administrative. Challenges to the British came from traditional leaders who wanted to govern in the same manner as those they challenged. The Western elite had different notions. They did not want to replace the British administration. They wanted instead to create a British political system, which they believed to be an open and democratic one, in India. With the formation of the Congress a dialogue began between the British and the Indian nationalists, a dialogue which lasted seventy years, which created modern Indian political institutions, and which left independent India with a strong democratic legacy.

While the political dialogue was developing during the post-Mutiny period, so too was the infrastructure which made British rule and Indian nationalist organization possible. Railroads and telegraph lines connected the major cities of the Empire. Moreover, India and Britain were brought closer together with the opening of the Suez Canal and with the intercontinental telegraph. These enabled the British government to supervise its empire more closely and gave the Viceroy and other British officials in India less discretionary power. The press grew by leaps and bounds, becoming the means of livelihood for educated Indians who could not secure government employment. In fact the press became the spokesman for new Indian political ideas, so much so that during the entire period from the Mutiny until Independence, the British repeatedly attempted to control the press. By the 1870s the press was officially felt to be seditious because it questioned British rule. British controls, confiscations, and arrests never stopped the press; they only angered Indians who had accepted British teachings on the freedom of the press.

Public policy and administrative development became a subject of discussion among Indians. In addition to revenue collection and law and order, the administration took on more service functions – railway, post and telegraph, public health, irrigation, etc. As the government became increasingly complex the number of civil servants and others associated with it grew rapidly. It became modern in terms of function and scope. Expanded services led to higher levels of expenditure. Land revenue still served as the major source of income, but other duties and tariffs were also imposed. Indian revenues were used not only for services to improve India, but also to finance imperial ventures in which Indian troops were involved and, later, Indian participation in World War I. As Indians became more vocal, they accused the British of destroying the Indian economy through high taxation and the import of European goods, while exporting raw materials. The 'drain theory' became an issue over which popular unrest could be aroused. Reminiscent of the American revolution, nationalists raised the cry of 'no taxation without representation'.

One way to view the political developments from 1880 to 1947 is as the growth of increased demands for participation in government and the emergence of the legislative arena. Lord Ripon, Viceroy of India from 1880 to 1884, was a British Liberal who, more than any other Viceroy before World War I, was sympathetic to Indian aspirations and who believed the Indians must be educated for self-government. On his own initiative, rather than because of Indian demands, he promulgated the 'Resolution on Local Self-Government' in 1882. His intention was to provide a set of district, municipal, and rural institutions in which the Western educated class of Indians could participate and thereby be schooled in the political and administrative arts of the local level with the idea that these skills would be useful in later years on higher levels. In contrast with the opinions of the majority on his subordinates, he was willing to see a drop in the level of efficiency in order to make the training real. He did not specify the structural details of the new local boards, but left room for variations based on local conditions. Generally, the institutions that emerged from this resolution were boards with a majority of non-officials who were both appointed and elected. The franchise was very restricted. Ripon expressed a preference for a non-official chairman, but in practice this occurred in only about one half of the cases. The variations in terms of official dominance were wide; some boards were composed entirely of nominated members, even though this was far from Ripon's intention (Tinker 1968: 48).

These boards exercised all the functions of local government. Restrictions on their utility as forums for learning the skills of modern, democratic government were the lack of funds available to implement their decisions and the close official supervision and control. Nevertheless, the fact that the Western-educated Indians formally participated in the political system for the first time in these institutions made them important.

Partly because of Ripon's generosity, the early Indian nationalists were not against British rule. They agreed with the British that the British conquest was the best thing that had ever happened to India and that only with British governance could India advance politically and culturally. What they wanted was not self-government but a share in the existing government. They asked for changes in the ICS competition to enable Indians to secure positions, for more Indian appointments to the executive councils at the center and in the provinces, and for the end of press and arms control. The British believed that the nationalists were an insignificant minority, representing only themselves, who could be ignored. This British belief continued well beyond World War I. The British justified their rule by claiming they were concerned about the good of the masses. What they failed to realize was that, although a minority, the Western-educated elite were becoming the spokesmen of Indian aspirations and it was they who could, and would, challenge British hegemony.

In 1892, the British reviewed the status of their government in India and passed the Indian Councils Act to amend the 1861 Act. The 1861 Indian Councils Act had retained the Executive Council of the Governor General and established the portfolio system, placing members in charge of specific departments. A Legislative Council was set up at the center which included the Executive Council plus six to twelve added members, at least one half of whom were non-officials. The Legislative Council could only discuss matters laid before it by the Viceroy. The 1892 Act increased the Legislative Council's authority to discuss the budget and to ask questions. Similar councils were established at the provincial level. Although most of the members of the councils were nominated, in some cases very select constituencies were allowed to elect members. Election opened the door to members of Congress who had not previously served on these councils, since the British had limited their Indian appointments to the traditional aristocracy. Quickly, Indians like G. K. Gokhale learned to use the Legislative Council as a forum in which to express the Western-educated elite's opinions and to press for further governmental reforms.

The turn of the century brought major changes in Indian political life. Lord Curzon, who served as Viceroy from 1899 to 1905, was an ardent imperialist. His policies regarding education and the partition of Bengal angered the nationalists, providing new causes around which to center their demands. A second generation of Indian leaders was emerging who had been educated politically by the early Congressmen and who had much stronger ambitions and demands. Many in this group did not accept their predecessors' maxim, what is West is best. Hindu revivalism had become a strong force on the Indian political scene. Its leaders were reinterpreting the Indian past in light of Western ideas and were attempting to create a new image of India as equal to the West. They offered an alternative to Western modes of government and political ideas by extolling the greatness of 'Mother India' and of native political institutions.

After Hindu revivalism gained a popular following, the Muslims began to reexamine their place in Indian society and the developing political system. They lagged behind the Hindus in Western education. After the Mutiny they had been in disfavor since the British believed they had been its leaders. The Muslims, by choice, had little representation in the early Congress. Suddenly they discovered that they were being left out. The specter of Hindu rule loomed on the horizon. In 1906, the first purely Muslim political association, the Muslim League, was formed to press Muslim demands for goverrnmental representation. The following year the Congress split into two factions, the 'moderates', who believed in British rule, and the 'extremists' who wanted self-government. The British perceived these new groups and new tensions as threats to their supremacy and once again set out to reform the government and meet some demands. This reform, and all subsequent ones until independence, gave too little and came too late to satisfy even the most moderate nationalists.

The Morley-Minto Reforms of 1909[3] set forth changes that were meant to be encouragement to the moderate forces and to the traditional elites, especially the Muslims. They were intended to stop the growth of what the British saw as anarchy fomented by Western-educated Hindus. This act extended the principle of elected members to the Viceroy's Council and to the provincial councils. The provincial constituencies were not structured on strict geographic grounds but were modified to secure due representation of all important interests such as commerce groups or religious minorities. At the center, official members still retained a majority on the Council, but in the provinces officials were outnumbered by a combination of elected and appointed non-officials. The Indians saw these changes as steps toward a British system of parliamentary government, following the same path as the British themselves had followed. The British categorically denied that their intention was to advance India toward self-government. They professed to see these changes as an expanded *durbar* (Coupland 1944: 25–27). In retrospect it appears that the Indians' sense of the dynamics of political development was more accurate than that of the British. Once the principle of representation was granted, its coexistence with an autocratic government created an anomaly.

Equally important to Indian political development was the principle of separate electorates conceded in the 1909 Act. The British felt that India could not be a unified nation because of the numerous religions coexisting on the subcontinent. Further, they perceived that the real trouble makers who were challenging British supremacy were the Hindus. They were inclined to give favors to the Muslim community in return for loyalty – the principle of divide and rule. Under the system of separate electorates a disproportionate number of seats were reserved for Muslims elected by exclusively Muslim constituencies. This encouraged political separatism and granted a privilege which the Muslims zealously guarded in the future to the detriment of national unity.

The functions of the Legislative Council were extended under the Act. The most important change was that legislators were allowed to discuss a wider variety of topics and to make non-binding resolutions. But the Governor General in Executive Council still retained final authority in financial and other sensitive areas such as defense.[4]

The Indians' perception of their role in government radically altered during World War I and the period immediately following. They contributed both men and materials to the war effort to prove their loyalty to the Crown. In exchange, they expected further constitutional advances. Anti-British activity was held in abeyance during the war years. At the close of the War, especially after President Wilson's Fourteen Points which included the idea of self-determination for all nations, the Indians expected immediate advances toward self-government. Instead the British enacted the Rowlatt Acts which extended wartime powers of internment and trial without jury. The nationalists were sure that these acts were aimed to silence them. Then, a British General fired on a prohibited meeting in Amritsar called to protest these Acts, killing 379 Indians. Immediately, the British proclaimed martial law and instituted severe punitive measures, such as public flogging, in the Punjab. With the so-called Jallianwalla Bagh massacre, Indo-British relations were at their lowest point since the Mutiny. It was against this background that the Montagu-Chelmsford Reforms, the next stage in institutional development, were passed and that Mahatma Gandhi became the leader of the first national civil disobedience movement.

The Montagu-Chelmsford Report was issued in 1918. Its reforms were embodied in the Government of India Act of 1919. The three principles underlying these reforms were the recognition of self-government as the eventual goal of British policy, the achievement of this goal by stages corresponding to the growth of Indian responsibility and ability, and the authority of the British to judge this progress. At the center, the Legislative Council was replaced by a Legislative Assembly of 106 elected and forty nominated members. The franchise for electing these members was restricted to about one million people. The Executive Council remained unresponsible to the Assembly, but three Indians sat on the Council of seven (excluding the Viceroy). Authority to act on certain subjects and sources of revenue was split between the center and the provinces, whereas previously the center had ultimate control in all areas.

The real advance came in the provinces. Enlarged legislative assemblies were created and about five million were enfranchised mainly on the basis of property qualifications. The reforms instituted a system of 'dyarchy' for the provincial governments. Under this system the functions of government were split into 'reserved' and 'transferred' categories. Reserved functions generally pertained to law and order and were handled by officers who were not responsible to the legislative assemblies. Transferred functions generally pertained to nation-building and were handled by ministers responsible to the assemblies. This was the first time that Indians were allowed to exercise responsible government.

There were many efforts to give vitality to local governments after the war. Rural government at the sub-district level received particular attention and statutory schemes utilizing the idea of *panchayat*s proliferated. However, these institutions never became viable under colonial auspices. The fate of the municipal boards was better. The system of dyarchy eliminated official control of municipal and district boards, so that these institutions of local government, although limited in scope, became genuine political arenas (Tinker 1968: 106–125). The character of municipal government has not altered drastically since that time.

In 1920, M. K. Gandhi launched the first nationwide civil disobedience movement demanding home rule. Although the movement failed, it had important implications for future developments. New groups entered the political arena. Local leaders began to create local power bases. These men became more important as regional and communal considerations outweighed national ones. Between periods of highly organized nation-wide protest, political action was centered in small areas and the concern was not independence, but rather the problem of coexistence faced by people with different religions and cultures. Throughout the 1920s, Hindu-Muslim antagonism increased. This made the British feel their rule was justified since they alone could preserve order. Indian politicians realized there could be no constitutional advance unless the communities unified, but despite concerted efforts, unity proved impossible. Neither Hindus nor Muslims wanted the other group to have much political power.

By this time, Indians had lost faith in Britain. Up through the war, Indians had believed that the British people, if not their representatives in India, identified with Indian aspirations for self-determination. But the war years, the failure of civil disobedience, and the appointment of the Simon Commission dispelled this belief.

By 1929, Indian pressure for further constitutional advance had boiled over. Led by the young Jawaharlal Nehru, the new demands included complete independence. To appease Indian popular opinion, the Viceroy announced that Britain's goal for India was dominion status. However, he did not set a timetable for the realization of this goal as the Indians demanded. In 1930, Gandhi once again led a civil disobedience movement, this time for independence. The British then held three round table conferences where British and Indian representatives discussed future government reforms. The result of these conferences was the 1935 Government of India Act.

The institutions established by the 1935 Act have served as a basis for those of independent India. This act committed India to federalism and to parliamentary government. While the separation of powers under the 1919 Act had been based on the principle of decentralization, in 1935 it was based on federalism. The central or federal government had a bicameral legislature which was carefully constructed to balance diverse interests arising from the communal situation and from the existence of the princely states. The upper house would be composed of representatives of the princely states. Indirect election by communities was the method used to elect the lower house, the representatives of British India. The structure was dyarchical, with two lists of subjects, one of which was to be handled by ministers responsible to the legislature, the other of which was to be handled by officials. This part of the act was never put into effect because the necessary number of princely states did not accede to it.

Schedules were drawn up to define the spheres of activity of the center and of the provinces. There was also a concurrent schedule of subjects on which either authority might legislate. Residual powers were given neither to the center nor the states; rather the Governor General had discretion in these cases. A federal Court consisting of a Chief Justice and six other judges was established to deal with constitutional questions of federalism and to take certain types of appeals from provincial high courts.

The provinces were made legal entities for the first time. The dyarchical system was abolished and fully responsible provincial government was established on a parliamentary model with a council of ministers responsible to legislative assemblies. Some provinces had unicameral legislatures while others had bicameral ones. Suffrage was limited by property qualifications. The electorate for the legislative assemblies of all the provinces numbered about thirty million. In accord with the Communal Award of 1932, the principle of separate electorates and weightages for minority groups was extended and fully institutionalized with the expanded electorate. The provincial governor did retain a few powers, mainly those concerning the protection of British civil servants and their salaries, British business interests, and minorities. Elections for the provincial legislatures were held in 1937.

Historically the decade from 1937 until independence was a period of crisis in India and Britain. Immersed in a global war, Britain refused to meet Indian demands for immediate independence. After its overwhelming victory in the 1937 elections, the Congress believed it represented all Indians and continually refused to recognize the increasingly great cleavages in Indian society. In 1940, Mohammed Ali Jinnah, leader of the Muslim League, called for a separate Islamic state. The forties were marked by conferences and attempts to unite a deeply divided nation – all of which failed. When independence was granted on August 20, 1947, two new nations were created – the secular state of India and the Islamic state of Pakistan. Partition of the subcontinent was accompanied by rioting, looting, and bloodshed as many of the Muslims in India fled to Pakistan and many Hindus living in Pakistan came to India.

SINCE 1947

Despite its bloody birth, India emerged as the largest democracy in the world. Under the British 'Cabinet Mission Plan' of 1946, the members of the provincial assemblies elected a constituent assembly to draft a constitution for India. At independence, this body assumed the dual task of governance and of producing a constitution. Its administration managed to maintain law and order, to settle the millions of refugees from Pakistan, and to keep the nation from disintegrating without resorting to a dictatorship or to military control. Further, when Gandhi was assassinated in 1948 by a Hindu fanatic, the leaders preserved order and used his death to unite the Assembly to produce a secular, democratic, Western-type constitution.

Congressmen, almost all of whom had served in the Government, dominated the Constituent Assembly. Well-schooled in British ideas and principles of government, these men debated for three years on what kind of government should be instituted. Two major problems which had plagued all previous efforts at constitution-making no longer counted as serious factors. Partition eliminated the Hindu-Muslim conflict and the Assembly, under the iron hand of Sadar Patel, integrated the princely states into the provinces. In the end, the Assembly produced a long, extremely complex document. This constitution promulgated on Republic Day, January 26, 1950, is still in force today, a testimony to the farsightedness of its framers, the high quality of the document, and the strength of the British legacy. That it has survived so well is remarkable indeed in comparison with the fate of other newly independent nations.

In drafting the Constitution, the Constituent Assembly did not take any radical directions, rather it followed the institutional lines which had been developed under British rule, particularly in the 1935 Act. In fact, 250 out of 395 articles are taken verbatim or with minor changes from the act (Hardgrave 1970: 44). The Constitution established a federal system with a parliamentary form of government. The central or federal level is termed the union. An indirectly elected president serves as the head of state, fulfilling the functions of a British monarch. A Council of Ministers with a prime minister at the head exercises the powers of government at the union level. The members of the Council must be members of Parliament and they are collectively responsible to that body. Parliament is bicameral. The upper house, known as the Council of States or *Rajya Sabha,* consists of twelve members nominated by the president and not more than 238 representatives of the states indirectly elected by the state legislatures. This body cannot be dissolved. One third of its membership is replaced every two years. The lower house, known as the House of the People or *Lok Sabha,* consists of not more than 500 members chosen by direct election from territorial constituencies of roughly equal population. The life of the House of the People, unless dissolved sooner, is five years.

The Constitution includes the constitutions of the states. The president appoints a governor for each state. The governor exercises the executive powers of the state through a council of ministers headed by a chief minister. The state council is collectively responsible to the state legislative assembly. Both unicameral and bicameral legislatures exist. Unicameral legislatures and the lower houses of bicameral legislatures are known as legislative assemblies. They are composed of between sixty and 500 members directly elected from territorial constitutencies of roughly equal populations. Upper houses are known as legislative councils and their size is limited to one third that of the legislative assemby. Special electorates composed of local government office holders, university graduates, school teachers, and members of the legislative assembly choose various portions of the legislative councils with the governor nominating the remainders. Real power resides in the legislative assembly which has a five year life, unless it is dissolved sooner.

Areas in which each legislature may act are enumerated in three lists: the union list specified the Parliament's exclusive domain, the state list specifies the state's exclusive domain, and the concurrent list enumerates areas in which either Parliament or the state legislatures may act. The Constitution gives the residuary powers to Parliament. It further strengthens the hand of the Union government in federal relationships by making provision for a proclamation of emergency under which the power to make laws for any part of India is conferred on Parliament. In spite of these advantages in power that the Constitution gives to the Union government, the federal aspect of the Indian political system is very real. In practice the Union government must depend on the essentially voluntary implementation of many of its programs by the states. This process involves considerable bargaining between the Union and the states in which the states hold a powerful position.

The Constitution establishes a judiciary that is much like that found in the 1935 Act. On the union level there is a Supreme Court consisting of a Chief Justice and several other judges. Its primary function is to handle cases arising from the federal nature of the Constitution, but it also has appellate jurisdiction in cases on appeal from state high courts. Below the state high courts are various subordinate civil and criminal courts of the constituent territorial units. District judges preside in these courts.

The civil service structure is complex because it combines elements of the old unitary civil service under the British and of the new federal setup. In brief, there are all-India services whose members can hold posts in either the union bureaucracy or the state bureaucracies. In addition each state has its own services whose members work only in the state bureaucracy. Public service commissions function on both levels to insure unbiased recruitment, testing, and discipline of civil servants.

The Constitution recognizes that certain groups in Indian society need special protection. These groups are the untouchables and certain tribals, officially known respectively as the Scheduled Castes and Scheduled Tribes. The Constitution reserves a number of seats in the House of the People and in the state legislative assemblies for members of these groups.

As we have seen, there has been a steady growth of the franchise throughout Indian constitutional development. But the change from the franchise of thirty million under the 1935 Act to the universal adult suffrage of the Constitution is in the nature of a quantum jump. This is perhaps the most important change introduced by the Constitution. It cannot be considered as a mere matter of numbers because of the profound impact on the nature of Indian politics that it has had. Other related and important electoral changes are the end of separate electorates and weightage. One man, one vote is the rule and the dynamics of mass democratic politics are beginning to have an impact.

Since the Constitution was enacted in 1950 there have been several territorial realignments among the states, but no radicial changes have been made in the Constitution. The most important structural change has been the development of *panchayati raj* institutions on the local level. The impetus for this development issued from the failure of the community development programs to increase agricultural production and to eliminate the stagnation of the rural areas. In 1957, a study team looked into this problem and concluded that the peasants lacked a feeling of participation in these programs. To be effective the programs had to arise from the people themselves. The team devised a three-tiered structure of elected councils at the district, development block and village levels in order to obtain popular participation and support. This scheme hit a very responsive chord in Indian political life and within a short time most of the states enacted *panchayati raj* (rule of the councils) legislation along the lines suggested by the report. The councils were empowered to impose certain taxes and they received grants to dispense for development purposes. The effect of *panchayati raj* upon agricultural development has been mixed and difficult to evaluate. But its effect on politics has been great. It created new arenas of political activity. Political parties have used the institutions to forge links with village political leaders. *Panchayati raj* has enabled large numbers to go beyond the passive act of voting and to participate actively in the Indian political system.

This account of the institutional framework does not present a total picture of political life in independent India. Despite the stated roles of the institutions, political realities and the arenas of power have been influenced by personalities, events, and movements. The legacy of British administrative rule, the tendency to look to Britain as the model for all political ideas and processes, and the power of the Congress party elite who had led the nationalist movement were important factors in the early post-independence period. The Westernized, eloquent Jawaharlal Nehru, Prime Minister from the inception of constiturional government until his death in 1964, epitomized this early style. Mass participation, local power bases, and more Indian ways of operation characterize the new style which has gained ground rapidly since Nehru's death. Perhaps for the first time in India's long political history, the Indian masses are becoming a viable political force. The challenge to the Indian political system is whether it can meet the demands of these newly politicized groups.

NOTES

1. India is an agricultural society. Land and its produce traditionally have been the bases of political power. The villages, the smallest economic units, serve as the building blocks for all political organization. While the village units have been self-sufficient (or nearly so) economically, the political order has been of wider dimensions. Revenue obtained from the land supported the political super-structure. The question of who 'owned' the land – the peasant, the village headman, or the king – is a thorny one. In fact, it is best to disregard the Western concept of ownership as there was no clear cut land ownership. Rather all elements of society have had the right to a traditional share of the produce of the land. Produce was divided among the cultivator, the service castes, the landlords, and the ruling power. The centrality of land and its produce meant that most of the disputes in the political and legal systems concerned who had the rights to what share.
2. Even in Akbar's time, the *mansabdari* system was not established throughout the empire. For example, the Rajput kings maintained a degree of autonomy which resembled the older system.
3. The Liberal Secretary of State for India, John Morley, and Governor General Lord Minto broadened the representative character of the government in India. Their changes, commonly known as the Morley-Minto Reforms, were enacted into law as the Indian Councils Act of 1909.
4. In 1909 the Royal Commission Upon Decentralisation reported on the state of local government. The Commission found that the intentions of Ripon's Resolution on Local Self-Government had been subverted by official control. British officials had allowed no significant freedom. The Commission endorsed Ripon's views and set forth more detailed regulations for the structure of local boards in an attempt to put his intentions into action. However, these regulations did not result in significant strides toward independence in local government. Official control remained, stifling initiative.

JYOTIRINDRA DAS GUPTA

10

Practice and Theory of Language Planning: The Indian Policy Process

Although no comprehensive document can be discovered which initially laid down a step-wise progression of the sequences of language planning in India, the language policies which have been pursued by the national political authority in the period since independence reveal upon close examination a rather unified structure. Like most cases of language planning, what one can discover in the Indian case is a connected set of policy measures which, in intent and in effect, have converged to an approximation of a deliberate direction of language resources towards a stated purpose, within a defined time schedule, in a fairly coordinated manner, and guided by a specified public authority. Since the policy area subsumed under language policy differs significantly from the policy area covered by economic planning, we should not expect an exact correspondence between the processes of planning applied to the problems of both areas. For policy studies, however, it is interesting how a shift in policy area may account for the differences in policy processes, particularly public planning processes.[1]

PLANNING AND POLICY PRIORITY

Policy areas may be defined in terms of the classes of problems handled by the policy makers. Problems related to national security, economic development, law and order, distribution of power, participation, and income are normally considered as universally agreed spheres of policy attention and action. Any political authority, not matter how recent in origin, or how different its context of operation, can fall back on comparative experience in such policy areas in different parts of the world, cutting across time, scale, and ideology. On the other hand, problems relating to ethnic conciliation, language development, or cultural transformation are neither regarded as normal preserves of policy action nor can they readily draw on recipes from historical or lateral precedents.

For a developing country like India, one acute burden of language planning is that problems of security, productivity, welfare, and integration impinge on the national policy makers all at the same point in time. In other words, language planning has to be considered in the context of the competing claims of the other policy areas within the general framework of over-all political planning.[2] The nature of the competing policy areas may be appreciated better if one turns to the set of problems which the new republic of India inherited at the outset.

The inherited set of problems, as perceived by the political authorities in India, may be classified as those relating to the survival of the polity, socialized development of the economy, political integration of the national community, and impressing a stamp of authenticity on national life and behavior. Given this fourfold aspiration, it is conceivable that the ranking of the national language question never acquired priority over the first two categories because by common consensus it apparently belonged to the third and the fourth categories. This priority ordering was apparent not merely in the stated declarations of the ruling authorities, it was also reflected in the public behavior of the political parties and interest groups with, of course, the solitary exception of the language associations and a variety of ad hoc language demand groups in different parts of India.

PROBLEMS OF LANGUAGE POLICY PLANNING IN INDIA

The national government assuming power in 1947 inherited the nationalist movement's language objectives which were to define the language policy area. Those objectives were translated into formal constitutional provisions in the Constitution enacted in 1950. It should be noted that the Indian Constitution defines the political structure at the federal as well as the state level.[3] The federal structure outlined in the Constitution limits the authority of the national parliament and invests the states with a significant degree of autonomy. The exact extent of authority of the national legislature is determined by the balance of political bargaining between the two sets of legislative authorities.

Any consideration of language policy in India has to take into account this duality of authority and the limited scope of the national legislature in defining and pursuing a national language policy. The scope of authority of the national legislature is also circumscribed by other factors. The Supreme Court, as the guardian of the Constitution and in its capacity of arbitrating between the states and the federal government, restricts the freedom of Parliament. The nature of parliamentary government based on the cabinet system offers at least two important constraints: the leading party has to seek a broad coalition of voter support; and the legislative leadership, by virtue of its identification with the executive leadership, has to take into consideration the feasibility of a policy measure before adopting it. Add to this the massive burdens of politics of a large multiethnic, multilingual, plural society struggling with the most pressing poverty situation in the world, and the constraints on language planning in India will be obvious.

The constraints mentioned above affect the ruling authorities' capacity for action as well as the activities of the demand groups concerned with language policy. For our purpose, we will consider language policy as a process in which several events are linked in a sequence (Das Gupta 1973). First, language demands expressed in organized form by voluntary organizations, including associations, parties, and movements, may be considered as the impulses for policy. Secondly, these impulses are processed by the legislatures which treat them in the context of other competing demands emerging from the general political scene. Once an ordered ranking of values has been reached, obviously in terms of the political ordering of the leading group in the legislature, the relative place of the language policy area is established and appropriate legislation is sought.

Whether the legislated policy will have the appropriate executive attention, in terms of implementation in extent and time, is likely to depend on several factors. The degree of specificity in the legislation and the urgency of intent behind it will tend to influence the congruence between legislation and implementation. The other factors to take into account will be the executive capability and the ability of the demand groups to keep the pressure on the administration continuously with an unwavering intensity. At the same time, the capacity of the policy makers to generate continuous feedback from the policy publics and to act accordingly will be important factors determining the success of language policy or of a coordinated set of policies subsumed under the category of language planning.

In the specific case of India, the objectives of the nationalist movement regarding the task of replacement of English by Hindi as the official language of the federation and the use of regional languages as the official languages of the states were coded into constitutional law (Das Gupta 1970: 137). The provisions of the Constitution pertaining to the federal level may be classified into the following categories: nominating the official language of the Union; designating the uses of this language for transaction of business in the national legislature, legislation, and judicial proceedings at the higher level; and the promotion of the official language inot a more developed and widely accepted language of national communication. Functionally, these provisions can be said to include policy issues relating to language selection, transfer,[4] and development.

POLICY ELABORATION AND IMPLEMENTATION

When the makers of the Indian Constitution declared their choice of official language in favor of Hindi and sought to lay down some general rules of timing, scope of use, and patterns of development of Hindi, they cast their legal language in the form of a normative exhortation rather than immediate imperative. The function of the Indian constitutional declaration can be seen as a record of consensus on general language goals, enumeration of public responsibility for achieving these goals, and an implicit incentive to language planning for the coordination of the explicit language tasks under the auspices of the central political authority. Each of these steps needed subsequent elaboration through relevant policy structures so that proper authorities could be created to handle the problems raised by the general declarations – thus specifying general goals into specific objectives. Instrumental sub-goals needed to be defined; offices and roles were to be devised; lines of action were to be laid down; and control systems were to be instituted (Das Gupta 1969: 578–596).

All these functions presuppose the willingness to recognize the existence of a body of information pertaining to the problems of official language policy with special reference to the available language resource and the proper manner of developing this resource. The responsibility of preparing this body of information was assigned to an advisory committee of experts composed of scholars and reformers. The Report of the Official Language Commission of 1956 was considered by Parliament, and, in 1958, a Committee of Parliament examined and revised the policy recommendations of the Commission. On the basis of this review, the Presidential Order of 1960 gave directions for the implementation of the recommendations.

What is interesting from the perspective of the policy process is that despite the fifteen-year deadline there was no noticeable hurry in implementing the constitutional proposals. If the constitutional document gave the impression of urgency, neither the legislative nor the executive authorities seemed to share that sense of urgency. In the order of national policy priorities, there were other pressing issues on the agenda which gained the major share of attention. Also within the legislature, the support for Hindi policy was less extensive than what was expected before independence. Anyway, the level of intensity was lower than expected.

The low salience of the federal official language issue for the national policy makers in the fifties was also, in part, due to the high salience of the politics related to the issue of reorganization of the states within the federation along linguistic lines.[5] Language politics during this decade were confined to specific regions where the basic conflict was intraregional rather than national. Fortunately for the national political authority, the timing of these regional conflicts was staggered throughout the decade and not cumulatively reinforced at one point of time. But these conflicts did demand an important part of the national authority's attention. The share of attention gained by these demands perhaps accounted for the relative loss of policy energy for the promotion and development of Hindi.

POLICY STRUCTURE

By the beginning of the sixties, the linguistic reorganization of states was largely accomplished, and the policy planners at the national level were once again able to cencentrate attention on the Hindi question. The Presidential Order of 1960 served as a formal incentive for the implementation of the official language policy. Under the Indian system of policy-making, an order of the President implies an initiative of the cabinet which combines both executive and legislative leadership in one body. Constitutional directives are implemented by the parliamentary system through the cabinet led by the Prime Minister. The cabinet members are invested with the executive responsibility of managing their administrative departments, and the cabinet as a body is collectively responsible to Parliament. Being in charge of over-all policy planning for the federal government, it is the cabinet that formally decides which sector of policy deserves what measure of priority and allocation of resources. As for the expected mode of operation, it is assumed that, given the limited volume of national resources and alternative demands on them emerging from competing policy sectors, the policy planners normally tend to arrange their scale of priority in such a manner that it satisfies their norm of a 'good enough' solution. Thus the demands of the language sector are treated in the context of other sectors just as within the language sector the state of competition of rival demands tends to influence the relative share of resources commanded by the policy planners. By resources, we mean not merely the physical resources but also the political resources of influence, authority, and institutional capability accessible to the policy planners in a given time and situation.

By 1960, the policy planners realized that only five more years remained out of the fifteen-year deadline for changeover to Hindi as the official language and that nothing much had been done in the fifties in this direction; they resolved to increase the pace of organized public effort for Hindi promotion and development. From the very beginning the Ministry of Education within the national cabinet was assigned the major task of implementing the objectives of language planning for Hindi. However, during the fifties, the Ministry of Education, due to the constraints discussed before and due to the personal lack of warmth for the cause of Hindi on the part of the Minister, mainly relied on allocating grants to voluntary associations working for Hindi. Organizationally, the Ministry of Education itself remained content with the creation of a small unit of its secretariat called the Hindi Section which was subsequently raised to the status of the Hindi Division. The strategy pursued in the fifties was one of routine coordination of the work assigned to non-governmental agencies and the section's own work. Most of this work was directed to preparation of scientific and technical terminology and promotion of Hindi. The Hindi Division occupied a minor position in the Ministry's work, and its funding represented a minor share of the Ministry's budget.

A series of protests emerging from the Hindi voluntary associations, increasing pressure from the pro-Hindi legislators, and the plain fact of inadequate preparation for the change-over made the national planners aware of the need to create proper institutional structures for stepping up the pace of work. In 1960, the Central Hindi Directorate was created under the auspices of the Ministry, and in 1961 the Commission for Scientific and Technical Terminology was added as a separate but related organization. The working budgets of these organizations are much larger than those of their predecessors, and they enjoy a larger degree of independence within the administrative setting of the Ministry of Education.

The Directorate is responsible for the general task of Hindi promotion.[6] It initiates and controls programs for development and propagation in several ways: translation of books; coordination of book programs including dictionaries and encyclopaedias; translation of administrative manuals and documents; coordination of Hindi teaching and examination systems; standardization of keyboards for typewriters and teleprinters; conducting information centers; incentive systems for authors, publishers, journalists, and students; and a variety of other related tasks. The Commission, until it was merged with the Directorate in 1972, was devoted exclusively to the production and control of scientific and technical terminology. Each organization has maintained its own publication program and both have worked in close cooperation with the specifically educationally oriented organizations like the Hindi institutes, university cells, training centers, etc.

Proliferation of organizations and expansion of work in each of the organizations often create a complex problem of coordination, and this over-all responsibility of coordination and control is vested in the Language Division of the Ministry of Education.[7] However, important sectors of Hindi promotion and development work lie outside the control of this ministry, since they are under the auspices of the Ministries of Home Affairs (Interior), Law and Information, and Broadcasting. Inter-ministry coordination systems have been instituted. Substantial work is done in the Hindi states, and control systems of the central cabinet are not always sufficient to coordinate work at the state level. Periodic consultation and informal coordination seeks to take care of the problems at that level of operation.

POLICY OUTPUT

As the complexity of the language policy structure increases, it becomes difficult to evaluate the extent of productiveness of the policy process. The stepping up of the pace of lexical and literary products in Hindi is easy to discern (Ministry of Education 1969). However, the more important question is what use has been made of these products in order to enable Hindi to become the actual official language of the Union. Measured by the number of Hindi words, books, dictionaries, encyclopaedias, lectures, and exhortations, the progressive development of Hindi under the official auspices has been impressive. Since the sixties, increasing public expenditure in the field of Hindi production has satisfied a large clientele who apparently derived financial and intellectual gains as a result of this policy. Language associations concerned with Hindi and the Hindi-speaking intelligentsia were loaded with subsidies. Leaders of these groups were increasingly coopted into the production planning processes with high remunerations in financial and public status terms (Das Gupta 1970: 168–169).

Paradoxically, none of these impressive gains in Hindi production and development could be said to be directly related to the question of bringing Hindi closer to the unrivaled role of the official language of the Union. In fact, the stepping up of the pace of Hindi production and its promotion created strong resentment from the non-Hindi political groups, who demanded a legal guarantee that the fifteen-year deadline would not be followed. Their demand that the use of English should be continued as one of the languages for official transactions was granted by the passage of the Official Languages Act of 1963 and further reinforced by the Official Languages (Amendment) Act of 1967.[8] By permitting the use of English indefinitely along with Hindi, the national legislature demonstrated that in spite of considerable product-gains, Hindi is not any closer to being accepted as the only official language of the Union than it was before.

Though these legislative decisions have frustrated the Hindi hard liners' attempt to remove English from official use and have evoked some strong rhetoric against the ruling group in the legislature, no large-scale opposition to these decisions has materialized. Some attempts were made to create an opposition when these laws were enacted, but the general tactics of spirited mobilization failed. If it was difficult to mobilize support for the Hindi hard line at the beginning of 1968 when the 1967 Act was published, it became still harder to generate support during the early seventies when the ruling group in the national legislature seemed to be more confident than ever of its own strength and multilingual support base.

However, the Acts of 1963 and 1967, when read with the Government Resolution adopted by both houses of parliament, clearly indicate that the content of official language policy accepted by the national government can be divided in several parts. The question of coexistence of Hindi and English, though debated more often in public and often generating considerable political heat, constitutes only one part. The second part concerns the progressive use of Hindi for various official purposes of the Union. The third part consists of the promotion and development of Hindi and is therefore closely related to the second part. The fourth part is related to the question of ensuring justice among the various language groups as a result of language change in official transactions and administrative business.

As we have seen above, the first part of the policy question has been resolved in favor of a two-language formula in order to reconcile the contending claims regarding the relative facility and authority of diverse language communities of the nation. At the same time, accelerated efforts have been made in the late sixties to implement the second and the third parts of the policy question. Politically, this acceleration was made possible because, as a result of the recognition of a dual language policy, relatively higher investment in Hindi appeared to evoke less suspicion in the non-Hindi population. Similarly, within the administration, the pro-English officials felt less threatened and assumed that a larger investment of resources for Hindi and its greater use, while benefiting the Hindi speakers, will not necessarily make them or their like worse off.

DIVISION OF DOMAINS

The key phrase used in the official documents concerning Hindi policy is the 'progressive use of Hindi'. Until the early sixties, the non-Hindi public and the political groups interpreted this phrase as signifying the progressive decline of their power, authority, control, share of jobs and resources, and facility of communication in the public sector of the national life. After the legislation and the Resolution of 1967, the cogency of this interpretation has lost some of its ground. Moreover, two decades of political experience have apparently brought home the lesson that the national political authorities' interest in promoting the use of Hindi is, at one level, more symbolic than substantive and at another level, more directed to serving the Hindi clientele than necessarily depriving the non-Hindi clientele.

In Parliament, no one is forced to speak Hindi. Legislation is introduced in English, and in the future it may be introduced in English and Hindi. All acts, resolutions, orders, rules, notifications, official papers laid before the national legislature, and other documents of importance are required to be issued bilingually. At best, this requirement provides employment to a growing profession of translators; at worst, it delays the preparation of documents. It does not, however, cause any serious deprivation to the non-Hindi public. If the Hindi versions are mostly unused even by the Hindi public, these may serve either as training grounds for later generations' use or as museum pieces for future historians of nationalist ego or ethnic rivalry. Also, it is interesting to note that surveys of documents that have been issued in English and in Hindi-English bilingual versions indicate that, while the quantity of the latter have increased in the

Table 10.1 *Language versions of official documents: Government of India, 1968–69*[a]

Documents	First quarter		Second quarter		Third quarter	
	Hindi and English	English only	Hindi and English	English only	Hindi and English	English only
Group A						
Notifications	1,941	454	2,614	351	2,165	213
Official papers laid before national legislature	1,732	667	315	135	673	25
General orders	188	174	440	211	264	183
Group B						
Contracts	–	38	–	47	4	105
Permits	–	59	–	84	–	5
Forms of tender	1	30	–	41	6	82

[a] From: Government of India, Ministry of Home Affairs, *Annual Assessment Report, 1968–69,* p. 22.

field of general papers, orders, and notifications, no such comparable increase has been noticeable in the more technical fields of transaction involving contracts, licenses, and tenders. Where caution and precision are highly valued, chances are rarely taken, and the logic of business presumably gains a premium on the progress of Hindi. A comparison of the items in groups A and B in Table 10.1 provides a good example.

It is this kind of pragmatic discretion in implementing language policy that seems to assure the non-Hindi public that the expansion of the domain of Hindi transaction poses no serious threat. On the other hand, the fact that documents are provided in Hindi may be useful for the Hindi public, especially for that part of it which is growing up with mostly Hindi literacy and education. One useful result of the policy of progressive use of Hindi can be found in the increasing number of letters in Hindi transmitted to the Union

Government that are being replied to in Hindi. These letters include representations from the employees, especially of the lower ranks, of the national government and communications from the Hindi states. It is worth noting in this connection that five large states of the federation have Hindi as their official language and conduct most of their educational activities in Hindi.

Comparable progress in the use of Hindi is yet to be noticed in the sphere of official recording of files and drafting. The administrative instructions of July, 1968, permit the officials to exercise a choice between Hindi and English for noting on files and drafting. The language of this instruction circulated by the Ministry of Home Affairs says that 'there can be no restriction on the use of either Hindi or English' for this purpose, and that the employee 'himself should not be asked to provide translations.' What the instruction does not mention is the simple administrative fact that most senior officers are neither incapable of drafting in Hindi or, even when they can do so, they are unwilling to switch from English to Hindi.[9] Since these officers set the norms for the junior personnel, the latter simply follow the established pattern. This is not merely the case at the federal level of government; the pattern is followed in the same way even in the secretariats of the Hindi states despite the fact that most of the officials and almost all of the clientele groups in these states are Hindi speaking. The federal government has intensified the training program of its staff in Hindi and has provided monetary and other incentives to attract increasing numbers of employees who have no previous knowledge of using Hindi for official transactions. These are normally short courses, and the major incentive for taking these courses would seem to be the expectation that they provide one more qualification for promotion. Even the reports of the ministry in charge of the training program recognize that these courses do not generate enough confidence to enable one to switch from the familiar ways of drafting in one language to another, especially when many of the statutes, codes, manuals, handbooks, and other standard aids to official transactions are either yet to be translated or exist in indifferent translations of doubtful utility. In any event, like all administrative hierarchies, the Indian administration follows the rule of downward percolation of norms; and, as long as the upper-level officials will continue their preference for using

English for office work, lower-level training is unlikely to alter the familiar and rewarding routine. Moreover, the choice offered by the 1967 Act and Resolution, together with the 1968 instruction, have seemingly reinforced the routine.

Both in theory and practice, a division of domain between English and Hindi has become a reality of Indian political life at the federal level. Even when the use of Hindi has grown over two decades, it has carved its own domain of expansion useful to a large Hindi clientele. The increasing stock of Hindi translations, lexical products, codifying works, standardization efforts, mechanical equipment such as Hindi typewriters and teleprinters, Nagari script reforms, and the creation of a large group of language personnel, made possible by a substantial investment of funds channeled mainly through the Ministries of Education, Home Affairs, Information and Broadcasting, and Law have considerably contributed to this growth. Curiously, these investments have not generated any significant opposition from the non-Hindi political groups. In the fiscal year 1970–71, the Ministry of Education alone spent more than 23 million rupees for language development, almost all of which was invested in Hindi promotion and development.

One reason why such increasing investment was not significantly challenged when the status of Hindi evoked so much resentment could possibly be that the increasing emphasis on a dual language policy effectively reduced the perception of the threat of Hindi dominance. Gains for Hindi were no longer counted as losses for the non-Hindi regions. This point of view weighs heavily in the consideration of our four part policy question relating to inter-community sense of justice.

Secondly, the late sixties also witnessed for the first time a national investment plan for the promotion of the regional languages of all the states of India. The basic objective of this plan was the production of university-level books in order to facilitate changeover from English to Indian language media of higher education.[10] This plan of awarding 10 million rupees to be spread over a period of six years to each of the states (except Nagaland, Jammu and Kashmir, and the Union Territories) appeared to convince the states that the central resources were intended to develop all the major Indian languages and not simply Hindi. The grants awarded to the states,

Table 10.2 *Central grants for developing regional languages, 1968–71*[a] [in hundred thousand rupees]

States	Grants 1968–69	1969–70	Allocation 1970–71
Hindi States			
Bihar	5.00	2.00	5.00
Harayana	2.00	–	5.00
Madhya Pradesh	–	7.00	5.00
Rajasthan	5.00	4.00	5.00
Uttar Pradesh	2.00	3.00	5.00
Non-Hindi States			
Andra Pradesh	10.00	9.00	15.00
Assam	1.00	4.00	5.00
Gujarat	–	–	5.00
Mysore	5.00	7.00	5.00
Maharashtra	1.00	–	5.00
Orissa	–	4.00	5.00
Punjab	–	1.50	5.00
Kerala	0.43	7.00	5.00
Tamilnadu	2.72	9.34	5.00
W. Bengal	0.33	2.00	5.00

[a]From: Government of India, Ministry of Education, *University Level Books in Indian Languages,* 1971, p. 2.

including the Hindi states, are listed in Table 10.2. In fact, the state governments had never expected so much money to spend on their language development. Some of them hurriedly planned to spend the annual grants, while others were at a loss trying to determine how to allocate it rationally.

The image of the national political authority remained consistent with the states' expectation that the financially worse-off regional languages should have federal support, and that in distributing resources no single language community should enjoy a monopoly of status, resource, and glory. It was this minimal notion of intercommunity justice that the new national leadership of the late sixties had publicly endorsed and continued to convince the states through the early seventies that it is interested in pursuing it. The actual inter-state allocation may not have satisfied the states equally, but they have not disputed the principle governing this allocation in the context of the nation as a whole.[11] This principle of distribution, together with the principle of division of language domain at the federal level, appears to have contributed to a reduction of salience of language conflict at the national arena; nevertheless partial conflicts between two states or one state and the federal government or two language communities within one state have not disappeared.

LANGUAGE PLANNING: PRACTICE AND THEORY

Language planning in India operates at many levels. We have concentrated on a level that is most visible, nationally relevant, affects maximal sectors of political life, and evokes national attention. At this level, planning connects a series of policy episodes consisting of language selection for federal official use, promotion and development of the selected language, division of domain in national use, allocation of relative status among contending languages, impressing a sense of reasonable justice among language communites, and ensuring the congruence of these measures with the other social, economic, and political policy objectives of the national political community. Federal language planning, however, does not include several other dimensions of language planning that are carried on at the level of state politics or local politics. Similarly, language planning excludes those important areas of language growth and change which occur as a result of efforts and endeavors generated outside of the public realm.

In a developing country such as India more attention is focused on the federal government because of the obvious greater command of resources, political and economic, which enables it to coordinate scarce national resources for common objectives. Federal coordinate planning carried on under the framework of parliamentary democracy is obviously different in scope, method, content, and rules of efficiency estimation from the kind of superordinate planning that is unitary, monolithic, dictatorial, technocratic, and total.[12] Language planning in India shares the general style of coordinate planning pursued in other policy areas but differs from the latter in several respects. To begin with an account of advantage,[13] language planning demands only a small part of the national resource compared to the needs of general economic planning. Secondly, because of relatively less factor constraints, the major barriers to language planning are political rahter than economic. This is not to suggest that political constraints are more malleable than the economic ones but rather to indicate that the kinds of prudence and strategies needed for language planning are significantly different from the ones required for economic planning. Thirdly, the social cost of delay in language planning is relatively easier to compensate or tolerate than is likely to be the case in economic planning in a poor country.

As we have noted in this analysis of Indian language planning, the ideal pattern and time table set up by the nationalist movement for displacing English has been significantly modified without much difficulty. Priority ordering in nationalist rhetoric is determined by aspiration rather than a hard balancing of scarce resources to be allocated to contending claimants. Language planning as an act of public policy cannot afford to follow merely ideological priority rules independent of the rules of investment and power allocation determined by economic and political priorities. Public needs and claims have been stated in terms different from the pre-independence patterns. Language planning in India has recognized the changing course of language demands emerging from the public policies in the post-independence decades.

In this sense Indian language planning has not followed a theory of planning where the goals are assumed to be given and the planner's job is merely instrumental. The process followed in this case has been to recognize the national goals in the context of the initial conditional constraints of the early years of independence, modify these goals in accordance with the contemporary flow of intimations from the national community, and then to work out serial steps of compromise in order to conciliate the contending demand groups, and thus to proceed to coordinate policy measures in a relatively coherent sequence. If this does not measure up to the theory of synoptic planning, it seems to approximate a theory of planning[14] more consistent with the demands of a democratic polity based on a plural society. This theory regards planning as an organizational device to process diverse demands in a framework of reconciling conflicting groups and interests in a manner that allows the attainment of a feasible and coherent sequence of objectives in a reasonable order of time.

NOTES

1. A useful survey of problems of policy analysis is contained in Rose (1973: 67–94).
2. For an elaboration of problems of language planning, see Jernudd and Das Gupta (1971). A useful discussion of policy problems in developmental planning is contained in Higgins et al. (1971: 319–378)
3. For an analysis of Indian federalism in relation to language problems, see Roy (1962).
4. The notion of transfer includes the question of promoting the using of one language from one use to another, implying an elevation or decline of relative language status and increase or decrease of functions.
5. For a configuration of issues impinging on the authorities when the politics of states' reorganization engaged their attention, see Kothari (1970: 322).
6. The outline of organizational functions is derived from various surveys we conducted in 1970–71 as a part of the International Language Planning Survey. A fuller report is in preparation.
7. Inter-ministry coordination, however, is the responsibility of the Home Ministry and the Cabinet.
8. Article 343 of the Constitution authorizes Parliament to provide by law for the use of English language after the fifteen-year deadline (beyond 1965) for such purposes as may be specified in the law. The Act of 1963 provides that English may continue to be used, in addition to Hindi, even after January, 1965, for all federal purposes and for the transaction of business in Parliament. The amendment Act of 1967 provides for the use of English for communication between the federal and the state governments and non-Hindi states until the latter opt for corresponding in Hindi.
9. These and the subsequent materials in this paragraph are derived from our project interviews and from departmental surveys in 1970–71 and part of 1972.
10. The new trend of federal concern for the development of regional languages was associated with a general concern for the educational function of these laguages in the states. The Report of the Education Commission of 1964–66, followed by the National Policy of Education in 1968, reiterated this emphasis.
11. Clause 4 of the Government of India Resolution of January 18, 1968, states the necessity of ensuring that 'the just claims and interests of people

belonging to different parts of the country in regard to the public services of the Union are fully safeguarded'.

12. For an elaboration of the contrasting theories of planning, see Mannheim (1951).
13. The relative advantages are specifically mentioned here because in most writings on planning it is generally assumed that economic planning is easier to deal with because of the easy measurability of the economic phenomena. This assumption is more uncritically asserted by the non-economists than the economists. See Fishman (1973: 22).
14. Contemporary planning analysis is gradually coming to recognize the value of 'softer' theories of planning. A useful discussion of this type of planning is Kornai (1970: 1–19). Another instructive discussion is Kaplan (1973: 41–61). For discussions and citations on the links between general planning literature and problems of language planning, see Jernudd and Das Gupta (1971).

MAHADEV L. APTE

Language Controversies in the Indian Parliament (Lok Sabha): 1952–1960

In the history of modern India, especially since the beginning of the twentieth century, linguistic issues have figured prominently in the socio-cultural, economic, and political domains. The Congress party, even while fighting for independence from the British, was obliged to pay attention to the linguistic questions, and to arrive at a solution. The party recognized the strong feelings of linguistic identity and endorsed the principle of establishing administrative units on linguistic grounds (Harrison 1960: 276ff.; Morris-Jones 1957: 20–21).

After independence the linguistic issues became even more dominant and the Congress government constantly faced problems arising out of linguistic controversies. These reached a climax in 1956 and were solved to a considerable degree with the reorganization of Indian provinces on linguistic criteria although some issues continued to be debated.

The purpose of this paper is to examine one facet of this complex phenomenon, namely the role of the Indian Parliament in the linguistic controversies. The major focus is on the first eight years during which the country constantly faced one linguistic problem after another. The aim is to show in broad outlines how the debates in the Indian Parliament reflect this constant preoccupation of the country with linguistic issues. In addition, such other aspects of the debates as the techniques used by Members of Parliament (hereafter MPs) to draw attention to the pressing linguistic issues, the very linguistic nature of the debates themselves, and the symbolic behavior of the MPs are also discussed. Thus the goal is to demonstrate the nature and degree of relationship between the peak periods of linguistic controversies in the country and the moods and the workings of Parliament on such occasions.

The reports of the parliamentary debates for the years 1952–1960 constitute the primary source for this investigation. These are the Hansard verbatim reports of the daily transactions during all sessions of the Indian Parliament.

The debates in the Indian Parliament have often reflected the multilingual nature of India in a variety of ways. During the first eight years the primary concern of many MPs, especially those who represented non-Hindi constituencies, was to make sure that the demands of their people for the creation of linguistic states were fulfilled. The other major issue which drew the attention of almost all MPs was that of Hindi, which was designated by the Indian constitution as the future 'official language'.

The first linguistic state created by the Congress government, as early as 1953, was that of Andhra Pradesh. Subsequently, the government appointed the States Reorganization Commission in December, 1953, and after receiving the recommendations of that Commission in 1955, the creation of other states, primarily on linguistic bases, took place in 1956.

The debates until 1956 clearly indicate that MPs frequently commented on these two major issues. However, after 1956 when the majority of linguistic states had been created, only those MPs who represented the constituencies which were dissatisfied with their fate, especially the Marathi- and Gujarati-speaking constituencies in the bilingual Bombay state,[1] continued to debate the reorganization issue. While MPs from other parts of India occasionally participated in such discussions it seems that the majority of them were satisfied with the outcome of the linguistic reorganization of the country. After 1960, however, even the MPs of the Marathi and Gujarati constituencies stopped complaining because by then separate states for these two linguistic groups had been created. Thus in the sixties, focus was on the issue of 'official language'. Although other issues were discussed, it is realistic to say that the first half of the sixties was mainly devoted to solving the problem of the official language.

During the first eight years the MPs from the Hindi regions were primarily concerned with the constitutional goal of implementing Hindi as the sole official language of the country by 1965. They had no basic interest in the creation of linguistic states because it was obvious that all of North India where Hindi and its various dialects were spoken would not be formed into a single state and that the preindependence division of this region into four provinces – Bihar, Madhya Pradesh, Rajasthan, and Uttar Pradesh – would be maintained with some boundary adjustments. They kept the government busy with inquiries about the progress of Hindi. On the other hand, MPs from certain minority groups, especially the Anglo-Indians, and from some South Indian provinces were apprehensive about the constitutional provision regarding the official language. They therefore kept urging the Hindi protagonists to be patient, and to postpone the implementation of the constitutional goal.

To summarize then, the following major trends were dominant in the fifties: (1) linguistic autonomy to the major linguistic regions within the limitations of the Constitution; (2) achievement of maximum territory for each linguistic state, hence the great concern over the boundaries of the proposed states in the early fifties; and (3) development of Hindi in various domains so that it could replace English. This, of course, does not mean that MPs were not concerned with other linguistic issues. For example, recognition of regional languages as having equal status with Hindi and equal treatment by the central government to all languages in terms of financial support for their development was the concern of many MPs. Those MPs who represented various minority linguistic groups without a regional basis continued to raise questions about their linguistic status,[2] the protection of their linguistic rights in the context of newly emerging linguistic states, and the government's interest in developing minority languages. The last was particularly the concern of MPs representing tribal areas.

FREQUENCY AND SUBSTANTIVE NATURE OF LINGUISTIC DEBATES IN THE PARLIAMENT

The considerable time devoted to discussing linguistic issues during the Parliament's early years is not surprising in view of the fact that these issues were on the forefront. The most difficult and controversial task of reorganizing the country on linguistic criteria was accomplished during this period.

During the very first session of the Parliament in 1952, Mr. Tushar Chatterjee, a Communist MP from West Bengal, submitted the following resolution to the house.

'This House is of the opinion that immediate steps should be taken to redistribute the states on a linguistic basis and that the boundaries of the existing states be readjusted accordingly (Government of India, Parliamentary Debates; July 7, 1952).'

The Congress government was not yet prepared to undertake this difficult task, and the party leaders were having second thoughts about the reorganization of the states, especially after the report of the Dar Commission[3] which recommended the postponement of the creation of linguistic states (Gopal 1966: 73; Harrison 1960: 281). Therefore, the Congress party had no desire to support the motion. Although the resolution for reorganization was defeated by a vote of 261 to 77, the debate on the resolution was clearly a harbinger of things to come. As many as twenty-two amendments to the orginal motion were submitted and more than fifty MPs spoke on it during the debate which lasted for two days. Many MPs supported the motion and some claimed areas from other provinces for their own future linguistic states. Questions were raised about which linguistic states would include the cities of Madras and Bombay. The Telugu and Tamil MPs claimed Madras while Marathi and Gujarati MPs claimed Bombay. MPs accused each other of either falsifying information or misrepresenting it. Terms such as 'linguism' and 'linguomaniacs' were frequently used by the Congress MPs to label those who took the pro-linguistic states position. Thus, the debate clearly demonstrated the strong feelings of the MPs on the question of linguistic states. And although the Congress party was not in favor of the motion, Prime Minister Nehru made a long speech in which he assured the Parliament that necessary action for the reorganization of states would be taken at the appropriate time. Interestingly enough, in January, 1953, the annual Congress party session, 'passed a resolution on linguistic states that was a hocus-pocus reaffirming the linguistic commitment but evading definite pledges beyond the formation of a separate Andhra. Nehru spoke ominously of further linguistic reorganization as opening a "Pandora's Box" . . . (Harrison 1960: 285).'

In August, 1953, a bill for the creation of the first linguistic state of Andhra Pradesh was introduced in the Parliament. The bill was introduced because the hands of the Congress government were forced by the events towards the end of 1952; the death of Potti Shri Ramulu during his fast for the creation of a Telugu-speaking state, and the subsequent riots which took place in the Andhra Pradesh region. The debate on the Andhra Pradesh bill lasted for eleven days. Among those who participated, a substantial number of MPs represented Andhra Pradesh and other southern regions as these were the areas primarily affected by the bill.

The trends exhibited earlier during the debate of the previous year became even more apparent. There were frequent accusations and counter-accsations by MPs against each other and against the government on factual matters involving the creation of the new state. The representatives of the Telugu speakers were somewhat dissatisfied because the new state included only eight Telugu-speaking districts and not the remaining four which at that time were part of the princely state of Hyderabad. Among the MPs from the Telugu region, there were further disagreements on which city should be the capital of the new state. The district of Bellary was the bone of bitter contention between the Telugu and Kannada MPs as both claimed that it belonged to them.

It is interesting to note the types of arguments presented by the MPs for claiming various linguistically complex border areas for their respective future linguistic states. Many used historical evidence and in this were challenged by others. The issues even came down to such specifics as which kings belonged to which linguistic region. One MP, for example, claimed that a famous king by the name of Krishna Deva Raya was a Telugu king and the statement was immediately challenged by the Tamil and Kannada MPs, each group claiming the king to be from their linguistic region!

Plebiscite was often suggested as the solution for including disputed border territories into one or another state. This claim was equally vehemently denied by others on the ground that if all such problems were to be solved by plebiscite the country would be in chaos.

The tenor of the debate clearly reflected the thinking of the MPs. They felt that the creation of linguistic states was imminent now that the first such state was coming into existence. They also felt that they should now start claiming in earnest those border territories which they thought rightfully belonged to the linguistic regions they represented, but which might be claimed by the neighboring regions.

There were a few MPs, especially of the opposition parties, who criticized the government for their stop-gap solutions. For example, Mr. Gopalan, a Communist MP, blamed the Congress government for not stating the general principle on which the creation of Andhra Pradesh was based. On the other hand, it appears that government leaders were hoping that ad hoc decisions could be taken when and if the need arose, and that the total problem could be postponed for some more time. This, of course, did not work. Towards the end of 1953, Prime Minister Nehru announced that a commission had been appointed to look into the question of the reorganization of states and to make a report to Parliament no later than June 30, 1955.

A few MPs representing minority groups which had nothing to gain and everything to lose by the creation of linguistic states opposed the creation of Andhra Pradesh, not only in self-interest, but also because of a genuine apprehension that once the redistribution of the existing provinces began, there would be no way of anticipating where and how the process would end. Their feeling was that the fissiparous tendencies would ultimately destroy the unity of the country. One MP who forcefully expressed these views was Mr. Frank Anthony who represented the Anglo-Indian community. The primary concern of his community was to retain English in India.

The States Reorganization Commission submitted its report to the Government in October, 1955. It was based on extensive research of various records, representations received by the Commission, and on a substantial number of interviews it conducted with persons in various walks of life from all parts of India.

The reactions to the report were diverse, but the strongest response occurred in Bombay city which was besieged by riots on linguistic issues in November, 1955, and remained under constant tension during the next six months. The primary reason for the riots was the recommendation of the Commission that Bombay should not be included into the Marathi-speaking state of Maharasthtra. Another reason was that the Commission had rejected a single state for the Marathi-speaking population and instead suggested two separate states.

In December, 1955, the entire report of the Commission was placed before Parliament so that suggestions and views of the MPs could be taken into consideration for the final framing of the bill. Over two hundred MPs participated in the debate which lasted for seven days.

Once the debate began, the division among the MPs was obvious. Those who were satisfied with the principal recommendations of the Commission tried to justify the report while those who were not tried to show how wrong the Commission was in arriving at certain conclusions and recommendations. All kinds of facts and documents, such as census data, judgments of High Courts, and reports of the previous commissions, were used both to support and to refute the recommendations of the Commission. There were constant references to history, culture, and the wishes of the people to justify claims and counter-claims.

It appears that most of the debate was primarily justifications for demands for either accepting or changing the recommendations of the Commission. Occasionally, some comments reflected the thinking of the individual MPs on broader linguistic issues. For example, some South Indian MPs regretted the fact that the Commission had not given enough thought to the balance between the Northern and Southern zones and had not considered dividing the country along those lines. The statuses of various mother tongues became a major issue. For example, Punjabi was labeled a dialect which the supporters of a Punjabi state vehemently refuted. On the other hand, Konkani, which was traditionally considered a dialect of Marathi, was declared to be a language.

This particular debate was often emotional and argumentative. The following two excerpts from the debate give us a glimpse of these moods. The first is about the border areas (Government of India, Parliamentary Debates: December 20, 1955).

Shri Jaipal Singh: . . . We won 11 seats on this specific issue. And here is my hon. friend from Dhenkanal and West Guttuck, and here are a few other members, who had the impertinence to tell us that the people want to go to another State.

Shri Sarangdhar Das (Dhenkanal-West Cuttack): It is impertinence on your part.

Shri Jaipal Singh: All right, it is an impertinent claim.

Shri B. Das (Jaipur-Keonjhar): Why should my hon. friend Shri Jaipal Singh say 'impertinent'?

An. Hon. Member: It is unparliamentary.

Shri Jaipal Singh: May I just point out that it is not a pertinent claim? I think I know the English language as much as my hon. colleague knows [interruptions] . . . .

The second excerpt is about the coexistence of various linguistic groups (Government of India, Parliamentary Debates: December 20, 1955).

Shri Frank Anthony: . . . If we accept the theory that the Mahrattas cannot live with the Gujaratis, and that the Gujaratis cannot live with the Mahrattas, if we accept the principle that a language spoken by millions and millions of people cannot burgeon or flourish, and that it cannot reach its full stature. . . .

Shri Joachim Alva: Are not the Anglo-Indians fleeing this land because they want to go back to the land where only the English language is spoken?

Shri Frank Anthony: My hon. friend has in his rather typical way tried to bring in something which is utterly irrelevant.

Shri Joachim Alva: It is very simple and relevant.

Mr. Chairman: If it is irrelevant, the hon. member need not reply to it.

Shri Frank Anthony: I shall defer to your very good advice. . . .

There were in this debate a few voices of restraint and of opposition to the whole process of linguistic reorganization of the states but they were drowned in the enthusiastic support for the basic principle, and in the vehement arguments for changing the recommendations of the Commission so as to satisfy those who were disgruntled. The most controversial recommendations in this debate were: (1) the future of Bombay city; (2) settlement of certain border areas; (3) creation of two states each for the Marathi-speaking and the Telugu-speaking peoples; and (4) separation of the Punjabi- from the Hindi-speaking populations.

Two more extensive debates took place on this issue. The first was in April, 1956, when the Home Minister Mr. G. B. Pant submitted a motion to the House to send the report and the bill to a select committee for final consideration in view of the various opinions expressed in the Parliament, in various state legislatures, and also in the country at large. The debate on this motion lasted for three days. The select committee was to submit its recommendations by the middle of May, 1956.

The last debate took place in July, 1956, when the final bill was submitted by the Home Minister to Parliament. The debate this time lasted for thirteen days. About one hundred MPs participated in it. The most significant event in this debate was the recommendation of 180 MPs for changing the provisions of the bill regarding Bombay city.

During the next three years, the question of the bilingual Bombay state was raised several times in various debates, especially by many independent MPs who were elected on that very issue in 1957. The bilingual Bombay state was debated in the Parliament until 1960 when two separate linguistic states were carved out of it, and the linguistic reorganization problem was put to rest except for isolated issues such as the separation of Punjab into the states of Punjab and Harayana Prant in the late sixties.

TECHNIQUES FOR DRAWING ATTENTION TO LINGUISTIC ISSUES IN THE PARLIAMENT

Although parliamentary democracy is only twenty-odd years old in India, the rules, regulations, and conventions for the conduct of business in Parliament were well established by the time it opened in 1952. The principles of debate were primarily modeled after those of the House of Commons in England (Morris-Jones 1957: 201 n.). Many elected MPs were experienced politicians who had been members of the Central Legislative Assembly during the thirties and forties. Thus most MPs were aware of the limits within which they could draw attention to specific linguistic issues. Many therefore used the techniques described below for this goal.[4]

Questions. The most popular technique to draw attention to linguistic matters was to submit questions to be answered during the Question Hour. An MP submitting a Starred Question – a question which could be answered orally during the session – was allowed to ask supplementary questions. MPs regularly took advantage of this procedure and elicited from the Government factual information regarding various linguistic issues. Questions were also 'asked to evoke statements of policies' (Morris-Jones 1957: 317). For example, during the fifties, those who were staunch supporters of the Hindi movement asked questions forcing the government to present factual information about the progress made for the development and propogation of Hindi. Often, MPs would ask the same question at regular intervals to judge the progress of Hindi in regard to such activities as: the creation of a technical vocabulary; translations of various central acts and criminal and civil procedure codes; the appointment of a special commission for its propogation; the preparation of an encyclopedia; use of Hindi in courts, postal forms, and at railway stations; and proficiency in Hindi as a requirement for personnel in foreign service. Often, MPs who asked these questions accused the government of not going fast enough for achieving the goal of replacing English by Hindi as set forth in the Constitution. On the other hand, MPs from South India argued that the government was going too fast. Such polar views frequently resulted in heated arguments between the pro- and anti-Hindi segments in Parliament.

The question hour was utilized not only by the Hindi partisans but also by others who had to guard the linguistic interests of their own constituencies. There were frequent questions about the developments of tribal languages, government subsidies given not only to Hindi, but also to other regional languages, etc. For example, an MP from Gujarat raised the question twice in 1956 about the unfair treatment given to Gujarati becasue it was not one of the languages selected by the government for study at central universities. Exclusion of languages in similar situations was interpreted as an indication of backwardness or underdevelopment and such decisions were vigorously challenged. Thus, the MP from Gujarat wanted to know if the government would include 'the study of Gujarati which is equally advanced' (Government of India, Parliamentary Debates: August 3, 1956). An MP from Kerala raised similar questions when he found that Malayalam was not included in overseas broadcasting or for study at central universities. In 1957, when a question was asked by an MP from the Hindi region about government money spent on the English-Hindi dictionary and plans to print it, several MPs from

South India raised the question of the government preparing similar dictionaries for other regional languages (Government of India, Parliamentary Debates: May 16, 1957).

Adjournment motions. A technique that was occasionally used by MPs to bring linguistic issues to the forefront was to give notice of an adjournment motion. However, this was done only when there were major events such as riots, agitations, police-firings, or protests concerning linguistic controversies. Such adjournment motions were rarely allowed by the Speaker, but they served the purpose of demonstrating that the MPs in whose regions such events occurred, or others who were concerned, were doing something about them. For example, in August, 1952, a motion for adjournment was brought before the house by a member because of anti-Hindi riots in Madras. The motion was disallowed by the Speaker. In December, 1952, adjournment motions were submitted twice: once when the condition of Potti Shri Ramulu who was fasting for the creation of a Telugu-speaking state became critical, and the second time immediately after his death. In both cases, the motions were submitted by several MPs from the Telugu region. In the first instance Prime Minister Nehru made a statement saying that the Parliament could not be forced to decide major issues by such methods. The Speaker thereafter disallowed both the motion and the related questions. As a result, several MPs including those from the Telugu-speaking region walked out of Parliament in protest of what they called the 'callous attitude' of the government. Similar adjournment motions were brought before the house on several other occasions, notable among which were the linguistic riots in Bombay and Ahmedabad in 1956. Although such adjournment motions were not allowed they served the function of symbolic protests by the MPs. Short Notice Questions and the technique of Calling Attention to Matters of Urgent Public Importance were used similarly to draw attention to linguistic controversies and events arising out of them.

Debates on President's Address. The President's Address on the opening day of every session provided another opportunity for raising important linguistic issues. The President of India delivered an address to the joint session of both the upper and the lower houses of Parliament at the beginning of every session. This address represented the official government position on national and international events, outlined future plans, reviewed events of previous years and the progress made in various domains. A motion was then made to express thanks to the President for his address, followed by a debate on the government's policies. At most such debates during the fifties many amendments were submitted to express dissatisfaction towards the government's policies and actions regarding linguistic issues. Often, such amendments were submitted by the opposition MPs and many discussed the linguistic problems in their speeches during the debates. Although such amendments were generally defeated, they served the function of injecting language problems into the general debates and enabled the MPs to express their dissatisfaction of the governmental policies in such matters.

Since the President's Address was put before the house both in Hindi and English, comments were often made on these versions. At the opening of the first session of the second parliament in 1957, a Hindi-speaking MP commented on the Hindi version of the President's Address and claimed that it was bad. He implied that the speech was first written in English and was then translated into Hindi. Another MP simply said that it was wrong, while a Communist MP facetiously remarked that the translation was in 'official' Hindi (Government of India, Parliamentary Debates: May 14, 1957). In 1957, the debate on the President's Address lasted for three days and MPs from the bilingual Bombay state added several amendments to the original motion thus expressing their unhappiness both over the creation of the bilingual state and also over the government's decision about border settlements. One MP added an amendment expressing his displeasure about the lack of firm policy with regard to replacing English with Hindi as the official language.

Debates on Demands for Grants. MPs not only had the opportunity to introduce linguistic issues into the debate on the President's Address, but also to do so while debating Demands for Grants for various ministries. The established practice was for the government to place before the Parliament Demands for Grants for a particular ministry. Once this is done MPs submit Cut Motions to the Speaker. These Cut Motions request symbolic cuts of anywhere from one to a hundred rupees for particular demands and state reasons for such cuts. They are all submitted, and a general debate ensues, at the end of which the minister in charge of that particular ministry replies to the various criticisms and comments.

During the fifties, no ministry escaped from the Cut Motions submitted by MPs of the Opposition Parties. Many of them were made on account of language issues, since all ministries were in some way involved with language problems. The number of Cut Motions was generally higher for the Ministries of Education and Scientific Research, Broadcasting and Information, and Home, because of their direct involvement in linguistic matters. However, linguistic problems were not necessarily restricted to them alone. In 1958, the Minister for Broadcasting and Information, while replying to the debate, observed that 'There is a tendency to drag in the present linguistic controversy into anything or any subject that comes up' (Government of India, Parliamentary Debates: April 7, 1958). Although no systematic statistical data on submissions of Cut Motions because of dissatisfaction with the government's language policies have been collected, it is safe to assume that once the major linguistic controversies were solved, fewer Cut Motions on linguistic grounds were introduced.

Comments during speeches by MPs. A popular technique among the MPs was to comment on each other's linguistic competence. Many such comments were not necessarily relevant to what the person was saying. The tendency to comment in this fashion was widespread during the fifties, primarily because the question of the official language was not yet resolved satisfactorily. Also prominent was the question of what kind of Hindi should be used in the debates. MPs therefore commented on the abilities of others to speak 'proper' or 'correct' Hindi or English and offered their views on the linguistic competence of others. For example, in 1956, Mr. Tandon, a staunch supporter of Hindi, expressed the opinion in a speech given in Hindi during the debate on Demands for Grants for the Ministry of Education that it was a shameful thing that many members who spoke in English did not make the effort to learn even 'broken' Hindi. He said that if they spoke Hindi the situation could not be worse than speaking English, because even Englishmen would not understand the kind of English that was spoken in Parliament (Government of India, Parliamentary Debates: April 16, 1956). On the other hand, an MP from South India on another occasion asserted that 'English, though not the mother tongue, is the language in which we are more well versed than our own mother tongues' (Government of India, Parliamentary Debates: August 20, 1957).

LINGUISTIC NATURE OF PARLIAMENTARY DEBATES

As if all other techniques were not sufficient to draw attention to linguistic issues, the daily transactions in Parliament also served as a constant reminder of the linguistic diversity and its political implications.

According to the provisions of the Indian Constitution, only English or Hindi could be used for speeches in Parliament. Only when MPs did not know either language were they permitted by the Speaker to use their mother tongue. In the fifties, there were only about half a dozen occasions when MPs spoke in their mother tongues. In some cases such speeches were simultaneously translated into either English or Hindi by their MP friends. Otherwise most of the time MPs spoke in English. However, many from the Hindi-speaking area made it a regular practice to speak Hindi which created problems. There was a tendency on the part of those from South India to complain that they did not always understand speeches in Hindi. Others raised the question of translations of both English and Hindi speeches. The Speaker announced that translations of the summaries of speeches and of the questions and answers would be provided on a very limited basis, but only in response to genuine requests. Sometimes MPs raised hypothetical questions. On the fourth day of the first session in 1952, an MP from South India inquired about getting translations of speeches delivered in languages other than Hindustani or English. The Speaker responded that the problem would be dealt with if and when it arose and warned the MPs not to raise imaginary difficulties (Government of India, Parliamentary Debates: May 13, 1952). However he himself expressed the suspicion that some MPs might attempt to use the privilege of speaking in the mother tongue for reasons other than lack of knwoledge of either English or Hindi.

There were occasions which proved that the Speaker's suspicions were justified since MPs occasionally got carried away by their linguistic patriotism. One MP from Tamilnad made the following statement in English during the first session in 1952. 'On a point of information, I want to put a question in Tamil and I do not know Hindi and English well. How can I do that?' The Speaker responded: 'The hon. member's statement in the House that he does not know English sufficiently well, is not very convincing, but if he wants it in any other language, he should in that case request some obliging friend of his to get the translation. It cannot be done by the Parliament secretariat' (Government of India, Parliamentary Debates: June 20, 1952).

Since Hindi was to replace English in fifteen years, and since the Congress party was primarily responsible for that decision, many MPs expected that the Congress party leaders would know Hindi and speak it. However, many did not and thus were often criticized by the staunch supporters of Hindi.

During the Question Hour, MPs who asked their questions in Hindi always insisted that the answers should also be given in Hindi. Although many ministers tried to do so, they were not always successful. Frequently a minister would start to answer the question in Hindi and would then switch to English. This switching was also criticized. On the other hand, those ministers from non-Hindi regions who made an effort to speak in Hindi were ridiculed by MPs from South India. Note for example the following remarks by Mr. Gurupadaswamy, an MP from South India, during the debate on the appointment of a Hindi commission in 1955. He was trying to emphasize the point that Hindi was being forced on non-Hindi speakers too soon.

Shri M. S. Gurupadaswamy: . . . I am willing to support the policy of the Govt. in respect to propogating Hindi, but I cannot understand their madness for imposing and spreading Hindi in this manner.

Shri U. M. Trivedi: Is it parliamentary to use the word 'madness'? [Interruptions].

Shri M. S. Gurupadaswamy: I am seeing certain Deputy Ministers now and then getting up and reading out Hindi speeches just like parrots and peacocks . . . [Interruptions].

Pandit Thakur Das Bhargawa: May I submit that the hon. member is offending the sentiments of those who speak in Hindi. It is not correct, moreover to say all that when the official language is Hindi. (Government of India, Parliamentary Debates: September 27, 1955).

Some MPs from South India felt that if a subject pertaining to their constituency or one in which they were interested was being discussed in Hindi, and if they claimed that they did not understand it, those making the speech should switch to English. Such a request was actually made by two MPs during the debate on the bill for creating the state of Andhra Pradesh in 1953. An MP from north India began his speech in Hindi about a certain territory which was to be the part of the new state and two MPs from that particular region requested that since he was talking about their region, he should speak English so that they could understand. He obliged by changing over to English! (Government of India, Parliamentary Debates: August 23, 1953).

Despite the emphasis on Hindi by north Indian MPs, the total time of Hindi reporting during the first few years of Parliament was rather limited. From 1952 to 1954 the average number of minutes of Hindi reporting per day was as follows (Morris-Jones 1957: 145):

House of the People, 1952–1954	*Average No. of Minutes of Hindi reporting per day*
First Session	36
Second Session	35
Third Session	58
Fourth Session	39
Fifth Session	34

The length of the day's sittings averaged about five hours.

Since not all MPs, government ministers, and other officers of the Parliament understood Hindi, occasionally there were problems which could not be resolved. During a session in 1955, an MP from north India used the word *domukhi* 'double-mouthed' in his Hindi speech. Others objected to his usage claiming that it was derogatory. Although the word was later expunged as directed by the Speaker, at the time it was uttered, the Deputy Speaker, a South Indian, was in the chair, and as he did not know the meaning of the word he could not rule on it and postponed the ruling until the Speaker who knew Hindi well was in the chair (Government of India, Parliamentary Debates: November 30, 1955).

There was often considerable switching between English and Hindi not only during the Question Hour, but also during speech-making. An MP from north India while delivering a speech in English became very agitated and switched from English to Hindi in the middle of his speech, and immediately another MP raised a point of order asking if it was permissible and parliamentary to switch languages in the middle of a speech! The Deputy Speaker who was in the Chair did not give a ruling, but simply ignored the remark (Government of India, Parliamentary Debates: November 30, 1955).

Many Hindi-speaking MPs considered it their duty to deliver their speeches in Hindi although they used English to comment on or to interrupt the speeches of others. There were occasions when an MP giving his speech in Hindi, if interrupted by another with a comment in English, would reply in English, and then continue his speech in Hindi. Situations were rare in which MPs while giving a speech in English, if interrupted by a comment in Hindi, would reply in Hindi. Such occasions often led to humorous exchanges in which the Speaker of the House also participated. For example, Mr. P. L. Kuril, an MP from Uttar Pradesh, announced in Hindi at the beginning of his speech that he wanted to present his speech in English, but the last time he spoke in English, his friends said to him that since he lived in Uttar Pradesh (a Hindi region), he should speak in Hindi despite the fact that he did not know Hindi well. As soon as these introductory remarks were made, another MP commented that what Mr. Kuril was speaking was anything but Hindi. The Speaker replied, 'At least it is not English!' And Mr. Kuril himself commented in English: 'There is practically no difference between Hindi and Urdu' (Government of India, Parliamentary Debates: June 27, 1952).

Many MPs from the Hindi-speaking region had definite opinions about what was Hindi. They expressed dissatisfaction with those who spoke Urdu. But others claimed that there was no difference between Hindi and Urdu. During the entire term of the first Parliament, Maulana Abul Kalam Azad, a Muslim, was the Minister of Education and he always spoke in Urdu. The protagonists of Sanskritized Hindi were not happy about this and a few even indirectly suggested that Mr. Azad was favoring the propogation of Hindustani[5] by appropriating government grants to institutions to spread Hindustani at the expense of Hindi. Even Nehru, who spoke a much more Persianized than Sanskritized Hindi, did not escape such criticisms. This was beneficial for the MPs from South India who used such argument as a lever for delaying the replacement of English by Hindi.

Many MPs commented on official Hindi translations of legal documents, acts, and codes, and on Hindi used for news and other broadcasts on All-India Radio. On one occasion, during the debate on the Demands for Grants for the Ministry of Broadcasting and Information, there was a general criticism on the kind of Hindi that was being used on the radio. Prime Minister Nehru had just then publicy remarked that All-India Radio was 'murdering Hindi', and many MPs referred to his comment. Nehru's remarks were prompted because his speech delivered in Persianized Hindi was presented on the radio in Sanskritized Hindi.

During the fifties both the Speaker and the Deputy Speaker were keen in implementing the provisions of the Constitution as far as possible. They believed that since the Constitution had set down a period of transition from English to Hindi, and since it was expected that Hindi would replace English after fifteen years, members of Parliament should make a conscious and serious effort to at least understand it. When Mr. Ayyanger from South India was elected to the position of Speaker after the death of the Speaker, Mr. Mavlankar, in 1956, he announced at the first session of the second Parliament that from then on he was going to conduct business in Hindi as far as possible. He had learned Hindi because during the term of the first Parliament, he was often hindered in his job by his lack of proficiency in Hindi.

The Speaker allowed for translations to be provided immediately when answers to questions were given in Hindi during the first couple of years. Generally, MPs from South India insisted on such translations claiming that they did not understand Hindi. However, by 1954, the Speaker had decided that he would not continue this practice. Translations in English were always available from the parliamentary secretary after the debates, but these were not very useful for asking supplementary questions at the right time. On one such occasion during the Question Hour, the Speaker refused to provide a translation of the government's reply to a South Indian MP's question and announced that now that the Constitution had declared Hindi to be the official language, everybody should make an effort to at least understand it. He further added: 'I feel hurt when members laugh at an attempt to speak in Hindi. Hon. members have taken an oath to be faithful to the Constitution . . .' and that 'it should be their earnest and serious effort to see that Hindi is developed. That is why I feel hurt. It is natural that when we are having a process of transition, there will be difficulties' (Government of India, Parliamentary Debates: December 2, 1954). But the Speaker could be flexible. By convention MPs were not allowed to read their speeches (Lok Sabha Handbook for Members 1967: 104) They could make notes and refer to them, but they could not continuously read from them. However, the Speaker occasionally allowed newly elected MPs to read their 'Maiden Speeches' as it was their first experience in Parliament. Some MPs who wanted to make a genuine effort to speak in Hindi wished to read their speeches since they could not speak Hindi fluently. On such occasions, the Speaker overlooked the fact that they almost read their speeches.

Despite the attempts of the Speaker and the Deputy Speaker to stick to the provisions of the Constitution, the extremist tendencies persisted. Just as South Indian MPs often claimed that they did not know Hindi and therefore wanted translations of answers in Hindi, MPs who were strong protagonists of Hindi constantly asked even those ministers who did not know any Hindi to speak it and answer questions in it.

CONCLUSION

The discussion above demonstrates that the Indian Parliament was greatly preoccupied with language problems during the fifties. This constant concern seems justified in some ways when it is realized that language is one of the most important social institutions and that linguistic identity plays a dominant role in any sociocultural and political interaction. It is to the credit of the Indian Parliament that it contributed substantially towards accomplishing the major task of reorganizing the country on linguistic principles, especially in view of the fact that the Congress government was reluctant to undertake such a potentially fissiparous task. Since Parliament is a representative body of the Indian people, it is but natural that there should be a relationship between the variety of symbolic and substantive patterns of behavior on the part of the MPs and the continued focus on language issues in the country at large. The first eight years indeed represented the peak period of linguistic activity and were the natural consequence of what the people were led to believe by the Congress Party.

This is not to say that the Indian Parliament did not face any linguistic problems in the sixties. But somehow the great intensity of passions in linguistic matters which was at a constant high ebb in the fifties was dissipated later on. And once the official language problem was resolved in the sixties, the Indian Parliament appears to have diverted its attention to other issues. Language controversies from then on seem to occupy the attention of the Parliament only occasionally.

NOTES

1. Although linguistic states were created for the speakers of most major regional languages, the Marathi and Gujarati speakers were denied this privilege. Instead, a bilingual Bombay state was created which included both these groups and the city of Bombay which had become a disputed territory from the very beginning of the linguistic reorganization process after independence. The States Reorganization Commission in its report emphasized the 'cosmopolitan' nature of Bombay and recommended against its inclusion in the Marathi-speaking state of Maharashtra. The Marathi speakers did not have an absolute majority in the city, their population being only forty-three percent. The next largest group was that of Gujarati speakers constituting about seventeen percent. The rest of the population represented other language groups. No other city in India was so controversial. The various decisions taken by the Congress government about Bombay kept on shifting during 1955–56 until it was included in the bilingual state formed by the recommendation of many MPs during the final reading of the states reorganization bill. However, this decision was changed four years later and the linguistic states of Maharashtra and Gujarat were created in 1960 with Bombay city going to Maharashtra.

2. The question of the status of Sindhi, which did not have any regional basis since Sindhi speakers were scattered all over India, was raised as early as 1953 in the Parliament by a Sindhi-speaking MP from Bombay. He wanted to know if petitions had been submitted to the government for the inclusion of Sindhi in the VIIIth Schedule of the constitution and what decision the government intended to take in the matter. This question continued to be raised until 1967 when the Constitution was amended to include Sindhi in the VIIIth Schedule thus fulfilling the goal of Sindhi speakers to raise the status of their language. Similar attempts were made by speakers of Konkani and some other languages. It is interesting to note that Urdu which was in a similar position to Sindhi was, however, included in the VIIIth Schedule. For a detailed discussion of how extralinguistic factors affected the status of languages and interlingual communication, see Apte (1970).
3. In 1948 a Linguistic Provinces Commission consisting of four members was appointed by the Constituent Assembly on the recommendation of a drafting committee which had begun work on a new constitution for India. The Commission was directed to examine and report on the feasibility of forming linguistic provinees, especially in South India. It was popularly known as the Dar Commission because of its chairman, Mr. S. K. Dar, who was a retired judge of the Allahabad High Court. For a detailed discussion of the Commission's report, see Gopal (1966: 71–78).
4. It is difficult to present statistical information on how often MPs of different political parties used the various techniques to draw attention to linguistic issues since the verbatim reports do not list the party affiliations with the names of MPs. However, my overall impression after reviewing the reports of eight years is that most of these techniques, except perhaps the questions, were more frequently used by MPs of the opposition parties such as the Communists, Socialists, Jan–Sangh, and also by MPs elected independently. A few Congress MPs devoted to 'linguism' did use these techniques, but such occasions were infrequent. However, when it came to asking questions during the Question Hour, MPs of all parties were equally interested in getting information on the policies of the government on language matters, and on the progress of the various language-related projects and activities undertaken by the government. In such endeavors, linguistic regionalism of the MPs from non-Hindi regions was just as prevalent as that of the Hindi protagonsists from all political parties.
5. Hindustani is a cover term for varieties of Hindu and Urdu. The major difference between Hindi and Urdu is at the phonological and lexical levels. It is most noticeable in writing since Hindi uses Devanagari script while Urdu uses Arabic script. Many Hindi-speaking MPs in Parliament had a missionary zeal for implementing Sanskritized Hindi in Devanagari script which they thought was to be the official language of India. They were therefore unhappy over the government's efforts to help Hindustani. In reality very few people speak either Urdu or Hindi exclusively. Often it is a mixture. Only

highly Sanskritized formal Hindi speech and a highly Persianized formal Urdu speech represent the polar versions. They are even more so in writing for the reasons stated above. Gandhi recognized this situation and therefore preferred the term Hindustani and wanted to propogate this variety of the language. When he realized that he could not get along with the Hindi and Urdu literary elites with this position, he founded a separate institution called Hindustani Prachar Sabha for the dissemination of Hindustani. The Congress leaders including Nehru were still under the influence of Gandhi's philosophy during the fifties, and hence were in constant conflict with the group of Hindi protagonists in the Parliament. For a further discussion on Hindustani and Hindi-Urdu rivalry see Das Gupta (1970: 111–112, 120).

ROBERT L. KIDDER 12

Language and Litigation in South India

Numerous sources of cleavage in the Indian social fabric have been described and debated at length. Caste and religion occupied center stage in this debate for many years. More recently, especially since independence, language has thrust itself into contention as it has grown into an important locus of political organization, power, and overt political activism. Political boundaries have been redrawn in accordance with general linguistic groupings. Various language 'agitations' have periodically produced alarmed warnings of imminent balkanization. Sixteen official state languages appear to create tremendous problems of national integration. English becomes a temporary ally of local linguistic nationalism for groups opposed to nationwide adoption of a rival indigenous language, Hindi. English, the language of aliens and local elites, is promoted as the only language capable of sustaining national unity, even though it remains largely incomprehensible to the majority of citizens.

How does this linguistic confusion affect India's courts of law? Courts can, after all, be thought of as integral parts of political systems. So it is reasonable to ask whether, and in what ways, linguistic diversity influences their structure and functioning.

A number of approaches could be taken toward this questioning. One would be to analyze the possible political uses to which linguistic partisans put the courts, and the responses of courts to these efforts. Another would be to consider the effects of official and de facto linguistic practices in courts upon their functions as experienced by actors within the system, particularly the clients. Stated idealistically the questions turn on the issue of justice – is the quality of justice strained by practices which make it impossible for most actors to comprehend the language of proceedings? Stated behavioristically, how do actors respond to structured linguistic 'blackout', and what are the consequences of their response patterns for the judicial system? I will take this latter approach in this essay.

THE RESEARCH SITE – BANGALORE

During 1969 and 1970, I conducted the research on which this paper is based in the city of Bangalore, Karnataka (then known as Mysore State), and in some of the surrounding towns. At the time, Bangalore's population was approximately 1.7 million and rising rapidly as the city acquired more and more heavy industry. The city, as capital of Karnataka state, has a heterogeneous population in almost all senses of the word. It has both a large industrial population and a large bureaucratic population. It is as religiously mixed as any other Indian city. And both its pre-growth condition and the recent rapid in-migration have made it a linguistic kaleidoscope. The two major linguistic groups, Kannada and Tamil, vie with each other for claim to majority status, although Kannada won the main political battle by having Bangalore included in a Kannada-speaking state. In addition to these two, however, are large groups of Telegu and Malayali speakers, smaller groups of Marathis, and enclaves of merchants and industrialists of a variety of tongues dominated by Gujarati.

Within the major linguistic groups are further divisions of large, well-organized caste groups, some of which cross linguistic boundaries and some of which intentionally do not. Linguistic diversity, then, is only one of many sources of differentiation in Bangalore.

With respect to its courts, Bangalore's legal jurisdiction includes many surrounding agricultural communities representing Kannada, Tamil, and Telegu. The city's courts receive cases from all of these areas in addition to cases arising within the city. One frequent source of litigation from these areas, aside from the usual land disputes, has been the city's encroachment on agricultural lands as it expands to make way for more industry and housing developments.

Bangalore's courts are organized following the national pattern: lower courts of original jurisdiction are organized hierarchically according to type and size of case handled. They are presided over by a

District Court whose judge hears some original cases and some appeals. Above him is the state's High Court, located in Bangalore, which hears only appeals and constitutional questions and is responsible for the administration of all courts in the state. Above the High Court is the national Supreme Court in Delhi.

METHODOLOGY

The method underlying this study was eclectic and inductive, centering around systematic field observational techniques. Many hours were spent taking verbatim notes of observations in both the High Court and lower courts both in Bangalore and in surrounding towns. Observations focused almost exclusively on courts hearing civil rather than criminal cases, and the findings presented here deal only with litigation in civil courts.

Conversations with lawyers in their offices, at their Bar Association Canteen, and at local clubs were also noted verbatim. Since I had only rudimentary grasp of Tamil and Kannada, I employed a variety of assistants and interviewers to gather different kinds of data. In addition to my own interviews with litigants who could speak English, I employed a multilingual law student with several years of experience as a court clerk to conduct partially structured interviews with non-English-speaking litigants whom he selected by casual contact on the court compound over a four-month period. He also kept detailed notes on his conversations with litigants, and I kept notes on discussions with him about his interviews.

Questionnaires completed by seventy-five lawyers and over three hundred law students provided further information. And when most of the lawyers given the questionnaire (over six hundred) refused to complete it, valuable information was gained from many who sought out the researcher to explain why they could not give a 'true picture' of their experiences within the limits of the questionnaire.

Local 'influentials', including thirty caste association leaders, were interviewed extensively to determine the degree and style of their involvement with courts, lawyers, and litigation. In addition, seven interviewers conducted a sample survey of over 1,700 Bangalore households, asking questions about involvements with the courts and lawyers. For the purposes of this study, the survey results provide additional commentary in the form of casual remarks made to the interviewers during the interviews.

LANGUAGE IN BANGALORE'S COURTS

The 'blackout' mentioned above refers to the fact that in Bangalore, as elsewhere in India, the official language of the courts is English. Those in the legal profession receive their training in English. Legal journals are all published in English. Court opinions are rendered and recorded in English. Official documents and records are kept mainly in English. And more importantly for actors in the courts, English is the language in which courts carry on most of the business of adjudication.

The predominance of English can, of course, be traced back to the development of the courts and the legal profession under the British. The Indian legal profession formed and developed around an elitist career ideal which began with a trip to England to earn a coveted English law degree. Although only a minority of legal practitioners achieved this ideal, it was they who set the standard for legal practice in India. And their standard included promotion of English legal doctrines, procedures, and the language in which these doctrines were born. It was their grasp of English which enabled them to practice anywhere in the imperial Indian legal system, and which gave them hope that their aspirations to the ultimate professional achievement of a high court judgeship (or even advocacy in England before the Privy Council) might eventually be realized as Indians increasingly replaced Englishmen in these positions.

However it came about, English does dominate the official procedures of Indian courts. And to add to the potential for linguistic difficulties, many courts, particularly in urban areas, receive cases from parties of diverse native tongues. Hence courts officials may be alienated from clients not only by the official status of English but by their own limitations with local languages.

Thus, the potential for linguistic impact in Indian courts is significant. The purpose of this study is to examine specific Indian courts in order to determine whether, and to what extent, this potential actually intrudes upon the operations of these courts.

LANGUAGE AND LITIGATION

The first task here is to modify the description of linguistic 'blackout' provided above. While it is true that English is both the official language of the courts and a language in which all lawyers have facility, the actual language of court procedures varies depending on the level of court. In general, the higher the court, the more English predominates as the medium of interaction.

Thus, in a small town with the lowest level 'Munsiff's-Magistrate's Court', one can expect to find the entire proceedings conducted in the language of that town. This means that not only the testimony of witnesses but also the remarks of the judge to the advocates and their remarks to him and to each other will all take place in the local language. The clerk reads the calendar in that language, makes announcements in it, and gives directives in it. Witnesses are sworn in using a translation from the English. The judge uses the local language for announcements of decisions and verdicts. The only intrusion of English into such proceedings comes from the need of the judge to translate all testimony into English for the official record. In most low-level rural courts, this was handled by the judge listening to a sequence of testimony on one subject and then reciting to the clerk a capsulized English summary of what the witness had said. The opposing lawyers assisted in the construction of this summary by correcting the judge's errors as they occurred.

Courts of the same level in Bangalore city followed the same procedures when possible. There was, however, a tendency towards more use of English between lawyers and judges, particularly when the languages of the opponents were different.

As one moves up the ladder of courts in Bangalore, he encounters increasing use of English. In the High Court, local languages have no place whatsoever, except in the rare case where a witness is recalled in order to repeat his testimony. In such a case, his words are immediately translated, and his meaning is discussed informally by lawyers and judges alike in English.

In between the High Court and the Munsiff's Court are gradations of English usage, so that even in lower courts of original jurisdiction, lawyers, clerks, and judges often vacillate between local languages and English, using English to convey the more precise legal meanings of points they have been making in local languages. In gencral, for most original suits, English is used to promote legal points, and the higher the court, the more likely it is that English will also be used to discuss factual matters.

Courts in urban areas and larger towns encounter problems with the diverse linguistic origins of witnesses who come before them. If a judge or court reporter does not understand the language of a witness, a translator is called in to translate the testimony sentence by sentence as it is delivered. Such translators are not necessarily hired for that purpose – often they are persons with other roles at court who are known to be competent in particular languages.

In summary, then, the average litigant can expect to encounter more and more linguistic 'blackout' the higher he goes in the pursuit of adjudicatory resolution of this grievance. But just how important is this blackout in affecting his ability to achieve just treatment, the way he experiences his treatment in court, and the ways he relates to the other actors in the judicial system?

LINGUISTIC AND LEGALISTIC BLACKOUT – COMPLEMENTARY PROCESSES

A narrow conception of language might lead to the conclusion that linguistic elitism in the courts could only be harmful to the court's ability to function as a legitimate arbiter of disputes. If a litigant cannot understand what is going on around him, how is he to develop that sense of trust and confidence upon which the institution builds legitimacy? If a decision given in an incomprehensible tongue and resulting from an incomprehensible process goes against him, how can he be convinced that he has been treated fairly? Further, how can he explain to his relatives and associates what happened to him? Will he respect the judicial process? Will he abide by its directives so that the conflict on which the litigation was based will cease? Would not the local language be much better in assuring full and satisfactory participation on the part of the litigant?

I shall argue here that the courts studied do not achieve legitimacy in the eyes of litigants, many of whom lose, through the process of litigation, much of their trust in the ability fof the courts to provide 'justice'; and that rather than accepting unfavorable decisions as final and bindings, litigants approach courts, instead, from a manipulative point of view. The process ultimately functions to force litigants into acceptance of compromise in the face of the court's failure to achieve adjudicative effectiveness. However, I shall also argue that the role of linguistic elitism and heterogeneity in producing this pattern of court use and function is only marginal at most. I will attempt to demonstrate that the use of English is just one aspect of a structure of practices and relationships which characterizes litigation wherever it occurs under English-born provisions of legal procedure. To put it in practical terms, a mere shift from English to local languages in the courts studied would have no significant impact on the court's image, its ability to engender trust, or on its ability to function adjudicatively.

THE EXPERIENCE OF LITIGATION

Interviews with a great variety of litigants engaged in litigation at the time of the interviews reveals that the experience of litigation is an experience of constant intrigue in which almost no other actor is completely trusted. The social world of the court is perceived as a labyrinth of obstacles obstructing the litigant's presentation of his 'clearcut' case to an honest judge. This social world is a maze of alternatives for the litigant whose every choice is accompanied by apprehensions of miscalculations.

The cast of characters on this stage includes the opponent, the lawyers for the two sides, the judge, the judge's clerk, lawyers' clerks, vendors of legal stamps, record keepers, court peons, notaries, typists, nearby astrologers, and other litigants who may or may not be able to give advice or assistance. Learning to conduct litigation means, among other things, learning the structures of relationships between all these actors and the possible effects of that structure on one's own fortunes. Becoming a litigant also means acquiring a new role among one's relatives, friends, and neighbors – a role whose ramifications are gradually learned as litigation consumes more and more of the litigants's time and resources.

Most litigation in Bangalore results in either prolonged delay or out-of-court settlement. I have, elsewhere, discussed the factors which make it nearly impossible for the courts to impose settlements to which the litigants themselves refuse to consent (Kidder 1973). In essence, the Bangalore courts function to produce negotiated settlements even though most of those who approach the courts for the first time fully expect to be supported triumphantly by favorable, 'just', and effective decisions.

The contradiction between a litigant's expectations and the actual capacity of the system to produce cloture and finality raises problems of stage management for those who preside over the process. Between the lawyer and his client, in particular, it creates severe problems of credibility. The most common experience a litigant faces in court is the postponement of his case. Delay of proceedings is almost always to the advantage of one of the opponents (e.g. for the one in possession of a piece of disputed land). The courts are always overcrowded with a docket of cases that could not possible be finished in the normally allotted time. And lawyers generally carry more clients than they could possible service on any given day, since they know that the average case will more often than not be postponed, and since the court's administrative procedures give at best only an hour's advance notice that a case will be called as scheduled.

The problem for the lawyer is to convince his client to stay with him. Lawyers' fees are charged in a variety of ways, usually including a charge for each court appearance regardless of whether the case is actually heard or postponed. Whatever the fee agreement is, it almost always means more money for the lawyer the longer the case drags on. Simultaneously, of course, the longer the delay, the more anxious the client becomes. In other words, built into the fee structure of the legal profession is a constant source of frustration and grounds for suspicion that the lawyer is not acting in the client's best interests. The lawyer, like all professionals who deal with clients, has the job of projecting a credible, salable image of expertise. His expertise is called into question each time he comes away from a hearing empty-handed. He must, therefore, convince the client that, in fact, each postponed hearing went exactly as planned and contributed to the client's ultimate victory in some incremental fashion known only to the expert.

Interviews with both lawyers and litigants demonstrated that this question of expertise is one of the most serious and ubiquitous problems faced by lawyers. Most of the litigants' interviews indicated some degree of anxiety that their lawyer was actually working in collusion with their opponents to defeat them. On the lawyers' side, this problem was experienced as one of constant aggravation from clients to 'do the impossible' by making the courts move faster or making an opponent yield from a relatively impregnable legal-strategic position. Lawyers complained about their constant worry that clients would shift to other lawyers, that clients would not follow their advice because of lack of trust.

The client's naïve lay expectations create a 'cooling out' problem for the lawyer. With as much tact as possible, beginning with the client's first inquiry and continuing throughout the litigation, the lawyer must induce the client to revise his expectations downward. In this, the lawyer is walking a tightrope between losing the client by too much discouragement and losing him through apparently inadequate expertise as reflected in failure to win expected results.

The average first-time litigant comes to a lawyer with a clearcut common-sense notion about his legal rights and how they should be presented before a 'just' court of law. He makes a whole cluster of assumptions about which facts are important, which evidence pertinent, and what in fact did occur between himself and his opponent. Cautiously, gently, but inevitably, his lawyer must question the client, challenge him on facts, and reorganize the available information into a coherent, legally-presentable theory of events. Almost invariably, the story which emerges for presentation in court looks twisted, distorted, and illogical to the client. He may understand in some abstract sense that only his lawyer's version of the story has any chance in court, but he will still be left with a sense of participating in a lie. And since it is a 'lie' constructed for him by his lawyer, the best image the lawyer can hope to achieve is that of an effective liar who lies only on behalf of the client. But since the relationship rests on finite economic exchange rather than limitless personal devotion, it takes little in the way of unfulfilled expectations to stir a client's doubt about anything told him by his lawyer. The fee structure is thus just one source of alienation between client and lawyer. The lawyer must, in addition, cope with lay naïveté concerning the viability of claims and the relevance of facts.

Lawyers were observed responding to this structured image management dilemma in a variety of ways. One tactic, especially used with clients employing a lawyer for the first time, was the systematic treatment of the client as if he were a child or servant. Often, during interviews at lawyers' offices, I found myself being served tea or fruits which had been humbly fetched by a waiting client on command of the lawyer. The degree and type of servitude varied depending on the social status of the client. Thus, the author spent a day sight-seeing with one lawyer and his family and discovered part-way along that the chauffeur and car were provided by a wealthy hotel owner being defended by the lawyer. This was not some unusual expression of gratitude – the lawyer's wife complained loudly about 'these ungrateful clients who send their cars with only two or three litres of petrol' and expect the lawyer to pay for the rest. A common sight around all courts is the lawyer, brow furrowed in apparent deep thought, walking along followed at a few paces by an anxious-looking client who is earnestly lugging his lawyer's briefcase.

In a variety of ways, then, the lawyer encourages conspicuous gestures of recognition that the lawyer-client relationship is a paternalistic one. Again, he obviously walks a tight-rope by such behavior – risking the client's resentment on the one hand and damage to his own image of power and expertise on the other if he cannot command suitable deference.

Another technique of image-management centers on behavior in court. Recognized by lawyers as lamentably necessary is the practice of putting on a show for the client. Clients develop numerous, partially-informed notions about what must happen in court in order for them to win. The lawyers repeatedly expressed resentment in interviews about the ridiculous things they often find themselves doing in court in order to please. It is the same as the resentment Becker says jazz musicians have against 'squares' who pressure them to play inartistically (1963: 85–95).

The most common technique is the use of strident oratory. It is not uncommon to enter a court and find one lawyer holding forth at great length about miscellaneous seemingly unrelated aspects of the case being heard. Great emotion is projected. The advocate will be gesturing angrily first at the opponent, then at his lawyer, often even at the judge. Such rhetoric is not confined to concluding remarks. It occurs even at the most preliminary phases of cases and may concern only some simple procedural issue. Other lawyers present in court snicker among themselves or look knowingly at each other and the judge, expressing in-group awareness of the charade. Although there were clear instances of animosity between members of the Bangalore bar, I found no case in which courtroom rhetoric produced resentment on the part of a target opponent lawyer. Their relationships were rather more similar to those between American professional wrestlers who rarely take each other's postutring seriously.

The lawyers generally feel that their clients will be satisfied with nothing less than the most vigorous possible assertion of their claims. And judging from interviews with clients, they are probably right. The expressed mistrust of lawyers generally centers around the charge that for one reason or another the lawyer 'does not care' about the client's problem. The ideal lawyer, as seen by litigants in the midst of litigation, is one who is personally involved as well as highly experienced – hence the need to produce a show of personal involvement.

Staging such as this reaches its purest form in the observed practice of double talk. When a client could not understand English, this was apparently not necessary. But in cases where English was spoken, especially in the High Court, some of the most famous lawyers in the state were observed engaging in long speeches of apparently profound content which were actually loaded with non-sequiturs, unfinished sentences, and illogical transitions from one subject to another.

At first I felt as confused as clients must feel by all this. I wondered whether my lack of legal training was beginning to show, or perhaps the type of English being spoken was so different from that to which I was accustomed. But frequent on-the-spot attempts to get clarification from other lawyers who were listening in led to the conclusion that nonsense was indeed being used in a skilled and self-cconscious way to impress a client. In response to whispered questions, 'What did that mean?', the usual response was 'Nothing. He is just going on, you see. That man (pointing) is his client.' Such explanations were spoken either matter-of-factly or with awe and respect depending on the reputation of the rhetorician for success in the profession.

This double-talk method often coincided with another – the citation of cases or precedent. Having a common-law foundation, the Indian courts, like those in the U.S. and England, are inclined to place formal importance on the earlier decisions of courts in determining the direction present decisions should take. In practice, in the Bangalore courts, especially in appeals cases, this has lead to a 'battle of the books'. When a trial reaches this stage, the lawyers' table will be piled high with old reports. Senior lawyers have their juniors and clerks scurrying conspicuously around the court library extracting tomes in an apparent search for 'the case' which will guarantee their client's success. Hearings are likely to turn into seemingly endless verbatim readings of cases purported to bear on the present case.

To a certain extent this has legal effectiveness, because, as Marc Galanter has argued (Galanter 1967), Indian appeals courts have created a tremendous problem for themselves by over-responding to arguments when rendering opinions. The result has been the creation of an almost endless supply of precedents, and it is the lawyer's responsibility to construct a pattern of them favorable to his client.

Word about the 'cases' circulates among new clients as they spend time around courts. Naïve clients can be heard boasting that they have 'all the cases' on their side (experienced litigants discard such glib notions of certainty). The result is that lawyers feel pressure to 'argue the cases' even when there is little of relevance in them. Again, the lawvers understand and sympathize with a colleague who spends hour after hour droning through cases in support of his client. They know, as was obvious from many comments made by litigants during our interviews, that novice clients often judge a lawyer's devotion to the case by the length of time he spends presenting cases. Several litigants actually reported having changed lawyers midway through a case because they felt cheated when their opponents' lawyers spent more time presenting more cases then their own lawyers had. Lawyers often commented on how ridiculous such an evaluation was since their professional view leads them to believe that relevance of the case is far more important than numbers.

Like rhetorical style and treatment as an inferior, the 'cases' bear exaggerated importance to the client because they are tangible, quantifiable elements in an otherwise bewildering set of events. Since they initially opt for litigation in the belief that it functions adjudicatively as officially presented, they are unable to perceive that they are engaged in a battle of strategy in which the court's official actions bear minor significance compared to the interests and actions of the various actors who inhabit the court world. As their goal of victory and vindication continues to elude them, they search for clues which will tell them how far they have moved along their erroneously conceived path to success.

Since the courts cannot exert the decisive influence for which they are designed, legal personnel find themselves engaged in an exercise in mystification which has the dual purpose of sustaining the institution on which their livelihoods depend and giving them the leeway needed to arrange nogotiated settlements which leave their images of expertise intact.

It should be clear here that the use of English is just one of a whole battery of techniques of mystification, such as those discussed above. Its use is similar to the use of Latin in high church ceremony. Laymen are impressed by the unknown and believe, based on fragmentary information from various sources, that certain sounds indicate progress in the right direction. The professional elite alone can give authoritative progress reports, and these are expressed in terms of the practical results which are of greatest concern to the supplicant. The mystification which is maintained in the courts does not depend on the use of English – it is the mystification of elite discourse, and could be just as effectively perpetuated in any of the local languages.

That this is a feature of legal institutions generally in highly differentiated societies seems confirmed in Jerome Frank's comment on jargon in American law: 'Legal jargon . . . aids in keeping the law to a class of exclusive professionals (lawyers). This legal jargon is unintelligible to the man on the street (Frank 1949: 258).' As long as the lawyer remains an elite expert interceding on behalf of a naïve layman in an institution which operates on the basis of privileged information, specialized procedures, and elevated ideological reasoning, the client is at the lawyer's mercy and can only judge results as they trickle out of the legal black box.

The general conclusion, then, is that English usage in courts constitutes little more of political significance than an additional weapon in the arsenal of elitism.

LITIGATION ELITES

There is, however, an important modification of this conclusion which must be made. Some of those who engage in litigation in Bangalore develop what I have called 'careers in litigation' (Kidder 1971). A fraction of those who litigate develop such expertise in legal jargon, such keen awareness of legal procedure, and such an extensive network of contacts and influence in the court system as well as their own communities that they become 'court birds'. These individuals recognize the manipulative potential of court procedures and develop careers which incorporate litigation into overall strategies for economic and social mobility.

One would probably be inclined to list such entrepreneurial activity as dependent on 'illegitimate opportunity structures' (see Cloward and Ohlin 1961: 145–152, 161–186) if one contrasts it with the formal rationale of litigation. Furthermore, the use of English in courts may produce inequalities of illegitimate opportunity. It is possible that one of the prerequisites for a career in litigation, or more generally for successful use of litigation in furtherance of entrepreneurial activities, is a command of English. English could become a differentiating factor because in order to establish such a career, it is necessary to become as privy to the secrets of courtroom mystery as the experts themselves are. Those who become 'court birds' actually develop such thorough knowledge of the courts that they become regular providers of legal services to less experienced litigants. They serve as touts helping clients find lawyers. The direct people to the 'proper office' for particular services. They help people draft documents and find necessary records.

In other words, success in this illegitimate opportunity structure depends on the erasure of differences between the litigant and the experts. Litigation must be made into a predictable process, which it is not for the majority of litigants. The use of English probably limits the potential pool of career litigants because it could serve as the residual source of mystification blocking the aspirant's entry into the inner circle.

But once again, English should not be over-emphasized as a qualifier because career litigants generally were already the occupants of local elite positions before they moved into litigation. Most of them could speak some English. But most were also caste leaders, charity organizers, 'social workers', or village officials whose positions and activities gave them special opportunities to develop 'influence' in various social settings which could be translated into advantages for themselves. As I have discussed elsewhere (Kidder 1974), their use of litigation fits into an overall strategy of mobility which depends on these multiple bases of influence. Manipulation of court processes to force concessions from an opponent is made possible not only by command of English, but also by the reserves of 'influence' the entrepreneurs can call up when needed. Their ability with English, combined with their extensive knowledge of both the formal law and actual procedure, give them a sense of control over their lawyers which naïve clients never exhibited. Some even spoke of their lawyers as pawns to be used strategically under the client's strict guidance. This was particularly true of small cases in which career litigants would hire inexpensive young lawyers and completely direct the case from the sidelines.

Knowledge of English, then, helps these men break the mystery of litigation and turn it into a strategic tool. And it is a tool which these careerists can use most effectively against the inexperienced who are still cloaked in the fog of legal mystification. Thus a certain amount of the litigation in Bangalore's courts must be described as the victimization of those who rely on the courts for protection by those who have discovered the courts' inner mechanisms. But, in addition to English, a career in litigation depends also on learning the legal language and the context within which it is used. This means the development of privileged access, and in order to gain this, one needs an elite base of operations to begin with. Once again, then, English is an adjunct of elitism. In this case, however, it serves a selective function in determining who shall take advantage of the courts as 'illegitimate opportunity structures'.

THE FUNCTIONS OF AMBIGUITY

In analyzing general sociopolitical structures, Murray Edelman has dealt with the problem presented here by pointing out the predictability of schisms between legal *language* and legal *meanings*. It is a schism between the clarity and precision of the words and the ambiguity of their application by legal elites (Edelman 1964: 138–142). A statutory standard 'means what its administrators do about it', and 'administrators and judges proceed as if the language is ambiguous . . .' even though, 'when faced with an abstract discussion of law, the same judges or administrators are likely to talk quite sincerely as if statutory language does have a clear mening'. The most the layman can hope to get from legal discourse is the false comfort of 'assuming that there is a mechanical, precise, objective definition of law'. Effective users of the system, on the other hand, use it as 'a vocabulary in which they justify their actions to accord with this lay assumption'. For them and their lawyers, linguistic ambiguity 'is the most useful attribute of legal language' because it allows the promotion of their own interests based on the influence they can muster.

The result is a process which 'satisfies both pressure groups and the mass audience' because of their different perspectives on linguistically defined events. To Edelman, 'a language form which facilitates this result is functional' because it provides conflict resolution while at the same time permitting self-expression and the symbolic satisfaction of various reference groups.

The impression of functional orderliness and mutual satisfaction in Edelman's analysis may be due in part to his focus on the relations between organized interest groups and governmental administrators. By studying litigation in Bangalore, we can see that 'satisfaction' is not always a regular outcome of direct experience with linguistic ambiguity. We can also see that the fact of ambiguity in the litigation context is a function of the uncertainty which arises when previously norm-bound relationships disintegrate into normlessness. In such a context, linguistic ambiguity is a source of aggravation and anxiety to lawyers who must mediate between the two worlds of meaning. To the client who ultimately yields to compromise, someone is to blame for the failure of his 'clearcut case'. He gives in, not simply to Edelman's ambiguity of interpretation, but to the functionally limitless permutations of strategic maneuver furnished to all litigants by the procedures of courts. Those who usher him through the experience develop elaborate techniques for protecting themselves from his frustration and they employ the myth of legal precision in the act.

There is no quarrel here with Edelman's portrayal of legal ambiguity. Knowledge of English alone would help the client very little, for, as Edelman argues, the words mean nothing outside the context of the court's routine and emerging social processes. But the litigation studied here represents conflicting claims among members of Edelman's 'mass audience', and his comforting visions of symbolic satisfaction and conflict resolution seem to be washed out by the preponderant role of power and privilege. What would help our client most are the same advantages that help any party in a relationship freed of normative restraint – i.e. resources of combat such as wealth, alliances, 'inside information', and free time.

CONCLUSION

English persists as the official language of the courts in Bangalore. It does so in spite of the general inability of the population to use the language. Its use does not, however, materially affect the actual functioning of the courts or the responses of litigants to them because adversarial procedures, rules of evidence, grounds for postponement, and a whole host of other features of litigation have transformed the courts' actual function from adjudication to delay, negotiation, and compromise. The elitism of legal specialization and differentiation serves to mask this adjudicative impotence and English is only one of many devices by which the mask is maintained.

A handful of laymen break through the mask and learn to use the contradictions in the legal system to their own entrepreneurial advantage. To do so, they must know English. But their knowledge of English is only one in a cluster of elite skills and statuses which they use to move from success to success.

The 'language barrier' in court, therefore, is only a secondary influence on the court's effects in Indian society. The chief barrier between citizens and a sense of satisfaction with their justice system is the elitism of a profession which must operate in a highly unpredictable context and must therefore erect and maintain self-protective images of expertise.

F. G. BAILEY

13

'I-Speech' in Orissa

Courts of law and councils and committees have certain things in common, and this makes it possible to consider them together and to discuss their connection with linguistic diversity.

Firstly, they are all scenes of contest. Litigants argue their case before a judge. In councils and committees diverse points of view are, as the word is, 'contested'. Each side attempts to assert and to convince their opponents or some third party of the correctness of their definition of what happened or what should have happened or what might be done, or prevented, and so on. Thus courts, councils, and committees require a pair of antagonists[1] : to that extent they have a common form.

These three kinds of institution also display one process. This is the sequence of claim and counter-claim, a series of offers and counter-offers, which, according to the norm of the institution,[2] should terminate in a decision.

Thirdly, all three kinds of institution, are, in some sense of the word, peaceful. They all provide arenas for contest, but the contest is 'jaw' and not 'war'. The only weapons allowed (at least in theory) are words and arguments; and, while sometimes the tokens of language may stand for other direct resources at the disposal of an antagonist outside the present arena, it is also the case that the skilful and appropriate use of language itself becomes a source of power and can, up to a point, compensate for deficiencies in other forms of power.

To hold one's own in such an arena requires the capacity to use the appropriate language or style of language with skill and subtlety. This is not only a matter of staying within the formal rules which lay down arguments which may be properly used in that arena and which penalize failure to observe these rules; it also involves the ability to transmit or to understand unspoken messages that lie behind the spoken, the hints and the veiled threats — in short, the capacity to communicate one message while apparently saying something else.

In these circumstances it seems obvious that only those contestants are equally and fairly matched who speak the relevant language with the same level of skill. The disadvantaged contestant, provided that he realizes what is happening, will be that much the less inclined to grant legitimacy to the presiding institution (because it is 'unfair' to him), and then will the more readily resort to forms of coercion other than the verbal, if he has them at his disposal.

Thus, other things being equal, linguistic discontinuities put in peril that social consent upon which the successful working of courts, councils, and committees depends. At the very least, they continue to symbolize differences in culture, which may render more difficult the legitimacy of judicial and governmental councils. They may also, unless special measures are taken, directly disadvantage speakers of 'inferior' languages.

Undoubtedly diversity of linguistic competence goes along with different access to power. In Bisipara[3] there is a caste of Untouchables called Pan. The population of the region in which Bisipara is settled is predominantly Adibasi (five in eight persons) and there are reserved jobs in administration and scholarships to be shared between Adibasis and Untouchables. Yet many more Pans is Bisipara are able to make use of these privileged opportunities than is the case in Adibasi (Kond) villages. The reason is that the Pans of Bisipara grow up speaking Oriya, and this is also the language of education and administration. The majority of Konds, on the other hand, use Kui in the home and need to pick up Oriya as a second language. Consequently in the competition for minor administrative appointments and for scholarships to schools, they are much disadvantaged.

People in Orissa are not slow to grasp the significance of language as a means of obtaining power. Orissa was colonized partly from Madras and partly from Bengal, and over large parts of the province the administrators imported by the imperial power were Bengalis.[4] From two decades before the turn of the century, Oriyas conducted a campaign to separate the Oriya-speaking areas from Bengal and to have their own province. Eventually, in 1911, these areas were divided from Bengal to form a joint province with Bihar. Later, in 1936, Oriyas were allowed to form a separate province. In 1956 there was a state-wide outbreak of violence occasioned by a proposal to readjust state boundaries in conformity with the languages spoken. In fact at the time Orissa stood to lose only very small enclaves of territory: nevertheless there was considerable violence.

People at the time I was in Orissa (during the 1950s) saw these agitations from two different points of view. For the more romantic the identity of Oriyas and Oriya culture was involved in the language: indeed, for some language had an intrinsic value and was seen as an end in itself. Language was a token of nationist values: this explains the outbreak of violence in 1956, since very little of material value was at stake. From the other point of view, language is a means to an end, and by this reckoning Oriyas (in the nineteenth century) had been unable to get positions of power in the administrations, because Bengalis monopolized the civil services. To gain such positions and to operate effectively from them, one had to be a fluent speaker of Bengali.

Recounting these events, it becomes clear that asking for the effects of linguistic factors on politics is only half the question. If the congregation which is involved with a court of law or a council speaks more than one language, steps may be taken to minimize or cancel out the effect this might have on the distribution of political resources. Also, if linguistic diversity imperils the legitimacy upon which judicial and conciliar institutions depend, a range of policies may be adopted to buttress this legitimacy.

Obviously the process will be circular. The diversity of languages sets the problem for language-policy decisions in councils and courts, but once those institutions make a decision about acceptable languages, this feeds back upon the diversity. If the courts decide that Hindi will be the language of justice, then budding advocates will learn Hindi and this may effect educational policies and eventually the pattern of language distribution in that society.

I shall discuss one part of this process, asking how the range of policy decisions about languages in courts and councils connects with the social context in which those institutions operate. The decisions which a council makes about linguistic diversity (counteracting it, encouraging it, ignoring it, etc.) depend upon how that council stands in relation to the society or community – whether it governs or serves or represents or exploits or whatever else it does.

This requires two main questions. What are the different categories of language-policy which a council or a court may adopt? Secondly, what dimension should be used to discriminated between different kinds of courts and councils? Once these are established, we can begin to look for connections.

THE LANGUAGE-POLICY VARIABLE

I shall argue that language discontinuities are found everywhere, both in polyglot and 'monolingual' societies, since even in the latter some institutions require participants to be skilled in an esoteric language or, more usually, an esoteric form of everyday language.

The different institutions which I encountered in Orissa (between 1952 and 1959) exhibit a range of choices in their policy about language. By that time the state included within its boundaries most areas where Oriya was spoken. Nor was there any language group which approached in size the Oriya speakers.

Nevertheless for many people Oriya was a second language, if they spoke it at all. On the borders with neighboring states other major Indian languages were spoken: to the south, Telugu; to the west and northwest, varieties of Hindi; and to the north, there were Bengali-speakers. Secondly, throughout the upland regions of the state diverse tribal languages (mostly unwritten) were used.[5] Thirdly, the variety increases because in certain contexts people were expected to use English, although there were very few native speakers of this language in the state.

English was the official language of the Orissa Legislative Assembly, but a member (MLA) was free, with the Speaker's consent, to address the House in another language.[6] There are obvious constraints. To influence listeners in the chamber and cause them to change their minds then clearly the MLA must use a language which his fellows understand. For this reason, Oriya was much the most common tongue in which the House was addressed, since all but a very few members could understand and speak it. But it was also common to hear English used by those who spoke fluent Oriya, in spite of the fact that some members did not understand English. A small group of MLAs, representing the Jharkhand Party and coming from the extreme northwestern areas of the state bordering on Bihar, consistently used Hindi to address the House. Their speeches were received with mild derision, the Oriyas repeating, as if sniggering, the Hindi form transcribed as 'hai'. Reports of the proceedings of the House, bills and formal speeches by ministers were printed in English and in Oriya, while questions were printed in either English or Oriya according to the language used by the questioner.[7]

Bisipara, the village in which I lived, has a traditional panchayat, which met to settle disputes between villagers and also to decide upon common policies and to put them into practice. All adult men were entitled to attend this council, providing they did not belong to one or other of the untouchable castes. Untouchables sometimes used the council to settle disputes, but they were compelled to stand apart, to present their evidence and receive the judgment, without being allowed to enter into the deliberations. Women were treated in the same way.

The language situation was relatively simple. Bisipara is a village of Oriya speakers: it is located in an area in which most of the inhabitants (five out of eight) are native speakers of Kui, the language of the Konds, most of whom, however, can also speak Oriya. None of the villagers knew English or Hindi. Many of the Oriya speakers in Bisipara, especially those aged about thirty and upwards, could also understand and make themselves understood in Kui. Oriya was generally the language used in the panchayat. Occasionally the panchayat met to settle disputes between Konds who were one-time vassals of the Bisipara headman. He arbitrated the dispute between his 'subjects', sometimes using Kui to meet the needs of an elderly plaintiff or defendant unable to cope adequately with Oriya. On rare occasions Kond women gave evidence and this was usually done in Kui, since few of these women spoke Oriya.

The situation in formal courts of law was more complicated. I have printed reports from tribunals which investigated complaints about the 1952 election. It is clear that the proceedings were conducted in a variety of languages, according to the capacity of those giving evidence, but the summing up and the decisions were entirely in English. Even in the lower courts – say at District level – the judge or magistrate presiding was likely to use English to hear arguments from those counsels who spoke that language, and to deliver his judgements. Nevertheless, as in the case of the Orissa assembly and of the Bisipara panchayat, there was a good deal of flexibility, depending upon the linguistic capacities of the judge or magistrate and of those whom he was addressing. The formal judgment, designed to enter the record as a precedent for future cases, was in English. But if the judge wished to lecture the plaintiff or the defendant or both, he would need to do so in a language which they understood, and sometimes this could only be done through an interpreter.

The lower level courts in the Kond region at certain periods strove to avoid formality. The administrators saw themselves as benevolent autocrats, making extensive use of their own discretion to avoid the use of intermediaries. They would accept verbal complaints; they discouraged legal practitioners; they allowed Kond forms of oath to be used; and they permitted themselves to refer disputes back to tribal panchayats. Interpreters were used and at least one of the officers (Ollenbach, who 'reigned' 1901–1924) could speak the Kui language.[8]

At this descriptive level, our survey of language choices is itself babel and we need to identify some dimensions of variation.

The main distinction is between I-speech and N-speech. 'N-speech' stands for 'natural speech', for a language which is, ideally, within everyone's capacity, because it is an everyday language. An N-speech policy is in force when an institution[9] takes pains to allow those who are before it to use their own language. Insofar as the Orissa assembly permits its members to use their mother-tongue (if necessary) on the floor of the House, it is following an N-speech policy. So also is the Bisipara panchayat is shifting easily between Oriya and Kui, as the occasion requires. The formal courts of law are also employing an N-speech policy in hearing evidence (but not in delivering judgment and handing down precedent). Finally the European officials in the Kondmals were trying to put into practice N-speech principles.

There are two varieties of N-Speech. One is a A-speech (which stands for 'all-speech') and the other is M-speech ('majority-speech').

To follow an A-speech policy in a polyglot society, the institution must not only permit but also in practice usually provide technical devices which allow participants to use their own language to good effect. These devices take the form of translators and interpreters, or regulations insisting that judges and magistrates and administrative officials should learn the languages of the region in which they are working, and so forth. The extreme example, not reached in any institution in Orissa, is the device of simultaneous translation into several languages.

An M-speech policy makes use of the language most frequently found among those who form the congregration for that particular institution. This definition rests upon the number of speakers (there are, of course, more than a few difficulties in determining the boundaries of a language). 'Majority', in this context, does not refer to the exercise of political power. For example, English was the language of the higher courts and of such higher councils as existed at the time when the British ruled India, but this is *not* an example of M-speech. On the other hand, that the Oriya-speaking members of the Orissa assembly barrack Hindi speakers is evidence that they would like an M-speech policy within Orissa (but not within India).

The European officials in the Kondmals, seeing themselves as the protectors of Konds against the dominance of Oriya traders and exploiters, insisted on a A-speech policy in their judicial and administrative activities, resisting pressures towards M-speech.

Both varieties of N-speech contrast with I-speech ('institution-speech'). An I-speech policy is in force when an institution requires its participants to learn an esoteric language. Sometimes this is literally true. There were periods in different parts of India when Persian and later English were the official court languages and the effect was to create a class of specialists whose services were needed by the ordinary N-speaker to gain access to the courts. But this is only a special case of a situation found everywhere: most courts of law, and, as I will argue, many kinds of council, require the knowledge of an esoteric language, or more commonly an esoteric variant of ordinary language, before they can be used effectively. In this wide sense 'language' means a set of rules regulating communication: for example, the rules which courts lay down about permissible and unpermissible evidence, acceptable and unacceptable lines of questioning, and so forth. The phrase 'unparliamentary language' refers to the same phenomenon. Thus 'language', as used here, may comprise both form and content.

A consequence of accepting the notion of I-speech is to make all societies multilingual. Our basic problem is that of discontinuity in communication and how this is handled by courts and councils, and it is clear that such discontinuities exists within what is conventionally called 'one language': between regional dialects, between class-dialects, and, as in the present case, between different levels of expertise. The difference between the babel of New Guinea and the relatively less varied Orissa and so-called monolingual England becomes one of degree and not one of kind. Finally, on a thoroughly practical level, transcending this distinction should make us realize that if ever the day comes when everyone in India speaks Hindi and only Hindi, and everyone in New Guinea speaks Pidgin and only Pidgin, their troubles in communicating and the need for courts and councils to cope with language discontinuities will *not* have come to an end.

Let me summarize this in a diagram:[10]

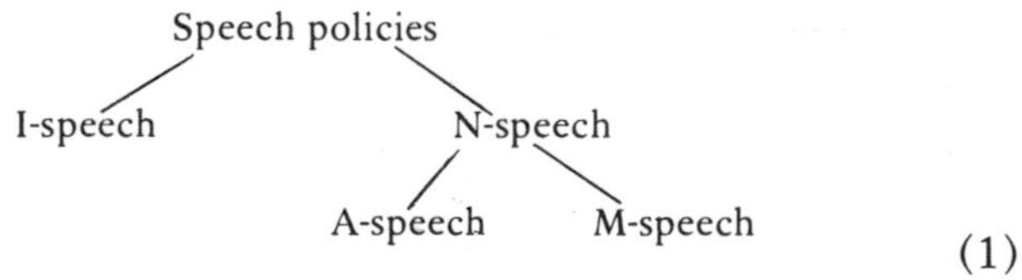

(1)

LEGITIMACY AND POWER

It may be argued that if courts of law limit the forms of argument that may be used and create a type of communication which is radically different from N-speech, this is because the law is a very precise, technical and complex matter, which can only be expressed in N-speech at the cost of considerable distortion and with great loss of efficiency. To use ordinary speech in the law courts would be like attempting to rewrite a manual of algebra in ordinary English. The argument is that technical factors set absolute constraints on the language used in courts of law, and it is only within these constraints that the language can be used for symbolic purposes, that is, for making claims about power. In explaining the language which is used in courts of law, this argument runs, technical factors with regard to content provide a system of constraint which is hierarchically above symbolic factors. Even if the lawyers wished to simplify their language and so remove the power symbolism, it would be impossible for them to do so.

This assertion is to be doubted (but not dismissed out-of-hand) because it may itself be a claim about the power and the legitimacy of the institution (the law courts). Courts of law and councils have sanctions at their disposal, but at the same time their *raison d'être* is the process of persuasion and compromise, through which the contestants agree which verdict to accept, even when they do not feel pleased with it. Indeed, there are some councils which are virtually without sanctions, as in the case of the traditional village panchayat in India, and in practice, if certain contestants decide to ignore the decision, there is not very much that the court can do about it (Bailey 1960: 97, case 31). But even when there is an effective 'last resort' sanction, which transcends and eliminates the process of persuasion, courts or councils employing it too frequently are considered to be failures. Legislatures which do no more than regularly endorse decisions made elsewhere (the 'rubber stamp') or which too often permit decisions to be made through filibusters or walkouts become derisory.

The legitimacy of the institution and whatever willingness the contestants have to play within its rules are enhanced (up to a point) by the custom of giving the institution an aura of the sacred. The rules and the procedures, special patterns of seating, convention about clothing, which range from the medieval absurdities of an English judge to the feeling that someone who comes to a committee meeting on a hot day in bathing trunks is not to be taken seriously, all serve to bring home to the participants and others that the meetings of this institution are events of a kind different from 'ordinary life', something slightly mysterious and not to be questioned, an entity embodying an ultimate truth and an eternal verity, endowed with 'dignity' or even 'majesty' against which there should be no offense.

The effect of these ritual usages is to 'domesticate' the contestants to make them feel separated from the world of relatively narrow sectarian interests, from which they have come or which they represent, and to concentrate their feelings on the 'numinous' quality of the institution before which they are appearing.[11]

My argument is that I-speech policies are to be explained not so much by appeal to technical difficulties of communication caused by complicated subject matter, but rather by its symbolic functions. I-speech is one device among several for making apparent (or at least making a claim) that the institution stands above the conflicting sectarian interests in the society (where, of course, N-speech prevails). Certainly the capacity to communicate does have something to do with the matter, and the use of Pidgin is an obvious example. Given mutually unintelligible languages, without Pidgin there would be no communication and no debate. But my argument suggests that even if there were an N-speech available throughout the region, we should expect this speech to become increasingly modified for use in courts and legislatures until eventually an I-speech emerged.

I deal now with a second dimension in the relationship between councils and their clienteles. One was legitimacy: that is, the extent to which the clientele accept that institution as at least appropriate, and at most beyond question. The other dimension is power, which produces firstly a distinction between two types of council which I have elsewhere called 'arena' and 'elite' (Bailey 1965). Both these are 'superordinate' councils in the sense that the activities of their members vary according to their relationship with a congregation which, in varying degrees, acknowledges the council's authority. Elite councils exemplify the situation of oligarchy, and the members of such councils are not responsible to their clientele and take decisions, whether benign or otherwise, without being formally constrained by the wishes of those whom they rule. The other type of council does not wield power, but is rather a forum in which debate takes place between the representatives delegated by sectarian interests in the clientele. In this case the contestants in the arena must pay attention to the wishes of their clientele and their performance is judged by their capacity to satisfy these wishes.

A third situation is that of the 'subordinated' council, one which is under the close control of a superior authority. The local councils which are the creation of colonial governments and sometimes of the successors of these governments are examples. In their case the relevant 'congregation' is very often not the people whom they are supposed to represent or administer, but the controlling authority which overlooks their actions and their deliberations. In practice all but 'sovereign' councils are theoretically in this position (a committee is so, by definition), but I have separated out the 'subordinated' council as the one to which the regulations formally allow very little discretion to make their own decisions. My discussion mainly concerns 'superordinate' councils.

These two dimensions, in order to keep the matter simple, are given only two values: all power as against no power; and total legitimacy as against no legitimacy. It need hardly be said that this representation is a long way from the real world and that all kinds of 'mixes' are possible both as to the 'nature' of councils, measured by the statistical frequency of what they do, and as to normative claims about how the councils should be.

	0	Legitimacy	1
	1	2	Arena
Power			
	3	4	Elite
	1		

(2)

A few examples, however, will indicate that the real world does contain phenomena which roughly fit into one box or the other. For example, Bisipara's traditional panchayat can be placed firstly on the righthand side of the diagram, that of legitimacy, since the villagers, as clientele, do not readily countenance alternatives to it: with reference both to dispute settling and decisions about the management of village affairs, they usually place the alternative institutions (government courts of law, government officials, and the so-called statutory panchayat established under government auspices) on the lefthand (negative) side of the line of legitimacy. (It must be remembered that I am speaking of the period 1952–1959.) Secondly the traditional panchayat tends to operate in cell 2, as an arena institution, at least when discussing matters internal to the village (which is divided by factions [see Bailey (1968: 281–284)]). From the point of view of their subordination to the Administration (and especially after the creation of the statutory panchayats) the traditional panchayats were mostly in cell 1. Conversely the newly formed statutory panchayat, so the village cynics said, was extremely unresponsive to the needs and demands of the villagers, served the interests of its members alone and is therefore to be placed in cell 3, as a body exercising power but without the consent of those over whom the power was exercised. (Of course, its members might claim a place in cell 4.) Thirdly, returning to the traditional panchayat and going back, let us say, to the turn of the century, this institution, insofar as it affected the lives of the Untouchables of the village, is to be placed in cell 4, since that particular clientele neither envisaged an alternative institution nor had any voice in its proceedings. Lastly any council which its clientele and their representatives feel should be abolished, or changed, is to be placed in cell 1. For example, there were in India in the 1950s regional councils, intended to regulate affairs affecting more than one state. Orissa belonged to the Eastern Council and most Oriya politicians who bothered to talk about it considered it mostly a waste of time and potentially a nuisance or even occasionally a menace.

LANGUAGE-POLICY, POWER, AND LEGITIMACY

Some preliminary statements about the connections between language-policy and these different kinds of superordinate council are possible. I-speech is very likely to be found in cell 4. It is also possible in cell 2, if the sectarian interests, which encounter one another through their protagonists in the arena which 2 provides, are relatively well matched: in effect the participants agree to develop an esoteric language, so that no one of them will have an advantage over the others, because his language is used in the council and theirs is not: in doing so they signal their acceptance of the council as legitimate. Conversely, if power is not evenly distributed (as, for example, between Oriya and Hindi or between Oriya and any of the tribal languages in Orissa) then an M-speech policy is likely to predominate. A third possibility is that if the interested parties are evenly matched, and the technical apparatus is available, an A-speech policy may be adopted. On the lefthand side of the diagram, in cell 3 chances of I-speech are lower. A challenge to the existing elite may take the form of symbolically challenging its I-speech, a situation discussed later. As for cell 1, since the contestants doubt such a council's usefulness in achieving anything they need, they have no incentive to sacrifice an element of the legitimacy of their own sectarian interest,[12] by allowing someone else's language or an I-speech to be used.

But in certain situations a position in cell 1 will encourage the use of an I-speech. This is the case of *subordinate* councils. Fundamentally, I-speech is a way of selectively blocking communication. This act of blocking has both symbolic and practical aspects. (From the position of cell 4, the use of I-speech is both a symbolic way of telling the 'unwashed' to keep out, and of preventing them from offering communications or from eavesdropping; this exclusion has potentially disruptive consequences, as I will argue shortly.) From the position of cell 1, in the case of a subordinate council, the use of I-speech may also be a practical means of excluding those in power from gaining too close a look at what the members of the subordinated council have in mind. This is the familiar phenomenon of thieves' *argot*, and, indeed, of any minority which fears persecution. But, in addition to this practical protective function, here too there can be symbolic overtones: in particular the declaration to oneself and one's peers that outsiders really do not belong to the moral community: 'black speech' in contemporary America has this symbolic function, as does the prisoner-of-war game of addressing the foulest obscenities to a jailer (in a language which he does not understand) in the tones of utmost deference and respect. Academic disciplines too, especially perhaps the social sciences, are not entirely innocent of bolstering self-respect by making themselves emperor's clothes out of I-speech.

Since I-speech may be found both in cell 1 and cell 4, it suggest the following over-simple formula: extremes of power (very powerful or powerless) encourage a council to adopt an I-speech policy.

This formulation is insufficient (not wrong) because it deals with states of affairs rather than with movement or process. There are likely to be different claims about what the language policy should be. For example, Hindi speakers in the Orissa legislative assembly were making a statement about the position of Hindi as the national language of India: I suspect that some of those fluent speakers of Oriya who deliberately chose to address the House in English did so partly to assert that Hindi should *not* be the national language of India. (In other words, English should continue as a kind of I-speech in cell 2, thus denying unfair advantages to native speakers of Hindi, the M-language for India.) When such claims exist, then the probability is that some of them will succeed and so bring about changes in language policy, which either reflect or in some cases influence those changes in power and legitimacy which are summarized in the diagram.

Diagram 2, if we consider moves only between two cells (2 to 4 or 2 to 1 and so on) generates 12 kinds of shift, horizontal, vertical and diagonal. One task (for which I do not have time) would be to consider all 12 moves, to work out whether any are unthinkable, and then to see which of those possible in theory occur in practice. Further patterns can be generated if there is any reason to believe that a second move regularly accompanies the first. For example, a legitimate elite council (cell 4) may have its legitimacy challenged (cell 3) and may reemerge as a legitimate arena council (cell 2) in which the former members of 4 now represent only a sectarian interest (and agree that they do so) and enter into contest with their former challengers. Another likely shift would be from 4 to 3 to 1: that is, the outcome of the challenge is to reduce that council to an unimportant arena. Clearly many other shifts either in legitimacy or in power or in both can be envisaged.

Two different kinds of questions can be asked about such movements. Firstly we can treat the cells as representing the claims which people make about a council or a court. Such statements have two elements: firstly there is an assertion about what ought to be the nature of the council under consideration (that is, in which cell would a 'proper' council be placed); secondly the statement claims to define what situation in fact exists. If the two parts of the claim name different cells, then a shift is envisaged.

This mode of using the framework is potentially extremely complicated, and much more so than the one I will describe shortly. The complications arise because (given that one must explain why one claim rather than another is made) one man's claim will depend partly on what his opponent's claim was (or, even more difficult, what he expects it to be). Furthermore, if we treat the cells as claims, we become involved in questions of bluff. Certainly these questions will have to be faced at some stage, but at the beginning it will be easier to treat moves between cells as representing not claims but rather the outcomes of contests; what I have elsewhere called 'encounters' (Bailey 1969: 29, Ch. 6). For example, on meeting an instance of a move from cell 2 to cell 4, we ask: What has such a move to do with language policy?

The discussion which follows concerns superordinate councils.

FROM ARENA TO ELITE, BOTH LEGITIMATE (2 TO 4)

A legitimate council must be in some way distanced from its clientele, or rather from the particular sections of this clientele, since the councillors must be seen to stand at least partly for the whole society and not exclusively for particular sectarian interests: otherwise its legitimacy, the consent upon which the council depends, is diminished. Even in the case of arena councils, the members must be domesticated and re-educated so that at least some part of the sectarian value which they represent is sacrificed to create a whole. This process must lessen the hold which their clientele have over the councillors, and to this extent they move towards forming an elite council.

Members come to the Orissa Legislative Assembly, pledged to fight for the interests of their constituents (or of some section of them), and in varying degrees they learn to think of the interests of a larger collectivity. At least, when they are detected letting down their constituents, they claim to be thinking of the good of Orissa (although others might say that they are serving their own personal interests). Obviously the motivations for such behavior vary from one person to another, and are unlikely to be wholly one thing or the other even within a single person: but, I am arguing, because councils can only achieve legitimacy by separating themselves from their clientele, the council members must learn to serve the corporate interests of the council itself: and the more they do so, the more they transform it from being an arena council into an elite council.

Part of the process of re-education and domestication is learning to express oneself (and eventually to think) in I-speech. Of course, not everyone learns it to the same degree, and in any case the movement towards cell 4 is periodically interrupted by elections and, in places like Orissa, by not infrequent agitations designed to remind the legislators that they are there to represent sectarian interests. Nevertheless, once elected, for five years the effectiveness of the legislator depends on his ability to manipulate his fellow council members and the administrators, and the language which manipulates them is not N-speech but I-speech. By the use of this language, the legislator signals his worthiness to belong to the company of oligarchs. The more frequently he uses N-speech (unless he happens to be formidable because he really does have a power base among his clientele – typically shown by his capacity to organize agitations), he brands himzelf as the kind of outsider to whom no favors should be granted and from whom, when possible, people are tempted to withhold even his legitimate rights.

In fact the Orissa Legislative Assembly, at least at the time at which I knew it (1959), had made only the slightest move in the direction of cell 4. There were a number of reasons for this, in addition to the elections and agitations mentioned above. Firstly, there were not a few people who would have questioned my placing the Assembly on the righthand side of the diagram, indicating legitimacy. For many villagers it lay somewhere between cell 1 and cell 3, and this instilled in the legislators not only a feeling of personal insecurity but also some doubts about the legitimacy of the institution. Furthermore there were attacks from among the elite itself, questioning the value of the parliamentary form of democracy, in particular majority voting: prominent among them were followers of J. P. Narayan (Bailey 1965: 2–5). Some of the legislators themselves shared these views, especially when they were on the losing side in a vote. For many people, to get the institution firmly defined as part of cell 2 was task enough and any measures which were seen to separate each member from his own clientele (such as an increase in I-speech) endangered an already precarious legitimacy.

Furthermore, even if circumstances had been favorable for greater development of I-speech, most of the members would have had neither the time nor the sophistication to acquire very much of it.

The following propositions emerge from this discussion:

(1) In the case of an arena council, the legitimacy or usefulness of which is in some doubt in the minds of the clientele (a tendency towards cell 1), any striking development of I-speech will be a signal to the clientele that their representatives are no longer serving the clientele's interests (but possibly their own – cell 3). In this situation, since the clientele have the power, no development of I-speech is likely.

(2) Conversely, if the arena council is seen to serve a useful purpose (one thinks of the bargaining between trade union leaders and management in industry), then the clientele will give their representatives the right to operate in an I-speech, because this is the most effective way of getting the prizes, in spite of the fact that such speech lessens the hold which the clientele have upon their representatives and, in extreme cases, opens the way for these representatives to ally themselves horizontally (that is, with each other) and so take a move in the direction of becoming an elite council.

(3) The development of an I-speech is both a sign of that working of the iron law of oligarchy and a means of educating the oligarchs into accepting the legitimacy of their privileged position. This process can continue to the extent that oligarchs in fact have a collective basis of power, and that each one of them does not depend on his own sectarian support.

Similar propositions can be made about judicial institutions; for example about the courts which were in theory available to the villagers of Bisipara, when in dispute with one another.

In the 1950s the government set up statutory elected panchayats. I have remarked earlier that the Bisipara villagers classified their statutory panchayat in cell 3, as exercising totally illegitimate power and serving its own interests. The villagers believed that the government intended that this body of men should also act to settle disputes, but, as they said, they preferred to go to their own traditional panchayat. Strictly speaking, therefore, the question of the language used by the statutory panchayat in its judicial capacity must be hypothetical. By my reasoning, if they had attempted to copy the manner of government law courts (that is, develop an I-speech) they would have further undermined their own legitimacy.

To have been tolerated at all, they would have had to operate in N-speech.

There is no doubt that the traditional village panchayat was considered legitimate by the villagers. To be legitimate it had to distance itself from its clientele. But the distancing, so far as it went, was achieved not by developing a distinctive I-speech but by such devices as meeting in a sacred place and having certain rules of procedure (which is, in fact, a step in the direction of I-speech). But N-speech was in fact the medium of communication and this indicates that in the end the clientele (that is, the plaintiff and the defendant) are relatively powerful. In other words, such a panchayat lacks an efficient means of sanctioning people: for the most part it depends on getting wrongdoers to agree that they have done wrong. To have made claims through the use of I-speech to a cell 4 position, in the absence of other changes in power distribution, would have moved the council towards cell 3.

My third example is that of the government court, which has the power to tell a wrongdoer what he must do and punish him if he does not. These courts, compared to the traditional panchayat, employ I-speech, which can be used effectively only by trained personnel (petition writers, advocates and the judges and magistrates). They can afford to distance themselves from their clientele in this way because they have the power to do so. I-speech is a way of claiming or symbolizing both the neutrality of justice and, at the same time, the authority of the court: I-speech means 'numen'[13], at least in the eyes of the court itself.

To summarize. For any legitimate superordinate council cell 4 is a magnet towards which it is drawn. This process is reversed if the councillors are reminded, often enough, that they depend for power on those they represent (and, of course, if this happens to be true). In such situations I-speech has two kinds of significance: claims for and against it are symbolic statements about the power context in which the council operates and its increasing use is evidence that the council's position is moving from arena (2) towards elite (4). Secondly the I-speech itself is a kind of power resource, for the simple reason that I-speech contributes towards legitimacy (up to a point) and legitimate power is less costly than contested power (that is, legitimacy frees political resources for investment elsewhere).

In the next section we consider what happens when legitimacy is challenged.

FROM LEGITIMATE TO CONTESTED SITUATIONS

If councils and courts which are accepted by their congregations as legitimate tend to move towards cell 4, it follows that any *reverse* is not a tendency but occurs only when someone takes steps to bring it about. Can such a challenge be represented merely as a move from 4 back towards 2, or does the very fact of contest move the council, at least for the time being, into cell 3? If the latter is correct, the familiar distinction between rebellion and revolution is over-simplified, because all situations of rebellion have in them a strand of revolution. This comes about in the following way: the rebels may claim that they fully accept the present institutions and wish only to remove the incumbents who are doing a bad job; the riposte of those in power must be that they themselves are in fact doing a good job and therefore the claim of the so called rebels to respect existing institutions must be false and they are in fact revolutionaries.

Let us explore the situation further. I-speech encourages the tendency to move from cell 2 to cell 4, and this movement becomes more dangerous the further it goes. Several steps are needed to set out this argument. Firstly (and by definition), a council or a committee or a court has a congregation. I do not mean that it is necessarily responsible to outsiders, but I do mean that its actions and decisions have consequences for that congregation and there is therefore always the possibility of 'feedback'. The purely 'elite' council, having absolute power over a congregation, is useful for thinking but certainly has never existed. It follows that all kinds of council, in varying degrees according to the cell in which they are placed, need to take some account of the effect their decisions have upon the congregation, because the reactions of the members of this congregation may in turn affect the council.

The intensification of I-speech renders councils and courts progressively more insensitive to the fate of congregations. Having one's own language insulates one from those who do not speak that language, and, more importantly, the language sets constraint upon the kinds of messages that can be fed back to the councillors. I-speech is above all a mechanism for excluding things: excluding not only messages, but also people and ideas and change itself. By its very nature it is a device for putting an end to argument, like the Swat Saint who holds up the Koran (Can he read it?) and ends an argument by saying 'This is Islamic law . . .!' (Barth 1959: 98). Brahmans are said to do the same with Sanskrit texts.[14] Indeed, any fully developed I-speech is filled with efficient ways of getting quickly to uncontestable normative themes, and thus silencing the opposition by making them appear in favor of sin. An attempt to do this in N-speech must, other things being equal, be less effective because N-speech lacks the required numinous quality, and is ill-adapted for the expression of 'eternal verities'.

The same stablilizing authoritarianism is achieved in the recruitment of persons. Only those who speak the language and who therefore see the world in the same way can find a place among the elite. As I-speech comes more into being, the degree of challenge *within the system* diminishes, since the challengers have to make use of I-speech and must of necessity become like the incumbents. This lies behind the familiar complaint (not always accurate) that in parliamentary democracies there is never very much to choose between one party or the other.

The outcome is that when a council reaches reaches the point of being too insensitive to what is happening to its congregation, the message of the danger cannot be transmitted in I-speech. In other words, up to a point I-speech promotes legitimacy and beyond that point, where communication (in a broad sense) has stopped, the effect is the opposite: the council ceases to be legitimate because the congregation is not getting what it wants.

Such a situation is revolutionary. This does not necessarily mean literal violence and, indeed, our discussion does not deal with that situation. We envisage contests being carried on still in words and debate, but if the analysis given above is correct, it follows that certain fundamental rules of debate already encoded in the existing I-speech must be abolished. Or, to put it another way, since the existing I-speech cannot carry the message which the protestors want to deliver, if there is to be any debate at all, it must tend to use an N-speech.

There are two other reasons why such situations encourage at least the temporary use of N-speech. Firstly the reason for the protest is the failure of the elite council to perceive the effects of their decisions on the congregation. In other words, to the extent that there is a protest, the elite have mis-read the power distribution and assumed a greater degree of consent than existed. The congregation turns out to be a locus of power and those who emerged to lead the protest will be anxious to symbolize their responsiveness to the congregation's needs. N-speech is clearly an appropriate code for doing this.

The former elite (now a contested ruling group located, initially at least, in cell 3) must acquiesce in the use of N-speech, if they elect to have a debate rather than resort to force. If they do so, to that extent they *implicitly* acknowledge (although they may claim otherwise) that they are no longer *numen* (representing the collectivity) but are in fact, as their opponents allege, one among several interested sectarian parties, bargaining with others to get the best advantage for themselves, and not laying down the law for all concerned from the position of a neutral and disinterested authority.

The second reason why N-speech is likely in such situations is that I-speech is one element in the *sacra* which buttressed the legitimacy of the elite while it was still in cell 4. An open contempt for the *sacra,* including the I-speech, is what is most strikingly revolutionary in such situations. This is the familiar phenomenon of four-letter words on august occasions in august institutions or of the studied disrespect sometimes shown to parliamentary institutions by newly-established dictators.

To summarize. The more developed and esoteric the form of I-speech, the more likely are its users to be insulated from the real world, and the less likely is an orderly (that is, within the canons of I-speech itself) move back towards cell 2. Elite councils do not voluntarily transform themselves into arena councils. When such transformations occur, they take place via cell 3: that is, the encrustation of I-speech (and I-think and I-culture) must be chipped away by an episode of relative disorder and revolution before a new legitimacy can be created for an arena council (cell 2): then the whole process can begin over again.

CONCLUSION

My discussion has generated questions rather than answers. For example, I do not claim that councils must follow this path from 2 to 4 to 3 and so on. All the framework suggests is that, of a given situation, one can ask about the extent to which these paths are being followed and about the extent to which the situation, at any one time, is symbolized by the actual use of or by a campaign to promote the use of one or another mix of I-speech and N-speech.

I think it is also clear that the mainsprings of such movements are not to be found in language, and certainly not in language alone. Language policy symbolizes a power-legitimacy situation, or a claim about what the situation is or should be. To this extent it may also be instrumental, a way of altering situations. Languages of themselves also create certain situations, as in the 'sealing-off tendencies' of I-speech. But language is only one among many political resources, and indeed (unless we take 'language' in the very broadest sense of any kind of message-exchange) one among many ways of symbolizing political claims. We can point out the effect of an I-speech policy or an N-speech policy, or we can deduce from the fact that one or other of these policies is in force what the pattern of power distribution must be, but it is clear that when we ask these questions or make these statements about actual situations, we can only predict their outcomes by taking into account many other factors (both symbolic and otherwise) besides language distribution.

ACKNOWLEDGEMENTS

I offer my thanks to those who assisted my attempts to unravel some of the confusions in this essay. Besides those who took part in the conference, my gratitude goes also to colleagues at UCSD: David Jordan, Ted Schwartz, and Mel Spiro.

NOTES

1. Those who think of committee and council deliberations as the exudation of common wisdom may find this statement in poor taste. I do not mean that every such gathering is likely to be a slanging match: only that decisions are reached by coming to a 'verdict' which selects between two or more different and contested possibilities.
2. This qualifying phrase is inserted in order to cover those many situations in which deliberations meander on and vanish into the sand, no decision having been reached. Councils which favor decisions by consensus are especially likely to behave in this way. Alternatively one might say that the implicit decision is to reach no decision (Bailey 1965).
3. The background to these examples, together with a more detailed description of them, will be found in Bailey (1957, 1960). A summary account is given in Bailey (1964).
4. See Bailey (1963), especially Chapter 7.
5. According to the *Statistical Outline of Orissa (1957),* in a population of around 15 million, there were 12 million Oriya speakers, 300,000 Telugu speakers, 120,000 Hindi speakers, 90,000 Bengali speakers, and the bulk of the remainder spoke one or another of about 20 tribal languages, the largest of which was Kond (listed as Konda, Kui, and Kondh) with around 500,000 speakers.
6. Article 186 in the *Rules of Procedure* states: 'The business of the Assembly shall be transacted in English provided that any memberr may address the Assembly in Oriya or in Hindi and further that the Speaker may permit any member who cannot adequately express himself in any of the aforesaid languages to address the Assembly in his mother-tongue.'
7. So far as I can see from the printed records in my possession, questions asked by those MLAs who habitually spoke Hindi were translated and printed in Oriya.
8. My authority for this is a manuscript on the Konds written by H. W. Alderson, who served as Sub-Divisional Officer in the Kondmals between 1929 and 1936. He records that the Angul Laws Regulations of 1897 (the Kondmals was then part of Angul District), while intended to be a 'charter for the peoples' liberties', were based upon regulations drawn up for Baluchistan: thus their application called for frequent acts of translation and so allowed local officers considerable discretion in their application.
9. It is, of course, too simple to suppose that particular institutions have single language-policies. See the discussion below.
10. I have distinguished I-speech from M-speech according to the numbers of people allowed to use their 'native' speech: thus in the case of A-speech, notionally everyone has this right; in the case of M-speech, the largest single group is privileged; and in the case of I-speech, because of the relatively heavy investment in learning it, only a skilled few are permitted *direct*

participation in courts or councils. This dimension, therefore, is sociolinguistic rather than strictly linguistic.

An alternative strategy, which I have neither the skill nor the time to follow, would be to construct, for particular cultures, strictly linguistic characteristics for I-speech, A-speech, and M-speech: for example, A-speech, through the need to communicate with people speaking a different language, might become a 'grunt' language, excessively simple and able to convey only a restricted range of messages; M-speech, on the other hand, being a natural language may be the vehicle for song and poetry, sophisticated and subtle thoughts, shaded nuances and so on, a language good for playing upon the emotions; finally, following this flight of fancy, I-speech is also subtle and sophisticated, but adapted solely to the matter in hand (conducting contests and determining their result), a language of logic and intellect rather than of the emotions.

11. See Bailey (1972b). *Numen* ('nod', 'command', 'will', 'the divine will', the 'supreme authority', etc.) stands for the interests of the collectivity in adjudicating between two contestants.
12. Compare Leach (1954: 290). When there are constant changes in political federations, 'peculiarity of language serves to uphold the continuing unity of the village community in the face of rapid shifts of power in the external political world.'
13. See note 11.
14. A one-time colleague, a Sanskritist, encountered great resistance to this researches from certain Brahmans in Nepal. It transpired that they feared that he would discover and reveal that they were unable to read the sacred books (in Sanskrit) with which they impressed their clientele.

PART THREE

Papua New Guinea

Introduction to Part Three

The linguistic situation in Papua New Guinea differs from that of both Tanzania and India. The political uses to which language is put, however, bear a striking resemblance to those found in the other two countries.

In Chapter 14, Sankoff shows how social processes seize upon linguistic disparities and systematically manipulate them into highly structured systems of speech varieties which mirror and reinforce social class and power distinctions. In pre-colonial times, Papua New Guinea exhibited extreme linguistic diversity, but very little linguistic inequality. Papua New Guinea, with a population of just over two million, has more than seven hundred separate languages. Today, unlike the pre-colonial situation, this diversity has become the basis for linguistic stratification. Drawing on her knowledge of the Buang villages of Morobe District, Sankoff shows how the coming of colonialism began to transform the configuration of political power at the local level and consequently the linguistic patterns. Despite the clear stratification between Europeans and New Guineans, vertical mobility was possible for those indigenes who had the skills which were requisite in a colonial economy. The ability to speak a pidgin was such an avenue to mobility. In the more recent past, knowledge of such languages was not enough – English now overlays the Papua New Guinean linguistic mosaic. English has become the elite language, and one pidgin, *Tok Pisin,* has become the language of solidarity among the urban population.

The literature on political development makes the assumption that the existence of multiple languages in a country represents a barrier to vertical and horizontal communication and integration. Staats and

Conti, in Chapter 15, considering the evolution of contemporary councils and courts in Papua New Guinea, argue as Sankoff did that multiple languages were not a barrier in pre-colonial times, but that they have increasingly become so. In spite of great variation in indigenous political forms, Staats and Conti find that smallness of scale, absense of hereditary leaders, and existence of 'big men' distinguish New Guinea societies from those of Tanzania and India. The establishment of colonial control over these societies meant that new political offices were superimposed on existing ones and that the bases of authority of 'big men' were undercut. The contemporary task of the Papua New Guinea government is the blending of indigenous and colonial political cultures – a task deeply intertwined with the complexities of the linguistic profile of Papua New Guinea in the 1970s.

Lang's discussion in Chapter 16 of the role of interpreters in local courts in New Guinea provides ample evidence for the points raised in the two overview chapters. Before the arrival of the modern colonial powers, interpreters as such did not exist – people either made use of trade languages, they learned each other's languages, or they conducted intersocietal affairs at a non-verbal level. There was, in short, no single language whose superiority was acknowledged and whose use conferred social power on the user. Colonial officials relied on a few trusted individuals to act as intermediaries between themselves and the native population. These interpreters had access to new ideas and new contacts, but especially they had a new ability in language which was a resource they could put to use in multiple contexts. For example, over ten percent of the members of the present House of Assembly, Lang points out, are former interpreters. Lang's analysis is directed to the role of the court interpreters. His thesis is that the interpreter is both translator proper and intermediary – a position, he argues, which is a function of the interpreter's own self-perception reinforced by the behavior of his clients.

Salisbury, in Chapter 17, is concerned with a specific case of bilingualism in New Guinea, that of the Tolai, the wealthiest, best educated, and politically most advanced of all the New Guinea ethnic groups. In the Tolai case, the usual pattern whereby a national language steadily preempts the growing number of situations that are defined as interlingual is qualified. The Tolai experience confirms the proposition that the specialization of a language to particular domains is indeed a comparatively stable pattern of coping with the pressure of several languages. But it is not inevitable that it is the vernacular which becomes more restrictive. The attitude toward the national language determines whether it is the language that expands or not. If the language is disvalued, as Tok Pisin was between 1920 and 1960, then its use will be the one that is limited to the local area. If the language is highly valued, as was the case for Tok Pisin even relative to English in 1971, then that language can maintain its wide usage and may even become a special elite language. Bilingualism may thus serve as a useful skill to preserve the exclusiveness of the group of monolinguals.

GILLIAN SANKOFF

14

Political Power and Linguistic Inequality in Papua New Guinea

Perhaps the major task of sociolinguistics is to reconcile the essentially neutral, or arbitrary, nature of linguistic difference and of linguistic change, with the social stratification of languages and levels of speech unmistakeable in any complex speech community. Indulging in personification, we might term this the study of how social processes seize upon linguistic disparities which are intrinsically symmetric, and upon innocuous linguistic processes constantly operating in any language, and systematically manipulate them into a highly structured system of speech varieties which mirrors and reinforces social class and power distinctions. The object of this essay is to focus upon some of these transformations as I have studied them in Papua New Guinea. The theme is general, though I will draw most heavily on my own experience in Lae, in the Buang area (Mumeng Subdistrict, Morobe District), and in the Morobe District in general.[2]

In the next section I will review some notions of linguistic relativity and show how and to what extent these are exemplified by the socially symmetric relationship of languages and dialects in the precolonial situation, or, at present, among local languages. In the third section I will briefly summarize the state of sociolinguistic knowledge about the other extreme: the class structure of language in present-day urban North America. In the fourth section I will sketch typical political organization at the village level in New Guinea, and the changes which have occurred in the power structure since the colonial period. The fifth section will discuss rhetorical aspects of political behavior and will trace the integration of the dichotomy between local languages (Tok Ples) and the colonial lingua franca (Tok Pisin)[3] into relationships of power and authority. Finally, in the last section, I will discuss the deepening of linguistic stratification accompanying the current spread of English.

I should point out that I have not confined my analysis to language usage in village meetings, village courts, and other village bodies, and thereby avoid at least two misleading assumptions: (1) that ultimate or at least the major political decisions are made within such institutions; and (2) that such institutions are recognized by all as the legitimate structures in which political problems are concentrated. I hope my attempt at a power and class analysis of language will help put these questions in a broader perspective.

LINGUISTIC RELATIVITY AND VILLAGE NEW GUINEA

The basic tenet of linguistic relativity is that all natural languages are on an equal footing in terms of their capacities for human communication. There is no denying, of course, that some languages are used in cultural contexts and for purposes for which other languages are not, and that they are to some extent adapted or specialized to these purposes and contexts. This adaptation is, however, largely a matter of lexical proliferation and stylistic elaboration; there is no evidence that in terms of the basic machinery of a language considered as a code for transmitting messages, i.e. the phonology, morphology, syntax, or even the overall semantic organization, any one language is inherently superior, more logical, accurate or efficient, or in any way preferable to any other language. Thus stereotypes such as that French is a particularly beautiful or precise language, that English is inherently better suited to scientific thinking, that non-standard English is illogical, etc., have no basis in linguistic science. No language, by virtue of its inherent structure, bestows any general cognitive advantage on its speakers.

Extreme linguistic relativism needs a good deal of qualification, such as is provided by the evolutionary perspective of Berlin and Kay (1969), Kay (1971), Berlin (1972), or the functionally adaptive and ethnographic perspectives of Hymes (1961; 1966; 1972). Situations of prolonged bilingualism (Gumperz and Wilson 1971), situations of language contact, of the use of *lingue franche* and especially of

Map 14.1 *Linguistic divisions of Papua New Guinea*

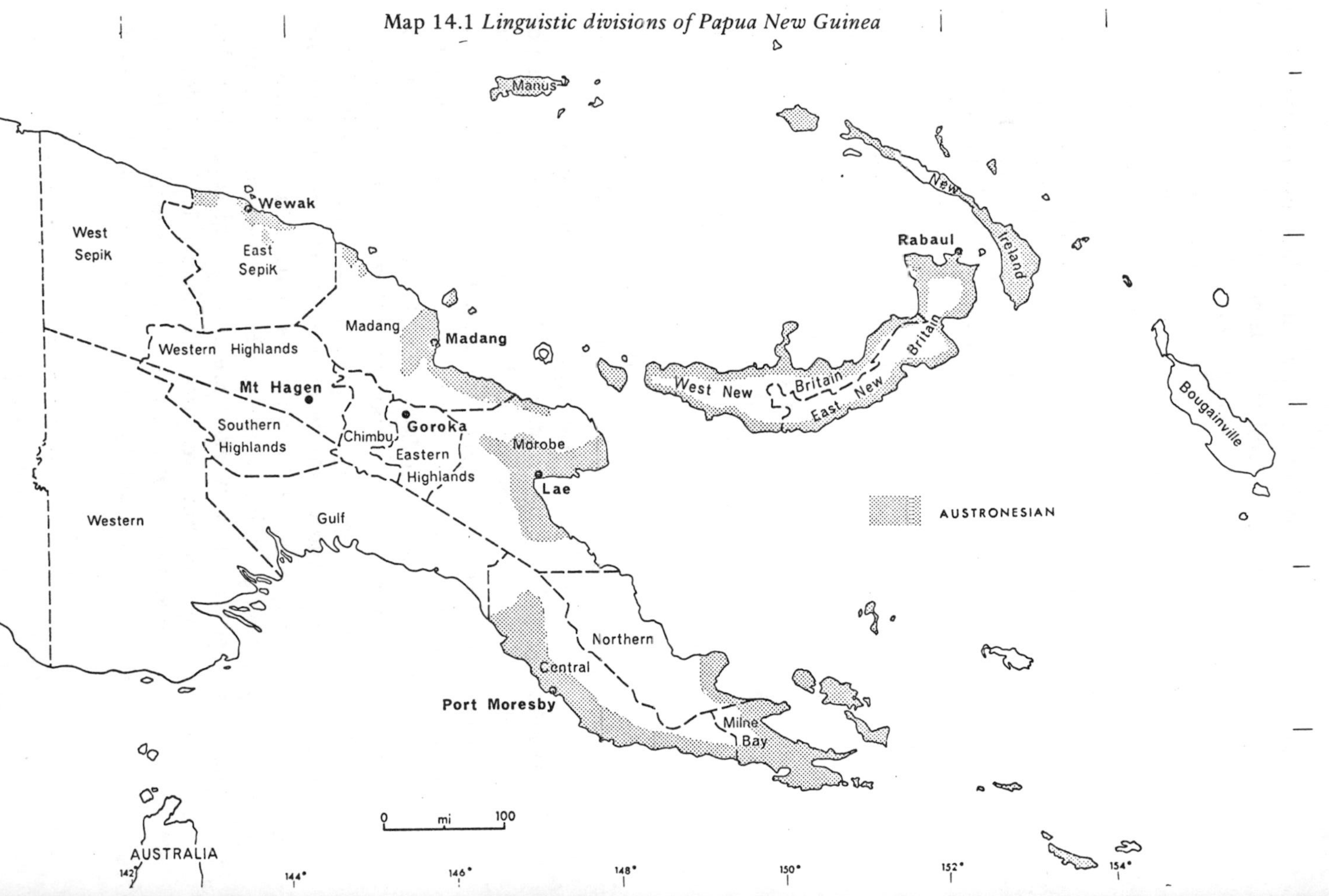

pidgins seem to lead to certain types of reduction in surface complexities of the languages used (Ferguson 1971; Kay and Sankoff 1972; Hymes 1971; Traugott 1973). Nevertheless it is important to stress the great consensus among linguists regarding the scientific validity of the relativist position on grammar, viewed as a code or instrument for communication – a point that few non-linguists realize.

Anyone familiar with western speech communities knows that in various periods and in various regions, people have been willing to accept the superiority of Greek, Latin, French, German, English, or Russian over their own language as being linguistically justified. Even more widespread are opinions that Parisian French, Oxford English, High German, etc., are inherently more comprehensible, more logical, and more beautiful than provincial or non-standard varieties and dialects. The historical record incontrovertibly shows that these languages and varieties have spread because of the political and economic dominance of their speakers, and one would be hard put to argue that, for example, the Germanic dialects were better adapted to warfare and thus helped their speakers to dominate the Celts. But the *attitudes* and *opinions* of those who come to accept the 'superiority' of these various languages and varieties are not solely or even largely a matter of accepting a common standard for wider communication purposes, but are based above all on scientifically unfounded notions of structural and logical superiority. Indeed it is common to attribute the political and economic inferiority of speakers of non-standard varieties to mental and communicative incapabilities deriving from sloppy or illogical language, as the abundant literature on compensatory language education programs alone would attest.

The linguistic situation in Papua New Guinea, including attitudes towards language, has been strikingly different from the picture I have just painted. Especially in pre-colonial times, a situation of extreme diversity, but very little inequality, had not been obscured by imperialism, social stratification, or nationalism. The linguistic diversity and the great differences in even major grammatical features between languages whose speakers are in geographical proximity have been noted by numerous authors (cf. Capell 1971; Hooley and McElhanon 1970; Wurm 1971a). These major language differences, it should be noted, occur among groups having very similar cultures.

Wurm (1960: 129) estimates approximately 700 separate languages for Papua New Guinea. With a total population of approximately 2,150,000 (Territory of Papua and New Guinea Population Census 1966, Preliminary Bulletin No. 20), this averages out to about one language per 3,000 people. As Wurm (1960: 132) points out, however, the distribution is fairly uneven, with almost a million people speaking just over 100 languages (an average of 10,000 people per language), and with some languages claiming as many as 60,000 (Chimbu) or 100,000 (Enga dialects). Many of the remaining 500 languages have very few speakers, 'mostly ranging from a few dozen to a few hundred' (Wurm 1960: 133).

The languages of Papua New Guinea belong to two large language families: the Austronesian languages which are distributed throughout the Pacific; and the non-Austronesian or Papuan languages, unrelated to any other known language family. The largest language groups are mainly Papuan, found predominantly in the center of the Papua New Guinea mainland as well as in the centers of many of the smaller islands. Though not all languages in the coastal areas are Austronesian, this is where they are concentrated, the only large inland groups of Austronesian speakers being in the Markham Valley and the subcoastal areas of the southern Morobe District. Many Austronesian groups are very small pockets on the coast, surrounded by Papuan speakers. This distribution tends to suggest that Austronesian speaking peoples arrived in Melanesia after the Papuan speakers, occupying many of the coastal areas and forcing Papuan speakers inland. The large size of many of the interior Papuan speaking groups in the Highlands would also suggest a relatively recent and rapid expansion.

In most areas other than the wide valleys of the Highlands, then, linguistic groups tend to be relatively small, and even withing the Highlands, dialect differentiation is such that neighboring groups often speak perceptibly different dialects. Thus it is a reasonable assumption that most New Guineans living before the colonial period had personal experience of linguistic diversity, without having ventured very far from their home villages. We may well ask, however, what this linguistic diversity implied in social terms, i.e. what were the social parameters which made for a considerable degree of linguistic diversity, coupled with a fair degree of knowledge of other varieties on the part of many people.

Haudricourt (1961) has described a state of what he called 'egalitarian bilingualism' in precolonial New Caledonia, resulting from social contacts such as intermarriage between small groups. Hollyman (1962) sees this type of bilingualism as responsible for a tendency he has noted in some Melanesian languages toward extensive borrowing, particularly at the phonological and lexical levels. Certainly neighboring groups in Papua New Guinea had contact througth intermarriage, trade, and warfare, leading to a certain amount of bilingualism or competence in other dialects, depending on the degree of linguistic difference among neighboring groups. Clearly women who married into other language or other dialect villages would have this competence, as might their children, particularly if visiting of affines were kept up. And the fact that linguistic differentiation exists even on the level of neighboring villages speaking the same 'dialect' has been pointed to in several studies of disparate geographical areas and language groups including the Eastern Highlands Kainantu area (McKaughan 1964; 1971), the Dani in West Irian (Bromley 1967), both Papuan speaking groups, and the Austronesian Buang of the Huon Gulf hinterland (Sankoff 1968; 1969). On bilingualism in the Highlands, see Wurm and Laycock (1961). Thus it is quite possible that a sizeable minority of New Guinean women have had the experience of being at least to some degree linguistic 'foreigners' in the village into which they have married.

Given this general situation, we might well ask why such contacts did not lead to a *lessening* of linguistic differences, through dialect or language leveling. Here we may find that the explanation lies at least in part in cultural attitudes and behavior with respect to language. Salisbury (1962), for example, describes the importance which the Siane attach to the distinctiveness of their own language from neighboring languages. Given the degree of bilingualism Salisbury describes for the Siane, it appears that contacts with and awareness of other languages have led not to leveling but to heightened consciousness of and pride in difference.[4]

This type of situation also prevails among speakers of Buang, a total population of approximately 8,000–9,000 whose traditional home is along the slopes of the Snake River Valley in the Morobe District southwest of Lae. Twenty-three villages are strung out over a distance of approximately fifteen miles, and they are divided into three major dialects recognized by all: the eight headwaters villages speaking a dialect we shall refer to as A, the ten central villages speaking dialect B, and the five lower villages speaking dialect C, a 'dialect' (according to the folk view) which is sufficiently different to rank as a separate language (Sankoff 1968, 1969; Hooley and McElhanon 1970). Within each of A, B, and C, speakers recognize subgroupings which further differentiate each dialect. Features they use in illustrating differences include lexical items, vowel length and diphthongization, and consonant shifts and correspondences. Thus a resident of a village in dialect A is likely to state that there are three main divisions of A, citing lexical and phonological differences; that there is another dialect B, which is somewhat more difficult to understand, again citing lexical and phonological differences; and that there is a third dialect C which is quite difficult to understand, citing probably only one or two lexical differences.

Knowledge of these related language varieties fades out with distance, but within such a system of recognizably related varieties, speakers will insist that their own variety is the best, that it is the easiest and clearest to understand, that it is in fact understood by people from miles around, that it is the easiest to learn, and so on. Other varieties are judged to be some kind of corruption or aberration from the speaker's own, and imitations occasion much mirth on the part of any local audience. The point is that each village feels its own dialect to be the best, and accentuates its particular features especially in contrast with those other varieties it is most familiar with, i.e. the closest ones, geographically and usually also in terms of degree of similarity.

This situation is, in a sense, a confirmation of the relativist position. Here language diversity is at least as marked as in Europe, for example, but lacking stratified societies, far-reaching empires, and nationalist consciousness, this horizontal diversity is not accompanied by any linguistic stratification. Everyone is ethnocentric about his own variety, but since the groups which agree with him, and analogous groups, are all very small, since people know that other people think their own is the best, and since within a region there is no consensus that a particular variety is the best, the situation is certainly an egalitarian one.

The question of whether in pre-colonial times there existed any non-egalitarian situations with respect to language use and attitudes brings forth three possible affirmative answers, all of which revolve around the idea of language as a resource. The language of ritual, of sorcery and of spells has been discussed in several of the classic ethnographies on Papua and New Guinea, the best known being Malinowski's *Coral Gardens and their Magic,* Volume 2 (1935). Malinowski's analysis of the language of Trobriand magic stresses the importance of what he calls 'weirdness' in giving language its power. He notes that 'a great deal of the vocabulary of magic, its grammar and its prosody, falls into line with the deeply ingrained belief that magical speech must be cast in another mould, because it is derived from other sources and produces different effects from ordinary speech' (p. 218).

Nevertheless, his analysis of the magical formulae shows that magical language is based on ordinary language, but involves lexical, phonological, and grammatical elaboration, including literary devices such as 'use of metaphor, opposition, repetition, negative comparison, imperative and question with answer' (p. 222). There is, to my knowledge, no other description, for any other language of Papua New Guinea, of the exact nature of a ritual speech variety and of its differences from everyday speech as detailed as Malinowski's Trobriand analysis. Various authors mention 'esoteric formulae' or 'nonsense syllables' when discussing spells; the language used may be supposed to be that of the gods or ghosts, but not that of other groups. Fortune, for example, in *Sorcerers of Dobu,* states that: 'The words of Dobuan magic are not words of ordinary speech. They form a secret esoteric language, a language of power (1963: 130).'

Differential access to magical language and the power it brings may be determined by sex, as well as by social position and personality, attributes which have to do with whether or not, or to what extent, and individual is taught such language by local experts. In any case, such language does not appear to constitute an entirely separate code, but to be either limited in scope (sets of nonsense syllables) or some sort of elaboration or alteration of normal speech as in the Trobriand case.

The second case of a non-egalitarian situation with respect to language concerns the linguistic skills of political and economic leaders in pre-colonial Papua New Guinea. It appears that many such men may have possessed extraordinary linguistic resources, both in terms of rhetorical skills and in terms of bilingualism. Salisbury (1962) mentions bilingualism as a high-status characteristic among Siane, and biographical material on some current leaders in New Guinea also tends to give supporting evidence. Handabe Tiabe (Member of the House of Assembly, Tari Open Electorate, 1964–1967) would appear to fit into the category of a 'traditional leader' (Hughes and Van der Veur 1965: 408). He cannot speak Tok Pisin or Police Motu, but his multilingualism in Tari area languages is probably a mark of local big man status, and may well have helped to increase his vote among linguistic groups other than his own. Another contemporary politician noted for his linguistic skills in local languages is Stoi Umut, former Rai Coast Open Member of the House of Assembly. Harding (1965: 199) notes that Umut's trilinguality in Komba, Selepet, and Timbe is an important aspect of the ethnic base of his popularity. The multilingualism of these current politicians in local languages offers some indication that the traditional leaders of the past also outstripped their fellows in such skills. The Gahuku leader Makis (Read 1965) would appear to be one example.

Bilingualism was useful to traditional big men in at least two ways: most obviously as a means of talking with politicians and others away from home, and second as one in a battery of rhetorical skills used in speechmaking in their own villages or areas. Skill in oratory has long been recognized as a crucial attribute of Melanesian big men, who must know when to speak in public (optimally after consensus has been reached so as not to lose face by taking an unpopular position), how to harangue and convince an audience, how to hold the floor without being interrupted (speaking forcefully, articulately, retaining the audience's interest), and so on.

A third situation of linguistic inequality could be seen in the realm of commerce. Knowledge of the lingua franca of the traders in the coastal areas where long distance trading circuits were in operation was obviously an advantage and probably formed the only clear case where a particular language was commonly agreed to be in ascension or to have higher status than others. It is important to note, however, that this case remains within the entirely practical realm of language as a resource. Trading visits were often of fairly long duration, and of considerable economic and social importance. To be able to communicate with the traders was advantageous, but learning 'their' language (generally a pidginized version thereof) did not carry the added connotations that 'their' language was in any way inherently better. Even magical language could be seen in this light and probably was, since spells had commercial value in many areas of Papua New Guinea, and were a means or resource to be applied to a particular end.

In summary, it would appear that the best reconstruction we can make of the pre-colonial sociolinguistic situation is one in which the basic relationship of languages and dialects was a socially symmetric one. Language was viewed as being essentially pragmatic, as means to communicate with natural or supernatural beings, whether local or foreign and people learned and used languages as a function of their personal exposure and interest. Differential size of the various language groups can be seen therefore not as a result of the general prestige and/or economic utility of these languages, but rather as a result of the differential rate of expansion of the populations speaking them and of their success in competing with other populations for material resources such as land.

In the few situations where linguistic differences within a community displayed a nascent correlation with power differentials, it is clear that the language disparities must be considered to be the dependent variable. Aggressive and intelligent individuals would learn ritual languages, *lingue franche,* neighboring languages, etc., as just one aspect of their economic and political striving. Moreover, whereas rhetorical skills are directly observable, power must be inferred rather indirectly. Hence it is difficult to know whether rhetorical talents lead to political power, or whether, as is more likely, the oratorical behavior of leaders is in part a result of the deliberate development of rhetorical skills by aspirants to leadership positions, and in part a reflection of the self-confidence of leaders and of the respect they enjoy within their communities as a result of their political or economic position. This does not, I believe, contradict Reay's (1959: Ch.5; 1964) observations about the importance of rhetorical skills as a prerequisite for Kuma leadership. Reay notes that Kuma rhetoric is a highly developed art, and that 'a man who makes accomplished speeches is likely to be sought as a leader in public affairs' (1964: 244). She also gives evidence, however, that men who seek positions of leadership work hard to practice their rhetorical skills (cf. the case cited in 1964: 251); the Kuma 'Rhetoric Thumper' was thus not only in important ways an achieved position, but the linguistic skills it demanded were also consciously developed by aspiring politicians.

THE SOCIAL STRATIFICATION OF LANGUAGE

The New Guinea case described in the preceding section showed that language is not only a resource but also a symbol of identity. The question we now wish to ask is under what circumstances does the identity function become inverted in such a way that a particular group becomes alienated from its own language or language variety and begins to regard it as inferior to some other language or language variety. Do these tend to be circumstances in which it is quite clear that some other group, speaking some other language or language variety, is economically and politically dominant? Are there circumstances in which access to a particular language or language variety works to create and maintain real differences in power and wealth?

In the same way that even slight speech differences in Papua New Guinea serve to place an individual in terms of his geographical origin, language is a sensitive indicator of social position (and to some extent geographical origin) in contemporary North America. Particular varieties of or features in English are associated with various ethnic and racial groups, and there are some marked regional differences. Even holding constant race, geography, and ethnic groups, linguistic differences have also been found to correlate with class in several studies of large urban centers (e.g. Labov 1966a; Cedergren 1972; Sankoff and Cedergren 1971). The linguistic features which differentiate the population in this way often seem to be arbitrary and quite inconsequential from the point of view of communication. Thus pronunciation of /r/ in preconsonantal and final position (e.g. 'cart' and 'car', respectively) has been at various times a low and a high prestige feature in American English (McDavid 1948).

A phenomenon which regularly co-occurs with class-based differentiation of speech is an attitude of linguistic insecurity and linguistic alienation on the part of at least some of those who speak non-prestige varieties. The well known hypercorrection of some segments of the 'middle' class and of people who have undergone rapid social mobility without adequate opportunity to learn the linguistic behavior appropriate to their new station is evidence of such insecurity. People recognize that they have stigmatized features in their speech, but in lamenting this state of affairs, the way they talk about it tends to show that they *accept* a standard external to their own behavior; that is, they acquiesce in another group's definition of features in their speech or of the whole code itself as being inherently inferior (Labov 1966b; Laberge and Chaisson-Lavoie 1971). This is a type of 'mystification' in which a symbol (language, or particular features of language) takes on *in its own right* the negative evaluation of the object (in this case a group of people) with which it has become associated. Acceptance of such mystification is self-defeating, since other symbols can always be found if and when the group in question manages to alter the present set of offending behaviors.[5]

There are two mutually reinforcing phenomena here: first, the extent to which lack of knowledge of a particular language or language variety blocks access to other resources or goods within a society – education, jobs, wealth, political positions, and so on; and second, the extent to which the inferior political and economic position of a particular group results in a devaluing of its language or language variety, and in feelings of inferiority and worthlessness on the part of its speakers. In its extreme form, this set of attitudes is similar to the 'complexe de colonisé' described by Fanon (1961). A quotation from a volume published by the Académie canadienne-française illustrates this syndrome with respect to Quebec or Canadian French:

'J'affirme que la langue n'est pas d'abord un moyen de communication mais bien l'outil de la pensée. La pauvreté d'expression que l'on constate chez les nôtres, leurs lacunes dans les domaines culturels, leur impuissance à créer, proviennent d'une incapacité de concevoir. Une langue amoindrie, rapetissée, déformée, tronquée et méconaissable, ne produira jamais que des cerveaux incultes' (Roy 1960: 112).

(*Translation:* I maintain that language is not principally a means of communication, but in fact the vehicle of thought. The poverty of expression which we note among our own people, their cultural gaps, their lack of creativity, come from a conceptual incapacity. A language which is diminished, shrunken, deformed, truncated, and unrecognizable will never produce anything but uncultivated minds.)

It seems clear that the latter phenomenon, the devaluation of a speech variety to reflect the socioeconomic position of its speakers, is primary, and that the converse, the negative consequences of speaking a given variety, is but a derivative effect. Historically, the changing political and economic fortunes of countries or nations have been followed, with a certain lag, by a reevaluation of their languages. However, it would be difficult to find a clear case where the change in status of a language variety led to a change in the socioeconomic status of its speakers.

Many other factors are of course involved, including whether the situation is one of different dialects or different languages. When it is necessary for a group of people to learn another language for the practical reasons mentioned earlier, this may or may not lead to language loss, and the variable tenacity of different linguistic groups in maintaining their languages is difficult to explain in terms of purely economic criteria (cf. Hymes 1966 on two Amerindian groups). In the single language situation, the characteristics of 'good' or 'correct' speech can be broadly or narrowly defined to broaden or reduce acceptance of those whose speech is more or less divergent from the prestige form. Entrance examinations can be deliberately manipulated to exclude all 'non-U' (Ross 1954) applicants, who are bound to give themselves away sooner or later.[6] And of course the prestige features themselves can be changed when the wrong people acquire them, or simply as a result of a new geographical or social center of prestige.

It is also the case that when differential linguistic knowledge becomes important in providing access to other goods and resources, social structure also determines differential access to the resource of language itself. Thus language is at once a symbol of an individual's place in the society, since it represents the opportunities he has had for learning language varieties, the people he has been in contact with, and so on; and a resource providing access to particular activities and opportunities, and blocking access to others.

THE CHANGING POWER STRUCTURE IN PAPUA NEW GUINEA

Having briefly reviewed some of the characteristics of a highly stratified sociolinguistic situation, let us return to a consideration in greater detail of politics in Papua New Guinea, beginning with a closer look at traditional political organization.

As mentioned in the second section of this paper and as is widely recognized, the 'big man' system was the pivotal political institution over much of Papua New Guinea. Becoming a big man involved political manipulation of lending and borrowing relationships involved in trade, whether local (e.g. bridewealth) or foreign (e.g. the Enga *Moka* or the Trobriand *Kula*). It also involved being a war leader (this is obviously the skill about which least is known), and being able to attract and hold a loyal following who would accept one's leadership and not defect to another leader. Community activities requiring leadership included decision-making regarding large communal gardens, especially in preparation for feasts (whose timetable and other associated planning also had to be decided), trading and warfare expeditions, settling of local disputes, arranging marriages, and so forth. The men's house was a key institution here, and the men's house group (under the leadership of a particular big man) could presumably be relied on for economic assistance and moral backing in time of need. The system has been described as a highly competitive one involving considerable rivalry among actual and potential big men. Big man status in most of New Guinea was not hereditary though having an influential backer (usually a father or uncle) was a decided advantage for any young man.

What were the traditional sources of power in New Guinea, and what resources could a powerful man draw on? In Buang society, probably the most important were land and labor. Yam growing was the prestigious activity, and large and well tended yam gardens required both. Land was managed by the kin group, but individual inheritance of particular fields or portions of fields meant that some people found themselves with more and better land than others. Labor was more difficult, as it depended not only upon the demographic vagaries of one's close family, but even more upon clever manipulation of available kin, trade, and friendship ties. The rich and powerful man who had successfully managed his marriage(s) and his inherited resources could always count on finding a ready work force when he needed a roof thatched or a large garden cleared. He could entertain such work parties in style, with pork from his own herd or hunted in the forest – and he could also entertain distant trade friends, having the time and resources to cultivate such contacts.

Thus in any community there were influential and powerful men (Tok Pisin *bigpela man*) with large and well tended gardens, possibly more than one wife, many pigs, the authority to direct community activities and command a large labor force, likely having a better command of foreign languages than their fellows as well as a larger collection of traded goods, particularly the highly visible clay pots from the coast. Big men could, through a combination of seniority and astute political behavior, become managers of the garden and forest land of their descent group. There were also the men referred to in Tok Pisin as *rabis man* ('inconsequential men'), people whose gardens were more modest, who more often found themselves clearing other people's gardens than vice versa. These people were not poor, or in a condition of servitude to the more powerful – they simply did not command the resources and authority that the *bigpela man* could.

The coming of colonialism immediately began to transform the configuration of power. The localized and unstable community influence wielded by individual big men was dwarfed by the (relatively) unified and absolute power of the colonial authority. How did this affect the big man system? Since colonial authority, including missionary influence and the power brought to bear by commercial interests, was exercised only in connection with certain matters, such as warfare, taxation, religion, paid labor, and relations with non-New Guineans, and was only sporadically viable except in town and government stations, the big man tradition was able to continue, albeit in a somewhat modified fashion. Indeed, the cessation of warfare permitted a certain expansion of the influence of particular big men from the local to the regional level, as discussed for example by Salisbury (1964) and as has been noted in the case of several cargo cult leaders (e.g. Lawrence 1964; Schwartz 1962).

Nevertheless, power with respect to all matters of a non-local nature was clearly vested in the colonial triumvirate of government, mission, and business. This was understood by all concerned from the earliest stages of colonization. It was most apparent and most significant in towns, government stations, missionary outposts, and commercial enterprises such as plantations and mines.

Despite the clear stratification between Europeans and New Guineans, correlated with exaggerated power disparities, there were some possibilities for vertical movement for New Guineans within the colonial power structure. *Bosboi* ('foremen'), *Blak misin* ('evangelists'), and *plis man* (*plis boi*) ('police sergeants') are examples of some of the positions whose incumbents often had a great deal of influence and control over other New Guineans within colonial institutions. These distinctions entailed prestige and authority through their closer association with the true power holders, not only within town and station communities, but extending back to their home rural populations.

Today, skills such as literacy, accounting, the ability to drive a truck, and knowledge of the language(s) of the wider arena(s) can be of immense benefit to those who possess them, and can lead to much larger differences among villagers than could possibly have existed in the pre-colonial society. These differences may even be measurable in traditional resources such as land, as when a local entrepreneur gains permanent control of large tracts of good gardening land for cash crop production. Differences also come to exist among areas rich in resources usable by the colonial system and/or cloese to the new centers of power and those not so endowed.

Today, young Buang men in their twenties who cultivate the traditional virtues and take pride in their yam gardens refer to themselves as *rabis* men, in contrast to their peers who decide to go away to work and earn money. The sophistication of the retired policeman or other ex-official in the workings of the colonial society, his fluent Tok Pisin in dealing with representatives of this society, his well educated children who return home only for brief visits on vacation from 'good' jobs in the city, have not failed to impress those who stayed at home. Indeed, political astuteness became synonymous with the ability to further big man status locally, using achievements and associations within the colonial world while simultaneously improving one's situation within the urban or station community by using the economic resources or political support of the people from one's local area (cf. Sankoff 1968: 52–54).

The changes brought by the colonial society have made for some fundamental alterations in village level politics, though a number of formal aspects have remained the same. In some Buang villages the men's house has fallen into disuse, but there are still 'big men' in the sense of influential leaders whose opinions carry weight in meetings, who can recommend courses of political or economic action which others will follow, and who can organize a large labor force for community work of various sorts. But both political issues and the resources used in deciding them have undergone fundamental changes. First, the scope of decision-making at the village level has had to expand to take in issues of wider arenas – the regional and national levels and the questions which their agents raise. These include questions like the support of local Lutheran religious officials and of Buang Lutheran officials in other areas of New Guinea, preparation for a visit by the health inspection team of the Local Government Council, members of which include one representative from each one or two villages, participation in the agricultural cooperative, work on roads or airstrip, and response to questions about national policies raised by the travelling Member of the House of Assembly, as well as traditional matters such as settling marital or other family disputes, deciding where and when to carry out communal garden plantings, and so on.

Second, decisions emanating from these wider arenas can have important effects at the local level in ways which completely surpass any possible input from the local level. Geography alone has had a huge effect on access to markets for local producers, as well as access to schools, jobs, and the like. Thus distance from the town of Mumeng and a major road to the coast is inversely proportional to emigration to urban centers in Buang villages. Thus in 1967, 47 percent of the dialect C villages' population was living elsewhere compared with 39 percent in dialect B and only 20 percent in dialect A. By 1971 there was one Buang university student – from dialect C. Economic decisions made internationally (e.g. the World Coffee Agreement) or in another country (e.g. Australian decisions regarding imports of sugar) or even at other levels or in other areas of New Guinea (e.g. the decision about where to put a road or a bridge or a factory) can have effects whose magnitude at the local level is greater than that of decisions taken at the local level.

TOK PISIN IN COLONIAL NEW GUINEA

The birth of Tok Pisin coincided more or less with the beginning of the colonial period in New Guinea, gaining a foothold in the Rabaul area of New Britain, the site of the German colonial capital, in the 1880s (Laycock 1970b; Salisbury 1967). It has been from this earliest period the language of colonization. It has always been spoken principally in what is referred to as the 'New Guinea side', i.e. the ex-German territory (current island Districts of Manus, New Ireland, East and West New Britain, and Bougainville, and mainland Districts of East and West Sepik, Madang, Morobe, Chimbu, and Eastern and Western Highlands, as shown on Map 14.1, see page 285. Papua, the ex-British territory which was administered jointly with New Guinea since the Second World War (present Western, Gulf, Central, Northern, Milne Bay and Southern Highlands Districts), has used Hiri Motu[7] as a lingua franca. In 1966, of the approximately 1,500,000 Papuans and New Guineans age 10 and over, 36.5 percent spoke Tok Pisin and 8.1 percent spoke Hiri Motu (Territory of Papua and New Guinea Population Census 1966, Preliminary Bulletin No. 20, Table 14). Table 14.1 shows the number and proportion of current Tok Pisin speakers by district.

The first Buang men to learn Tok Pisin acquired it in what has now become the classic tradition – as indentured laborers on a plantation.[8] The plantations at this stage, just before the First World War, were German, and the men were taken by ship to New Britain where they worked for seven years before being returned home. Buang men also worked as carriers on 'patrols' of various sorts – including trips of exploration for minerals and police patrols, sometimes in reprisal for an incident in which other villagers had harmed or killed someone in the former 'patrol' category. The most important source of learning Tok Pisin was the Bulolo gold rush in the early 1930s. Because of its relative proximity to Buang territory, it attracted dozens of Buang men to their first opportunity to earn money and the things it could buy.

In retrospect, men who had worked for Europeans during that time had almost nothing good to say about the experience. They complained of long hours, hard masters whose whims were difficult to understand or comply with, and low rates of pay. Some of them

Table 14.1 *Papua New Guinean Tok Pisin speakers by district*[a]

District	No. of Tok Pisin speakers age 10 and over	Percentage of the age 10 and over population speaking Tok Pisin
New Ireland	32,550	94.2
Manus	11,784	89.2
East Sepik	79,680	76.6
West New Britain	21,026	75.7
East New Britain	48,464	69.5
Bougainville	31,843	68.0
West Sepik	45,208	67.4
Madang	62,426	61.5
Morobe	65,634	47.1
Central	25,630	28.2
Eastern Highlands	35,237	26.3
Northern	7,267	19.1
Chimbu	20,706	17.4
Western Highlands	26,385	13.0
Gulf	2,873	8.0
Southern Highlands	9,592	7.7
Milne Bay	3,547	5.2
Western	1,844	4.5

[a] Figures from the 1966 population census

escaped and came home; others stayed in order to be able to earn more money, or out of fear of reprisals, and learned more about how the colonial society worked.

We can only extrapolate as to the effects on local level politics of these early returnees, with their goods and their knowledge. Men who were part of this group say that they gave many of their goods away; like more recent returnees in areas of Papua New Guinea where the first return of indentured laborers has occurred when an anthropologist was there to observe it, probably they found their goods rapidly integrated into the distribution system controlled by older men who had not been away. But knowledge was another matter, and especially valuable was the knowledge of Tok Pisin, referred to as *bubum ayez* ('the white men's language'), the language which permitted access to the colonial society. Indeed, knowledge of Tok Pisin was originally the criterion for appointment as a *luluai* or *tultul* (village officials given military caps and expected to translate the words of visiting government officials, to assemble the population for censuses and tax collection – in other words to be the official brokers between the village and the secular colonial society).

The regimented character of the contacts between villagers and visiting whites in the early colonial period, added to the highly disciplinary tone of contacts between master and servant (the primary work relationship known to Buang workers up to and including the present, though the style of most current masters probably differs considerably from the earlier ones we are discussing here), made for a strong association between Tok Pisin and authoritarian behavior. Tok Pisin was demonstrably a language in which one could give orders and expect to be obeyed, even if the persons to whom the orders were given displayed little comprehension (as was the case for most workers during the early phases of their indenture). Though as we shall see below Tok Pisin is now a common demoninator, even a language of equality among urban New Guineans from diverse linguistic groups, it has retained its associations with and connotations of power and authority at the village level, learned by each new generation in the context of giving orders and shouting at people, as well as in playful imitation of such contexts.

The extent to which returned laborers used Tok Pisin in the village context during this early period remains unknown, but it is likely that they at least repeated common expressions of the *kiap* (patrol officer) or other visiting dignitary, explaining to the others what they meant. Certainly the high degree of comprehension of Tok Pisin among people under fifty in Buang villages today (including women and people who have not been away or to school) would attest to the early use of Tok Pisin locally, at least to some extent. There is some sex difference in comprehension of Tok Pisin, though this is not extreme, but education makes for very little difference in competence in Tok Pisin. Tok Pisin is definitely not a school language, but a language introduced in the sphere of outside work which has been integrated to some extent into village life. Hearing a father instructing his daughter who can barely toddle, '*Yu kam!*' ('come on!') is not at all uncommon, and children's games include epithets such as *bladi* ('bloody') and *yupela klia* ('you guys get out of the way').

Village meetings are, however, the most common context for the use of Tok Pisin, particularly the *lain* morning meetings where people (particularly women) are supposed to line up and receive orders about the work they are to do later in the day; and the 'special events' meetings often called to discuss economic (cash economy) matters. The forced regimentation of the *lain* borrows the symbolism of 'lining up' (as indeed have a number of millenarian religious movements in Papua New Guinea) as well as the language of the prototype – village visits or 'patrols' by government officers. Men will get up and harangue the crowd alternately in Tok Pisin and Tok Ples (in this case Buang) regarding issues like absenteeism at the *lain*, work not properly done, orders not followed, and so forth.

The literary rhetorical devices used in the oratory at this and other kinds of village meetings are many. Synonymy through borrowing is particularly frequent. One device is code switching (cf. Sankoff 1972), where whole passages are spoken in one language, then followed by making the same point in a slightly different way in another. (In the present context, the two languages are always Buang and Tok Pisin.[9]) Or the dire consequences to befall someone who violates a condition stated in an if-clause in one language are explained in the other, as in sentence (1) below.

(1) ŋau ti ŋmodo (Buang), bai ol ikot stret long yu (Tok Pisin).
'If you're the only one sitting down (i.e. doing nothing), they'll take you straight to court.'

Table 14.2 *Language used in speeches in eight village meetings*[a]

	Language used		
Speakers	Buang	Tok Pisin	Total Speeches
The 'government' leader	9	9	13
The 'economic' leader	12	11	17
Others	75	17	86
Total	96	37	116

[a] From Sankoff (1968: 191).

Though people being shouted at, harangued, or sworn at in Tok Pisin do not necessarily take this behavior very seriously on all occasions, neither can it be completely disregarded, since its use reflects the village power structure. Table 14.2 compares language use in eight village meetings of the *lain* and 'special event' type. We see that the two most influential men in the village used Tok Pisin more frequently than all the others combined, and that they frequently switched codes during a speech. 'Special events' meetings sometimes use a device clearly borrowed from the 'officer on patrol' situation, i.e. the formal use of an interpreter. Formal interpreters may even be used when the 'visiting dignitary' is himself a Buang. In such a case the 'visiting dignitary' speaks Tok Pisin throughout the meeting, the translator repeating at short intervals in Buang.

The meetings discussed above are 'political' in the sense that they are held in order to make decisions regarding future action which will affect a number of people. And some participants are more powerful or influential than others in that their opinions are more likely to hold sway, and in that the decisions taken at the group level are more likely to favor their personal interests. It is not principally a man's behavior at public meetings which *creates* this kind of power for him, though it is important in providing justifications, assuaging those who might be against the course of action, and validating support in terms of agreement by other speakers.

For the past thirty years or so, Buang parents have seen the acquisition of Tok Pisin as perhaps *the* chief resource which will gain their children access to the riches of the colonial society, and have been anxious that they learn it. Its obvious usefulness and the relative ease with which it could be learned, however, made it the type of practical resource which was readily within the grasp of almost anyone. The last four or five years have shown a growing awareness that, on the contrary, Tok Pisin does not get you far enough in the new society, that it is not the white man's language after all. It is English that must be known.

The introduction of English, to be discussed in the next section, has put the position of Tok Pisin into clearer relief. Thus though Tok Pisin has indeed been the language of colonization, it has been far more. From its earliest usage, it has been the lingua franca of New Guineans of diverse ethnic backgrounds. It is the language of much

Table 14.3 *Language distribution in the seven largest towns of Papua New Guinea (expatriates excluded)*[a]

Major towns of Papua New Guinea	% of Hiri Motu speakers 1966	% of Tok Pisin speakers 1966	% of English speakers 1966	Total Papua New Guinean population 1966	Total Papua New Guinean population 1971
Port Moresby (Central)	77.8	54.9	64.4	31,983	50,988
Lae (Morobe)	14.8	94.2	36.1	13,341	28,494
Rabaul (E. New Britain)	11.9	97.1	37.4	6,925	20,700
Madang (Madang)	8.0	96.2	30.8	7,398	13,472
Wewak (E. Sepik)	5.2	96.2	27.8	7,967	11,383
Goroka (E. Highlands)	14.3	89.6	31.6	3,890	9,238
Mount Hagen (W. Highlands)	13.5	82.7	27.0	2,764	8,398
Total				74,268	141,973

a Language figures from 1966 Population Census (Tables 33 of Preliminary Bulletins 23, 27 31, 32, 33, 35 and Table 32 of Preliminary Bulletin 29); Population figures from 1971 Population Census (Preliminary Bulletin 1) provided for comparison, 1971 language figures being not yet available.

everyday life in towns such as Lae, Rabaul, Madang, Goroka, Wewak, and Mt. Hagen, in most of which over 90 percent of the people speak it (Table 14.3), and it is increasingly used in Port Moresby and other Papuan centers. Though from the village perspective it may have been considered the white man's language, its integrating and solidarity functions in the activities of multi-ethnic New Guinean urban and commercial life have been increasing.

ENGLISH AND THE DEEPENING LINGUISTIC STRATIFICATION OF PAPUA NEW GUINEA

The dramatic introduction of English in the past ten years has again symbolized, or perhaps even fostered, the changing social structure of Papua New Guinea. It is a scarce resource – to have your children learn it, you must send them to school early and pay for them to stay there for many years.

Though in the past Tok Pisin was conceived at the village level as an important resource for getting on in the colonial society, its accessibility made its integration into village life relatively undisruptive. Big men could use it as an added resource in rhetoric; signs could be posted on competitive festive occasions stating the cost of the food being distributed; its understanding by virtually everyone within a reasonably short time span meant that it could be more useful than symbolic.

Permanent or relatively permanent urban living is also a novel phenomenon in Papua New Guinea. It is here that the resource of learning English is chiefly possible. But accompanying the spread of English as an elite language is also the spread of Tok Pisin as a general language of solidarity among the urban population. It is the language in which a growing minority of urban children and adolescents are most fluent and it has become the native language of many (Sankoff 1973). Many highly educated New Guineans who are perfectly fluent in English use Tok Pisin in relaxed, informal situations with friends. Some of its proponents whom I talked to about it in 1971 waxed very enthusiastic about its communicative usefulness, its solidarity function, and the fluency of their children in it, as indicated in the following quotations:

(2) Em, long Pisin olsem tok ples bilong yumi yet.
'That's right, Tok Pisin is like our real language.'

(3) Ol i no harim Tok Ples na ol i Tok Pisin tasol olsem na, Tok Pisin bilong ol i no inap ron o mekim wonem; em i klia.
'They (the children) don't understand Tok Ples, just Tok Pisin, you know, and their Tok Pisin doesn't wander or go off the mark; it's clear.'

(4) Ating bihain bai Tok Ples bai inogat ia. Bai i Pisin na Inglis tasol.
'Maybe after a long time there won't be any more Tok Ples. Just Pisin and English.'

Nevertheless the current situation is one in which English is reinforcing and clarifying urban social stratification, as indicated by the figures presented in Table 14.3. Already in 1966, over 30 percent of the Papua New Guinean population of most major towns spoke English (though a cautionary note is necessary: many of those who claimed to speak English when enumerated in the census may not have commanded a very fluent or functional English). The language figures for the 1971 census are not available at time of writing, but it is clear from the figures on the population of major towns that the high level of urban growth in the 1966–1971 period will have produced many more English *and* Tok Pisin speakers.

Currently, in every town, there are always new migrants or transients (e.g. market vendors or village people visiting urban relatives) who speak only Tok Ples, with little or halting Tok Pisin or none at all. These are the *bus kanaka* ('bush natives'), the country bumpkins who are increasingly ashamed of their Tok Ples. Next is the bulk of the urban proletariat – mostly Tok Pisin speaking, and working at service jobs or as manual laborers. They may resent being spoken to in Tok Pisin by a white person or a Chinese, or sometimes even by a Papuan, regarding it as an insult even if they do not speak English. Then there are the English speakers, who tend to be fairly young and who work in stores or offices, or in technically skilled jobs, or as teachers. Among these people, it is recognized that there are many degrees of fluency in speaking English, and that speaking it 'well' is a difficult but worthwhile task.

What appears to have happened is that the original Tok Ples/Tok

Pisin dichotomy has been largely replaced by Tok Pisin/English as a symbolic marker of power and status in the urban society. For now, the landless and virtually resourceless urban proletariat is linguistically symbolized by the feature (– English), the learning of any English at all being a scarce resource. But as English instruction spreads, Standard 6 educated speakers will increasingly find that (+ English) is not a useful resource. Speaking English 'well' (i.e. having the amount of schooling that fluency in English can symbolize) will increasingly come to mark the elite.

Though the distinction between Tok Pisin and English is still very clear, there are some signs that the urban New Guinea linguistic situation is moving toward what has been characterized as a 'post-creole continuum' (De Camp 1971) in other colonial and ex-colonial situations. As educated and powerful New Guineans replace Europeans in high government posts, as agresssive rural migrants succeed in setting up profitable enterprises, as school-leavers from various levels enter the public service, Standard English, English spoken as a second language with varying degrees of fluency and correctness, highly anglicized Tok Pisin, the more classical Tok Pisin of migrants, and the creolized Tok Pisin of the urban born coexist and loosely reflect the merging social stratification of urban New Guineans.

To return briefly to formal institutions, it is likely that the correlation between education, speaking English, and office holding at every level will increase, as villagers as well as urbanites feel that the most equipped person to deal with the 'outside' is the person with the most education, who can speak the language of the educated and sophisticated men with whom he will have to deal.

Prolonged exposure to a situation where a knowledge of English is a clear advantage will probably not lead to the loss of many local languages, since there is every indication that a majority of people will continue to use Tok Ples or Tok Pisin in family and informal contexts. But the symmetrically egalitarian relationship which existed among local languages – Tok Ples – has already been irrevocably altered by the spread of Tok Pisin and of English. That some speakers are more equal than others will probably lead many to the anti-relativist position that some languages, and particularly some language varieties ('good' English), are more equal than others. And will lay the way open to the classic, erroneous but treacherously seductive argument that it is this unfortunate 'linguistic inferiority' (symbolizing, for some, even *cognitive* inferiority) which is the *cause* of poverty and powerlessness.

NOTES

1. Papua New Guinea is a newly self-governing nation of some $2\frac{1}{2}$ million people, situated north of Australia and east of Indonesia (see Map 14.1, page 285). New Guinea was a former German colony which came under Australian rule in 1914; Papua was a former British colony which passed to Australian rule in 1906. They were jointly administered by Australia from 1946 – 1973 under United Nations supervision.
2. I wish to thank the many New Guineans without whose generosity and hospitality during my three visits to New Guinea (July 1966-August 1967; July-August 1968; June-September 1971) this essay would not have been possible. I also thank the Canada Council for sponsoring the first two visits.
3. Tok Pisin is variously referred to in the literature as Melanesian Pidgin (Hall 1943; Mihalic 1971; Brash 1971), Neo-Melanesian (Mihalic 1957), and New Guinea Pidgin (Wurm 1971b; Laycock 1970a). I follow the usage of its speakers in referring to it as Tok Pisin.
4. On language as a symbol of identity in bilingual situations, cf. Gumperz (1969); Cumperz and Hernández (1969); Jackson (1972: Ch. 6).
5. Cf. Weinreich, Labov, and Herzog (1968) on change in status of features.
6. Michener's epic novel *Hawaii* describes in a moving historical vignette the application of such entrance tests to keep Chinese children out of white schools.
7. Hiri Motu, formerly known as Police Motu, is the name of the somewhat pidginized version of the language of the Motuan traders, later also propagated by the police in Papua.
8. In some areas of New Guinea, the missions were important agents in the spread and use of Tok Pisin, e.g. the Roman Catholics in the Sepik area (note in Table 14.1 the East Sepik District today counts more Tok Pisin speakers in terms of absolute numbers than any other). In other areas, however, missions used and spread as *lingue franche* a number of Austronesian and Papuan languages. Kate, for example, whose native speakers number less than a thousand, is now said to be spoken by more than 40,000 Lutherans in the Morobe and Eastern Highlands districts (Wurm 1966). Other mission languages include 'Jabem and Graged by the Lutherans; Weda (in the Milne Bay District) by the Anglicans; Dobu (also in the Milne Bay District) by the Methodists; Kuanua (in New Britain and New Ireland) by the Roman Catholics and the Methodists; Toaripi by the Anglicans and the Roman Catholics, and Kiwai (in the Fly Delta area) by the Anglicans' (Wurm 1966:

141). Since the government has been discouraging the use of such languages, once widely used in the schools, by refusing to subsidize mission schools unless government linguistic guidelines are followed, use and spread of such mission *lingue franche* has been declining.

9. Laycock (1966) provides texts showing switching between Tok Pisin and Abelam.

STEVEN STAATS and EUGENE A. CONTI 15

The Evolution of Courts, Councils, and Legislatures in Papua New Guinea

The evolution of courts, councils, and legislatures in Papua New Guinea is the result of the interplay of two forces: one is the nature of the indigenous political institutions which exist in the country and the other is the attempt by the Australian government to create governmental institutions, originally for the purposes of overt control and more recently in preparation for independence. A set of contemporary political institutions has emerged out of this interplay of local systems of government and colonial policy. Because internal self-government is so recent, it is too soon to discern the impact of the national government's policies and ethos on the country's political institutions. It is certain that some indigenous and colonial influences on courts, councils, and legislatures will recede with time as they have elsewhere in the third world. And it is equally certain that the orientation of the new national government will become more influential in molding the country's institutions. However, the base from which the new government proceeds is this interplay of the indigenous and the colonial. That interplay is the subject of this chapter.

Australia has interacted directly with Papua New Guinea for over a century. Portuguese explorers had sighted New Guinea in 1512, but it was not until 1793 that an official of the British East India Company formally took possession of the eastern part of the island of New Guinea for Britain (Mair 1970: 10). Holland claimed the western end of the island and Britain acquiesced in that arrangement. Throughout the nineteenth century, Britain refused to actively pursue annexation of the eastern end of the island although she was repeatedly urged to do so by explorers. Towards the end of the century, plantation owners from Australia began recruiting labor in

New Guinea and pressed the British government to annex the territory. The British refused to act until the Australian colonies themselves – whom they saw as the chief beneficiaries of annexation – contributed financially to the costs of administration. The colonies refused. In the early 1880s however, a German trading company began operating trading stations on the island. Spurred by these competitive activities, the Australian colonies agreed to make a financial contribution towards administering the territory if Britain annexed it. Britain proclaimed the protectorate of British New Guinea over the southern part of the eastern half of the island. Within ten days Germany annexed the northern part of the eastern half (Legge 1956: 28).

Both northern and southern parts soon came under Australian authority. In 1906 the British protectorate, now renamed Papua, was transferred to Australia. During World War I, the German colony was occupied by Australian forces and in 1920 Australia was given a League of Nations Mandate for the territory (Stanner 1953). The northern and southern parts were separately administered by Australia until 1942 when, following the Japanese invasion of the island, the civil administrations were replaced by a joint military administration, ANGAU (Australian New Guinea Administrative Unit). After the second world war, the former mandated territory became a United Nations Trust Territory again administered by Australia. The administrative union of the two parts continued after 1949 as the responsibility of the Department of External Territories in Australia. In New Guinea, Australian administrative headquarters were in Port Moresby.

The shape of New Guinea has often been compared to that of a great elongated bird. Approximately one half of the island, from 141 degrees longitude eastwards, constitutes contemporary Papua New Guinea. The northern part, which was the Trust Territory of New Guinea, includes the Bismarck Archipelago, with its three main islands of New Britain, New Ireland, and Manus, and the two northernmost islands of the Solomon group, Bougainville and Buka. The southern part of New Guinea covers the former Australian territory of Papua. New Guinea has a population of approximately three million inhabitants, including some eighty to one hundred thousand expatriates, most of whom live in the fast growing urban centers such as Port Moresby (Howlett 1967: 6). Topographically, New Guinea is extremely rugged. The main island is dominated by a central spine of great mountain ranges which are the eastern extremity of the great arc of rugged mountains that runs through the Himalayas and Malaya into the Pacific. In addition, there is a second chain of ranges along the north coast, running from the border of West Irian (Indonesian New Guinea) to the Huon Peninsula and reappearing in New Britain (Howlett 1967: 24). The majority of the population live at relatively temperate altitudes in the neighborhood of 5,000 feet (Howlett 1967: 6). The population is usually classified according to linguistic criteria; this classification is discussed in Chapter 14.

The economy of New Guinea consists of subsistence and commercial sectors. The commercial sector is dominated by plantation agriculture and mining (Fisk 1966: 34). Indigenes are involved in the monetary sector primarily through the provision of labor. In 1968, the indigenous wage labor force was estimated at 100,000 (Staats 1970: 17). It is growing rapidly. Indigenes are also estimated to produce one quarter of the copra and cocoa and one half of the coffee exports (Schaffer 1971: 1). The extent of expatriate supremacy in the economy can be gauged from the following statistics: in 1972–73, the expatriate 1.5 percent of the population received approximately 52 percent of the income from commercial agriculture and 90 to 95 percent of that accruing from industry, commerce, and services (Crocombe 1969: 57). This expatriate preeminence in economic affairs has parallels in the political sphere as we shall see below. It has been estimated that the copper deposits on Bougainville are amongst the largest in the world. The wealth of the area is evident from the fact that Conzinc Rio Tinto (Australia) Limited, the main shareholder in Bougainville, will recover its cash outlay of some $300 million (Australian) within the first five years of operation (Treadgold 1971: 163).

In the next section of this paper, Australian policy toward New Guinea is reviewed. Then, the following section deals with local councils and courts. Juxtaposing official policy with local realities allows us to see the interplay of the two forces. The final section looks at the evolution of the national legislature as it reflects this interplay.

AUSTRALIAN POLICY TOWARDS NEW GUINEA

Sir Joseph Cook's statement to the Permanent Mandates Commission of the League of Nations in 1925 that Australia's New Guinea policy 'has never been formally expressed in a comprehensive way within the limits of a single document' was indicative of the general tenor of Australian administration prior to World War I (Colebatch 1968: 106). The main concern was to penetrate and establish effective jurisdiction in all areas. A dual policy of encouraging European economic enterprise and of protecting the indigenous inhabitants was followed. In both aspects, the administrations found themselves frustrated by lack of funds and a shortage of adequate personnel.

World War II may be considered as a watershed in Australia's approach to New Guinea's political evolution (Staats 1973: 16–23). The redefined approach emerged in the context of Australia's views on colonial questions particularly as they were enunciated by External Affairs Minister Herbert V. Evatt and Edward John Ward, Minister for Transport and External Territories. Evatt was emphatic in his support for the principle of self-determination for colonial peoples. Ward exhibited a willingness to allocate more funds for native medical and educational facilities. More importantly, he showed a preoccupation with the welfare of the indigenous peoples which he regarded as the government's primary concern. This preoccupation was reflected in specific policy recommendations. First, the indenture system was to be abolished within five years, or earlier if possible, and conditions of work, wage rates, methods of recruitment, penalties for violation of contract, and a number of other matters pertaining to native labor were to be improved (Staats 1973). Secondly, the amount and type of European enterprise in the territories would be strictly controlled. Thirdly, the government proposed to make an effort to improve and expand native agriculture, and to encourage native production of commodities not then produced.

The Labor government of which Evatt and Ward were members was defeated at the polls in 1949. The achievements of their government in relation to New Guinea lay largely in a redefinition of certain major aspects of Australia's responsibilities to the territories, namely, the acceptance of the broad principles of trusteeship, recognition of the need for a more active development policy than had been pursued in the past, and amelioration of the conditions of native labor.

The Liberal and Country Party government which came to power in 1949 placed a greater emphasis on the role of private enterprise in New Guinea's development as well as formulating the purposes and direction of Australian policy with greater clarity than had been done previously. Hasluck, who held a wide range of government and academic positions and who was minister for Territories from 1951 to 1963, argued that Australia was formally bound by a 'sacred obligation' to 'promote the progressive development' of her dependent peoples 'towards self-government or independence as may be appropriate to the particular circumstances of each territory and its peoples . . .' (1958: 83). But this obligation, while it spelled out the end objective fairly clearly, left the means of its achievement substantially to the discretion of the administering authority. It is, therefore, from the choice of means that the distinctive elements of Australia's policy emerged. Its basic premise lies in Hasluck's definition of the word 'self-determination':

'Self-determination can only be the true choice of a preferred choice if the person making the choice is in a position to know clearly what are the alternatives before him and what are the full implications of each choice that is made. . . . We have . . . to interpret the meaning of the word simply as a right to choose by those who are capable of making a choice and who, having made it, are also capable of maintaining without impairment the advantages which they expect to follow from their choice' (Hasluck 1958: 83).

In Hasluck's view, therefore, the essential precondition to self-determination was that the people be 'capable of making a choice'. This aim was conceived in terms of a problem in social transformation:

'Unless there is a society with its own values, its own cohesion, its own standards of conduct and its own loyalties, the indigenous peoples will never be able to take over from the trustee those responsibilities in regard to just treatment and protection from abuses and the safeguarding of human rights and liberties which are at present confided to the administering power' (Hasluck 1958: 81).

Hasluck sought through his policies to create a social climate conducive to the development of a tradition of respect for law, order, and the fundamental rights of the individual.

Although distinct limitations on the ability of the administration to control the pace and direction of change were recognized, Hasluck nonetheless evolved a very definite policy designed to avoid what he considered to be the main pitfalls in the process of evolution. This approach, called the policy of 'balanced development', dictated that social and economic advancement must go together. A 'solid, well-constructed economy, capable of sustaining the social services that are necessary for the advancement of these people' was needed (Commonwealth of Australia Parliamentary Debates 1955: 1330). In the political arena, lasting progress 'will be achieved only if training in the arts and practices of government is accompanied by cultural changes which produce a society of individuals who have gained an appreciation of democratic values' (Commonwealth of Australia Parliamentary Debates 1960: 25). This implied that political training must begin at the level of local affairs. The advantages of proceeding in this manner were explained as follows:

'Insofar as it entails working upwards from the village population this system of political development is slower than one which concentrates on the advancement of an educated elite only, but, because it means education in citizenship for the people as a whole, the gains it makes are more likely to be sound (Commonwealth of Australia Parliamentary Debates 1960: 26).'

This last statement brings out clearly one of the key features in the Australian program for New Guinea's advancement towards self-government, namely, to concentrate on the general development of the population as a whole, rather than on the creation of an elite with its potential for domination.

The exogenous factors precipitating a change in Australian policy towards New Guinea in recent years are numerous. First, the United Nations General Assembly's resolution of 1960 on granting independence for colonial peoples stipulated that immediate steps were to be taken by all colonial powers to prepare for independence. The Committee of Seventeen, appointed to supervise the carrying out of the resolution, emphasized that the inadequacy of political, economic, social, or educational preparedness should never serve as a pretext for delaying independence.

Australia was served notice that it too was regarded as a colonial power, that the anticolonial block would keep up the pressure until New Guinea became independent, and that the relatively 'primitive' nature of New Guinea society would not be tolerated indefinitely as a reason for withholding independence. The campaign reached a peak in 1962 when the U.N. visiting mission to New Guinea, whose observations are known as the Foot Report, abandoned the customary tone of general approval combined with minor criticism, and launched a comprehensive attack on the assumptions and results of Hasluck's policy of balanced development. It demanded 'crash programs' in every field to train people who could manage the political, administrative, judicial, and technical institutions of an independent New Guinea (Staats 1970: 21–25; 1973: 18–21).

Finally came the expulsion of the Dutch from adjoining West New Guinea. The Australian government had always supported the Dutch presence on legal as well as on practical grounds: Holland was the owner of West New Guinea and was far better qualified to administer it than Indonesia. But the Dutch were forced out by an Indonesian political and military offensive in 1961–62 which drew strength from the international anticolonial bloc.

While it is impossible to assess the relative importance of these factors, there can be little doubt that they influenced the government. For instance, the changing attitude towards the U.N. was probably due to a feeling of exposure on the part of the government. Australia did not wish to change its policies but realized that unless it presented them to the U.N. with greater diplomacy it would invite attack from the anticolonial powers. In December, 1960, Australia had abstained from the vote on the declaration on colonial rule and emphasized instead the unique primitiveness of New Guinea. Less than a year later it not only voted for the establishment of the Committee of Seventeen, but sought and obtained a seat on the committee. This change of tactics (at this stage there was no change in policy) can only be interpreted as a reaction to the pressure being put on Australia and as evidence of a desire to moderate the vehemence of the anticolonial drive by working from the inside.

It must be emphasized that the change was not a neat switch from one clearly defined policy to another; rather, it was a change in the way Australian policy makers looked at New Guinea, a change in focus (Colebatch 1968: 140). There had been a tendency to plan for the perfect society in New Guinea, with the granting of political independence as the climax to a long process of political, social, economic, and educational development. Stress was placed on the enormous difficulties to be overcome before a viable state could be established. Reflecting the changed focus after 1960, Prime Minister Menzies stated in June, 1961, that he would sooner grant independence to New Guinea too early, than allow hostilities to develop (Hughes 1964: 12). Accordingly, the administration embarked on a program of accelerated development in political, social, and educational fields, while the Australian delegation at the U.N. lobbied for maximum time in which to prepare New Guinea for independence.

LOCAL COUNCILS AND COURTS

Australian aspirations and programs are but one set of factors in the evolution of political institutions in New Guinea. The characteristics of her indigenous societies determine to a large extent the fate of those policies. The societies of New Guinea exhibit a political diversity exceeded perhaps only by the linguistic and ethnic diversity discussed in Chapter 14. This variation in societies, and particularly the variation in systems of local government, stems from a number of sources. First, the nature of indigenous political institutions was by no means uniform across the spectrum of New Guinea peoples. This diversity was only exaggerated by the differential application of colonial policy. Prior to 1949, as noted above, Papua and the mandated territory of New Guinea were under separate colonial administrative systems. In addition, there is variation among New Guinea peoples as to when colonial contact occurred and when colonial hegemony was firmly established. For example, by 1950 the Tolai of New Britain had been involved with alien colonial rule for eighty years (Epstein 1970: 429). In extreme contrast to the prolonged involvement of the Tolai is the case of the Maring peoples of Highland New Guinea who were contacted as recently as the 1950s and pacified only in the early 1960s (Lowman-Vayda 1968). Finally, even after the consolidation in 1949 of Papua and the Trust Territory of New Guinea, the implementation of Australian policies on local government proceeded differently across the colony. For instance, local government councils were established gradually from 1950 through the 1960s in various regions of New Guinea.

Nevertheless, it is possible – and desirable for the purposes of this chapter – to discuss some general characteristics and trends evident in both the indigenous politics and the implementation of the Australian-imposed system of local government. According to Mair, 'New Guinea political systems are characterized not only by their small scale but by the almost total absence of hereditary or even lifelong leaders' (1970: 8). The informal nature of politics in New Guinea societies has prompted some Western social scientists to treat these systems as the closest approximation to anarchy known to man (Mair 1970; Brown 1963). And a brief survey of the anthropological literature would seem to justify, to an extent, such a conclusion. Lawrence (1965–66) and Langness (1968) discuss political action among two different New Guinea peoples in terms of the 'security circle' concept. This security circle is a system of interpersonal relationships through which political action is carried out. 'Every individual is the nuclear figure of a security circle, the members of which are distributed within his political region . . . . At the same time, every individual is also a member of many other security circles, for there are as many security circles as there are people in the society' (Lawrence 1965–66: 379). While kinsmen, both affinal and consanguineal, form the nuclei of such groups, members are included on other bases also. Other writers (Kaberry 1965–66; Brown 1967) have discussed the acephalous, informal operation of political systems in New Guinea.

Another widespread feature of indigenous politics is the existence of a 'big man' leadership complex. To the extent that groups functioned as units, big men in leadership roles played a key part. Accession to the position of big man was seldom hereditary and was based, at different places and at different times, on a range of achieved statuses. Wealth, accumulated in yams and pigs (or shell money in coastal regions), often was the key to achieving big man status. The ability to coerce others by physical force sometimes allowed men to assume leadership positions. Frequently, oratorical skill, alone or in concert with the other qualities, would provide a basis for achieving status as big men. It should be emphasized, however, that rarely were these leadership positions part of formal political structures and just as rarely was there hereditary succession to a leadership role. Most big men made it on their own and in their own manner.

A variety of colonially directed political institutions were imposed on these small-scale, informal political systems. In Papua prior to 1949, the Australians had established two local political offices. 'Constables' were nominated by the Australian authorities to serve as the arm of colonial authority. In addition, 'councillors' were chosen or elected to advise the constables, informing them of native opinion. These councillors were without sanctioned authority from the colonial administration. An analogous system had been inherited by the Australians from the Germans in the mandated territory. The equivalent of the constable was the *luluai* who was assisted by local *tultul*s, functioning as councillors. In some regions there was an additional medical *tultul* who handled health-related matters. Brown (1963) has argued that under these conditions anarchy was replaced by satrapy. Salisbury (1964) and Burridge (1965–66) counter that while the *luluai* had the force of colonial authority behind him, he was at the same time subject to demands from the center. *Luluai*s thought by the Australian administrators to be uncooperative or unsuitable were removed from office and replaced by more tractable leaders. Consequently, the *luluai*-constable system may best be viewed as an extension of the colonial bureaucracy and not as an indigenous form of local government.

In 1949, a policy change occurred whereby a network of local government councils were to replace *luluai*s and constables. The ordinance under which these councils were to be organized empowered the councils to maintain peace, order, and good government and to establish rules to reach that end. The councils were given limited powers to levy taxes and to carry out local improvement projects. Taken at face value, the council concept would appear to be a step in the direction of responsible local government and authority. In practice, few councils represented the initiatives and interests of local leaders or populations (Salisbury 1964; Reay 1964). In addition, the gradual establishment of councils over a period of at least fifteen years in various regions created an overlap between the old *luluai* system and the more modern council system.

A Local Government Ordinance, passed in 1963 and made effective in January, 1965, made possible the inclusion of non-indigenous members on local councils. In mid-1969, 111 out 142 councils were multiracial in membership (Mair 1970). There has been resistance, notably among the Tolai, to this change in council composition (Epstein 1970). Local councils, already de facto dominated by colonial advisors, now also face domination by expatriate members. Epstein (1970), Salisbury (1964), and Reay (1964) detail the disillusionment and frustration apparent among native groups over the form and nature of local government bodies.

The evolution of a local court system in New Guinea somewhat parallels the development of local government institutions. As an official arm of colonial government, Courts of Native Affairs were established. Generally, these courts handled three types of cases: disputes involving a wider range than the local community; disputes which had been unsuccessfully resolved under the *luluai;* and all offenses resulting in bodily injury (Reay 1964). Court was held at subdistrict headquarters at regular intervals. In addition, magistrates would travel to local areas to hold court at various times.

Generally magistrates were apprised of local custom and 'law' by assessors who had no official role in the proceedings (Mair 1970: 76). A further involvement of local leaders in legal affairs was the operation of unofficial proceedings by *luluai*s and later local government councillors. These proceedings were tolerated but not officially sanctioned by the Australian administration. Strathern (1972) and Lang (Chapter 16) discuss the differences between these informal arrangements and officially sanctioned formal proceedings. At the time of the institution of local government councils, there was consideration given to extending formal status to the unofficial *luluai*/councillor hearings. It was not until 1966, however, that a formal system of local courts with limited jurisdiction not confined to native matters and partially staffed by indigenous magistrates and assistants was brought into existence.

THE DEVELOPMENT OF THE NATIONAL LEGISLATURE

The direct involvement of indigenous people in a legislature system in New Guinea is a comparatively recent phenomenon. Until the establishment of the House of Assembly in 1964, the Legislative and Executive Councils had served mainly as liaisons between expatriate interests and the administration (Staats 1973: 23–36).

In the pre-World War II period, each territory had an advisory Executive Council and a Legislative Council, with provision for nominated non-official members from among the European population. In Stanner's view the effect of this arrangement was to give the European population 'a share in and some hold on government' (Stanner 1945: 18).

In the post-war period, the long-term objective of increasing indigenous participation in government has already been referred to. Hasluck, in particular, saw representative government for the indigenous people as being an extremely distant goal:

'There is not at present, and cannot be for many years to come, any possibility of a Territory-wide franchise for the native people. They are separated into so many different language groups; they are at so many different stages of progress towards civilization; and there are so many who are still unaware or only partly aware of what a legislative council is that any attempt to form an electoral roll would be a travesty of any democratic principle and would only have the effect of allowing a very small minority of the people in a few regions to assume the representation of the interests of tens of thousands of people about whom they know less than do the officers of the Administration' (Hasluck 1956: 12–13).

In accordance with this view, the development of legislative institutions continued as before. A Legislative Council composed of official members and twelve non-official members, the latter group comprising three elected representatives of the European population, three nominated indigenes, and three persons nominated to represent other interests (generally mining, commerce, and planting), had been set up in 1949. An advisory Executive Council on which there was no non-official representation was also established at that time (Bettison 1965: 9). In 1960, the composition of the Legislative Council was changed to provide for a non-official majority (22 to 14), although elected members remained in a minority (12 to 24). At least five of the ten non-official appointees had to be indigenes. Of the twelve elected members, six were indigenes chosen by a system of indirect election, and six were non-indigenes chosen by a non-indigenous electorate (Parker 1966: 253). The Executive Council was replaced by an Administrator's Council consisting of three official and three non-official members (with at least two of the latter to be elected members).

This reorganization was largely stillborn as a result of the Foot Report in 1962. The official report of the U.N. Mission urged the development of 'representative, democratic government at the center to overcome the divisions which have so far bedeviled the Territory' and, to that end, suggested immediate preparations for the election of a representative Parliament of 100 members (U.N. Trusteeship Council 1962: 16). The changes effected by the Australian Government did not go as far as these recommendations, but in 1963 provision was made for the establishment of a House of Assembly with a majority of elected members (ten official and fifty-four elected members). A common electoral roll was established. Each voter could vote twice: once in one of ten special electorates where candidates had to be non-indigenes; and once in one of forty-four open electorates where there were no such racial restrictions (Parker 1966: 253). After the 1964 elections the House of Assembly consisted of twenty-six European and thirty-eight indigenous members (including the official representatives).

For the 1968 elections the number of elected members was increased to eighty-four. The special electorates were replaced by fifteen regional electorates in which anyone with at least an Intermediate Certificate standard of education could stand (Tudor 1969: 39). After the 1968 elections the House consisted of thirty European and sixty-four indigenous members. Changes in the Administrator's Council in 1963 increased its non-official membership from three to seven, all of whom were to be elected members of the House of Assembly. In addition provision was made for the appointment of fifteen Parliamentary Undersecretaries from elected members of the House (Parker 1966: 257). Ten undersecretaries were chosen after the 1964 elections. They were given administrative experience in government departments, but retained their right to criticize the Administration in the House.

In the 1972 election, 603 candidates stood for the ninety-seven House of Assembly positions. The result was a slim plurality for the

United Party, with the Pangu Party a strong second, then the People's Progressive Party, and assorted independents. The United Party, traditionally strongly tied to expatriate business interests, opposes rushing self-government. The Pangu Party raised the first radical voice for immediate self-government. Their appeal has mellowed somewhat as they have made extraordinary gains in power in the last few years. The Pangu Party effected a coalition after the 1972 election with the People's Progressive Party and gained most independent support to elect the first New Guinean Prime Minister, who then appointed a ministry of ten, with seven lower positions. These were in addition to four nominees from the Australian Administration from his cabinet.

The whole political process revolves now around the question of independence. Papua New Guinea reached self-government on December 1, 1973, with full independence to follow before 1976. Indigenous control of the 100 member House of Assembly, the Ministries (including the Prime Minister), and local councils are cited as evidence of New Guinea's readiness for independence. Some observers argue that Australia's desire to 'blend' New Guinean culture and society into some sort of unified whole has been a distinct failure. Various distinct and irreconcilable subsystems have merged: the indigenous systems themselves; an expatriate system of administrators and commericial operators; and a system of indigenous-expatriate relations, affected by European roles in missions, bureaucracy, and employment (Schaffer 1971: 4). The viable integration of these subsystems remains a problem for Papua New Guinea. Some observers consider secessionism and tribalism to be potentially the strongest and most divisive forces in New Guinean development, as two bloody and violent confrontations on Bougainville and New Britain have already demonstrated (Hastings 1968).

Local councils have followed the general pattern of Australian local government and acted as administrative instruments of the central government (Parker 1966: 251). In some cases the councils have been a forum for the discussion of political issues, e.g. land policy, demands for native courts, educational policy. On the Gazelle Peninsula of New Britain dissatisfaction with local government (in particular the establishment of a multiracial council to replace the native local government council) has been the focus of Tolai grievances on the land shortage and the 'masta-boi' character of race relations in the area. The conclusion remains, however, that while local government has had some role in increasing indigenous political participation, the Administration has functioned primarily in centralized bureaucratic terms.

This penchant for bureaucracy has been given a free rein in New Guinea. Some observers have criticized the bureaucracy for being too centralized for the needs of New Guinean society. While the process of localization has been slow, the administration has attracted most of the educated indigenes to its service. Since these indigenes will presumably be more nationally oriented than their less educated compatriots, it is to be expected that the administration, whether dominated by Australians or indigenes, will continue to act as a major integrative force in New Guinean society.

The House of Assembly has had a limited role as an integrative institution. It does provide a forum for the discussion of issues of national importance, but it has just as much served to provide a manifestation of the fragmented nature of New Guinean society. Local interests have predominated in the House, and political parties are only in the early stages of development. The low level of education of the elected members has helped to reinforce their parochial outlook. Certain attitudes on the part of the administration have added to these difficulties. For a long time it discouraged the formation of political parties. The more able members of the House have been co-opted by the administration through the system of under-secretaries and ministerial members. The effect has been to weaken the House as a possible basis for opposition to the Administration and to reinforce the training of the elite in bureaucratic values.

The evolution of local and national political institutions in New Guinea will doubtlessly continue over the next decades. At all levels the blending of native New Guinean and colonial Australian political values, ideals, and institutions should constitute the internal dynamics of that ongoing process.

RANIER LANG

Interpreters in Local Courts in Papua New Guinea

This paper reviews the status of interpreters in Papua New Guinea and analyzes one particular interpreter's performance in a court case. In the paper, I show the strengths and weaknesses of the present interpreting services in Papua New Guinea and consider what practical steps might be taken to improve these services; however, very little is said of the strengths, since there are few. Section 2 briefly sketches the history of modern interpreting services on a worldwide basis and compares it with the development of the interpreting services in Papua New Guinea. Section 3 focuses on the perfomance of Papua New Guinean interpreters in court, while section 4 provides the framework within which the interpreter's performance under analysis took place. Section 5 is an analysis of the methodological aspects of the performance under investigation. Section 6 concludes the paper with suggestions for improvement in the present interpreter services.

Section 4 and 5 are based on data collected in the Enga-speaking area of the Western Highlands.[1] The Enga number some 150,000 speakers and constitute one of the largest language groups in Papua New Guinea.[2] They have been studied extensively by anthropologists and geographers (Meggitt 1965; Waddell 1972). Data on their language is still scant (for a review see R. Lang 1970 and A. Lang 1971); the New Guinea Lutheran Mission – Missouri Synod has long carried out intensive work in the grammatical analysis of the language, but has only in recent years made determined efforts to analyze speech behavior not within the scope of classical grammatical analysis. As in many other Papua New Guinea societies public speech making and 'hidden talk' are highly developed among the Enga (Larson 1970;

Brennan 1970). They are no less fervent 'rhetoric thumpers' than the Kuma (Reay 1959: Ch. 5), and not being a good orator is a definite stumbling block (if not an overt disqualification) to becoming a 'big man'. But while this aspect of Highlands speech behavior has been amply reported on, a different aspect of it has generally been taken for granted and thus received little attention. It comes to the fore especially in both informal and formal court cases, where their talk is almost totally devoid of 'hidden talk' and rhetorical vehemence.[3] There they exhibit a matter-of-fact approach which observers have at times felt is pervasive of all Highlands cultures.[4]

HISTORICAL BACKGROUND

Papua New Guinea with its 700-odd languages would appear to be the ideal country for interpreters, where they would be needed, appreciated, trained, and in plentiful supply. Oddly enough, the real state of affairs attests to almost the opposite. Before the arrival of the modern colonial powers, interpreters as such did not appear to exist at all – people either made use of the existing trade languages such as had evolved (e.g. along the Rai coast) by learning these trade languages (Harding 1967: 203), or they learned each others' languages as in parts of the Highlands (Salisbury 1962), or they conducted their cross-tribal affairs at a non-verbal level (Hogbin 1947: 247).[5] Only with the arrival of outsiders and particularly with the arrival of the modern colonial powers did something like an interpreter's profession come into existence in Papua New Guinea. Expatriates generally came to rely on one (or a very few) trusted individual upon whom they bestowed the task of intermediary between themselves and the native population, and since certain categories of expatriates tended to stay at the same place for considerable lengths of time, these trusted individuals got enough practice in interpreting to become experts of a sort in this new skill.

The expatriate enterprises which most readily made use of such interpreters were the government and the missions. There appeared to be no training, however, for these interpreters and in a quite literal sense there could not be, since the expatriates themselves had not yet advanced enough to have interpreters in their home countries; this was doubly true then of the expatriates who had come to Papua New Guinea. Under these circumstances it is not surprising, therefore, that a peculiar type of interpreter should have evolved who differed in a number of respects from his European counterpart and preceded him by about 40 to 50 years.

With the rapid increase in international conferences after the first World War and the parallel decline of French as the language of diplomacy, there arose a very real need for trained interpreters. Initially these interpreters came from other professions, but had a natural talent for interpreting; they were lawyers, journalists, doctors, etc. But the pool such individuals was very limited and after the second world war and the establishment of supra-national agencies like the U.N., the demand for compenent interpreters was too great to be readily satisfied by a few gifted full-time amateur interpreters. It was at this point that interpreter training schools began to be established on a wider scale and organizations like the U.N. took on the advanced training and supervision of interpreters as well. With the development of interpreting as a profession came a gradual diversification into kinds of interpreting, each with its special skills and techniques. Initially there was a kind of simultaneous interpreting, *chuchotage,* in which the interpreter whispered into the ear of his client a simultaneous interpretation of what his partner was saying. But this had its limitations, especially in large gatherings where it was more convenient for a speaker to give his speech, the interpreter to make notes, and then give an interpretation at the conclusion of the speech; this was called consecutive interpretation. But here too there were limitations, since everything had to be rendered once in the original and at least once as an interpretation; the amount of time required for a meeting, therefore, would be twice as much as if the meeting had been interpreted simultaneously. As our electronic technology improved, so did the very real possibility of perfecting equipment that would allow simultaneous interpretation for large conferences either by the permanent installation of such equipment in specially designed meeting rooms or by portable sets. In addition to these two kinds of interpreting, there arose a steady need for liaison interpreters who would assist individuals from different nationalities to communicate in business meetings, sightseeing, or any other situation where two or three individuals might want to carry on a conversation rather than engage in speech making. The chief differenced between consecutive and liaison interpreting lay in the fact that the consecutive interpreter took notes, which meant that he had to evolve special note-taking techniques and that he was thus not limited by the duration of any given stretch of speech. There were minor differences as well, in that he had to have some oratorical skill, and that he had to have a high degree of analytical acumen, etc., but these could not be considered drawbacks for a liaison interpreter even though he had a lesser need of such skills.

Looking now at the New Guinea situation, consecutive interpreters in the above sense were out of the question, since most interpreters were either illiterate or barely literate. Most of the interpreting took place under adverse conditions on the outstations often with no electricity or an irregular supply of it,[6] which ruled out the use of mechanical equipment. There were thus only two kinds of interpreting available – *chuchotage* and liaison. *Chuchotage,* however, requires a degree of sophistication on the part of both the participants to a conversation and the interpreter, which could not be found in most situations in Papua New Guinea.[7] This then allowed only for the use of liaison interpreting. But since it could not always be avoided that speeches were given and had to be interpreted, the Papua New Guinea interpreter had to develop into a kind of consecutive interpreter minus the note-taking component.[8]

Interpreters have been employed on a permanent or semi-permanent basis by the government in Papua New Guinea since 1884[9] (Tomasetti 1973: 1). In German New Guinea *tultul*s were appointed in the villages to act as channels of communication between the colonial power and its subjects (Rowley 1958: 226), while in Papua the government employed a system of station interpreters. Later, when Australia was given responsibility for the administration of the Territory of New Guinea in 1921, a mixed system evolved whereby both station interpreters and *tultul*s were used (Tomasetti 1973: 2ff.). While the number of *tultul*s has declined in recent years, station interpreters have continued to serve a useful function. They continue to be influential in many parts of the country, especially in the Highlands, and the number of former interpreters who are now members in the House of Assembly has increased steadily over the years. In the first and second House of Assembly about 10 percent of the indigenous members were former interpreters, while in the present House their proportion has risen for the first time to nearly 12 percent.[10] Yet nowhere in the literature have interpreters been studied as interpreters, even though it is widely recognized that problems can (and do) arise through them. Mention is made of (accidental) misinterpretation, wilful distortion, and bribery, but nowhere is their role systematically analyzed. Nor is there any attempt made to assess their technical skills or to provide the data to assess them properly.[11]

As it was administration policy to rotate personnel rather frequently, administration officers soon realized that it would be a waste of time and effort to attempt to learn the local language as they would most likely soon be posted to another language area and would have to start all over again.[12] The immediate consequence of this was that there was no one who could have checked on the adequacy of the interpreter's performance. Thus, many an Administration employee may have had the uncomfortable feeling that not all was well but there was very little he could do about it. It is tempting, therefore, to posit that interpreters became as powerful as they are through exerting pressure on their (local) clients by threat (or enticement) to interpret for or against them.[13] Keesing and Keesing (1956), in discussing the Samoan situation, remark on the need to test 'the integrity of subordinates in a position to manipulate the facts on which decision-making rests' (1956: 127). This is undoubtedly a legitimate point and one which appears to be held by the majority of Papua New Guinea specialists. But it could well be that the decision is made long before the facts upon which it is to be made ever reach the official. Wolfers remarks on this when he points out that a 'careful study of the reasons for the political ascendancy of so many interpreters in the Highlands may, indeed, shock many a *kiap,* when he discovers that his interpreter is not popular because he is pro-government, but powerful because of his ability to control who sees the *kiap*, and what the latter hears (even in court)' (1968: 15).

Standard Enga practice about consulting the interpreter first,[14] before making an approach to the *kiap,*[15] makes it more than plausible that having control over who gets access to the official may be at least as important as the ability to control what facts reach the *kiap* through his interpretation.[16]

PAPUA NEW GUINEA INTERPRETERS IN COURTS

It should be stated at the outset that there are no court interpreters as such in Papua New Guinea.[17] But a good deal (if not most) of a regular government interpreter's performances take place while interpreting in court cases. The official language of the courts in Papua has been English from the beginning of colonial rule; with Australia assuming responsibility for the Territory of New Guinea, English also became the official language of the courts there. In Australia's annual report to the General Assembly of the United Nations for 1971 the following statement can be found regarding the official language of the court and the employment of interpreters in court cases.

'English is the official language of the Courts. However, evidence, etc., may be given in another language, in which case it is translated into English for the Court. Court interpreters are employed as necessary to assist the Presiding Judge or Magistrate. While no statutory qualifications are prescribed, considerable experience, a good educational background and competence in the relevant languages are sought in interpreters'[18] (Commonwealth of Australia 1972: 51).

Assuming now that such men existed who had this considerable experience, a good educational background, and competence in the relevant languages, how was the government to judge whether they had the requisite qualifications? What kinds of experience were required, and what was considered a good educational background? How was it to test for competence in the relevant languages if no government officer knew any of the local languages? If one looks at the biographies of interpreters in Papua New Guinea, one is struck by the kinds of 'considerable experience' which more often than not includes such things as cook and/or servant to one or more expatriates, coffee grower, trade store owner, and perhaps cattle owner.[19] The educational background more often than not contains statements to the effect that the person in question has no formal education, is illiterate, or taught himzelf to read and write. Their linguistic background almost invariably includes a command of their local language, of Neo-Melanesian, maybe Hiri Motu, possibly one or two additional local languages, and (rarely) some English. Competence in their own local language can no doubt be assumed as can most often their competence in Neo-Melanesian.[20] As for competence in any additional local languages, Tomasetti points out that there is no way at present to test for this (1973: 6). The practical consequence of this was that, with the exception of the Supreme Court, most lower courts conducted their proceedings in either Hiri Motu or Neo-Melanesian while the records were kept in English.

The fact that interpreters have no formal training has been recognized as a problem by the people teaching or administering the law (Barnett 1969: 160; Brown 1969: 203; cf. especially Johnson 1969: 89–94 and Minogue 1969: 105, 11ff.), but there have been no practical proposals as to how such training might be achieved. Regarding the selection of interpreters, officers of the Division of District Administration are advised that 'they should be selected carefully, having regard to ability, honesty, and loyalty' (Territory of Papua and New Guinea 1970: 30). Need I point out the essential vagueness of these selection criteria? The officers are further advised that is the job of the Magistrate 'to make sure that the defendent understands the language of any witness who gives evidence and that, if the defendent does not understand it, this evidence is interpreted to him; the defendant is entitled to hear every word which is said in court' (Ibid.: 115).

Government interpreters swear an interpreter's oath at the time of their first being employed as interpreters. If, however, a court has to use a private person, 'this person must swear that he can understand the language of the accused person and of the witness, and that he is competent to interpret it. He must also swear that he will interpret truly and correctly' (Ibid.: 115).

From my initial discussion of what it means to interpret, it will be clear how unrealistic such an oath is, especially in cases where more than one interpreter has to be employed. Selby (1963: 63–67) gives a vivid description of some of his experiences as a Supreme Court Justice and the problems involved in interpretation. Unfortunately, he had no way of directly checking the match between original and interpretation and in this he was no worse off than most other expatriates who had to rely on interpreters in their encounters with

Papua New Guineans; their only evidence for misinterpretation was usually of an indirect sort, e.g. the discrepancy between what they has asked and what they received as an answer. Although the discrepancy could undoubtedly have been due to the cultural gap, it was more likely than not due to inadequate interpretation.

I have recorded a large number of situations with interpreters at work and will present a detailed analysis of one such situation below. The findings derived from it, however, have validity beyond this single case, for interpreters working in many other situations use the same basic techniques and make the same mistakes.

THE TRIAL OF S.

S. was the youngest son of a widow and about 14 years old. There were no close relatives to take care of him at the time of the trial as his older brother was working as plantation laborer on the coast. S. had been engaging in a number of minor misdemeanors committed against members of his own clan. The clan had, therefore, lost patience about a year prior to the present event and had actually taken him to court, only to be told by the government officer that since S. was still a minor he could not take the case. This time S. had broken into a house and taken some money (not all of which belonged to K., the owner of the house), a belt, headbands, mother-of-pearl shells, and several other minor articles. The amount of money involved could never be clearly established, as the owner of the house (henceforth K. or complainant) did not really know how much had been left in his care by another clan member who was now in jail. When the theft was discovered, they immediately suspected S., who could not be found. Upon his discovery, he was subjected to threats of being taken to the government court to be jailed, and his hands were tied behind his back upon which he admitted the theft and revealed some of the places where he had hidden some of the stolen articles. It was obvious, however, that he did not reveal all, and angered by his stubbornness, the clan decided to make the trip into town for a court hearing where every effort was to be made to have S. jailed this time.

An official party of three – the village 'committee man'[21] (henceforth *komiti*) who knew Neo-Melanesian and had been a government interpreter himself, K., and S., both of whom knew only Enga – made the trip into town, where the usual procedure[22] was followed of first contacting one of the official government interpreters and informing him in Enga of the facts and their intentions. The interpreter, upon deciding that there was sufficient reason for a case, then ushered them into the courtroom where the government officer (henceforth *kiap*) in his capacity as Local Court Magistrate questioned the interpreter in Neo-Melanesian about the problem at hand. To this the interpreter gave an account of the facts as he understood them. From his behavior outside the court it had been evident that he considered S.'s guilt proven, and the case of the complainants worth his support. He related not only S.'s present offence, but also his previous brush with the law. His account of the old offence and the present one in fact integrated the two so well that the *kiap* could not immediately tell what the charges were supposed to be. He therefore questioned the interpreter further with the result that the interpreter found himself corrected in his answers to the *kiap* by the *komiti,* and finally suggested to the *kiap* that they question the litigants themselves. The *kiap* now sought to establish who was going to lay the charges and whether there were any witnesses. He received a satisfactory answer to the first question, but encountered difficulties with the second. This was brought about by improper answers, misinterpretation, misunderstandings, and subsequent attempts to resolve newly arisen problems.

Somehow it transpired that a certain amount of money was definitely involved in whatever charges they would finally decide to lay against S., and the *kiap* now tried to establish how much money had been stolen. Due to a gross error in interpretation which changed one pound ten shillings into ten pounds, almost the entire proceedings then dealt with the question of how much money was in fact involved. Any attempts to solve this problem created new confusion, some of which could have been avoided if both *kiap* and interpreter had followed some elementary rules of liaison interpreting behavior, such as I discuss in the sections to follow.

In bare outline, the following procedures and questions caused major problems in communication and lengthened what should have been a routine affair lasting not more than ten minutes into a major court session lasting nearly one and a half hours: filing of the formal charges against S.; whether the charges should be heard by the court in session or at some other time; who had ultimate responsibility over S.; whether S. knew what it meant to steal; K.'s testimony – what the circumstances of the theft were; the adequacy of the interpreter's interpretation; attempts at various stages of the trial to establish (a) how much money had been stolen, (b) how much of the money stolen had been returned, (c) whether S. should be charged over the amount of money stolen or merely the amount of money not yet recovered; K.'s evidence for the theft; whether S. was still a minor; evidence from S.'s previous appearance in court; final statements by the *komiti* and S.; and sentencing of S.

METHODOLOGICAL ASPECTS OF INTERPRETING

Interpreters, in Neo-Melanesian, are called *tanimtok* and to interpret is rendered as *tanim tok* ('to turn the talk'). This expression is taken over literally into Enga where an interpreter is called *pii kapilyingi akali* ('talk turn man') and to interpret is rendered as *pii kapilyingi* ('talk [to] turn'). It is a new profession which arose in response to the arrival of the modern colonial powers and the need to communicate with their representatives. Most of the interpreters initially were drawn from the ranks of the bright young men who had attached themselves to one of the early explorers' parties and been taken to the coast by them or into their employ where they could learn Neo-Melanesian, which stood them in good stead on their return home and the subsequent influx of ever more expatriates in need of communicating with the local populace. The mere fact that they were bilingual was the sole qualification necessary for them to be hired as interpreters. Additional qualifications were, of course, that they had seen more of the new ways and thus knew a great deal more than the average man about the expatriates (cf. Bettison et al. 1965: 508) so that they could in effect act as intermediaries as well as acting on their own initiative. Their role as interpreters was thus from the beginning contaminated as it were by their role as intermediaries, and an entire tradition of such interpreters *cum* intermediaries evolved and came to flourish. By doing a large amount of interpreting they could not help but also evolve certain techniques, and in what follows I will show the kinds of techniques used by one particular individual employed as a government interpreter at one of the sub-district headquarters in the Enga-speaking area. He had been an interpreter for a number of years, but clearly belonged to the second generation interpreters, those who had seen the art practiced by a number of others for a prolonged period of time. He was by no means an outstanding interpreter, for those are very few indeed; he was an average performer, good enough to satisfy his clients[23] and hold his job, and his performance can thus be viewed as of the kind one would most likely encounter in any situation involving an interpreter.[24] Nor were his clients very unusual, neither *kiap* nor the litigants – they were all individuals one could encounter any time in a local court. In fact, the occasion I am going to analyze is a thoroughly ordinary everyday affair – and that is precisely the justification for analyzing it in such detail.

There are three main parts to this section: firstly, an examination of the relationship of interpreter-clients; secondly, the kinds of misinterpretation that occur; thirdly, the interpreting techniques evolved by the interpreter. In the first part, after a discussion of the techniques used to distinguish between utterances that are interpreted and ones that are not, I go on to analyze the conflict that arises from the combination in one person of the role of interpreter (in the strict sense of the word, as a servant) and that of active intermediary; the practical consequences of this are shown in detail and the part concludes with a brief description of court behavior in Enga informal courts for purposes of comparison. The second part deals mainly with the reasons for misinterpretation. Four possible reasons are discussed in detail: carelessness, misunderstanding due to (a) auditory misperception, or (b) perceptual misperception, and wilful distortion. The third part concludes the section with a discussion of the specific interpreting techniques used by the interpreter; I point out that both interpreter and *kiap* made extensive use of paraphrases and that this was of particular importance in the case of questions, where I show that the interpreter had evolved a special technique of simplifying questions and how effective this technique was.

The interpreter and his clients. No interpreter can ever be viewed completely in isolation from the people whom he serves; in many ways his behavior as an interpreter depends on the behavior of his clients and on how they view him and each other through him. Do they want him to be an interpreter in the strict sense of the word or do they want him as an intermediary[25] as well? Do they view him with suspicion or do they view each other with suspicion? Do they regard the interpreter as the servant of one or the other party? How do they signal their attitudes and how does he? When is something that a party to the proceedings says to be interpreted, and when is an opinion privately expressed and not to be interpreted? When is something interpreted and when is it the interpreter's private opinion? And how is the potential ambiguity of such situations to be avoided?

There are a number of ways in which this ambiguity could be avoided. One obviously would be never to let the interpreter express any private opinion whatsoever, such that his clients would always be addressing each other directly, with the interpreter a mere mouthpiece. In terms of pronominal use it would mean that whenever one of his clients spoke in the first person the interpreter would do so too, when addressing his partner in the second person the interpreter would too, etc. This happened once in the trial I am discussing.[26]

(1) *Accused:* It's up to you whether you want to hit me or jail me.
Interpreter: It's up to you whether you want to hit me or jail me.

This mode of communication would be ruled out as soon as one allows the interpreter the auxiliary role of intermediary, and the fact that it was used just once out of at least 120 possible instances attests to the fact that the interpreter was considered as an intermediary as well by all parties concerned and that he was aware of this.

There are two major alternatives as to how this problem of ambiguity might be resolved from the interpreter's point of view, (a) by direct quotation:

(2a) *Interpreter:* He says: '. . .'.

or (b) by indirect quote:

(3a) *Interpreter:* He says that . . . .

From the point of view of his clients, the corresponding phrases would be:

(2b) *Client:* Tell him: '. . .'.

and

(3b) *Client:* Tell him that/Ask him whether . . . .

One would, for example, expect the interpreter to use the third person singular declarative form of the root *la-* ('utter') in order to express a sentence like (2a) as in (2c):

(2c) *Kiap:* How old is the boy?
Interpreter: He says: 'How old is the boy?'.
[('How old is the boy?') le-ly-a-mo[27]
— utter-PRES-3SG-DEC[28]]

(2c) is, in fact, the only example where the interpreter used *la*-'utter' in the declarative mood, i.e. where he vouched for the accuracy of his interpretation. In all other instances, and there are well over one hundred of them, he used the 'sensed' mode, a grammatical form which indicates that what the speaker communicates has to be qualified by the fact that the speaker only feels or senses the truth of that which he is saying. The practical consequence of this is that every statement that the interpreter interpreted into Enga was thusly qualified. In only one instance then, namely (2c), was there a claim made about the adequacy of the interpretation; in all others the claim was only to an approximation of the original.[29]

No such indeterminacy could be found in the utterances of the interpreter's Enga clients. In each case their version of (2b) indicated quite clearly that they wanted him to interpret precisely as they told him with no sensing implied.

(2f) *Komiti:* (You) say he says: 'I am saying I came in order to have him jailed.'!
[(I came in order to have him jailed) le-ly-o-na
— utter-PRES-1SG-QUO
le-ly-a-e

— utter-PRES-3SG-DEC
la-a!
— utter-IMP]

They used the construction 'quotative marker *-na,* followed by the imperative of "utter" ' more and more often as the trial went on and the confusion became greater. It was initially not used at all by the *komiti* (possibly because as a former interpreter he was under no illusions about the efficacy of the interpretation?) but from about halfway through the proceedings he too resorted to its use.

Thus, while there were a few problems with direct quotation they were not insurmountable and comparatively free of major ambiguities. Indirect quotation, on the other hand, is something interpreters everywhere are wary of, because of the problem of pronominal reference and the resultant misidentification of referents. The dangers lies in slipping from direct quotation into indirect quotation (3c), in forgetting to reverse pronouns (3d), and in having multiple third person referents (3e).

(3c) *Kiap:* Do you want me to conduct the trial?
Interpreter: I feel he says: 'Do you want him to conduct the trial?'.

(3d) *Complainant:* I went in search of S., found him and got him to return the goods to me and then I . . . .
Interpreter: He says: 'I went in search for S., found him and got him to return the goods to me and then he . . . .

(3e) *Complainant:* I went to the *komiti*'s house and told him about it and he said . . . .
Interpreter: He says he went to the *komiti*'s house and told him about it and he said . . . .[30]

Part of this problem resulted from the interpreter not being consistent in the use of either direct or indirect quotation. The remainder was due to his clients, Enga and expatriate alike, in not being consistent in their manner of communicating with each other through the interpreter. Most often the *kiap* would address the litigants directly in the second person but every once in a while he would slip and address the interpreter directly rather than the litigants, expecting the interpreter to make the pronominal change — in a number of instances the interpreter answered directly to the *kiap*'s question having thought the question was addressed to him.

(4) *Kiap:* And he returned the salt at the same time?
Interpreter: Yes.
Kiap: Ask him!

Sometimes the *kiap* would command the interpreter to ask one of the litigants something or other; at other times he would omit the command, so that there was a certain amount of inconsistency in his behavior.

I have remarked on the overtly signaled indeterminacy of all interpretation into Enga. No such indeterminacy is possible (or at least was not used by the interpreter) in the case of interpreting from Enga into Neo-Melanesian. Depending on the length of the passage almost every interpretation into Neo-Melanesian was signaled by either an introductory *em tok* ('he says') or closing *em tok* ('he says') or both.[31] It was sometimes strengthened by an added *olosem* which functioned both as a quotative marker and as an emphatic to mark utterances of special importance. Thus, the interpreter might begin his interpretation with *em tok* and close it with *em tok olosem.*

There were a number of instances where overt reference to the fact that something was interpreted was omitted, i.e. where *lalumu* or *em tok* neither preceded nor followed the interpretation. These were times when a client signaled either verbally or non-verbally that he had understood the original; where the opinion expressed in that which was to be interpreted coincided with the interpreter's personal opinion; where the interpreter continued after having been interrupted but where he integrated into his continuation material supplied to him by the person who had interrupted him; where the interpreter had to interpret a rhetorical question or an imperative/hortative which did not involve the root *la-* ('utter'); or where the interpretation involved such routine questions as 'name?', 'residence?', 'name of father?', etc. In the majority of such instances an overt interpretation marker was omitted, but in this too the interpreter was not entirely consistent. There was one area, though, where the interpreter was remarkably consistent, namely, if one of these interpretations without *lalumu* (but not *em tok*) did not immediately elicit the required response, the interpreter would repeat the interpretation with a *lalumu* following it. Only through this means did he unambiguously signal that he was speaking at the behest of someone else and that they were thus accountable to that someone else (in this case the *kiap*) and not to him.

I have remarked already on the conflict in the interpreter's role as either interpreter proper or intermediary, or both, and how this was brought about not only through the interpreter's perception of himself but was also reinforced by the behavior of his clients. I now analyze this behavior of the various parties concerned in relation to each other. Ideally, in liaison interpreting, the utterances are reasonably short – preferably containing not more than seven points[32] – and the sequence is either *client A, interpreter, client B, interpreter, client A, interpreter,* etc.; or *client A, interpreter, client A, interpreter, client A, interpreter,* etc.; or a mixture of the two where sometimes client A has several passages interpreted, then client B, etc.; but it should never be one where utterances of the two clients are immediately adjacent to each other without any interpretation in between. As I have already indicated this ideal sequencing rule was broken on a number of occasions, which should not be surprising, since the *komiti* had been an interpreter himself and was able to follow both sides with ease. But this was a minor problem.

A more serious problem arose from a feature of the above sequencing rule which indicates the direction of the flow of speech from one client to another through the interpreter and back. Thus, in the sequence *client A, interpreter, client B, interpreter,* etc., utterance *a* should turn into utterance *a'* and be received as such by client B whose response *b* should turn into *b'* and be received by client A as such. Similarly in the sequence *client A, interpreter, client A, interpreter,* etc., utterance *a* should turn into utterance *a'* and be received by client B as such, client A's next utterance a_1 should be turned into utterance a_1' and be received by client B as such, etc. Never should client A's utterance *a* turn into utterance *i* addressed to either client B or readdressed to client A, unless the interpreter was unable to either acoustically or perceptually perceive client A's utterance; in other words the interpreter may ask back to make sure he understands correctly so that he will be able to interpret adequately, but on no other occasion may he initiate an utterance on his own. This feature of the sequencing rule is to ensure that the clients will have a similitude of a direct interaction with each other as a two-party team rather than as two two-party teams, one consisting of client A and the interpreter, the other of client B and the interpreter where the interpreter is the pivot around which everything revolves. This is a very real danger in all liaison interpreting, that the partners to a conversation find themselves not partners to a conversation with one another but rather with the interpreter. And this is precisely what happened in a good many instances in the trial of S., with sometimes disastrous results. The litigants would address themselves to the interpreter or each other and not the *kiap,* the interpreter would address himself to either the *kiap* or the litigants, and the *kiap* would address himself to the interpreter. I will now discuss some of the reasons for this 'undisciplined' behavior and try to point out some of its practical consequences.

At the outset the reader should remember that the pecking order, from top to bottom, was *kiap,* interpreter, *komiti,* complainant, and accused; this scale also indicates who was most at ease with whom and as such it is also a scale of familiarity. The litigants, and foremost among them the *komiti,* most often turned to the interpreter directly in order to either correct his interpretation or add to something which had arisen out of an interaction between *kiap* and interpreter and which the *komiti* felt either left out crucial evidence or inadequately reflected their views. Once the *komiti* provided information which he felt was crucial but which he was afraid the *kiap* would not inquire about. In one instance the *kiap* felt he had not received a satisfactory answer to his question and he asked the question again and then once more. At this the complainant sensed a certain difficulty which might have to do with either the *kiap*'s being dense or some inadequacy in either the interpreter's interpretation or his understanding of the matter. Whatever it was, he turned to the interpreter and opened up with 'Look. . .'. Whenever they addressed each other the litigants did so in order to clear up a point among themselves. As this left the *kiap* entirely out of the picture and possibly because it violated some procedural rule in the court proceedings, such interaction between the litigants was each time immediately suppressed by him and in this sense at least not much additional confusion was introduced through a breaking of the sequencing rule. It was a constant battle, though, for the litigants to restrain themselves from interrupting or consulting with each other, and I will remark on this feature in more detail below.

When the interpreter himself initiated an exchange with the litigants (and some of them were very extensive indeed), it was for one of three basic reasons: (a) his own misunderstanding of the situation, aggravated by the fact that he considered the litigants in the wrong and causing undue confusion; (b) answers which in his opinion were unsatisfactory for the *kiap* and did not answer some question of his; and (c) a realization that he himself might be confused and that this should not be passed on to the *kiap.* It is no exaggeration when I say that in *every* instance where the interpreter initiated an exchange with the litigants rather than interpret what they had told him, the confusion on everybody's part was greater afterwards. I will remark on the exact mechnism for this added confusion below. Whenever the interpreter addressed himself to the *kiap* it was mostly in response to some question of the *kiap*'s addressed to the interpreter.

A few special instances are worth remarking upon, though, because they illustrate typical situations of interpreter-client interaction and because such situations are specially practiced in any interpreter training course overseas. They involve when and how an interpreter should apologize to his clients, when and how to interrupt them, verbal attacks or derogatory remarks by the interpreter about his clients, and vice versa.

There was one instance where the interpreter felt he ought to apologize to the *kiap* for an especially long interchange between him and the litigants, an interchange which had left the *kiap* wondering what it was all about since it had obviously involved more than a simple attempt to get an answer to his question. The interpreter therefore apologized and then explained the nature of the exchange (or the difficulty in getting a proper answer to the question). This was perfectly proper interpreter behavior.

Perfectly improper, however, are interruptions by the interpreter when his clients are in the midst of speaking. In only one situation may he do so, when his client forgets that there are physiological limits to his ability to process, retain, and recover information. If one of his clients, therefore, talks for too long involving too many points and thereby makes it impossible for the interpreter to perform his job of facilitating communication between two partners, then and only then may the interpreter interrupt but even this should be done surreptitiously, for example, by taking advantage of the little break that occurs when a speaker pauses to take a breath. He should treat this little break as if it had been a signal by the speaker that he had intended to pause here, even though it will be obvious to the interpreter that the speaker did in fact have no such intention. In the case under discussion this device was used once by the interpreter.[33] Most other times he was far less subtle and simply interrupted the litigants at will and in mid-speech when he felt they were straying off the subject.

Equally improper are derogatory remarks by the interpreter about any of his clients. Notice in this connection the following remark about the complainant by the interpreter to the *kiap*.

(5) *Interpreter:* I think he doesn't quite know himself what he wants.

This is as overt a violation of a basic rule of interpreter behavior as can be[34] and in this instance especially inappropriate, as the confusion which the interpreter here imputes to the complainant was in fact one that had been caused by himself and only existed in his own mind.

(5) prompted a very typical client's reaction in that the *kiap* now accused the interpreter of having possibly caused the existing confusion. Concerning such attacks by the client on the competence or adequacy of the interpreter's performance, beginning interpreters overseas undergoing a regular interpreter training course are advised to swallow their pride, to make sure that their interpretation was in fact adequate, and what the source of the confusion or anger of the particular client might be.[35] Here, too, the Enga interpreter acted contrary to professional standards – standards which he admittedly never has been told about – by immediately defending himself to the *kiap* and embarking on a lengthy recapitulation of his version of his questions and the complainant's answers to them hoping to show thereby that the confusion was indeed the complainant's creation.

Since it was the practice for people who wanted to see the *kiap* to check first with the interpreter,[36] it had also become a practice for the *kiap* to listen first to the interpreter's account of whatever matter was to be brought before him. The case in question is a perfectly good example of this behavior. A frequent lack of understanding of local customs also made them turn for help to their interpreters, and having to work together daily made them rely on each other as a team. It should not be surprising, therefore, if the *kiap* should more often than not turn to his interpreter for answers to his queries rather than to the litigants. (And it also explains to some extent why the *kiap* allowed the interpreter a relatively free hand to proceed with questions on his own.) The *kiap* did, in fact, query the interpreter extensively about the case throughout the trial and the interpreter responded to this in his own way, most often to answer the *kiap* directly from his background knowledge of the case.[37] Since his background knowledge of the case and his understanding of some basic facts of it were quite deficient, the *kiap's* understanding suffered as a consequence. That the interpreter's answers to the *kiap's* questions were not always up to par is indicated by the many interjections by the *komiti* described above. In a few instances the *kiap* was justified, though, in turning directly to the interpreter, such as when the defendant had answered in Enga *wane paono tene* ('one pound ten' = three dollars) and the interpreter interpreted *tri dola* ('three dollars'), a discrepancy in form which was noticed by the *kiap,* or when he wanted to make sure that he understood the interpreter's interpretation correctly. But by and large, the *kiap* was a willing participant to the 'conspiracy' between himself and the interpreter, and he thus unwittingly helped to sabotage the maintenance of a high standard of interpretation.

I will now comment briefly on what I believe is a built-in factor for malfunctioning in cases where the interpreter is permitted to proceed on his own, especially in court cases. Since the sequencing rule is broken and there is thus no direct interaction between an interpreter's clients, whatever one client communicates to the interpreter in an extended interchange between himself and the interpreter can only be relayed to the other partner via a summary by the interpreter. Thus, if the *kiap* asks a question *k*, and this is interpreted but the answer to *k* is not, and the interpreter instead begins to question further on his own (irrespective of whatever his intentions may be) the *kiap* will inevitably be confronted by a response which somehow does not quite make sense in the light of his question but which, if he had had access to the exchange between interpreter and litigant, would make (better) sense. Why should this be so? In the case of the trial under discussion, it was undoubtedly due to the fact that the interpreter did not necessarily interpret his own questions to the litigants along with their answers to these questions of his. What was happening, in other words, was that the interpreter presented a summary of their responses as a coherent body of statements which they were not in the original. What they were in the original was a by-and-large isolated set of responses to a coherent (and sometimes not so coherent) body of questions by the interpreter. Without this body of coherent questions, however, the answers seemed to lack motivation when presented in isolation and they appeared to be contextually out-of-place.

But even if the interpreter had attempted to present both his questions and their answers together, the extent to which he sometimes questioned would have made it well nigh impossible for him physiologically to do the exchange justice, as it would have been beyond his processing capabilities as a human being. Miller (1956) has shown the limits to our processing abilities and Bruner (1966: 324) has hypothesized that perception in less complex societies is more likely to fill the magic seven slots with the particularities of a certain object or event than with a domain of the alternative events that might have occurred. Both theses are borne out by the way the interpreter handled complex or longer stretches of speech: the maximum number of points correctly processed by the interpreter was seven and all were of the enumeration type. If either of his clients provided him with more than seven points (sometimes up to fifteen), he would manage to interpret a maximum of four correctly and an additional three points approximately correctly; the remainder would be either dropped completely from the interpretation or they would be substituted by entirely new points not contained at all in the original. The relationship between various points were ignored by the interpreter except for a very few instances.

I have remarked above on the difficulty the litigants had in restraining themselves from interrupting. To this might be added the difficulty of having to conform to an alien mode of conducting proceedings, and a comparison with an informal court[38] conducted back in the village over a theft that had occurred and involving almost the same set of participants (except for the *kiap*) would prove most instructive. First of all there was no limit to the participants. Anybody who felt he had something to say was allowed to and did so. Information which had already been supplied was readily given again if the need arose, as in the arrival of a casual newcomer who needed to be brought up-to-date on the event in question. Although the *komiti* was officially adjudicating the case, he did not impose his personality on the proceedings and force everybody to follow his mode of questioning or reasoning. In fact, he mostly sat and listened. No suggestion, however far removed it appeared to be from the case at hand, was ruled out-of-question – it was patiently followed up and reasoned through until it was considered irrelevant by everybody present. Nor was it considered out of order if somebody brought up again a point which had been argued through before and discarded – it was as if the first unamimous decision to pursue this particular point no longer had never been made. What was most pervasive was the seeming open-endedness of all decisions taken. Somehow[39] it transpired towards the end of the session that there was not enough evidence and the *komiti* dismissed the case, or rather was able to dismiss it.[40] The differences in actual and expected behavior of participants between the two types of court session are obvious.

Kinds of ministerpretation. So far I have not commented on the quality of interpretation in those instances where the interpreter attempted an interpretation in the narrow sense of the word, i.e. where he tried to do more than merely paraphrase from the original into the target language. I will first focus on the kinds of misinterpretation that arose and then on the interpreting techniques that the interpreter used whether consciously or unconsciously.

On the strictest terms there can be only two types of misinterpretation from the point of view of match between original and its interpretation: addition and omission. These two are not necessarily mutually exclusive and often occur in compound form. From the point of view of reasons for misinterpretation, there are essentially four: carelessness, misunderstanding due to auditory misperception, misunderstanding resulting from perceptual misperception, and wilful distortion.

In terms of omission, I have already remarked on the difficulties associated with the interpretation of lists comprising more than seven members. This was a problem throughout. Thus, when the complaint about the theft was filed and the *kiap* read the formal complaint to the *komiti* to get him to verify it under oath, the interpreter omitted (a) the name and origin of the person to file the complaint (= the *komiti* in this case), (b) the name of the person to be charged (= S. in this case), and (c) the name of the complainant.

In terms of addition, almost all of the additional material derived from the interpreter's background knowledge of the case and was usually prefaced to the interpretation to make one client's remarks more intelligible to the other. When the addition did not consist of such ancillary material, it was paraphrases of what he had interpreted already; some of these paraphrases were quite extensive and in most instances struck a different tone from that of the original. A few additions had no justification whatsoever (if one grants for the moment that any of the other additions were justified, which they were not), as in the filing of the formal complaint when he added that the *komiti* was charging S. because he had evidence for it, when in fact the charge only was an accusation that S. had committed a theft of a specific kind.

Misinterpretation due to carelessness made up the bulk of misinterpretations.[41] Most were harmless in and of themselves, but when found following each other could result in major distortions and unbelievable confusion. They could involve a subtle change of focus as in (6) or (7).

(6) *Kiap:* Don't talk!
Interpreter: Let this one talk!

(7) *Complainant:* I would think they are at home.
Interpreter: They left them at home.

Or they might involve a change from a statement of opinion to one of fact as in (7) or vice versa as in (8) and (9).

(8) *Interpreter:* Is there no witness at all?
Complainant: Right (= there is none at all).
Interpreter: I don't think they've got a witness.

(9) *Complainant:* I say I know he stashed it away.
Interpreter: I think he stashed it away.

Or they might introduce an ambiguity or remove one as in (10) and (11).

(10) *Kiap:* How much money was stolen?
Interpreter: How much money?[42]

(11) *Kiap:* Did you make only one trip to the house to steal or several?
Interpreter: Did you make only one trip to the house, yesterday, to steal or several trips?[43]
Complainant: No, I went only yesterday.

Others might have a different implication as in (12) and (13).

(12) *Kiap:* Alright, *komiti,* what do you want me to do with this boy?
Interpreter: Komiti, I'm asking you what you think in regard to the boy.

(13) *Kiap:* Do you have a witness for this?
Interpreter: Did you come together with a witness?

A few result from the substitution of a command by the reasons for that command, as in (14a) and (14b).

(14) *Komiti:* Lift up your arms!
Interpreter: Let him see the hairs under your arms![44]

(14b) *Kiap:* Come here!
Interpreter: He wants you to swear.

Yet others would result from a careless paraphrase which would invalidate an otherwise correct interpretation as in (15).

(15) *Kiap:* Do you steal knowingly?
Interpreter: Do you steal knowingly? Do you steal habitually?

And yet others resulted in an interpretation basically different from the original as in (16) and (17).

(16) *Kiap:* Were you present when 'x' was returned?
Interpreter: Were there several present when 'x' was returned or what did you (pl.) do?

(17) *Kiap:* What are your reasons for thinking he stole the money?
Interpreter: What do you think he did after he had stolen the money?[45]

Misinterpretation due to auditory misperception occurred only once.

(18) *Complainant:* One pound ten.
Interpreter: Ten pounds.

But the consequences of this one slip were disastrous. Throughout the proceedings the interpreter operated with this notion that the basic amount of ten pounds was involved and he tried to make things intelligible to himself and everybody else in these terms. Had the interpreter been accustomed to more rigorously enforced standards of interpreter behavior, the consequences would no doubt have been far less severe. But as it was, this initial misperception influenced the course of the entire trial and dominated it to its very end.[45]

Misinterpretation due to perceptual misperception did not occur too often and the consequences of this were not any greater than those caused by misinterpretation due to carelessness. On two occasions the misperception was caused by the *kiap*'s Neo-Melanesian not expressing his intentions properly, as when a question of his was meant to communicate whether S. knew what it meant to steal while his actual words conveyed rather whether S. knew how to steal or possibly what to steal. In another instance, the plaintiff communicated to the interpreter that not all the money stolen was his but that some of it he had been keeping for somebody now in jail. This the interpreter understood to mean that S. had committed two different thefts, and this was a point that never became satisfactorily disentangled during the trial.

Misinterpretation by wilful distortion occurred only when the interpreter's clients made some derogatory remark about him or some aspect of his interpretation which would have made it appear inadequate, or when he considered a statement by one of the parties to be totally unacceptable for some reason to the other party. Thus, when at one point he had neglected to interpret a statement by the complainant and the *kiap* later by chance asked a question about the very facts which had been stated by the complainant before, the complainant reacted angrily that he had asked the interpreter before to communicate a statement about these very facts – the interpreter tactfully omitted reference to this reprimand in his interpretation. He was following here a course of action recommended at some of the interpreter training schools overseas for precisely such situations. At another time, the *komiti* suggested that they lift S.'s *laplap* to check whether S. had any pubic hair (and thus was old enough to stand trial). The interpreter must have considered this a bit daring and his interpretation indicated only that the *komiti* considered S. to be quite old enough.

Technical aspects. I have variously remarked in this paper on the kinds of techniques which the interpreter could have used or did use. In this section, I would like now to discuss in more detail the purely technical skills exhibited by the interpreter in the execution of his duties. Before focusing on the interpreter exclusively, I would like to comment briefly on a technical feature exhibited by the *kiap*. This involved the ability to use paraphrases in order to make himself clear to both the interpreter and the litigants. It is a common experience of people traveling in a foreign country and trying to learn the language of the people of that country that, when they do not understand something the local inhabitants have said to them and inquire about the meaning of the utterance in question, the local inhabitants (instead of trying to paraphrase themselves) repeat the original utterance over again, only a bit louder this time and, failing the efficacy of this slight increase in volume, will increase it even further – with the unfortunate result that the foreigner will have people shout at him in the end, with no improvement in his comprehension. It is to the *kiap*'s credit that only once in this trial did he repeat the same question after he had received an unsatisfactory answer. Items involving notions possibly alien to the litigants, he would sometimes automatically paraphrase in asking a question as in (19).

(19) *Kiap:* Do you want me to hear this case or the district court? Do you want me to hear it or the big court?

In other instances when having received an unsatisfactory answer (which could have been due to misinterpretation, of course) to a WH[46] question he almost always rephrased the WH question as a yes-no question as in (20) and (21).

(20) *Kiap:* Who is his guardian?
(unsatisfactory answer)
Kiap: Is the *komiti* his guardian?

(21) *Kiap:* Why do you think *he* stole the five pounds?
(unsatisfactory answer).
Kiap: Did you see it with your own eyes?

The interpreter similarly took recourse to paraphrasing in order to facilitate understanding, but almost all of it occurred in the direction Neo-Melanesian to Enga. He was handicapped in this since he had to rely on his intuition of the *kiap*'s intentions in making a certain statement or asking a certain question. They almost always involved narrowing down the scope of an utterance. Sometimes he succeeded, sometimes the technique backfired and the response was to some aspect of the paraphrase which was of only marginal relevance to the utterance in the original. There is no doubt, however, that the interpreter relied extensively on paraphrase as a technical device available to him. Rather than enumerate every conceivable type of paraphrase used by him, I will analyze in more detail a particular class of utterances, questions, and how he handled them.

Before doing so, let me first remark briefly on some other techniques of minor importance of his. He had evolved a special technique to deal with vocatives, affirmative or negative responses involving only *mh, mm, ee* and other Enga responses equivalent to 'yes' or 'no', concepts from one client's domain which he figured would not be readily understood or appreciated by his counterpart or which could cause confusion, and items in one language for which he lacked the requisite equivalent in the other language. Thus, he would turn vocatives into sentences with an overt hypersentence[47] as in (22) and (23).

(22) *Kiap*: Alright S., ...
Interpreter: S., I sense he is asking you now . . . .

(23) *Kiap: Komiti,* . . . .
Interpreter: Komiti, he is talking to you now . . . .

'Mumbled' affirmative or negative responses he would turn into full sentences as in (24) and (25).

(24) *Complainant:* Mhmh (= yes).
Interpreter: He says: 'That's it, I'm finished.'

(25) *Complainant:* Mmmm (= no).
Interpreter: He says 'no'.

Items which he felt could cause confusion as in (26), where a confusion could have arisen over whether they were talking about a traditional or manufactured belt, he defined further.

(26) *Complainant:* . . . a belt . . . .
Interpreter: . . . a belt, one of the kind one can buy in the trade store with plenty of beads . . . .

Items for which he did not know the equivalent in the target language he would either define in terms of usage (27), in terms of 'kind of' relations (28), or by using the semantically closest equivalent (29).

(27) *Complainant:* . . . (the Enga term for a headband) . . . .
Interpreter: . . . some adornment we wear around the forehead.. . . .

(28) *Complainant:* . . . a packet of native salt . . . .
Interpreter: . . . something having to do with edible salt . . . .

(29) *Complainant:* . . . torch . . . .
Interpreter: . . . hurricane lamp . . . .

I will turn now to the way the interpreter handled questions. He was well aware of the fact that the Enga like to question obliquely and like to answer similarly. He knew that although the Enga operate with a notion of strict answerhood, they prefer not to make use of it except in very exceptional circumstances. He also knew from his experience as government interpreter that expatriates, generally, and the *kiap* during court cases, in particular, demanded adherence to the notion of strict answerhood, and that they could become very annoyed indeed if in their opinion someone was 'beating around the bush'. In his role as intermediary, he had evolved certain methods to avoid potential clashes due to differential application of the notion of strict answerhood between *kiap* and litigants. In the case of WH questions, therefore, the main danger lay in their potential open-endedness. He therefore tried to second-guess the *kiap* in almost every instance by narrowing down the scope of the WH question and turning it into a yes-no question or a disjunctive question. In this he succeeded well enough on a number of occasions by actually anticipating the *kiap*'s next question should he receive an unsatisfactory answer to his first question. Sometimes he would first faithfully interpret the *kiap*'s original WH question but then follow it up immediately by a non-WH paraphrase. (30) and (31) illustrate WH questions turned into yes-no and disjunctive questions respectively.

(30) *Kiap:* Who is your guardian?
Interpreter: Is he (= S.'s brother) your guardian?[48]

(31) *Kiap:* . . . who is speaking the truth?
Interpreter: . . . are you speaking the truth or is he?

One WH question involving a *verbum dicendi* was turned into an imperative (32) and this too was done deliberately, as can be seen from other examples discussed in a different context below.

(32) *Kiap:* Having thought about the matter, what do you have to say?
Interpreter: Having thought about the matter speak up!

That this trend away from WH questions was a conscious effort by the interpreter can be seen from the fact that nowhere did he turn a disjunctive or yes-no question into a WH question. He rather preferred to turn simple yes-no questions into disjunctive ones where the second disjunct would contain an overt element of negation ([33] and [34]) and he would sometimes 'reduce' other disjunctive questions by turning the second disjunct into an 'or not' version ([35] and [36]). Only once did he turn a regular yes-no question into a full-fledged disjunctive question (37).

(33) *Kiap:* Is it alright if I hear this case?
Interpreter: Do you want him to hear this case or not?

(34) *Kiap:* Did you steal the ten pounds?
Interpreter: Did you steal the ten pounds or didn't you?

(35) *Kiap:* Do you want me to hear this case or the district court? Do you want me to hear it or the big court?
Interpreter: Would you prefer to have the trial conducted by the *kiap* here or by the district judge? Would you prefer to have the trial here or not?

(36) *Kiap:* Is all of it missing or did you get some back?
Interpreter: Is all of it missing? Did you get some back or didn't you get some back?[49]

(37) *Kiap*: Is this correct?
Interpreter: Is this true or a lie?[50]

But, even with such reductions, he was not always successful in limiting the scope of the question sufficiently for the respondent to reply according to specifications. In a number of instances the respondent just would not answer to the point of the question, and this proved to be a most exasperating experience for everybody concerned. For these instances the interpreter made use of a rather effective technique which, in essence, involved the making explicit of one or more defining features of questions. Thus, he would make explicit the answer to be given: whether a disjunctive question was to be answered exclusively, or only a direct answer was desired.

He would specify a number of alternatives and then conclude with

(38) *Interpreter:* . . . according to those lines he wants you to answer him.

Or after having received an answer which was not an answer to the question asked (in any sense of the word), the interpreter emphatically repeated the question and concluded with

(39) *Interpreter:* . . . that is all he is interested in (= he wants an answer to this question and not some story which might be interesting but is irrelevant to the question at hand).

If, however, even such admonitions failed he took recourse to a device which was singularly effective – he would transform the question into conditional clauses followed by imperatives containing the possible correct answers as in (40) and (41).

(40) *Kiap* . . . is it true or not?
Interpreter: . . . did you take the money or didn't you? If you did, say: 'Yes, I took it'; if you didn't, say: 'If didn't take it'. Did you truly take it or didn't you take it?

(41) *Kiap:* Would you prefer to be jailed for six months or pay a fine or receive five lashes?
Interpreter: If you would prefer to be jailed for six months say so; if you want neither to be jailed nor receive five lashes say you want to pay the fine.

In both cases the answers were according to specifications, although in the case of (40) this created certain complications since the exact amount of money taken had never been satisfactorily established.

CONCLUSIONS

While I have discussed some shortcomings in the interpretation process, I hope to have shown that the interpreter was aware of the fact that interpreting consists of more than just having a knowledge of two languages and that there are certain techniques which greatly aid him in the solution of interpretation problems. I have also shown how an interpreter's clients can greatly aid him in the interpretation process, and conversely, how they can make his job almost impossible.

Though it is difficult at the time of writing (June 1973) to predict fully official government policy in regard to language problems once independence is achieved, and while this creates problems for someone trying to make specific suggestions for improving the present interpreter situation, it is possible, nevertheless, to suggest certain alternatives which the government would want to consider should it wish for such improvement. The imponderables are the attitude of the government of an independent Papua New Guinea in regard to universal literacy; literacy in what languages; whether to opt for an official national language (or several); which one(s); how much political education there shall be; whether it will place officers in their home areas; and whether it is interested at all in communicating with the people. Whatever its decisions, the need for interpreters will remain for some time to come.

Assuming that the situation will not change radically from what it is now, and that the government would wish to improve the interpreter services for the population-at-large, a number of alternatives could be considered. It could insist that all new interpreters undergo a brief training course at some institution in Papua New Guinea which could develop a section specializing in interpreter training. Depending on the efficacy of the training staff the training need not last too long – even for as little as two days – as they could concentrate on only the most elementary rules governing interpreting to ensure that the interpreters would in future avoid the more blatantly obvious mistakes. Thus, it could gradually phase out the old interpreters and replace them with ones having undergone some professional training. As a second alternative – and maybe complementary to the first one – the government could bring in present interpreters to the training center and thereby try to improve their future performances. Thirdly, and possibly complementary to the first two alternatives, it could send training officers to the places where interpreters are employed and teach them on the spot; this would have the additional advantage that the government officers too would receive some training (which they obviously need as has been demonstrated in the paper). Fourthly, it could ensure that all future government officers know about the specific problems of interpreting so that they are able to make the job as easy as possible for the interpreter and so that they could possibly teach some of the interpreting skills to interpreters with whom they happen to work. Fifthly, the government could prepare a booklet telling its officers how to select interpreters from a technical point of view, and how to train them (and themselves) in the basics of professional interpreting. The cost of any of these schemes, or a combination of several of them, would be modest if compared to the over-all cost of misinterpretation, in terms of the amount of time spent in clearing up misunderstandings or suffering from the effects of remaining misunderstandings.

NOTES

1. The data on Enga were collected from 1967 to 1969 while I was a research scholar at the Australian National University. I am indebted to the Administration of the (then) Territory of Papua and New Guinea as well as to the mission working in the area for their ready help and cooperation, and to the people of Kopetesa in the Laiagam sub-district for sharing their lives with us while my wife and I lived among them for 18 months. An Australian National University Postdoctoral Travelling Fellowship enabled me to study interpreter training methods in Germany and England. I am specially indebted to the director and his staff at the Sprachen- und Dolmetscherinstitut, München, and to Mr. A. T. Pilley of the Linguists' Club, London, for the kindness and interest shown in answering my many queries. Comments by Marilyn Strathern and Bill Tomasetti have substantially improved the paper.
2. Efforts are currently under way to convert the Enga-speaking area into a separate district. (*Papua New Guinea Post-Courier,* June 8, 1973, p. l.).
3. There are certain informal courts which involve opposing clans where the clan prestige is at stake. In these cases one does encounter 'typical' Highlands speech behavior, but these 'courts' are not very different in essence from many traditional encounters between opposing clans. But most informal courts are of the bread-and-butter variety.
   Marilyn Strathern has done a thorough study of informal courts in the Mt. Hagen area and gives an example of questioning behavior shown in such courts (1972a: 31–38); the similarities to questioning behavior exhibited by the Enga during informal courts are striking.
4. Meggitt (1967) is probably the most prominent and vocal on this score. That the thesis is vastly overstated and leaves out huge chunks of that which to the Enga, at least, seems most important need hardly be said. On this point, see also Strathern (1972b: 28).
   When I remark on the distinction between the two kinds of speech behavior I do not mean to be contradictory. Both kinds of behavior are real and, although not mutually exclusive, occur mostly in different contexts: formal speech making in situations involving open competition between clans; non-formal speech behavior in clan-internal affairs or ones involving expatriates.
5. What has variously been called interpreters for the pre-contact period, as in Hogbin (1947: 247), very likely were not interpreters in the technical sense of the word. See also Sankoff (1968: 118ff.).
   Genuine interpretation appears to have existed in the Eastern Highlands (Salisbury 1962: 3ff.), but interestingly enough it was not used to facilitate communication between individuals or groups, but rather to mark the special importance of a given situation. Interpretation in this case was redundant from the point of view of its more narrowly defined function of facilitating communication which otherwise would not be possible.

6. From 1880 to about 1950, most government stations did not have any supply to electricity at all.
7. When I speak of lack of sophistication, I do not mean this onesidedly as applying only to the Papua New Guinea interpreters. As I have pointed out above, the expatriates certainly lacked an appreciation of the true qualities of good interpretation and it takes considerably more skill and natural talent to do simultaneous interpretation than liaison interpretation. *Chuchotage* came into its own in the 20th century and its usefulness was comparatively short-lived, so that the knowledge of its existence (much less its main characteristics from the point of view of technique) never reached Papua New Guinea.
8. Since, as I remarked above, formal speech making is largely absent from these court cases and since to do the subject justice would require a paper twice the length of this one, I will not deal with the consecutive aspect of liaison interpreting.
   Mention should also be made that with the establishment of the House of Assembly in Papua New Guinea came the recognition that at least in this particular situation simultaneous interpretation was a desideratum, especially since English, Neo-Melanesian, and Hiri Motu were to be official languages. Accordingly, the House of Assembly was built with a simultaneous interpreter set-up and an attempt was made to recruit and train simultaneous interpretation was a desideratum, especially since English, Neo-Melanesian, and Hiri Motu were to be official languages. A Chief Interpreter was recruited but unfortunately he has been hampered very badly by a lack of interest in an appreciation of the true advantages of simultaneous interpretation by the people ultimately responsible for its smooth operation. The resultant lack of active cooperation on their part with the Chief Interpreter and his staff has resulted in a sadly neglected service of inferior quality.
   This behavior of the ultimate authorities stands in marked contrast to that exhibited by the authorities in places like Ceylon, Malaysia, Singapore, and Hong Kong (Pilley 1962, 1971).
9. I will not be concerned here with casual interpreters hired on the spot for a single (or few) performance(s).
10. It is only in connection with their sudden rise to official political power that some biographical data on some of the interpreters have become available. The spate of articles associated with the various House of Assembly elections contains data on their education, personality, and other qualifications. Cf. Chowning (1971: 59, 64ff.); Colebatch et al. (1971:240ff.); Fink (1965: 288ff.); Gostin et al. (1971: 107ff.); Hughes and van der Veur (1965: 408); Reay (1965: 162ff.); Watson (1965: 98ff.), and Wolfers (1967). Outside of the political sphere there are two references which contain biographical material – Anderson (1970: 37) and Glasse (1968: 136ff.). (I am indebted to Marilyn Strathern for this last reference.)
11. Criper (1965: 127ff.) and Reay (1965: 169ff.) are exceptions. Criper provides a transcript (in English translation) of a Chimbu interpreter's

interpretation. While the data he provides do not permit a detailed comparison between the Neo-Melanesian original and its Chimbu counterpart, they do permit an evaluation of the length of the stretches of speech the interpreter had to cope with. Criper marks two points as being incorrect, but it is not clear whether they are mistakes on the part of the interpreter or the patrol officer. Criper's data also show that the role of interpreter in New Guinea includes that of intermediary.

Reay carefully identifies each point of departure by the interpreter from the original and this allows us to consider the kinds of misinterpretation occuring, and the likely distortions in understanding that result from it.

Sankoff (1968: 125) mentions that Buang interpreters do 'phrase by phrase' interpretation, but unfortunately she does not elaborate on this.

12. Much of what I have to say is biased by my more extensive knowledge of the Highlands situation where first contact was made in the 1930s or later (Kopetesa, our field site, is in an area which was de-restricted in 1961) and where one tends to find large areas where only one (major) language is spoken. The coastal situation differs in this and administration officers in a good many instances were faced with two, three, or more different languages being spoken in the area for which they were responsible. This tended to inhibit further any attempts to learn the local language(s).

    The reader should also keep in mind that historically the equation *administration officer = expatriate* fits, but that this has changed in recent years as more and more Papua New Guineans have entered the public service as district administration field staff.
13. This is the hypothesis advanced by Keesing and Keesing in regard to the dependency of Samoan chiefs on their interpreters (1956: 127).
14. The practice of consulting the interpreter first (or the senior non-commissioned officer as the case may be), although not officially sanctioned, was nevertheless one which often was tolerated by the officials. This was true of most places where there was no police station as such, but only a government office.
15. *Kiap* is a term used freely in Papua New Guinea to denote district administration field staff.
16. This point is also illustrated by Downs (1972: 59ff.). Although Downs' book is a novel, it undoubtedly rests on his extensive experience as a government officer in the Eastern Highlands of Papua New Guinea.
17. Chris Vass informs me that there are now a few full-time Supreme Court interpreters in Port Moresby. But there are very likely station interpreters who have been elevated to the position of court interpreters rather than people who have undergone special training.
18. This statement, with negligible changes, can be traced through nearly fifty years of annual reports.
19. Their experience is considerable indeed, but hardly along the lines considered relevant for court interpreting by the people who wrote the annual reports.

20. This does not necessarily mean that the *kiap* would have been in a position to judge whether the interpreter's Neo-Melanesian was up to par, as many a *kiap*'s own command of Neo-Melanesian left something to be desired.
21. These 'committee men' are the village's lowest elected officials, introduced at the time the local government councils were created. They and/or the councillor function as the link between the village people and the official government structure.
22. Cf. note 14.
23. 'Clients' is a convenient cover-term for any and all parties with whom the interpreter deals professionally. It is meant to cover here: *kiap, komiti*, complainant, and accused.
24. This interpreter was an average performer in comparison to the other Enga interpreters whose performances I observed and recorded. Evidence from the literature about problems people have had in their encounters with interpreters elsewhere in Papua New Guinea suggest that from this point of view, too, this interpreter may be considered average.
25. Bill Tomasetti has brought to my attention two different functions involving the interpreter as intermediary: when he is acting (a) to assure linguistic accuracy, and (b) as a friend-of-the-court. These two functions are not distinguished from each other in this paper.
26. Except for a few instances, I shall cite in translation only so as not to burden the paper unnecessarily with what for our purposes are ancillary matters.
27. Enga is a language where the verb occurs inevitably in sentence-final position.
28. The following abbreviations are used in the interlinear:

1/2/3 = first/second/third person	PAST = past tense
AG = agentive	PRES = present tense
DEC = declarative	QUO = quotative
IMP = imperative	SENS = sensed mode
INF = infinitive	SG = singular

29. In few instances this claim was somewhat stronger by the additional use of the quotative suffix *-na*. This is a suffix which normally marks a passage as an exact quote but which is also used to highlight the importance of a given passage by giving it the aura of a quote. This was used whenever the *kiap* read off the formal charges against S., first when the complaint was filed and later when the complaint was rephrased.

Imba-me	namba-me	kosa	mende	la-la
you-AG	I-AG	court	a	utter-INF

epe-ly-o-na	le-1-e-no-na
come-PRES-1SG-QUO	utter-PRES-2SG-DEC-QUO

la-l-u-mu.
utter-PAST*-3SG-SENS

I feel that he is saying: 'You are saying: "I am coming in order to take someone to court."'
(*To express a present sensed action the past tense marker is used.)

Opa-na	la-l-u-mu . . .	(interpretation) . . .
this-QUO	utter-PAST-SG-SENS	

I feel he is speaking thusly: '(interpretation).'

30. In order to appreciate the multiple ambiguity involved, one has to keep in mind that in the Neo-Melanesian version the tense distinction between 'he says' and 'he said' was not overtly signified, nor was the distinction between 'say' and 'tell', and that it was a habit of the interpreter to insert a 'he says' in a longer stretch of interpretation in order to remind his client that he was still interpreting.
31. Examples from Neo-Melanesian are cited the way the Enga pronounce them when speaking Neo-Melanesian.
32. I am basing myself here on Miller (1956) and whatever empirical evidence there is in the corpus under analysis. I will remark on this in more detail below.
33. Interestingly enough, the interpreter interrupted his client here after the latter had made seven points and it looked like he was going to make at least as many more.
34. Chris Vass informs me that the interpreter's behavior here constitutes a violation of the rules of evidence recognized by the courts. While this paper is conceived as investigating interpreting behavior and its appropriateness from a strictly professional point of view, it is gratifying to note, nevertheless, that throughout the paper one kind of behavior or another which is judged inappropriate from an interpreter's point of view is also inappropriate from a legal point of view.
35. There are probably two reasons why the beginning interpreters are taught to swallow their pride – in one case because it is recognized that self-defence is a likely reaction and this would be in contradiction to the interpreter's role as a 'non-person', and on the other hand self-defence on the part of the interpreter is likely to provoke his clients further, which might cost him his job ultimately. Admittedly, the interpreter's position here is not an enviable one.
36. Cf. note 14.
37. Cf. note 34.
38. On the notion 'informal court', see Strathern (1972a).
39. I must apologize for the vagueness of this statement for I have not been able to analyze out the precise mechanism whereby the group arrived at its decision.
40. I would not have been surprised if the entire procedure had repeated itself the next day should someone have decided to bring up the matter once again. My observations regarding the open endedness of all decisions taken

coincide with the findings of Larson (1970) in his analysis of Enga rhetoric and those of Sackschewsky (1970) on the Enga clan meeting.

41. In the examples to follow, the careful reader might object and suggest that in the original the distortions might have been less severe due to the 'native idiom' and that I have merely emphasized the differences in the translation. Let me assure the reader that this is not the case, that for each example there was available to the interpreter a perfectly good and proper Enga (or Neo-Melanesian) alternative which would have expressed the *overt content* of the original infinitely better and which he could have used had he tried. Let me also point out that the consequences of these seemingly trivial slips were real – all one needs to do is look at the answers given. I have given only one response, in (11), because the majority of them are rather long and involved, and space does not permit an analysis of the answers (interesting as that might be in itself).
42. This was at a stage in the proceedings when there was active confusion about whether they were talking about the amount of money stolen, the amount of money returned, and the amount of money they were going to charge S. for.
43. The ambiguity introduced here consisted of the fact that the *kiap* was talking only about the theft for which S. was before the court now, while the introduced 'yesterday' then permitted a possible reference by contrast to previous thefts of S.'s, especially one committed a few days earlier.
44. This is used as an age-telling device, to determine whether a person is still a minor or not.
45. This is a very real problem for all interpreters since, with the exception possibly of simultaneous interpreters, what an interpreter interprets can only make sense to his clients if it makes sense to himself first. If, therefore, the interpreter misses a vital point at the beginning of an assigment, this is very likely going to introduce distortions in the rest of his performance. I myself have noticed this with professionally trained conference interpreters.
46. WH questions are questions involving interrogative pronouns and adverbs such as who, how, why, etc.
47. Hypersentences are sentences which make explicit the modality of sentences such as declaratives, interrogatives, imperatives, etc. Thus, the sentence *Go!* with its hypersentence would read *I hereby order you to go.* (The term is from Sadock (1969) and the concept shows many relationships to that of 'performative' as formulated by Austin (1965).)
48. Compare this to the *kiap*'s (later) question in (20).
49. This is admittedly different from (35) but the principle underlying this 'reduction' is obvious.
50. This system of paraphrasing worked fairly satisfactorily on the whole, which is not to say that the interpreter paraphrased every question, whether of the WH type or one of the others, or that it always worked one hundred percent. At times the interpreter became enamored by his paraphrase and

forgot about his initial rendering of the original, and when given an answer refering to his initial rendering of the original insisted that he be given an answer to his paraphrase as in the following sequence

Kiap: How do you know?
Interpreter: Who told you? Did you yourself see it?
Complainant: He himself told me.
Interpreter: You yourself didn't see it with your own eyes?

Here the complainant's answer would have answered both the *kiap*'s original question and the interpreter's admittedly careless interpretation of it.

RICHARD F. SALISBURY

Language and Politics of an Elite Group: The Tolai of New Britain

This case study of the wealthiest, best educated, and politically most advanced of all New Guinea ethnic groups tries to throw into relief some of the generalizations made about the relations between national and local languages in the political process, by looking at an exceptional case where, at first sight, the generalizations do not seem to apply. On closer analysis, however, the apparent exceptions reinforce the general rules by exemplifying their working in special circumstances. In most of New Guinea there has been a choice between a low status vernacular and a higher status pidgin language – with an obvious result of the spreading of the high status pidgin language. However, among the Tolai, the vernacular has had a higher status than Pidgin. Secondly, Tolai society has been in rapid flux. This has meant that attitudes to languages, which can be taken as relatively constant in less sophisticated areas, have been changing and responding to demographic and other sociocultural changes. In the third place, these changes are being explicitly manipulated and engineered by political groups within the society. Examining generalizations made on the basis of studies of relatively stable, bilingual situations, where attitudes to languages are seen as independently determined, in this sort of a complex situation can, I hope, lead to a better understanding of the simpler situations themselves.

The paper is, however, frankly ethnographic, covering personal field experiences between 1961 and 1971.[1] Fieldwork in 1961 was primarily focused on the economic and political development of this language group, living near the port town of Rabaul (Salisbury 1969). Further fieldwork in 1967, in both Rabaul and the national capital of Port Moresby, obtained data on elite linkages. In 1971, I worked in the area again, as a Special Adviser to the Administrator of Papua New Guinea on Tolai problems (see Salisbury 1971). Briefly, the problem was that an intense local sectarian conflict had developed over alternative relationships between the Tolai and the central government. All government mediation to date had failed to resolve the conflict. My report focused on the economic and political aspects of the difficulties. The present paper will rephrase the issues in terms of the linguistic issues involved.

THE 1961 LINGUISTIC SITUATION

Language use among the Tolai has been in flux for at least a hundred years, since traders first visited the coast (Salisbury 1967). Changes in multilingualism, diglossia, and innovation have accompanied all social changes, but there has also been a remarkable degree of historical continuity. Having discussed the history elsewhere (Salisbury 1969), let me here describe the 1961 situation with a minimum of history in order to better concentrate on post-1961 changes.

In 1961, all 35,000 Tolai spoke a single, mutually comprehensible language with three main dialects: a northern and a southern dialect differentiated by prenasalization of voiced stops in the north, and an outlying western dialect where /s/ appeared to replace some of the /t/'s found in other dialects. Variant words (e.g. *lolo/gogo* for a roll of shell money) had complementary local distributions; one kinship term used in the north but not in the south actually alters the whole structure of the terminology. A related but barely mutually comprehensible language was spoken on the nearby Duke of York Islands. Tolai was also spoken as a second language by numbers of non-Tolai. It had been used by the Methodist mission for teaching – Bibles and literature had been published in it for over fifty years – and Tolai-speaking ministers and preachers had converted other areas in much of the Bismarck Archipelago. Teenagers from other parts of the Bismarck Archipelago had come to the Methodist secondary school (George Brown College), to the Catholic seminary (St. Peter Chanel), to the administration schools of Malaguna Technical and Kerevat High and had acquired some Tolai from their fellow pupils, even though the language of instruction at all levels had been English since 1948. Among whites, few outside the missions spoke Tolai, but the missions used it for all local work. Tolai, in short, was one of the largest single language groups in New Guinea (after Enga and Chimbu) with some claims to be a lingua franca and to having literature published in it.

English had a limited distribution among the Tolai. After 1955, all pupils entering school received all their education in English after the first few grades. High school graduates who had done all their education in English began leaving school in about 1962: they comprised all such pupils by 1966. The group who had had a secondary education in Tolai began with the few who went to Malaguna Technical and the Catholic seminary in the mid-thirties. This slowly increasing flow dried up between 1941 and 1947 because of the war and Japanese occupation; it picked up slowly between 1947 and 1966. The first Tolai to attend university entered in 1962 and graduated in 1966. Nonetheless, with educational standards much lower elsewhere in New Guinea, the Tolai area graduated the major portion of all those with any high school education during the 1950s in New Guinea. It had also graduated most New Guineans with an education higher than grade 6 before World War II, but most of these had been educated in Tolai at George Brown College.

The third major language in the Tolai area was Pidgin. It was the lingua franca for the 10,000 immigrant indentured workers on plantations in the area, but Tolai had few relations with these men. They regarded them as inferior beings generally, and met them only in stores or on the streets on their days of leave. It was also the language spoken as a lingua franca by most whites, plantation managers, storekeepers, and government officials, although officials in technical departments tended to be less committed to the Territory and to learn it less. By 1961, there had begun an inflow of white service workers – insurance agents, garage owners, and airlines employees – who spoke no Pidgin. Pidgin itself includes many Tolai words, for it developed in the nineteenth century around Rabaul, but it has never been regarded by Tolai as more than a lingua franca. Most Tolai understand it, but speak it haltingly and infrequently. Only those who had been much involved in talking to other New Guineans or to Pidgin-speaking whites had acquired much fluency, or the ability to use it in public oratory. The chief group coming into this category were those who had worked outside the Rabaul area before the war or with the administration before or immediately after the war. In short, they were men who were at least over thirty-five. As can be realized, most of them had received only a primary education in Tolai and had no knowledge of English.

Political activity outside the colonial administrative structure in 1961 largely centered around the four Tolai local government councils. All had been running for ten years by then and together they included more Tolais, although 17 percent of the Tolai population had, for various reasons, refused to join councils. They were highly effective bodies, collecting taxes of about $8 per head, and participating in administrating medical aid posts, local primary schools, local markets, road maintenance, and a $1,000,000 cocoa processing project. A joint Tolai council co-ordinated their efforts and administered the central Rabaul market. Paralleling the council structure, and involving much the same sort of political discussions, was the structure of the Tolai Cocoa Project, involving fourteen local fermentery managers and directors, and a central management committee. Co-operatives included eighteen local groups, which combined in the New Britain Co-operative Association as the wholesale agent for buying merchandise and selling copra; its monthly meetings were another areal political forum.

All of these forums nominally involved decisions being taken by local groups under the supervision of, and with advice from, a government official. The official being unable to understand Tolai, the proceedings were held in Pidgin, and the minutes were usually written in that language (though not for the cocoa project). The role of the official varied and was gradually changing over time. At one extreme were cases where the meeting would not start until he was present, and most of the items on the agenda would be 'suggested' by him, or at least he would be asked to explain why the item was raised. At the other extreme were meetings where the council president would run all business, calling on the council clerk to present items, getting the minutes approved, and then attacking issues that the council was really involved in, and turning to the supervising official only for advice on tricky legal points.

Council (and project or co-op) presidents, the central foci of local politics, were all fluent orators in Pidgin (and in Tolai) in the forty to fifty year age range, with little education, but long experience in handling white men. The village councilors who made up the councils (and management committees) tended to be aged around thirty-five, to have somewhat more education, but not in English, and to be engaged in establishing themselves as cocoa planters in their villages. There tended to be considerable changeover in these officers, as there were limited prospects of upward mobility to replace council presidents who had established themselves as 'real big men' (Salisbury 1964). Council clerks were men with great influence, most being aged about thirty-five, and literate in English from a pre-war education.

Tolai council politics resembled closely in many ways the descriptions of other New Guinea councils in the literature. The ability of the president to maneuver in the informal meetings that preceded and followed official council sessions was vital. These were meetings conducted in the local language, involving issues and techniques of trade-offs, mediation, and caucusing that could be labeled traditional, if they were not also familiar to any committeeman in western society. The president, in short, had to be a real traditional big man politician; he had also to understand enough of parliamentary procedure and budgeting to be able to meet his supervisory official on equal terms and to use Pidgin to bamboozle him into permitting what his councilors wanted; if he had a clerk who worked with him he could really get things done. He was the epitome of the broker, manipulating support from below to obtain rewards from above, and using Pidgin to do so.

Fortunately most clerks were first-rate. As the first area with councils in New Guinea, the Tolai area included the Vunadidir Centre for training clerks. There was lively competition for obtaining the plum positions with councils near home; the vast majority of successful trainees had to leave home to start new councils in remote areas of the territory. With a few exceptions of excellent clerks posted away for special reasons like starting the first joint urban-rural council near Goroka in the Highlands, only the best stayed in the Tolai area.

Much the same picture applied in most other fields of government. A proportion of the English-speaking Tolai from pre-war days had become school inspectors and teachers, medical assistants, co-operative clerks, interpreters, land titles clerks, and agricultural assistants in their home area. As newcomers left high school with grade 8, grade 9, and finally grade 10 qualifications they were all rapidly absorbed by the civil service and posted all over the Territory as the first middle-range indigenous officials in a long-term process of 'localization'. Some many went, and the dangers of staffing offices in the Rabaul area solely with Tolai seemed so great to suspicious white administrators that over half of the indigenous officials and school-teachers in Rabaul came from *elsewhere* – mainly from around Port Moresby, the Territory capital.

The president of one of the councils had been elected to represent New Britain in the Legislature in Port Moresby. The Legislature still had a non-elected majority, however, and did most of its business in English (with simultaneous translation into Pidgin and Motu). The member clearly operated under difficulties by being a Pidgin speaker, although he was one of the most effective indigenous members of the Legislative Council.

CHANGES BY 1967

When I returned to both the Tolai area and the capital of Port Moresby in 1967, many changes had occurred. In Rabaul, the four councils had united into a single council, with offices located on the edge of the white town. Its president (and the presidents of the other major bodies referred to above) were still from the same group as in 1961 – only six years older and fewer in number. They were supported by some of the same council clerks, although others (and several school inspectors) had quit to seek advancement in the training program for local magistrates that was just beginning.

Councilors at the larger council were still roughly the same age, however, and included several who were literate in English and had experience in trade unions, teaching, or the cocoa project. The council had become highly effective, running major road repair projects, and having a budget of over $100,000. It still had its technical council advisor, and periodically the district agricultural officer, education officer, or co-operative officer, etc. attended for discussions of their specialties. When such an official spoke, his views were heeded. At a meeting I attended, for example, a proposal to hold a referendum concerning the conversion of the council to a multiracial one was warmly supported by councilors, but was dropped when the adviser said a referendum would be 'expensive'. This failure to hold such a referendum was the main trigger, as it turned out, of the 'problems' I went to investigate in 1971.

In another way, however, the problem was the efficiency of the council which had found that most budgetary and planning problems were most easily solved by executive action of the president, executive committee, and clerk without always seeking grass-roots approval. It was going too fast with social change for its constituents.

The council was also involved in the expansion of the white town of Rabaul, which was the second great change I noted. 'Development' in New Guinea had meant rapid expansion of social services – roads, schools, hospitals, parks, etc. – along an Australian model, with concomitant expansion of administering bureaucracies. It had also meant a surge of Australian-owned and operated business – banks, hotels, bookstores, record shops, garages and car-hire firms, biscuit manufacturing, sheet-metal working, etc. – and a construction boom for Australian-style housing. Very few of the flood of incoming whites spoke Pidgin; only English-speaking Tolai could be absorbed by these firms, and then almost exclusively at the bottom level as clerical help. English was increasingly being used in all activities around town, with Pidgin becoming the language of talking among (or to) migrant manual laborers and of government officials when relating to older Tolai.

The council was still run by Tolai who were competent in Pidgin (but not in English) and who related through officials who also spoke Pidgin.

But it was in Port Moresby, the capital, that changes were most obvious. The University of Papua New Guinea had just opened to accommodate the first of the new generation of English-language schooled students; approximately a third of the first class were Tolai. The second batch of local magistrate trainees were undergoing courses in law, while the first batch were returning to Port Moresby for periodic seminars. The first indigenous civil servants, who were candidates for promotion to top-level administrative positions, were taking crash staff-courses – the Tolais among them being aged about thirty. In banking, radio, trade unions, tourism, etc., individuals with the potentiality of being national organization president or representative were being groomed for the position. English fluency was clearly the key to success.

The Tolai-speaking group in Port Moresby was very extensive, and despite its range of ages, from seventeen to forty, was very closely knit. Its influence was apparent, and it became the object of suspicion among many other ethnic groupings in New Guinea, particularly the Highlanders. I entered this group as a Tolai-speaker, known to many individuals, and was asked to the first meeting of a proposed 'Tolai Progress Association' to advise them on 'what traditional customs should be preserved'. My speech in Tolai, suggesting that this goal, albeit laudable, did not exhaust the possible functions of such voluntary associations, was the first Tolai speech of the evening. The language was rapidly picked up by others, however, who rejected the identity *English = progress,* and picked up the theme of cultural identity. The organization eventually was named *Pal na Tabu Society.*

The same beginnings of rejecting the prevailing ideology that English alone is the language of progress and that traditional cultures and local languages are objectionable were also visible at the university as students changed from wearing shorts, long socks, and white shirts at the beginning of term to wearing thongs, laplaps, and Hawaiian shirts by the end. In the Legislature (now known as the House of Assembly), changes in constituency boundaries and the abolition of nominated members had reduced to one the number of Tolais in the House. He was an English speaker, aged thirty-five, who had been a school-inspector before entering politics. To speak only Pidgin had clearly been seen as a disadvantage by Tolai voters in 1964; but, by 1967, there was much criticism of the English-speaking member's lack of action on critical Tolai issues, notably land. The first suggestions of introducing vernacular courses in local history and so on into high schools were made by a Tolai at the administrative staff course, though these were drowned out (despite my own support) by the professionalized and brainwashed educators, white and black.

The brainwashing had, however, proceeded very far. With few exceptions the English-speaking Tolai felt that the Pidgin-speakers who ran local politics in Rabaul were ignorant country bumpkins. They, the progressive English-speaking elite, should go back and tell them how to progress – for example, how they should vote in the 1968 elections. Yet realities like the implications of the phenomenally high Tolai birthrate and the cut in the central government education budget were far more readily grasped by the locals than by the educated group. The latter felt that Port Moresby was where things were happening, but that they were still Tolai. Yet in their offices they spoke English, and even in a meeting entirely composed of Tolai speakers, they conducted business in English. A tribal voluntary association was, I would feel, vital to them to preserve for their own consciences this semblance of cultural identity. The fact that they were actually out of touch with Tolai affairs will appear later.

1971 FIELDWORK

When I arrived in 1971, there had been further major changes in language use. In the capital, the trend noticeable in 1967 for Pidgin to be utilized universally in the House of Assembly as a national language, whenever it was appropriate to stress one's patriotism, even though the speaker was fluent in English, was even more apparent. But at the university, what was immediately evident was the much greater fluency in *English* of the Tolai students as compared with 1967. In asking them their views of the political situation, I spoke in Tolai and they replied in kind. But they quite often switched by preference into English when the discussion centered on such topics as colonialism, dependence, racism, or oppression. Among Tolai friends in the public service at various levels, much the same switching occurred. We spoke in Tolai of family matters and events back home, but in English about administrative, economic, or political topics. I was concerned about this switching as I wished to learn, while talking to friends, and without prompting, the fashionable Tolai terms used in the local political disputes. I eventually had to experiment, using the terms familiar from 1961 – *a tinur warurung* ('solidarity'), *a warkurai kai ra tarai* ('authority'/'power to the people'), etc. – and found them accepted readily. If I had not known them as the standard expressions of non-English-speakers in 1961, I would have been embarrassed as they sounded so like translations of the black power language of the students.

In Rabaul, too, there had been marked changes. In technical government offices (as in business offices), the number of white staff who spoke only English continued high, but there were also large numbers of middle-range New Guinean staff whose language of business and social conversation was also English. A proportion of these were Tolai, but for many of these to switch to Tolai in the office seemed difficult, although informal gossip in Tolai came easily. The junior staff, newly graduated from high school, seemed most at home in switching between the two languages and to be the 'contact persons' when the general public came into offices. (I must qualify this: Tolai secretaries and waitresses lapsed into coy giggling when addressed by me in Tolai, although addressed in English they were very self-possessed, quiet, and 'proper'.) I must confess that 'English' offices struck me as efficient and smoothly working; there seemed a clear split between Tolai (used as a solidarity-producing language for gossip about non-busines topics) and English (the language of work in which the senior office staff were treated as equals and were not condescending). The public related in Tolai to only the bottom staff levels.

I would contrast these offices with those where senior white staff spoke Pidgin, which also tended to be offices which were more used by the public and to have more blue collar staff. English knowledge among the New Guinean and Tolai staff tended to show the same pattern as in the other offices – fluency among higher staff but difficulty of switching among senior Tolai, with less fluency but easier switching among juniors. Non-Tolai blue collar workers often used Pidgin among themselves or when talking to New Guinean white collar workers. Senior whites often addressed janitors or the general public using Pidgin, and were not always consistent in using English with white-collar workers. Indeed in many three-way conversations Pidgin became the lingua franca, even when, say, a member of the public and a middle-range office worker could have talked in Tolai but the third person was a white senior official. Tolai conversations in such offices seemed to me to have a feeling of being surreptitious. (I can remember being asked to come outside to talk in Tolai by one person in such an office.) I would characterize such offices as overtly much more out-going, friendly, cheerful, and haphazard. I also had the feeling that language use was an area of some strain in them and that use of Pidgin to a person implied some derogation of him (or condescension by the person who could speak English but did not do so) in a way that use of Tolai did not. At the same time, using Tolai informally seemed to signify an intention of excluding those people from the conversation who spoke only English and Pidgin.

I would note that many of these departments were proving among the most difficult to 'localize' – District Administration, Police, and Agriculture – due to the shortage of New Guineans trained for the top positions, at a time when the ability of senior white officers to communicate to the general public through Pidgin, coupled with their claims of greater training and experience, gave them added claims to stay on. In fact a major factor in the 'trouble' (*purpuruan*) that had caused my presence had been the role of the Pidgin-speaking council adviser at council meetings. Council meetings still were conducted in Pidgin, so that he and other technical experts could understand the proceedings, although all councilors spoke Tolai. It had been the intervention of the adviser in a meeting which I had attended in 1967 that had prevented having the referendum on changing the council to a multiracial one, thereby permitting this development to take place without grass-roots approval. The council adviser, in the black power terminology, was the main bastion of paternalism and colonialism. In administration terms, he was the last safeguard against council irresponsibility.

The suggestion emerges that where usage of a second language for specific technical purposes occurs, a bilingual situation can be a stable one even though associated with stratification. The use of a third language by speakers of the other two, in a variety of situations which cross-cut and blur the clear distinctions accepted for bilingual usage, makes for tensions and is unstable. The 'dichotomy' of English as a technical language and Tolai for all other purposes appeared in many other spheres. For example, most local court cases were being handled summarily in Tolai by the new local magistrates, but when cases required representation by barristers, this was all done in English. I was amazed, however, at the warmth of personal relationships observed between individual Tolai and members of the public solicitor's office who had represented them in court, even though English was the sole means of communication.

Most dramatic was the situation in local politics – the main object of my inquiry. As suggested earlier, one central issue in the disturbance around Rabaul had been the idea that decisions – political and economic – should be made locally by Tolai. Local politics, as a Tolai subject, would be expected to be discussed in Tolai. The Gazelle Local Government Council, the officially approved body, continued to operate as it had during the 1961–1967 period, including much use of Pidgin. The opposition group, the Mataungan, which claimed that the council was a puppet regime, had no non-Tolai present at its meetings. Meetings rotated around the rural villages, instead of being permanently located near town, and made much use of indigenous religious symbolism. Whereas traditionally (and in 1961) masked *tubuan*[2] figures would be present in a village for only a month every three years on the average (Salisbury 1966), in 1971 over half the villages had *tubuans* present. They were said to be 'the government of the people' (Salisbury 1969: 305), and their concern with preventing incest and adultery was contrasted with white-men's government failure to take cognizance of these crimes. I have no doubt that only Tolai was used at Mataungan meetings. I know, from personal acquaintance with many Mataungan members, that the major power base of the group was predominantly among the older non-English speaking conservative Tolai, supplemented by young, largely unemployed, Tolai who had not gone on to higher education or to skilled public service employment on account of deficient English language skills.

But the effectiveness of the Mataungan depended also on the excellent English of its four major spokesmen. These four had also created the image which the movement had in the English-language press in both Australia and New Guinea, of being a black-power, radical-leftist organization. Oskar Tammur, for example, the founder of the movement, had focused discontent over land shortages by occupying a plantation immediately on his return from military service in 1967. Elected to the House of Assembly, he had become known for his fiery eloquence in English. He had taken up previously inarticulate conservative fears of the speed with which the Gazelle Council was introducing change, and sponsored rallies as the self-styled 'Champion of the Oppressed' (emblazoned on his sweatshirt). At home, he is clearly a 'man of the people', living in a villlage, working at visiting constituents from dawn to long after dark, dressing simply and casually, often smoking twist tobacco, partly for preference and partly because money is very scarce. But villagers can also see that in the world of white-man's politics he can operate in English, can dominate reporters and even the Prime Minister and Leader of the Opposition from Australia, and is fully the equal of the senior administrator of the local area. Such a person who can bridge the gap between two arenas, each one defined as appropriate to a particular language, is ideally suited as the representative of those people who cannot themselves bridge the gap – either because of lack of language skills or because of lack of economic power. I believe a similar analysis could be made of the linguistic contribution of John Kaputin, the second best-known spokesman. He has had some business administration training at the University of Hawaii. His methods of achieving local popularity were very different – he was a star football player and man-about-town. In his relationships with expatriates or English-speaking New Guineans, however, he uses excellent English to discuss economic planning and related matters. But again he demonstrates to many local people the feasibility of the local economy being run in Tolai while the national economy is run in English – so long as the intermediary between the two can be fluent in both languages and can be a Tolai.

I would interject at this point the comment that my own role as a government consultant was a difficult one, both personally and for the Tolai situation. I found, for example, that when I was interviewed in Tolai after the 9 p.m. radio news about my mission, about fifty percent of the whole population heard me. I witnessed later how near universal is listening outside the house to the Tolai news, but how it is equally nearly universal for the radio to be switched off or to be ignored if the subsequent interviewee speaks in Pidgin or English. Official speeches by Matthias ToLiman, then the other local MHA and Ministerial Member for Education, and by Hosea ToWartovo, President of the Gazelle Council, were usually given in English or Pidgin and reported by the ABC in those languages, and so tended to receive little local attention. Tolai villagers mentally 'tune out' messages in Pidgin and in English as Australian propaganda or as referring to arenas that are locally irrelevant. They accept as important only messages given in Tolai, or messages about 'technical' matters (e.g. how to apply for a driving license) that come in English or Pidgin. Understanding of central government actions in 1971 was conveyed 'reliably' only by intermediaries such as Oskar and John, although many parts of this understanding were in reality factually inaccurate. Spreading accurate information about the central government (including ways to manipulate it) was something that I actually did, but at the risk of endangering my own local credibility as an independent observer and my relations with the other information brokers. I have discussed these issues elsewhere as ethical problems and as problems of role definition (Salisbury 1973).

The conveying of Tolai viewpoints to the central government presented the same issues in reverse. Expatriates generally interpreted all news of the Tolai selectively, in terms of their own fears of ethnic hostility, and in terms of the 'good/bad' impressions conveyed by the mass media. Most New Guinea papers reported the official speeches in English and Pidgin as 'good', and the black-power speeches of Oskar as 'bad' (Sydney papers mainly took the opposite polarity), with little knowledge of how positions were drawn locally among the Tolai. My interpreting (or expounding) the various local, Tolai language stances into English disconcerted many expatriates, who saw me as anti-white, while not endearing me to Tolai protagonists themselves who felt I should have overtly supported their personal stance, and not have presented both sides.

My personal commitment, I must add, is to the effect that local politics and economics *cannot* be divorced from national New Guinean issues. Local separatism and a rigid segregation of domains into a national, English-language level and a local, Tolai-language level is a retreatist action, refusing to face up to real problems. It requires positive action to break down the segregation of domains, to increase the degree of control over central government action by local bodies, and the amount of information supplied by central government to local people. It requires an *increase* in the number of information brokers and channels, not a concentration of communication (and hence power) in the hands of a small bilingual elite. Segregation may be more *comfortable,* especially for the elite brokers, but it is the comfort of stagnant authoritarianism. People know what the rules are, but questioning of the rules and innovation from outside are eliminated. Increasing information flows *in both directions* is essential, in my view. It will not make life comfortable, especially for those wedded to authoritarian positions of the right or the left, but without it decentralization of power is impossible. With increased flow people at the local level may know enough to see the wider implications of what they are doing, and they may be able to influence decisions taken by the center. To increase the flow, a first requirement is obviously a greater degree of bilingualism both centrally and locally. A second requirement is that the domains of local and central government not be cognized as 'us' against 'them'.

The question immediately arises of why, in the most educated and developed area of New Guinea, where some English-language schooling has been available for almost forty years, should there be a lack of bilingualism and a segregation of domains. The answer is tied to the pattern of national development. Most fluently bilingual Tolai, who could have been acting as information brokers at home, are not living in their home area. Those Tolai, who in 1961 were council clerks elsewhere in New Guinea, or in 1967 were civil servants receiving crash courses for training as administrators or magistrates, are now bank presidents or deputy ministers. Those who have completed their education since 1961 have not been promoted quite as fast, but have almost all been absorbed into the civil service or into teaching. Few have returned home, except some magistrates, doctors, and clerics, and they have disqualified themselves from direct political involvement.

These educated Tolai have their biggest concentration in the capital, where they provide solid support for the PANGU party, which in 1972 became the main party in a national coalition government. Their policy is one of national unity, speedy independence, localization of the civil service, and a slower pattern of economic development that is geared to New Guinean employment and self-sufficiency rather than to rapid, foreign-owned industrialization.[3] In many ways, their policy parallels that of Nyerere in Tanzania. They strongly support the anti-colonial elements of Mataungan policy, but in 1971 were becoming increasingly disturbed by the rejection of national policies and institutions, and the isolationism of that group; they did not support the local council but tolerated its members as being 'incompetent and uneducated traditionalists' who would be replaced in due course.

They had, by mid-1971, tried three times to mediate the disputes in their home area, twice during Christmas vacation in 1969 and 1970 when the university students in particular had gone home with a mission to 'educate people back home', and once in mid-1970 when a group of senior civil servants calling themselves Warmaram ('reconciliation') had been granted paid leave to spend time at home. The attempts had been ineffectual and may well have served to accentuate the identification of central government with English and 'them'. The students alienated local people by their know-it-all posture, and by their use of English classroom jargon rather than Tolai at crucial times. The term *tena minatoto* ('an expert at knowledge') had become a term of sarcasm, instead of being the ultimate accolade as in 1961. They had their sights set on government jobs, Port Moresby politicking, and urban Australian-style housing rather than on local issues. The public servants, despite the respect they still commanded as individuals, also found it difficult to see things through the eyes of local people and to talk in Tolai about national issues. They were suspect because of their wealth and comfortable housing. They were branded from the start as government stooges, attempting to discredit the Mataungan leadership, through the leakage of a seemingly official confidential letter from the Director of Information Services saying that those were their aims. They did, however, prepare an analysis of the situation very similar to my own later analysis, and they did recommend that more Tolai civil servants be posted to the Tolai area. When I returned from Rabaul, having prepared my draft report, I presented it to a group of Tolai in Port Moresby for criticism. I had been discussing politics almost exclusively in Tolai for the previous month, including two radio interviews, and expected to continue in Port Moresby. But after the social niceties in Tolai, everyone said that they were unable to discuss politics in Tolai and wanted to switch to English. I must confess that the discussion took place at a different level of sophistication than it might have had in Tolai, but I felt that the reality of some of the issues became obscured. Intellectually, the group agreed with my analysis and most of my recommendations. They disagreed strongly with my recommendation that Tolai-speaking civil servants be posted to all local positions in Rabaul, replacing the many Papuans who then served there. They argued that it would be difficult for a nationalist Tolai living at home; they could see themselves identified locally as undesirable central government agents.

Interestingly, the government also rejected this particular recommendation, while generally accepting most of the rest. The government's decision was based, however, on opposite grounds. For the Tolai to administer the Tolai area would, the government felt, promote separatism further. The crucial point that the local administrators would be bilingual in Tolai and English and would be able to convey an understanding of nationalism and national policy was missed. The experiment of greatly increasing communication flow did not take place, while the crystallization of Tolai exclusiveness did occur, with the replacement of the Pidgin-speaking council adviser by a Tolai administrative officer.

CONCLUSIONS

As a linguistic ethnography of a changing society, this study merely stops with my departure from Port Moresby in August, 1971. But in the realm of generalizations, some conclusions can be made regarding propositions about language and politics. These involve testing propositions made about the more typical situations of stable bilingualism, where local languages have low prestige and national languages have high prestige and are used in inter-language situations, and thereby widening the generality of those propositions.

The first normal pattern in such situations is for the national language to steadily preempt the growing number of situations that are defined as inter-lingual. The local language becomes restricted to situations defined as 'local' or even 'domestic'. Bilingualism is needed only by individuals who wish to move between loval and national situations. What the Tolai case shows is that specialization of a language to particular domains is indeed a comparatively stable pattern of coping with the presence of several languages. But it is not inevitable that it is the vernacular which becomes more restricted. The attitude toward the national language ensures whether it is the language that expands or not. If it is disvalued, as Pidgin was between

1920 and 1960, then its use will be the one that is specialized in the local area. If the vernacular is highly valued, as was the case even relative to English in 1971, then again the vernacular can maintain its wide usage and may even become a special elite language. Bilingualism may then become a useful skill to preserve the exclusiveness of the group of monolinguals.

A second proposition concerns attitudes towards languages. The Tolai case history, for ten years clearly, but also going back for one hundred years, has shown that language attitudes can change rapidly in New Guinea. Impressionistically, I would argue that it is only sketchy study so far that has delayed the recognizion of this (Salisbury 1962). More generally, attitudes towards language cannot *a priori* be taken as more fixed than other determinants of language use in politics. Specifically, attitudes may change as a result of changes in the numbers of people who have learned a second language or in the incidence of situations where one or more participants cannot speak a particular language. Attitude changes in their turn produce changes in incidence. The attraction away of nationalistic Tolai-English bilinguals into the civil service and out of their home area has had dramatic effects on demography. It has also involved further attitude changes as advocacy of national unity in English is being treated as having 'sold out' locally. But if attitudes here appear as determinant, it is equally possible to argue that attitudes can easily be politically manipulated.

Finally, there are generalizations to be made about the role of bilingual brokers. Typically the local bilingual was faced with monolingual representatives of the national language and culture, and served to represent local monolinguals and to gain for them (and for himself) as many benefits as he could from the central government, while restricting the officials to learning only what the locals wanted them to know. The Tolai modify this generalization. Widespread passive bilingualism in Pidgin, coupled with English-Pidgin bilingualism by officials, meant there was little to be gained by a Tolai-Pidgin bilingual broker. White officials closely controlled the information flow downwards; control of the upward flow of information was only possible by Tolai-Pidgin bilinguals who were extremely fluent in public speaking and so able to argue for benefits. Now that Tolai-English bilinguals occupy positions of power, and that Tolai monolinguals can easily communicate with them, the incentives to become English-speaking are all concerned with obtaining employment out of the area rather than with the possibilities for local area brokerage.

In short, the role of the bilingual broker in a multicultural country is a crucial one for investigation. But a knowledge of the languages alone is insufficient to predict who those brokers will be. It is determined more immediately by the possibilities open, by the limitations on communication, and by the benefits to be gained by the brokers themselves through increasing or restricting the flow of information. The extreme situation, of elite separatist bilinguals obtaining local support by appeal to local patriotism but actually producing encapsulation and local stagnation, is a situation that has been long known in French Canada.

The Tolai case, thus, not only tests and confirms propositions derived from the study of more typical situations, and widens their generality, but it also provides an approach to studying the very different problems faces by elite language groups in many newly independent states from the Congo to the Philippines.

NOTES

1. Fieldwork in 1961 was supported by the University of California Center for International Studies and by U. S. NIMH Grant 4192; in 1967 by McGill University, The Canada Coucil, and the University of Papua New Guinea; and in 1971 by His Honour the Administrator of Papua New Guinea.
2. These tall conical masks, worn above voluminous leaf-skirts, make the wearers resemble cassowary birds. They represent generalized ancestors, and each design is owned by a particular individual who periodically 'raises' the spirit of his *tubuan,* so that it may attend clan ceremonials. Salisbury (1966) gives more detail on ceremony organization and politics.
3. The Chief Minister, Mr. Michael Somare, outlined this policy (Government of Papua New Guinea 1973: 1411). It drastically modified the policy before local home rule of mainly encouraging foreign investment in capital-intensive industry. It was triggered by a World Bank report, endorsing the self-sufficiency stance previously urged by several advisers including the present author. This report was subsequently released by the Government Printer in February, 1973.

PART FOUR

Disciplinary Interests in Language and Politics

JOAN RUBIN

Language and Politics from a Sociolinguistic Point of View

SOCIOLINGUISTIC CONSIDERATIONS IN THE DEFINITION OF LANGUAGE

In the past ten years, sociolinguistic research has amplified our understanding of the concepts of language and communication within speech communities. Whereas linguistic theory continues to assume, as it always has, that it is useful for most purposes to ignore variation among the speakers of any one community, sociolinguistics argues that patterns of communication and linguistic change are reflections of the variation which is always extant in groups of interacting speakers. As a result, the traditional view held by many linguists that language is a monolithic static entity (or that it is useful to view it as such[1]) is being discarded by sociolinguists for one that now appears more realistic and relevant. This new view emphasizes the differences in linguistic competence and performance form individual, social, and historical points of view. As we learn more about how language variation reflects social change, these new insights are themselves helping to add new dimensions to our understanding of the nature of social and political processes.

This change in focus brought on through the development of sociolinguistics has resulted in the questioning of many traditional assumptions. The boundaries of a speech community, for example, are not to be assumed as given but are to be discovered through the empirical study of communication and interaction patterns. Instead of studying 'the language of a representative individual', as was customary in the past, sociolinguistics concentrates on patterns of similarities and differences within a community. It also considers not just *linguistic competence* (i.e. an individual's knowledge of the structural rules of a language) but also *communicative competence* (i.e. when and with what meaning particular structures are to be used). With a focus on not only the formal but also the functional aspects of language, a sociolinguistic definition of a speech community starts from the shared rules governing communication and interaction rather than from the shared rules of linguistic structure.

In studying a speech community, sociolinguistics tries to establish what the entire communication repertoire of a whole community is. Within any group of interacting individuals, there are rules as to when, with whom, and with what intention, particular varieties of speech are appropriate. Within any community there are shared rules for communication; but not all speakers necessarily have the same degrees of competence or even speak the same language(s). Different members of a speech community may have unequeal competence in using and understanding particular varieties in specific domains (e.g. educational, legal, religious, artistic, etc.). What they share as a community is a degree of agreement upon what varieties are the appropriate one(s) to use in particular situations. For example, although not everyone in a community may be able to write a sermon, there is likely to be a high degree of agreement within the community that 'sermon style' is the appropriate one for particular occasions. As another example of differential competence, we might discover that an engineer is unable to write out clear instructions for using a piece of equipment he has designed. It may be necessary to have the manual rewritten by someone who has greater skill in the particular language variety used by those who will operate the machine.

Thus, sociolinguistics has noted that it is not even necessary for speakers within a given speech community to share all the same languages or varieties. What is necessary for a speech community to exist is for all or most of the members to agree upon the rules for the appropriate usage of each of the varieties. For example, the members of a given religious community might agree that Latin is appropriate for use in church services even though few members of the community control it. The use of Latin in church fits in with the setting, the domain, the audience, etc. In Paraguay, certain administrative situations require the use of Spanish and not the local Indian language, Guarani. And as in the case of the liturgical use of Latin, there is a high degree of agreement that Spanish is the appropriate language for this setting, even though the particular individuals making this assertion may not speak or understand it. Kidder's paper in this volume (Chapter 12) suggests that clients expect lawyers to use a particular variety of English in their defense in certain South Indian courts. Deviation from this style, he suggests, might be interpreted as a lack of seriousness on the part of the advocate.

Within every speech community then, language knowledge and language usage may not be entirely uniform – nor do we start with the assumption that it is. In any community we are likely to find several languages (or varieties) along with rules as to how and when to use them. With this view of a speech community in mind, two questions emerge which are of immediate interest in the study of language and politics: (1) Given the fact that we may expect the rules of communicative competence to be shared (although there may be differing degrees of language knowledge), is it the case that such information is used in such a way that individuals have differential access to power based on their competence in particular varieties? and (2) Since, like any cultural phenomenon, rules of language use are subject to change, do individuals attempt to change the rules governing appropriate domains or to alter the degrees of competence required for a particular domain in order to enhance their own political advancement?

In addition to these insights which emerge from the new sociolinguistic perspective, some others are also of interest in the study of language and politics. It has been observed that linguistic devices of all kinds (phonological, grammatical, semantic) as well as whole languages can and are used to signify many kinds of social, cultural, and individual preferences and identities.

'Although members of all societies categorize each other through speech, groups differ in the linguistic means by which such organization is accomplished. What some groups accomplish by alternating between familiar and respectful personal pronouns, such as 'tu' and 'vous', others achieve by shifting between Mr. Smith and John. Still others may achieve similar ends by simply switching from a local dialect to a standard language' (Gumperz 1970: 7).

One of the most common communication patterns found across

many speech communities is that designated by the term *diglossia* (Ferguson 1959). *Diglossia* describes those situations where two languages coexist in the same speech community but differ in domains of use, attitudes toward each, and patterns of acquisition and proficiency. The examples given by Ferguson are colloquial and classical Arabic, creole and French in Haiti, *dhimotiki* and *katharevusa* in Greece, and Swiss and standard German in Switzerland. Looking at the Arabic example, we note that the differences between the classical language and any variety of colloquial Arabic are so great that it is impossible for a speaker of colloquial Arabic to understand the classical variety unless he has had formal instruction in it. If we used intelligibility to distinguish between languages, we would certainly conclude that these two varieties constitute different languages. Yet Ferguson chooses to class them together because the rules for when each of the varieties are to be used and the attitudes toward them are widely shared within the entire community. The concept of diglossia has been useful in gaining insights into the nature of an entire speech community which is really a whole despite significant differences among the varieties spoken.

The diglossia relationship which Ferguson first noted for related languages has also been found to obtain in situations where two unrelated languages coexist. In Paraguay, there are two such languages – Spanish and Guarani – which are spoken by the inhabitants of the country. Although not everyone is fluent in both languages (most can speak Guarani; about 60 percent speak Spanish), the rules for which is appropriate in specific domains and settings are generally shared by the entire community (Rubin 1968). Appropriate usage of one or another language turns out to be defined stylistically (by domain, social roles, attitudes, etc.) in much the same way as the appropriate uses of the *tu* pronoun in French or of such phrases as 'he done gone' by some speakers of nonstandard English. It is important to note that speech communities have available and actually use many possible kinds of linguistic devices to signal social, cultural, or individual meanings. As Sankoff has so eloquently pointed out in Chapter 14, language is a resource to be used for any social purpose.

Since language is so malleable and variable, we can conclude that it is a cultural resource available for manipulation by those who choose to use it. One of the ways in which this manipulation is manifested is in the very definition of a language. It is commonly believed that the boundaries between languages are relatively clear-cut and fixed. Those with greater sophistication would argue that languages are structural entities which have a life of their own – no matter how people try to change them, they will continue in the same direction. It turns out that defining these boundaries is not so simple a matter. Even in those definitions using only structural criteria, it can be shown that there is a fair degree of arbitrariness. Lunt (1959) has noted that cultural values affect linguistic descriptions and categorization of languages by linguists. 'Still, it comes as a surprise to find supposedly scholarly spokesmen from the Serbian and Bulgarian camps making diametrically opposed claims about one and the same local type of speech. One blandly classifies all Slavic spoken in southern Yugoslavia as South Serbian; the other with equally calm conviction calls them Western Bulgarian' (Lunt 1959: 21). We should note that not even linguists may be agreed that any particular speech act should be assigned to the same language. The establishment of boundaries even by structural criteria is not a clearcut decision and can be influenced by the values of the linguists themselves.

The definition of such boundaries may become even more complicated when languages of two different language families are spoken in the same community and when the speakers interact over a long period of time. Whereas linguists have held that the integrity of the structure of a particular language is maintained in the face of continual contact, evidence to the contrary is mounting. In a study of a single speech community in India, where two genetically unrelated languages belonging to the Dravidian and Indo-Aryan stock are spoken, Gumperz (1969) found that in the speech of bilingual speakers considerable merger between the two languages had occurred. On the basis of lexicon and phonology, the speech of individuals could clearly be assigned to one or the other language. However, on closer inspection Gumperz found that the structures of these two languages had in fact grown together due to usage by the same speech community. The kinds of morphemes and their order was identical in samples of speech clearly identifiable as Kannada or Marathi. Gumperz's study has extended our understanding of the malleability of language structures and of the influence of social communication on language structures.

Apart from the use of structure to define language boundaries, linguists have also attempted to establish objective criteria to define degrees of mutual intelligibility. Such tests assume that if two samples of speech belong to different languages, it will be possible merely on the grounds of intelligibility to assign these two samples to different languages. Even if there were no other problems with the concept of mutual intelligibility, the cut-off point for how much intelligibility constitutes the same language or dialect is not a simple matter. Unfortunately, this sort of test turns out to be influenced by both cultural views and historical habits. It turns out that intelligibility may depend on the desire to understand (Wolff 1959). If the people speaking a particular variety are a prestigeful or powerful group, one might find their language relatively easy to understand. On the other hand, if one has some sort of grievance against a particular group, intelligibility might be reduced. We should also note that there are some intriguing cases of non-reciprocal intelligibility (Spanish-Portuguese, for example) which cannot be explained entirely on structural grounds.

The definition of language boundaries is further complicated by political considerations. Even when two groups are linguistically close, they may wish to emphasize the differences between them. Thus, the Dutch and German varieties spoken at the Dutch-German border turn out to be very similar; yet speakers insist that their language is Dutch or German depending on their national allegiance. What is often important – not only for native speakers but also for linguists – are the political considerations rather than the linguistic bases for defining languages. Similarly, wide differences in intelligibility have not prevented peoples from emphasizing similarities. A classic case is the 'Chinese language' which consists of several unintelligible varieties. What makes this a single language is the fact that a common script and certain cultural heritage are shared. A recently discovered case of how cultural and political attitudes influence the definition of language boundaries is that of the so-called 'Quechua language' of Peru. Parker (1969) argues that Quechua is a language family consisting of at least two dialects. He suggests that the reason the very great diversity of Quechua is generally still not appreciated is due not simply to the lack of published descriptions of the language but also to the persistence of the notion that 'all present-day dialects are descendants of the Cuzco dialect of the Incas' (Parker 1973: 68). We might assume then that it is the historical image of Quechua origins that has maintained the myth of the homogeneity of Quechua, even among scholars, until recent times.

We may note then that the definitions of a language and of a speech community are to be based not simply upon language structure but also on social perceptions, values, and attitudes. That this is of interest to students of politics is clearly illustrated by some 'strange' statistics that appear in Apte's paper in this volume. Apte notes that 'the number of languages and dialects as listed in 1951 and 1961 are 782 and 1652'. How is it possible in the course of ten years for the number of languages and idalects to more than double? Surely, this cannot be due merely to the increase in linguistic knowledge in India. As Das Gupta and Gumperz (1968) have pointed out, whether you call your language Hindi, Urdu, Hindustani, Pushto, or Sindhi depends in large part on what the perceived political advantages are. That is, even the labels for a given linguistic competence can be manipulated to achieve particular advantages.

Given the malleability of even the name of a language, it is of interest for the study of language and politics to consider the attitudes and beliefs that people have about existing language varieties and to consider reactions to these varieties in order to really understand how different aspects of language can be used or manipulated for specific purposes. Salisbury, in his paper on the Tolai, and Wolfers in this volume both note that Pidgin is considered by the Tolai and many others in New Guinea as inferior. On the other hand, Sankoff notes that for many other New Guineans, Pidgin is used for communication between groups and is a sign of some degree of higher social status. If administrators fail to take these attitudes into account when making decisions about the languages of communication and education, their programs will likely suffer. Administrators need also to take into account the extent and spread of language competence, for success or failure in implementing decisions about language programs depends in part on the attitudes which the target population has toward the varieties selected.

THE LANGUAGE AND POLITICS RELATIONSHIP

This volume contains examples of a number of political uses of language. As Salisbury wisely points out in Chapter 17, the relationship between language and politics is constantly changing and is dependent upon a great many factors: language competency/ proficiency, opportunities to acquire varieties, social values associated with language(s) and with language proficiency, and opportunities to act as language brokers. And as Sankoff has further observed in Chapter 14, attitudes toward particular language markers can change significantly over time. In citing McDavid's evaluation (1948) of the pronunciation of /r/ in preconsonantal and final positions, she has called our attention to an example which demonstrates radical change in the social evaluation of a particular way of speaking.

The uses of language for political ends may either result from explicit language policy decisions or as a consequence of unlegislated customs which nonentheless have political effects. Among those situations considered in this volume are (1) the use of language to encourage participation in the political process and to mobilize populations, (2) the use of language as a boundary marker – both as a symbol of ethnic or national identity and as a means of excluding others, (3) the use of language for economic advantages, and (4) the use of language in the selection and transmission of information.

Encouraging participation and mobilization. One common language policy decision is the designation of a particular language for use in particular domains. Such a choice often rests on a desire to facilitate political participation by as much of the polity as possible. However, the decision may not be so simple when there are diverse language groups (however defined), when there is a diversity of language attitudes (often based on other socio-cultural values), and when these boundaries and attitudes are used to promote interests other than national participation. As Fishman (1972) has pointed out, language is often part of the message of nationalism. It is often used as a link with the glorious past; or as a justification for the authenticity of the nation; or to foster contrastive self-identification.

In Tanzania, the acquisition and use of Swahili has been successfully made a part of the process of nation-building. Speaking Swahili seems to be tantamount to good citizenship and to the goals of unity. But Tanzania has still found it useful to allow use of the mother tongue in some court proceedings. As DuBow points out in Chapter 5 the attempt to find an interfacing between the national-level use of Swahili as legal language and the local-level use of tribal languages in courts is not simple and may lead to some malfunctioning of the legal system. And as Jean O'Barr has shown in Chapter 4, the use of Swahili to promote Tanzania's egalitarian ideals may actually have quite a different effect at certain levels of the bureaucracy. In India, as is well known, the decision to make Hindi the national language has not been easy to implement for complex political, religous, and social reasons (Das Gupta 1970). While the use of some local languages at the regional level has led to an increase in mobilization of hitherto unenfranchised masses (Das Gupta 1970), such decisions have not been an unmixed blessing. Problems of boundary-marking remain; the relationship between languages and regions in India continues to be a heated issue and the boundaries between some regions are still in a state of flux. Bailey's paper (Chapter 13) offers a discussion of how the diversity of language competence in India is related to differential access to power and hence participation. While New Guinea has not yet resolved its problems of the language of national participation, it seems likely that the question will be complicated no matter whether the choice is English or Pidgin.

Language as a boundary-marker. The choice of a particular language for particular domains often rests on desires for boundary marking. In the process of deciding on a national language, policy makers may choose that variety which distinguishes it from its colonial heritage or from its neighbors (for example, the continued use of Guarani as a national symbol in South American Paraguay has a boundary marking intention in addition to a recognition of its function for national communication). Externally, a national language may serve as a symbol of national uniqueness and authenticity. However, boundaries may also be drawn within a nation by the use/choice of particular languages for particular domains. Such boundaries often limit political (and economic) access to those persons not possessing the requisite language comptetencies. In Chapter 22 Leibowitz traces the history of laws requiring knowledge of English in order to qualify for citizenship and voting. As he points out, such laws serve to control and manipulate people in a society. Further, he notes that: 'The decision to impose English reflected the popular attitudes toward the particular ethnic group and the degree of hostility evidenced toward that group's natural development.'

In other papers in this volume, we find examples of the use of language as a boundary marker. DuBow has provided a number of examples. In one instance, DuBow describes a tribesman who insisted on using his own language instead of Swahili in the courts – this in spite of the fact that he indicated knowledge of this language. Such usage might be interpreted as a symbol of resistance to complete incorporation into the national polity by insistance on an ethnic boundary. In another example, DuBow points out how existing language practices prevent interfacing between the courts. Noting how attempts to use one language throughout the courts may prevent communication of legal precedence, he suggests that some strategy to overcome the interfacing problems will have to be devised. Another kind of boundary in the courts which DuBow brings out is the way in which choice of courts may depend on which language a litigant or lawyer wants to or can use in court. The identification of particular levels of courts with particular languages often serves as a barrier to participation in the appropriate level of legal activity. A boundary can be effective if the level of proficiency of the participants is low, or if the opportunities or desires to learn are few, of if the desire to participate is not adequate.

Boundary marking is a double-edged sword. On the positive side, it may lead to some increase in loyalty (all other conditions being positive which they almost never are). On the negative side, it may create a potential field for resentment when participation is restricted through inadequate knowledge or proficiency in the language required.

Economic consequences. In addition to affecting political participation and identification, language policies and patterns of usage may have direct economic consequences. In a review of state laws relating to language requirements, Leibowitz (1970) demonstrated how such laws served to help keep people in certain jobs and in some cases served to delay their acquisition of adequate educations for advancement. In his paper in this volume, Leibowitz notes that where laws regarding language were related to the task to be performed in a reasonable fashion, one might find it difficult to question the economic motivation. But where such laws were more arbitrary, they might be seen as constituting some sort of control of the labor market. We would need a greater understanding of ethnic bias and the labor market to understand why the State of New York but not many others felt it necessary to require that exams for barbers must be in English of why Arkansas and Indiana (but not most others) require that bedding (and not other products) be labeled in English.

The paper by Kidder in this volume describes the use of English in the courts. Although not the major basis for choosing a lawyer, facility in the court with a particular kind of English does help to convince a client of the sincerity of his advocate. The use of English as a whole in the courts serves the economic advantage of an elite class who control the language and thus access to the bar. Whereas litigants can understand the language of court proceedings in Tanzania and may make more rational decisions regarding the activities of their advocate, Indian clients are more dependent on judging a lawyer's histrionics in the courtroom.

The use of language brokers turns up in all three of the countries discussed in this volume. As Das Gupta and Gumperz (1968) have pointed out, there had been linguistically-marked occupations for a long time in India. Access to these occupations was manipulated by the members of the occupations in order to allow them the economic advantages of elite groups. Manipulation of language skills remains an important political and economic strategy in India today. In New Guinea, as Lang and Salisbury point out (Chapter 16 and 17), language brokers play an important role in bridging the gap between the English-speaking world and the local arena. Such men gain political and economic prominence in part because of the ease with which they move back and forth between the two worlds. Salisbury emphasizes that in order to avoid the elitism which too few information brokers may lead to, he would recommend an increase in the number of information brokers and channels. In most complicated linguistic situations there is a need for language brokers. Das Gupta and Gumperz (1968) note that even in the United States there are means of translating complicated scientific discoveries into lay language. Language brokers turn up in Tanzania too as translators and court scribes.

Selection and transmission of information. The use of language in the selection and transmission of information has many political implications. Both William O'Barr and Swartz offer examples of where language is used to disguise the real meaning of the discourse. In O'Barr's example, the language used allows the members of the council to act as they see fit without outside interference. Such metaphoric use of language is widespread; one of the more common recent examples in the sociolinguistic literature is 'marking' style described for Black English by Mitchell-Kernan (1972). In the Swartz paper we see hyperbole used as a special sort of political resource. As he points out, 'by focusing attention on some aspects of reality rather than others it structures that reality in ways open to manipulation by users.' Thus the real meaning is manipulated.

By looking again at the role of brokers in Tanzania, DuBow points out that public writers have a very important role in rephrasing or rewriting the meaning of court proceedings and decisions which is often overlooked. Given the many complex language situations of the Tanzania courts, it may well be that translators are not selected with extreme care yet the outcome of the case is in large measure dependent on the translation of such brokers. Yash Ghai in the discussion at Quail Roost pointed out how much power such brokers may have when they reintroduce hot issues by restating them.

We need to recall that in all of these uses of languages, there are several phenomena which can be manipulated: (1) variation in language(s) may be used or created for political purposes, (2) variation in language competence may be used or created for political purposes, or (3) differential attitudes toward language varieties/markers can be used or created for power purposes.

Several examples of the first kind of manipulation can be found in this volume, that is, where differences in varieties of languages can be used or created for political purposes. Apte's paper (Chapter 11) shows that in India the number of people speaking a particular language can be manipulated to enhance the numerical strength of a particular group. It may also be the case that such a gross numerical difference between language affiliation may reflect perceived advantages on the part of the polity at different points in time. The paper by William O'Barr describes a deliberate use of a language style to keep people guessing about their intention and thus to obtain their own political goals. Finally, Kidder suggests some lawyers' use of language skills is part of a strategy to convince clients that they are taking the client's case seriously. Students of the relation between language and politics should always bear in mind the ever present option of *creating* variation in language for political purposes.

This volume also has several examples of the second kind of manipulation, that is, where differences in language *competence* are used or created for political purposes. Implicit in this kind of manipulation is that it is possible to legislate certain degrees of language competence so that particular groups are favored. It may also happen that particular degrees of competence may lead to particular kinds of access to power. Leibowitz has described a case where in manipulating voting and controlling access to education, one can make the level of competence so high that members of particular groups are kept out of certain arenas. Bailey (Chapter 13) points out that given the diversity of language competence in India, it is possible to note that this diversity is directly related to differential access to power. Sankoff (Chapter 14) notes in New Guinea that as education increases, speaking English well will increasingly come to mark the elite – that is, access to power will rest not merely on knowledge of this language but on the degree of knowledge which an individual obtains. South Indians have long objected to making proficiency in Hindi a major basis for national government since they recognize the handicap they would face as speakers of languages belonging to a completely different family. Their objection is that it would be difficult for them to match the degree of competency of a native speaker; therefore, they feel they would be limited in their access to civil service and other government benefits.

The third area of manipulation is a very complicated one and one not too well researched – that is, where differential attitudes toward language varieties are used or created for power purposes. Certainly, there are lots of examples where the symbolic value of a particular language is made important for nationalism. Yet, what we need to know are some of the complexities of the attitudes associated with particular languages or varieties. Is it the case that all varieties of Swahili bring political fame to politicians or are there varieties which are preferred to convey feelings of charisma, confidence, folksiness, etc. Salisbury gives us some idea of the social and political meanings which are attached to the use of particular languages in New Guinea offices: whereas in 1967 people used Pidgin as a national language to stress patriotism, in 1971, the use of Pidgin implied some derogation or condescension by the person who could speak English but did not do so. In order to assess properly how language attitudes are manipulated for political purposes, we need to know how members of the speech community feel about the different varieties of language of the speech community and what effects their use might have.

POSSIBILITIES FOR FUTURE RESEARCH

At Quail Roost, many people started out by thinking of language as a homogeneous entity and by discussing what I would call macrorelations between politics and language. As the conference continued, there developed a greater awareness of the kinds of variation in language that are subject to manipulation and change, i.e. such things as the range of varieties, the domains of usage, attitudes toward varieties of language, and the range of competence in varieties of standard-nonstandard style. And there remains a lot of room for further consideration of the relation between such linguistic variation and the use of power. Some questions which appear fruitful to me are:

(1) How is language ability part of the power of politicians? What degrees of ability in which varieties enhance his power? How are individuals excluded from particular positions because of their language abilities? Are there differences in effectiveness of leaders due to native versus non-native usage of language? In what domains is the politician expected or required to use these varieties? Are there varieties in the process of development/standardization for certain domains?

(2) What functions, if any, does the ability to code-switch play in politicical spheres?

(3) Are there brokers who, by controlling written or oral language competence, control access to information or interpretation of information? We have already seen several examples of these in the public writers in Tanzania, the English brokers in New Guinea, and the translators of court proceedings in all three countries. It would also be useful to try to consider how these individuals see their role. To what extent are they aware of manipulating the information? As we have seen in India, the manipulation of language seems to have been a highly conscious matter for a very long period of time.

(4) To what extent are politicians aware of the linkages between power and languages? Do they allow for opportunities for the polity to acquire competence in the variety chosen? Do they tolerate variation in this competence for at least some period of time? To what extent are they aware of the dilemma between facility in and attachment to one's own language and the needs for interfacing between distinct ethnic groups.

We need to think even further about what the boundaries of the speech community really are when defining who is being affected by the uses to which language is being put or in which group a politician is trying to use language as a political resource. Since, as Fishman (1968) has noted, 'language is a clue to societal change and development', students of political processes should be alerted to the potential source of information that uses of and changes in language can be.

Given the fact that so many variables about language can be manipulated, we can conclude that the relationship between language and politics is very rich one. Some of these relationships have already been studied in the area of language planning (i.e. the study of solutions to language problems by authorized government organizations). In the resolution of such problems, many political problems come to light and get attached to language problems. Indeed, decisions about language never seem to be simply related to mere communication problems but rather always to reflect other considerations. A discussion of this field and some of the political implications can be found in the recent volume edited by Rubin and Jernudd (1971). Many of the problems dealt with in this book relate to less formalized attention to language problems but which nonetheless permit manipulation of the same aspects of language. By attention to those places where language is legislated about and those where it slips in unintentionally, we can gain a fuller idea of the relationship. Additionally, we will learn a great deal about the flexibility of language varieties and language attitudes. It is of great interest to sociolinguistics to explore the extent to which and circumstances under which language variation is manipulable by sociopolitical interests. The study of the language and politics relationship can provide a clearer understanding of the basis for such manipulation. Sociolinguistics is just beginning to look at how language attitudes affect the entire communication process (cf. Shuy and Fasold 1973) and are manipulated for planning and development purposes. By looking at the language-politics relationship, sociolinguists stand to gain greater understanding of this process.

With the progress of sociolinguistics in recent years in understanding the nature of the speech community and with its further understanding of the nature of language variation, the study of language and politics can be a very rich and rewarding one, provided attention is focused on the complexities of both language and politics.

NOTE

1. A classic quotation from Chomsky (1965) demonstrates our point. Chomsky proposed that the proper object of study was '. . . an ideal speaker-listener, in a completely homogeneous speech community, who knows its language perfectly and is unaffected by such grammatically irrelevant conditions as memory limitations, distractions, shifts of attention and interest, and errors in applying his knowledge of the language in actual performance'.

WILLIAM O'BARR

Boundaries, Strategies, and Power Relations: Political Anthropology and Language

THE CONCERNS OF POLITICAL ANTHROPOLOGY

As a recognized sub-field of anthropology, political studies have a relatively short history. For such nineteenth century anthropologists as Maine, Morgan, and Tylor, a major goal — if not *the* major goal — in their research was describing and explaining the differences between Western societies and cultures and those of the 'primitive' world. Classical theorists, who in this period based their generalizations on the data of missionaries, explorers, traders, and colonial administrators rather than their own first-hand observations, attempted to formulate the stages through which society and government had evolved and to suggest the mechanisms which had produced these changes. Grand theory was the name of the game.

Around 1920, Bronislaw Malinowski ushered in a new era of anthropology earmarked by a revolutionary new approach to the collection of ethnographic data: the prolonged participant-observation field trip. Malinowski's own stint totalling more than two years in the Trobriand Islands set a precedent for future fieldworkers and still remains as a standard against which the length of fieldtrips is often judged. Based on first-hand observation, Malinowski produced copious descriptions and analyses of various aspects of Trobriand society and culture (e.g. myth, religion, economics, and so on). His detailed research in a particular society drew his attention away from the grandiose generalizations popular a generation earlier and focused instead upon the workings of various aspects of the sociocultural system which he studied. For Malinowski and innumerable social anthropologists who have worked in the tradition which he established, government is viewed as just one aspect of a total interrelated cultural system.

The first social anthropological volume to focus directly upon politics, a set of eight essays published under the title *African Political Systems* in 1940, reflects the sort of functionalist thinking which replaced the earlier evolutionary concerns. Noting the vastly different loci of power and government across societies – especially when exotic peoples were compared with more familiar Western societies – fieldworkers were instructed to look for functional rather than structural parallels of politics and government: 'In studying political organization, we have to deal with the maintenance or establishment of social order, within a territorial framework, by the organized exercise of coercive authority through the use, or the possibility of use, or physical force' (Radcliffe-Brown 1940: xiv). The major objective of their studies then was locating the various structural mechanisms which serve the political purposes of maintaining internal order and external peace.

Fortes and Evans-Pritchard noted three major groups (or types) of societies in Africa. There were, at one extreme, the centralized, complex, state-level societies and, at the other, the small-scale, hunting-and-gathering, highly-mobile societies. In between fell a vast array of societies (dubbed 'mid-range') which were definitely more complex than hunting-and-gathering bands but which lacked overarching governmental structure.

These typological concerns were elaborated in Middleton and Tait's collection entitled *Tribes Without Rulers* (1958) which attempted to clarify the nature of mid-range societies. The collection provided six studies in the tradition of *African Political Systems* and set up three major types of mid-range societies.

Attempts to define the varieties of political systems in the ethnographic world were not limited to British social anthropologists. American anthropologists, whose ethnographic studies had focused primarily on conquered and defeated North American Indians, had not provided much insight into the organization and working of indigenous governmental systems. The neo-evolutionists, however, working under the influence of Steward and White, provided some more universalistic and complete typologies of primitive social and political systems than had the British. Based upon many of Steward's ideas about the ecologically-based differences among primitive societies set out in the *Theory of Culture Change* (1955), Service's *Primitive Social Organization* (1962) proposed a four-fold typology covering *bands* (hunting-and-gathering societies with situational, ephemeral leaders and integrated primarily through ties of intermarriage among exogamous local groups), *tribes* (societies based on domesticated plants and/or animals whose patterns of leadership resemble bands and which are integrated through non-residential sodalities cross-cutting local communities), *chiefdoms* (more complex societies whose leadership offices are institutionalized and permanent and which are integrated through redistributional economies), and *states* (complex societies which have the ability to utilize force to back up decisions taken at the center). Responding to what he considered to be many of the incongruities in Service's scheme, Fried published his *Evolution of Political Society* (1967) which took issue with Service's concept of the tribe and proposed a more complex argument concerning the evolution of states. The Service-Fried dialogue on just how many really different types of socio-political systems are found ethnographically reached a plateau recently when Service published some concessions in which he claimed the most basic cleavages occurred among egalitarian, hierarchical, and archaic (state) societies (Service 1971: 157).

Whether approached from the vantage of British social anthropology or of American cultural evolutionism, there can be no mistaking the common interests shared on both sides of the Atlantic in defining the range and nature of political systems which differ radically from Western forms of government. This concern with the loci of power and authority, with the functions and structures of government, drew the attention of early political anthropologists away from the study of the political process itself and consequently from the roles which language can play in it. But political anthropology has undergone a great deal of growth in the last decade or so and the concerns of its contemporary practitioners have expanded and transformed its earlier foci.

The modern successor to the typological concerns is in many ways the sophisticated approach of Barth and his colleagues to the definition of *Ethnic Groups and Their Boundaries* (1969). Instead of assuming the primordial existence of 'tribes', Barth focuses upon the genesis and maintenance of boundary mechanisms in ethnic groups. As studies in his volume show, ethnic groups are not fixed in time and space; they are flexible, changing, and responsive to internal and external forces. This focus upon the processes of ethnic group formation and boundary maintenance reflects many of the earlier concerns in anthropology with what tribes are, how people maintain their allegiance to them, and how political life operates in those societies which lack such familiar accoutrements of government in the West as parliaments, congresses, monarchs, and presidents. Yet it goes beyond mere concern with the mechanisms for maintaining internal order and external peace by focusing upon the very processes by which social groups are generated and their boundaries maintained.[1]

A second set of research problems in contemporary political anthropology has focused on the nature of politics and political action across the gamut of societies known to anthropologists. The British have definitely been the leaders in these investigations. Well-trained ethnographers coming out of the various British universities in the last fifty years have produced detailed ethnographic studies of the nature of the political process in the particular societies in which they worked. And in addition to these often excellent descriptive accounts of political life which we have had on a piecemeal basis for some time, many of these anthropologists have concerned themselves recently with broader theoretical questions relating to the nature of politics. Gluckman and his students, in particular, working out of the University of Manchester have contributed significantly in this regard. Gluckman's views on conflict, rebellion versus revolution, and many other social processes have become widely accepted axioms in political anthropology. His notion, for example, that conflict is structurally endemic in all social systems has provided a theoretical stimulus for such penetrating analyses as his own work on Lozi law (Gluckman 1965), Turner's *Schism and Continuity* (1957), Marwick's *Sorcery in its Social Setting* (1965), and that of others.

Two of the contributors to this volume have added significantly through their own previously published works to our understanding of the political process along lines similar to those of Gluckman. Swartz has called for a deemphasis on structure and a sharper focus instead upon the political process itself, on the goals and tactics used in arenas of all sorts to succeed in political contests (Swartz et al. 1966; Swartz 1968). Bailey has produced, in addition to his very substantial ethnography of Indian village politics (Bailey 1963), a probing analysis of the nature of political behavior across societies (Bailey 1969). He has contributed a host of new ways of thinking about politics (such as his useful distinction between normative and pragmatic rules; see Bailey 1969: 4) the full implications and significance of which are still to be worked out. Yet, the approach of these two 'processual' anthropologists, and of others like them (for example the contributors to Swartz et al. 1966 and Swartz 1968), to the study of politics in human society is vastly different from the typologists of either the British or the American schools. Rather than being overly concerned with defining the range of types of governmental structures and political institutions, these anthropologists focus instead upon strategies, rules for winning political games, legitimacy, and such related issues.

Thus, political anthropology has in its history a dual concern with structure (e.g. the loci of government in different societies, boundaries, etc.) and process (e.g. political action). As we shall see shortly, these two traditions surface once again in the issues which are of interest to political anthropologists in the study of the language-politics relationships.

POLITICAL ANTHROPOLOGY AND LANGUAGE

Like politics, language has been of great interest to anthropologists. But those who have been interested in one of these have commonly not been concerned much with the other. Consequently, studies of the relationship between language and politics as such are not of long-standing concern to anthropology despite the fact that its holism and eclecticism would appear at first glance to be an appropriate spawning ground for such inquiry.

Anthropological studies of language are traditionally an American specialty. A host of insightful theorists and teachers, among them Boas, Sapir, Whorf, Bloomfield, Voegelin, Pike, Greenberg – to mention only a few – were responsible for this development. Perhaps because language proved less fragile and generally more resistive to change than political structure, or perhaps because it was of less concern to the agents of change, or – as is more likely – because of the interaction between both factors, it attracted the attention of many anthropologists who studied American Indians. Political organization, as noted earlier, was not so viable and reasonable an area of inquiry since most indigenous political systems of American Indian societies were, for all intents and purposes, defunct by the beginning of the twentieth century.

Among British anthropologists, language and linguistics were largely ignored until very recently indeed. Early British anthropologists in the period from 1850 to 1920, when the discipline was taking shape, tended to look on language as the subject matter of an already much more developed and autonomous academic discipline. Language, however, did enter, albeit peripherally, their discussions of the mental capacities of primitives and of the difficulties of obtaining reliable field data, but almost no attention was devoted by the early British anthropologists to language as an aspect, in its own right, of the total social and cultural system (Henson 1971). Malinowski, as ethnographer *par excellence,* set through his own example the precedent that fieldworkers should know and use native languages. But in addition to such pragmatic concerns, Malinowski stimulated some functionalist thinking about the uses of language in society and, together with J. R. Firth, is responsible for the development of the *context of situation* theory of meaning (Robins 1971). After Malinowski, Evans-Pritchard and his students worked through native languages to produce abundant ethnographies of many societies. From time to time, language was considered, more or less incidentally, as part of the total social and cultural system, but no significant attention was paid to it directly. Yet, their work remained isolated from broader developments in linguistics in America and in Europe. Fortes and Evans-Pritchard, for example, in the introduction to *African Politican Systems,* mention language only in the context of defining political communities (which were after all the objective of their studies):

'Community of language and culture, as we have indicated, does not necessarily give rise to political unity, any more than linguistic and cultural dissimilarity prevents political unity' (Fortes and Evans-Pritchard 1940: 23).

This position, that political structure is not necessarily coterminus with language communities, is reflected vividly in Leach's study of *Political Systems of Highland Burma:*

'. . . . persons who speak a different language, wear a different dress, worship different deities and so on are not regarded as foreigners entirely beyond the pale of social recognition . . . cultural attributes such as language, dress and ritual procedure are merely symbolic labels denoting the different sectors of a single extensive structural system . . . it is the underlying structural pattern and not the overt cultural pattern that has real significance' (Leach 1954: 17).

And Leach's dictum that language is merely a cultural attributed and should not be confused with the boundaries of the social system is reflected once again in Barth's approach to boundary maintenance mechanisms:

'. . . . most of the cultural matter that at any time is associated with a human population is *not* constrained by this boundary; it can vary, be learnt, and change without any critical relation to the boundary maintenance of the ethnic group. So when one traces thc history of an ethnic group through time, one is *not* simultaneously, in the same sense, tracing the history of "a culture". . . . (Barth 1969: 38).

While Barth admits, and many other social anthropologists would doubtlessly agree, that 'the interconnection between the diacriticia that are chosen for emphasis, the boundaries that are defined, and the differentiating values that are espoused, constitute a fascinating field for study' (1969: 35), very little attention has been paid to such relations. Beyond the strictly intuitive level, we know almost nothing about how language functions in boundary maintenance, how it differs (if indeed it does) from other diacriticia, and precisely under what circumstances it either is or is not employed in boundary definitions.

Within social anthropology recently, there has been a growing concern with the relationship between linguistic and social theory. This concern stems from the influence of Lévi-Strauss on what is known in some circles as 'post-functional British social anthropology' (Ardener 1971a). Lévi-Strauss' interest in linguistics grows out of a concern with what linguistics as a science can provide by way of analogous models for the understanding of social phenomena. Influenced heavily by the Prague school of structural linguistics, Lévi-Strauss has maintained that many of the models which the human mind employs in language are paralleled in social phenomena. His work has stimulated a significant number of anthropologists to look to linguistics for ideas which may provide new insights into society. These concerns are best reflected in the collection of essays which Ardener edited under the title *Social Anthropology and Language* (1971b).

While such concerns as those of Ardener and his colleagues portend the possibility of considerable insight into social reality, they do not parallel the concerns which the studies of language and politics in this volume reflect. The questions here are not *how is society like language?* but *how does language affect the social (political) process?* These are, I believe, complementary concerns. Each is an important area of inquiry in its own right; neither should be confused with the other. There are, within social anthropology, a few recent symposia which parallel rather closely the concerns of this volume. Of particular note is the book edited by J. Goody on *Literacy in Traditional Societies* (1968) which focuses on the effects of literacy upon the communications systems of preindustrial societies. By asking about the social consequences of literacy in society, by focusing on the ways in which the development or extension of literacy, whether pre-modern or resulting from recent colonialism and modernization, affects social systems, the Goody volume asks functional questions which are similar to the concerns expressed in this book.

The concerns of political anthropologists writing in this volume, and of the other contributors whose levels of analysis parallel the local-level focus of political anthropology, examine some of the myriad ways in which language and the political process intersect. The complexity of the topics in this volume defies any simple categorization. For the sake of convenience, however, rather than because these are distinct and analytically separate categories, I will consider their concerns under two headings: language as a boundary maintenance mechanism and language as a political resource.

LANGUAGE AS A BOUNDARY MAINTENANCE MECHANISM

Boundaries function to keep some people in while keeping others out. They encompass and thus describe by circumscription social groups. That individuals can and do cross such boundaries in no way dissolves the identity of such a group or its boundaries (Barth 1969: 9–10). Although, as the papers in Barth (1969) show, the specific mechanisms whereby boundaries are defined are highly variable, language is a frequent boundary maintaining mechanism. Language is to be found wherever humans live in social relationships. And because of its variability both within and between speech communities, it is a ready and likely candidate for use in defining boundaries. The papers in this volume show many such uses of language at both macro (societal) and micro (local) levels within social groups. It is used by governments to separate or unite and by local communities to symbolize their own social distinctiveness by separating themselves from others linguistically.

Governmental use of language to define boundaries. Jean O'Barr considers in Chapter 4 effects of Tanzania's language policy on political enfranchisement at various levels of the governmental bureaucracy. Tanzania's egalitarian ideals are reflected in its language policy which has as its ostensible aim the opening through Swahili of access to national and local political institutions as widely as possible. According to her analysis, O'Barr sees that the effect is *de facto* uneven at different levels of government. At the more local levels, moreover, enforcing the use of Swahili may in fact have the reverse of the intended effect since Swahili language knowledge is not even throughout all levels of Tanzanian society. Requiring a functional knowledge of the language for participation in political arenas, in effect, defines a boundary which impedes the political access of some citizens. In this particular case, however, the practical alternatives are probably less desirable and it does appear that Tanzania's policy will have the desired effects *in the long run.*

DuBow shows in Chapter 5 how this same language policy affects popular participation in the legal institutions. The move toward egalitarianism through Swahili use in courts is not, of course, without all sorts of attendant technical problems involving language: translation of laws formerly written in English, educating lawyers in the language in which they must operate, communication among levels of the court system, record keeping, and so on. The papers by Lang (Chapter 17) and Kidder (Chapter 12) also examine some of the kinds of problems that arise when the language of the court and of the litigant are not the same. Yet, as pointed out by Kidder, one should not jump to the conclusion that a mere shift of language will solve the difficulties in communication and understanding which are implicit in the differences which are to be found between the language of legal specialists and courts and the language of a community. Lawyers do not need separate languages to erect almost impermeable boundaries between themselves and their clients since legal jargon is quick to become unintelligible to most laymen. When considered from the perspective of social boundaries, Lang's analysis of one sort of linguistic mediator, the court interpreter, is particularly instructive. Upon the shoulders of such a broker rests a great deal of power, exercised perhaps at times beyond the level of his actual consciousness.

Regardless of the ability of laymen to participate in courtroom debates or to enter into dialogues with governmental representatives, one should not minimize the psychological effects which language policies handed down from above have upon individuals. One's language is intimately associated with the individual; new languages are difficult to learn; and language is a particularly easy tool to use in political control. Therefore, when language policies establish boundaries between people and government the effects are likely to be quite significant: alienation, distancing, and political impotence. When policies have egalitarian objectives, regardless of the actual difficulty in operating in such arenas, the psychological effects are likely to be the reverse. Thus, language can be used not only to establish real boundaries but to communicate *attitudes* and *feelings* of government toward people as well.

Local-level use of language to define political boundaries. The processes of boundary definition are initiated at local levels as well. At least two of the papers concern themselves with how and why local groups use language to define boundaries and separate themselves from others. In Chapter 13, Bailey examines some of the ways in which councils, through their language policies, either separate themselves from their constituents or utilize a language which is close to nary speech. In Chapter 7, I have tried to show how the members of one particular council which I studied have used double-talk as a device to separate themselves from the superordinate governmental structure. Each of these papers takes us some of the way in understanding how language can be used to erect boundaries, demonstrate internal solidarity, and maintain external exclusiveness.

Language is tremendously flexible and its variation is often used to mirror social differences. Yet, it is almost an axion of human society that differentiation is evaluated and ranked. Hierarchy is found everywhere superimposed upon difference. Two of the papers on New Guinea illustrate these processes in great detail: Sankoff (Chapter 14) shows how the colonially-introduced linguistic variation reflects social inequality and Salisbury, through a penetrating case study of the Tolai of New Britain (Chapter 18), shows the intricate interweaving of language with hierarchy.

Thus, wherever we turn language and social boundaries are closely connected. These processes are varied, yet all are a part of a larger use of language as a political resource to which we now turn our attention.

LANGUAGE AS A POLITICAL RESOURCE

Multifarious devices are employed by political actors to achieve their goals. It is hard to conceive of any political strategies which do not involve language in the sense that it is the essence of the communication system which underlies orderly social interaction. In some situations, however, the use of language to achieve political ends is more direct, overt, and complex. In various ways, the contributors to this symposium have suggested and discussed in varying degrees of detail at least four important and interrelated categories where language is a resource in political contests.

Communicating status. Recent studies in sociolinguistics are convincing us that there are few, if any, individuals who speak the same way to all individuals in all situations. Rather, individuals move along a continuum of speech styles, registers, dialects, or languages employing different phonological features, syntax, and vocabulary as they operate in alternative situations (see Rubin, Chapter 19). When a person selects from his speech continuum the appropriate style, degree of formality, etc. to be employed in a particular situation, he is thus communicating (however consciously or unconsciously) a set of status expectations. He is, as it were, defining the particular social personality he wishes to use from among the range of alternative possibilities in his repertoire. The hearer typically responds to what has been communicated on both overt and covert levels and the interaction proceeds upon the status relationships negotiated in such a fashion. On different occasions these same individuals must either establish or reestablish a status relationship in order for interaction to proceed. Verbal behavior is important in negotiating status relationships, but it is of course not the only cue which is used. The full range of language subtlety is brought into service here: status can be communicated through elaborate, formal greeting exchanges or through minute phonological distinctions. Among the papers in this volume, Salisbury's analysis of Tolai use of English, Tok Pisin, and their native language demostrates some of the relations between code-switching and the communication of status expectations. Among trilingual Tolai, code choice is not random. The choice of a particular code symbolizes bundles of expectations which define the parameters of the social interaction which will follow.[2]

Signaling power versus solidarity. Closely related to the use of language to communicate status is its function in signaling power versus solidarity. As mentioned earlier, differentiation in human society is almost always followed by evaluation. Being different presupposes that hierarchy will be imposed. Various linguistic devices can be used to symbolize the presenvce or absence of difference and, hence, of hierarchy or equality. One of the classic studies in sociolinguistics which demonstrates this is Brown and Gilman's 'The Pronouns of Power and Solidarity' (1960). In many Indo-European languages, a speaker has the choice of using the familiar (*tu-*) versus the formal (*vu-*) form of the second person pronoun. Once the first speaker makes his choice, the second one can either respond reciprocally or asymetrically. Parrying back and forth of *vu-* forms keeps the relationship on a formal level and maintains politeness and social distance; movement toward reciprocal *tu-* forms symbolizes greatest solidarity in interaction; and use of nonreciprocal *tu-/vu-* indicates hierarchy and power differentials. A variety of linguistic devices can be employed in conversational interaction to indicate and symbolize solidarity or inequality; they need not be so clear-cut and neat as the Indo-European pronomimal categories.

In a different sort of way, Bailey's analysis of institutional versus ordinary speech in formal political arenas can be seen as an analogous means of symbolizing solidarity between the council and its constitutency when ordinary speech is used or of symbolizing hierarchy when institutional speech develops. A careful reading of Bailey's paper with an eye to the relationships among language, hierarchy, and power will suggest many ideas about the ways in which language can signal power versus solidarity in formal institutions.

Rhetorical skills of individuals. In the hands of individual political actors, rhetorical skills become one of the chief devices for winning at politics. We are all familiar with the ways in which 'sweet-talking' politicians engender, through their verbal behavior, the trust and support of their followers and generate via the same their political personalities, dynamism, and – to use a much too overworked term nowadays – their charisma. But at levels even more common than the oratorical and verbal abilities of public politicians are the ordinary conversational interactions via which human beings engage in social intercourse with one another. Through the work of Goffman (1961, 1972), Garfinkel (1967), Sacks, Schegloff, and Jefferson (1974), and of others (see, for example, Sudnow 1972) engaged in such studies, we are beginning to have some insights into the nature of the social organization of conversation which governs verbal interactional systems. It appears that knowledge of the rules by which conversations proceed is not unevenly distributed across human populations for children, brain damaged adults, and the mentally retarded who are able to speak at all seem to utilize more or less the same rules for turn-taking in conversation.[3] While such evidence does support the notion that verbal interaction systems operate as a threshold phenomenon in the sense that individuals either do or do not have the knowledge and ability to participate in turn-taking conversational systems, it does appear that there are some techniques, however, for stealing turns in conversation, which, although they may be known across the population, may be differentially employed by individual actors in the system. Some persons may be more aggressive in using the rules, more self-aggrandizing, more anxious to 'win' in verbal exchanges. The work, especially of Sacks, Schegloff, and Jefferson already mentioned, provides a basis on which we can begin to ask questions about how the verbal skills of individuals are related to power and status in ordinary interaction.

More in line with the studies actually reported in this volume, we can see some examples of how individual verbal skills and rhetorical devices in the hands of individuals can become intertwined as part of the political process. Swartz's paper (Chapter 6) which considers uses of hyperbole in Bena courts is just such a study. The Bena, who are an otherwise quite literal-minded people, employ extreme hyperboles in local courts. Swartz has put forward the hypothesis that, in this particular cultural situation, hyperbole as a special rhetorical device may function as a political strategy for lost causes. By exaggeration beyond the bounds of ordinary reason, the litigant hopes to demonstrate and establish his claim. Were he not to do this, Swartz argues his cause would seem pedantic and umimportant. This insightful paper should serve as a stimulus toward thinking about the possible political used of such other devices as metaphor.

Focusing on categories of actors rather than devices per se, we find that a number of papers have considered political actors: court interpreters, lawyers, big men, government officials, and so on. How these men use language to convince, persuade, control, wield power, and otherwise work through strategies toward political goals provides a vast range of possible concerns for the student of language and politics. Their repertoire of political devices by no means stops at language, but the primal nature of language in human society means that a great many uses of language are likely to be found.

Manipulating and controlling others. In the hands of individual actors and of governments, language is a means of manipulating and controlling others. We have reviewed in other categories some of the ways in which individuals can use language to manipulate others in political arenas. From the local-level perspective of political anthropology, the most absolute manifestation of language in this function is through language policies which either give or, as is more common, deny access to political and economic arenas on the bais of language knowledge and abilities. With few exceptions, recent generations of anthropologists have worked in colonial situations in which superordinate governments may *establish* language policies stating which languages are to be used for education, for politics, for litigation, for economic interchange, for the dissemination of knowledge via the public media, and so on. In all three of the countries considered in detail in this volume, language is a significant political issue. This is because language controls access to political and other arenas, it is the key to change, and often the means of success in altogether traditional environments. I shall not comment further here on this issue for the papers throughout the book raise this question over and over again. I do wish to point out that Leibowitz's paper in Chapter 23 provides, via his examples from the use of language to manipulate and control in the United States of America, a cautionary note for India, Tanzania, and New Guinea as well as other newly independent countries to keep in mind. The pervasiveness and critical necessity of language makes it a likely tool for would-be manipulators and controllers.

FUTURE RESEARCH

The last decade or so has been a period of extraordinary growth within anthropology for the two subdisciplines (political anthropology and linguistic anthropology) where language-politics studies are most at home. Within each of them, a major focus has developed: processual studies in political anthropology and the study of the social context in which language is embedded for linguistics. It is in language and politics where these two developments meet and join efforts. With only a few exceptions, this remains uncharted territory. I have tried so suggest some of the kinds of topics which look promising at this point. At this early stage of our work, it is much too soon to comprehend the potentials and limitations of this new field. I suspect that in another decade or two, such will not be the case.

NOTES

1. It is perhaps an oversimplification of the concerns of Barth and his colleagues to insist too strongly that their studies are a contemporary and up-dated version of some of the earlier structural-functional studies of political systems in British anthropology. Their concerns certainly extend beyond the political into the bases of social organization itself. I believe it is important, however, to view a discipline's contemporary concerns with an eye toward the direction from which they have come. From the perspective of the history of political studies in social anthropology, Barth's concerns can be viewed as a more dynamic approach to the problem of defining the loci of political power and authority in human societies.
2. Shiela Seitel reports (personal communication) that the Haya of Tanzania often employ Swahili greetings in lieu of Haya greetings since the latter necessarily communicate more facts about the relative status of speakers. Code choice, in this particular case, is related to the choice of just what and how much the speaker wants to communicate about status. Soutworth (1972) reports that English is sometimes used in India for similar reasons.
3. Emanuel Schegloff in his lectures at the Linguistic Society of America Summer Institute, The University of Michigan, 1973.

MALCOLM E. JEWELL

20

Formal Institutional Studies and Language

Every political system in the world faces the problem of national integration, and the deeper the divisions within a society the more serious that problem is. Differences of language constitute only one of these sources of division; other include differences of race, religion, or caste. One of the basic functions of political institutions, such as legislatures, is to facilitate the integration of a political system, and students of such institutions are interested in studying whether and how they serve this function (Jewell forthcoming).

This paper is primarily concerned with legislative institutions and the problems of language diversity in a society. The laws passed by the legislature regarding the status and use of various languages may facilitate integration or acerbate conflicts among various language groups. The system of representation may or may not give the members of each language group as large a voice in the legislature as they believe they deserve. The legislature may serve as an arena in which conflicting demands of various language groups can be mediated or as a vehicle for control by one such group. The legislature is not the only political institution with an impact on language problems, but, because of its public and representative character, its impact may be particularly visible.

THE LEGISLATURE AS A COMMUNICATIONS SYSTEM

The differences in language that make the legislature's integrative function more important may also make its task more difficult. The legislature is, in one sense, a complex communications system, and communications are difficult and inefficient if the actors in the system cannot understand each other. If there is language diversity in a country, the legislators will speak and read more than a single language. It is not likely that each member of the legislature will be able to understand all of the languages that are native to the other members. For the legislature to do its work, the communications barrier must be overcome. One possible solution is to provide translation services to the legislature, for debate, hearings, and official documents. Another solution that may be feasible is to conduct all business in some language that is common to all, or most, members. The latter solution may have the effect of excluding from effective participation any legislator who cannot speak and understand such a common language. The problem of overcoming language barriers does not apply only to communications among members but to the member's communications with cabinet members, bureaucrats, constituents, and any other significant participants in the legislative process.

Communications problems may arise in any legislature whose members speak different languages, but special circumstances may make the problem particularly acute. The British government established legislative councils in a number of its colonies in the years prior to independence. In some of these, seats were allocated on an ethnic or nationality basis, with overrepresentation of persons with European backgrounds and underrepresentation of those with native (African or Asian) backgrounds. Generally the business of the legislative councils was conducted in English, a procedure that required non-English voters to choose English-speaking members if they wanted legislators who would understand what was going on in the council. An example of the English requirement for legislative councils can be found in the paper in this volume on Tanzania (Chapter 3). Jean O'Barr notes that the first legislative council in Tanzania in 1926 did not contain any African members; the governor asserted that 'no African could be found with a sufficient command of the English language to take part in the debates of the council.' When a legislative council was first established in Papua New Guinea in the 1950s, the Papuan members who did not have a good understanding of English were seriously handicapped because that was the only language used.

The language problem is also likely to be particularly acute in the legislature of a newly established country that has language diversity. At the start the legislature may lack the facilities and trained translators to provide oral and written translations. It may take time for consensus to develop on a common language to be used in the legislature and for the political leaders and potential leaders to become familiar with that language. O'Barr notes that the requirement of fluency in English was included in the first Tanzanian constitution, but was abandoned within a few years. A similar requirement persisted in Kenya and was applied during the 1969 election, in which a number of candidates failed to pass a required English proficiency test. A few examples suggest that English has persisted as the 'legislative language' in those former British colonies where there is no other language spoken in common by most educated persons who are potential members of the legislature. In Tanzania, where Swahili has become a very widely used national language, it has gradually replaced English as the standard means of communication in Parliament, and its use has eliminated the problems of inequality that resulted when English was being used.

LEGISLATIVE FUNCTIONS AND LANGUAGE

To study the relationships between legislative bodies and language problems, we need to examine more carefully the variety of functions that legislatures play. Legislative scholars recognize that these functions are numerous and that those legislative functions which assume great importance in some political systems may be of little or no importance in others. The literature on Western (and particularly American) legislatures has stressed the decision-making or law-making function. The fact that in many developing countries the legislature is not an important center of decision-making does not necessarily mean that it has no importance in the political system. It may mean that it is serving other, less obvious functions. Scholars are also increasingly concerned with how legislatures contribute to more basic functions of a political system, such as integration.

A common attribute of legislatures is that they have the formal authority to make laws. Some legislatures, like the American Congress, make crucial decisions about the content of laws. Some legislatures, including many in Europe and in some developing countries, accept cabinet decisions on major policy questions but modify and amend proposed legislation. Some legislatures are little more than rubber stamps. To the extent that any legislative body makes substantive decisions, a member must be able to understand the language of decision making in order to participate. This means not only participation in formal debate, but, more importantly, participation in informal negotiations that go on in committee or behind the scenes. Participation also requires the ability to read laws, reports of committees and agencies, and other pertinent material, some of which may not be translated into more than one language. For example, the fact that most written documents used by the legislature in Papua New Guinea are in English has created problems for those members with little or no understanding of English. It is also possible that poorly educated legislators will have difficulty understanding the legal language used in law-making, but this is not a problem unique to legislatures with language diversity.

The legislator who cannot understand the language(s) commonly used in the decision-making process is obviously handicapped in representing his constituents and advancing their interests. If major decisions are not made in the legislature, this is a less serious handicap for such legislators. If major decisions are made by the cabinet or by party leaders, it is pertinent to ask what legislators are recruited to the cabinet or to top party positions. It is possible that members who speak and understand only a minority language will not be recruited to such positions, and consequently the constituency they represent will lack a voice in the decision-making councils.

The function of legislative debate is an important one, but its importance is often misunderstood. In most legislatures it is rare for debate to change the minds of members, at least on important points. The major purpose of debate is to bring to the attention of the public, or of specialized publics, the views of legislators and the positions of legislative parties. The legislature provides the government with a forum in which to defend its policies and provides the opposition with a forum in which to question governmental leaders and criticize their policies. The freedom with which such debate is conducted is a good measure of the legislature's autonomy and vitality. Given these pruposes, it is more important that a legislator be understood than that he understand what others say. Legislative rules permitting a member to speak in his own language are of little value unless his views can be understood through translation. Perhaps the crucial question is whether those who report the debate in the media can understand what a member is saying. A more subtle problem might arise if either other legislators or the general public fails to fully understand points being made in the debate because of lack of language skills or faulty translation.

Apte's paper (Chapter 11) provides detailed examples of the problems of using both Hindi and English in the Indian Parliament. Members who did not understand Hindi often asked speakers to use English, while Hindi-speaking members often raised questions during the question hour in that language and demanded an answer in Hindi. It is also obvious from Apte's paper that the issue at stake was not only one of understanding the debate or using the language that a speaker felt most comfortable with. Those who used Hindi consistently in debate were often trying to emphasize their belief that the transition to Hindi as the official language should be accelerated, while those objecting to its being used were also making a political point. Particularly during the 1950s, when language questions were often in the forefront of political controversy, the tactics as well as the substance of debate were important.

Legislative scholars in recent years have been paying particular attention to the legitimizing function of the legislature, because of its importance in contributing to integration of a nation. 'The constitutional and traditional base of the legislature and the orderly procedure that it follows make legislative action appear legitimate; it has the quality of rectitude. It is regarded by the public as right and proper' (Jewell and Patterson 1973: 11). In a developing nation or any poorly integrated nation the legislature's ability to confer legitimacy on governmental decisions is particularly important because it may help that government to get its policies enforced and implemented. The legislature's ability to confer legitimacy depends on whether its actions are regarded by the public as 'right and proper'. The concept of legitimacy is closely connected to the concept of public support for government. If language difficulties create a barrier to effective participation by certain legislators and their constituents recognize that this barrier exists, it is possible that those constituents would question the legitimacy of legislative actions. Inadequate representation of language groups, discussed later in this chapter, could also erode public perceptions of legitimacy.

One of the functions of legislators is to serve as intermediaries between their constituents and government. The importance of this function, in both developed and developing systems, is becoming more evident as a result of recent research. Legislators defend and explain governmental policies to their constituents, thereby enhancing the likelihood of compliance with those policies. Legislators also act as spokesmen or intermediaries for individuals and groups in their constituency, carrying their demands for services to local, regional, and national bureacrats and even to cabinet members. They may be seeking better roads or schools for a town, the removal of a dishonest official, or the correction of a bureaucratic blunder or injustice against a citizen. (It is possible, of course, that they may be seeking a special favor for a wealthy or powerful constituent.) This intermediary role may be highly important for national integration, if the legislator is able to persuade bureaucrats to adapt policies to the needs of his constituency and persuade citizens to accept these policies.

To be an effective intermediary, the legislator must be able to communicate effectively at all levels, with his constituents, local bureaucrats, and officials at the national level. This means that he must be articulate, accessible to constituents, and bold and skillful in dealing with bureaucrats and cabinet members. In addition to these qualities, the legislator must be able to speak and understand well the languages used at each of these levels. If he does not fully understand the local language or dialect, he may not only misunderstand needs and demands but he may discourage citizens from approaching him. If he does not speak well the language of the bureaucrat, he may not only be misunderstood but also be scorned by officials who are well educated and often pompous. In any of the countries that were formerly British colonies, it might be expected that a lack of facility in English would handicap a legislator in communicating with many of the bureaucrats. In one sense or another, many legislators have to be able to speak two languages in order to be effective intermediaries, but in a bilingual of multilingual society this is absolutely necessary. Because of the importance of the intermediary role, a legislator's effectiveness is affected by the policy and practice of language use not only in the legislature but in the executive branch of government. In a federal system, such as that in India, it is possible that an effective legislator would have to be able to speak three languages, those dominant in his constituency, his state, and the nation.

REPRESENTATION OF LANGUAGE GROUPS

The legislature functions as a representative body, and this function contributes significantly to national integration. An effective system of legislative representation may contribute to the integration of minority groups in two ways. If these groups believe that they are fairly represented in the legislature, they may be more supportive of the political institutions and more willing to comply with governmental policies. Secondly, fair representation may give minority groups enough power in the legislature to bring about the adoption of policies that satisfy the demands of these groups well enough so that they will be supportive and compliant.

Legislative representation has an effect on any minority group. If those persons who speak a particular language are conscious of a common interest and seek policy outputs regarding the use of that language (or regarding other policies particularly affecting that language group), then legislative representation has implications for that group. There is no certainty that those persons who speak a minority language will have any such sense of identity or will seek any political goals. The larger its membership and the more concentrated it is geographically, the more likely a language group is to have such identity. A number of factors affect the legislative representation of a language group. One is geography. Unless a group is concentrated geographically, it is unlikely to be able to elect legislators responsive to its demands under any system of districting. The electoral laws, methods of apportionment, and slating practices of parties all have effects on the ability of members of a language group to get representation. Political scientists recognize that proportional representation systems benefit minorities more than single-member district plurality systems. District lines can sometimes be drawn to minimize (or maximize) a minority's share of seats. If parties are strong, the nominating or slating practices of a party may determine how many seats which minorities get. Any of these rules and practices that affect minorities in general can affect a language minority in particular. Finally, any law that requires candidates to meet a language requirement uniquely affects members of a language minority.

If these laws and practices make possible the election of legislators who are members of or who represent a particular minority language group, the role and behavior of these members deserve study. Does such a member perceive himself to be the representative of a particular language group or does he identify his constituency in different or broader terms? Does he act in such a way as to advance the interests of such a group, particularly on language questions that arise in the legislature? Do the legislators representing a language group meet together and coordinate their efforts on issues pertinent to their common constituents? It is also necessary to measure and evaluate the outputs of the legislative process. Are the representatives of minority language groups successful in getting laws adopted to implement their goals regarding language policy?

In order to make a thorough study of this topic, it would be necessary to study the practical effects of election and districting laws and party slating practices on the election of candidates representing language minorities. It would also be necessary to interview those who succeeded in winning elections, study their activities individually and collectively, and assess the output of the legislative process. Very little work has been done along those lines, just as very little systematic research has been done on the representation of other minority groups in the legislative systems of plural societies.

The Indian experience in the 1950s provides an outstanding example of the success of minority language groups in winning recognition and autonomy through the reorganization of a number of Indian states along linguistic lines, a process that was both complex and highly controversial. As Apte's paper in this volume illustrates, the Indian Parliament was the arena in which these issues were debated, and the MPs were effective representatives of these language groups. The MPs were sometimes elected specifically on the language issue, and they were very persistent in pressing these claims in Parliament. They used debates, question periods, motions, and other devices to advance their viewpoints. Because the government initially resisted the demand for state reorganization along linguistic lines, it can be argued that the Parliament played a major role in bringing about such a reorganization.

Although we have concentrated on the study of national legislative bodies, many of the same points are pertinent to the study of legislatures at other levels. At the local level there is much less likelihood that language diversity will be found in the community or among legislators. In state or provincial legislatures, however, such diversity is very possible, and it may be complicated by differences between the predominant national language and that which is predominant in the state. State legislative bodies may be less likely to have facilities and resources for translation and may be less likely to attract members who are well enough educated to handle more than one language.

HENRY L. BRETTON 21

Political Science, Language, and Politics

One major political science study where one would expect to find a thorough treatment of the language and politics relationship is Karl Deutsch's *The Nerves of Government* (1963), subtitled *Models of Communication and Control.* But the word language does not appear in the index nor is it found under 'communication'. Yet, the conceptual framework from which the basic ideas for the book are developed is derived from Norbert Wiener's work on 'cybernetics', clearly a language matter[1] (Wiener 1954). Another likely source of substantive enlightenment on language and politics, Lucien Pye's *Communications and Political Development* (1963), does not mention language except in the vaguest sense and then far too briefly, given the volume's focus on communication. These two illustrations are representative of general neglect of language by political scientists. Where language is considered, as elsewhere by Deutsch (1953) for instance, it is more likely treated as a social characteristic or expression than as the primary physical component of the human message system. Several explanations may be offered for this.

Even when political science is practiced under the label 'behavioral', it will more likely address itself to social relationships far above the level of individual communication and interaction. Yet that is the level where language as such is most meaningful and effective. Neither does the political scientist feel compelled to address the subject matter at that level nor does he feel obliged to consider language directly. Rather he feels quite comfortable treating it as an abstraction, a synonym for social interaction, or, as we have shown, communication. Treated in such a manner, the extreme complexity and the subtlety of language are in danger of escaping the political scientist's attention altogether.

But, the linguist, looking at politics, also must exercise great analytical skill and conceptual caution. It would not be helpful if only the focus on language is sharpened to the point of greatest possible clarity while the other component in the relationship, politics, remains blurred. Politics without specificity as for example to area, arena, sphere of social action or concern, or level of operation remains a most unproductive research target; it may prove to be a morass.

The critical level, then, where the language-politics relationship can be assessed most effectively, and most conclusively, is where language is actually spoken and heard. Yet, at that level, what is meant by 'politics'?

No matter how committed we may be to academically rigorous treatment of our subject matter, there remains the distinct possibility that politics, at the level of individual interaction, is an art. It may be an art of deception. Indeed, a survey of political science titles, *scholarly* books as well as articles and of titles in related disciplines, reveals that by 'politics' is meant an almost indefinite variety of things – not concepts, theories, paradigms, but *things* – hazy, vague, relationships difficult to isolate and identify, even the artful and the dodging. Often politics appears to mean muddling, or meddling, fudging the edges of otherwise logical and precise argument, manipulating in the dark, and by devious and secretive means; politics is finessing and deceiving. Or it means conducting irregularly what by non-political methods, or in a non-political context, would be conducted with regularity. Of course, the potentially embarrassing aspect of this is the distinct possibility that given the nature of the principal in the political act, the human being, the indistinctiveness of the term may reflect quite accurately its real meaning. It is obvious that the definitional problem, here barely touched upon, must be taken into account in the analysis of language as it relates to politics. To be sure, we must avoid the trap of indefinite regression but evidence abounds that we have a very long way to go before that danger becomes acute. Both language and politics still are discussed at levels far too ethereal for effective analysis.

Bernard Crick, comparing sexuality and politics – 'both activities in which the tacit understanding of presuppositions often makes more formal propositions unnecessary' – comments that 'both have much the same character of necessity in essence and unpredictability in form' (Crick 1964). Elsewhere Crick suggests, I believe with much justification, that 'politics' is the art of governing, i.e. assuring survival, by resorting to persuasion, suasion, manipulation, in place of application of sheer arbitrary and brute force. To him, totalitarian regimes are not political regimes, as they are far too direct, immediate, straightforward and explicit to qualify as *political.* Crick's understanding of politics is mentioned here because he offers an interesting distinction, namely that between governance as an art, which he deems *political,* and governance as a rigid system which, to him, is something else. Thus, even if we do distinguish – which we certainly must do – between general politics at all levels, in all situations, including marriage and debating teams, and on the other hand, governance, Crick reminds us that this too is loaded with definitional and conceptual difficulties.

Once we depart from the level of individual language contact to higher-level and broader social relations, entirely new problems are posed for the student of language and politics. There political speech may appear to be directed at one audience when in fact it is directed at another.[2] Or it may seem to relate to the present when in fact it is intended for the future. Christian Bay has drawn attention to the urgent need for differentiation between politics and pseudo-politics (Bay 1965). Torrents of words are being directed daily at alleged happenings which are actually sheer creatures of political inventiveness: they are conjured up for political effect only; they have no concrete basis in the real world. Yet it is this world of imagination which provides the background for much, if not most, political rhetoric.

Several of the contributions to this volume refer to political participation or participation in politics. In one respect, or context, the electorate in the United States participates in the determination of United States foreign policy as the people of India, for example, participate in foreign affairs in that country; alas, in both instances, and typically everywhere, this kind of participation is quite remote if not a pseudo-event. At the level of decision-making, at the national as well as at the lower levels, language purportedly or seemingly employed in a participant capacity may in fact have no such quality.

Instead, it may be more part of a ritual commonly referred to as popular participation in government.

THE LANGUAGE SITUATION AND POLITICS

Language is at the same time a delicate, sophisticated instrument and a blunt tool. It serves as a direct means of communication from man to man and it serves as an issue, or a foil, to achieve social and political goals. Whatever function we consider, it is necessary to keep in mind the enormous potential of language as a multi-purpose instrument: the same phrase, the same figure of speech can convey substantitally different meanings in different situations. Doob, for example, illustrates the great differences which exist between the range of associations evoked by such ordinary words as *eye, heart, head,* and *liver* in French and Bambara (Doob 1961: 192). Communication across such language (and hence cultural) barriers opens a wide range of possible misunderstandings, whether unintended or not.

Language is a key to power and wealth for many. As Latin once served as the secret code of power, beyond the reach of the masses, like French at the German courts and in Russia later on, so English, French, or Portuguese serve as codes of power in most of Africa today. The spread of any of these languages, or the degree to which they have penetrated Africa, and, most crucial, the degree to which any of them may serve as keys to social or economic change, tells us much about the language situation against which background the full import of the political potential and meaning of language must be gauged. Clearly, extent of literacy within a given sphere of authority, or social power, places some limits on the potential uses of language within a political community, particularly as an instrument of government and administration. Insofar as language may provide the key to income, and beyond to power and influence, the prevailing language situation may be controlling (Bretton 1973).

Many 'languages' and 'language groups' now appear to have originated during the colonial period for administrative convenience. Hermassi, in his analysis of elite development and behavior in North Africa, cites the military 'conqueror-ethnologist' who generated classifications of ethnic units to facilitate French control, and eventually conquest, of a given area. Much of the linguistic landscape of Africa, and probably elsewhere in former colonial areas, may well be the product of such an exercise, with profound consequences for both language and politics. Seen in this way, language serves the functions of imperial design and of colonial administrative convenience. In that respect, and more consequential for social behavior, language has been and continues to be used to secure, or assure, socio-psychological control over subject peoples.

Other political functions of language of special interest to us relate to preservation of the identity of cultural or ethnic minorities – to the 'centripetal' drives supportive of national unification goals as well as the 'centrifugal' forces tending to spin off secessionist groups seeking their own separate existence. Language also serves to secure class advantages and maintain class distinctions. In Tanzania, Swahili has been described as the instrument of socialism because it is said to be the language of the people (Whiteley 1971: 155). Swahili in East Africa has also served as an instrument of religious mobilization, as have Hausa and Arabic in West and North Africa.

SECOND LANGUAGES[3]

The fragmented nature of the indigenous African language grid, combined with the emergence during the last century of governmental and administrative systems which transcend the tribal-traditional worlds, makes possession of a second language a vital necessity if not a *sine qua non* for almost anyone wishing to participate actively in the modern political process anywhere on the continent. To 'know' a second language is useful; better still is to be able to *understand* not just the vocabulary and grammar of the language but the customs and conventions usually associated with its use. Two illustrations underscore the problem. The first is that of a Hindu, in Paris – probably apocryphal – who addresses a police officer with these words: 'Brigadier, vous êtes une vache.' A compliment to be sure, but also an embarrassment. The second illustration was offered in the course of a debate in the Ghana Parliament on the problems posed in transmission of government directives by lower-level clerks unable to fully comprehend the language in which directives were being sent down.

'A certain young man attended an interview and he was asked to explain what was meant by this: "The Government of Nigera has placed a ban on all South African goods because of their apartheid policy." This was a simple sentence. When the man was asked to translate into Fante or Twi, he said: "Nigeria Aban ato nsa afre South African Aban de wo, bobo baan wo Nigeria na yebobo pata ama woatsena ase. . . ." Meaning literally, that the Government of Nigera has invited the South African Government to come and play band in Nigeria and they will raise a shed for them to sit under' (Government of Ghana Parliamentary Debates 1965: 450).[4]

When secondary languages, either indigenous lingua francas or colonially-imposed European languages, are spoken across different cultural traditions, there is no guarantee that a word in such a language carries anything like the same meaning across the cultural boundaries. It is doubtful whether – as second languages in Africa – French, English, or Portuguese convey the same meanings in all parts of the continent where they are spoken. Should we not expect variation in the French spoken in Paris, Dakar, and Madagascar? Just how great are the differences between the English spoken in Nairobi and Lagos from each other and from that spoken in England or America? And when Paden (1968), for example, asserts that Hausa 'is able to deal with "patent medicine", "Western democracy", and "nuclear devices", surely he does not mean to suggest that local renditions of Western ideas, be they technological or political, mesh easily with the cultural framework into which they are being translated. I am told that the reverse difficulties also obtain, as, for example, the anthropologists' attempts to render the complexities of African indigenous medicines in a European language where these concepts, as well as a vocabulary sufficient for expressing them, are foreign.

It is assumed, by some writers at least, that second languages are immune from the social afflictions and corrupting influences which tend to attack first languages. The following comment from a Foreign Area Studies Handbook prepared at American University exemplifies this notion.

'Because Swahili is the indigenous language of few and the second language of many, it is also apolitical and thereby of enhanced usefulness. Speaking Swahili is in no way an indication of an attachment to a single society, region or political party, a problem faced in many other African countries where the language of a dominant indigenous group comes to have political significance when it is a second language elsewhere' (American University 1967: 144).

There is of course no such thing as an 'apolitical' language as there is no such thing as an 'apolitical' person. As we have stated above, politics is human relations, and language is an organic component of such relations. It is simply impossible to disassociate languages from the contexts in which they are learned and used. While Swahili may be above specific ethnic associations, although this is itself doubtful given the patterns of knowledge of the language within the country, it carries close associations with Tanzanian nationalism, not to mention political educational requirements, the politics surrounding the spread of Islam, and the like. Neither Swahili nor other languages can be disassociated from human influences and choices, from value judgements, and from deliberate policy decisions by officials and administrators, that is, by political personages.

Second languages, then, represent no easy solution to the communication problems of multilingual countries. There may be a considerable efficiency loss where a European language or a second African one *must* be spoken, regardless of the degree of control on the users' part. Students of policy and decision-making can ill afford not to assess that efficiency component with the greatest care. The most sensitive aspect of the second language syndrome is, of course, the problem of choosing official languages, a problem which we will discuss at some length below.

POLITICAL THOUGHT AND THEORY

If political thought and theory actually influences political behavior, shapes social institutions, and determines social processes, can it be assumed that a language medium suitable for these purposes is available and at work? If we consider the enormous institution-building demands placed upon the indigenous languages in developing societies today, and considering both the lack of technical elaboration in vocabulary to express these new ideas and the different sorts of philosophical systems rooted in different languages, it is possible that linkages between thought and practice may be quite precarious and possibly inadequate for many practical purposes. If one further considers changes in the mode of production, ongoing incisive demographic changes, and the social and cultural consequences flowing from these, the burdens placed upon indigenous languages in developing countries with respect to the formulation of relevant social thought and theory may prove to be far beyond the present capacity of most of them. This is, of course, as true for economics or religion as it is for politics. As linguists are wont to point out, language changes more slowly than most other parts of the cultural system. The lag between changes elsewhere and in language may in fact play a key role in the disruption, confusion, and disorganization often observed as a counterpart to social and political change.

My reservations are reinforced by considering the implications of the Sapir-Whorf hypothesis which holds that 'perceptions and thoughts and views of nature and of the world in general on the part of any given body of speakers is controlled, for the most part unconsciously, by their language . . .' (Hertzler 1965: 119–120). Martin Landau offers a corollary which suggests that users of markedly different grammars are pointed by these grammars towards different types of observations and different evaluations of externally similar acts of observation (Landau 1965). A group of social scientists and philosophers, twenty years ago, alerted us to the possibility that thought and theory are shaped not so much by what we prefer to call the intellect but by the structure of language (Henle 1958). Landau's comments on the Sapir-Whorf hypothesis are especially salient here.

'Whorf's principle refers to natural languages which carry the patterns of their respective cultures and as such contain the unconscious assumptions and concealed premises through which their uses make contact with nature: the categories and concepts, the images and models of a natural language are the unquestioned "givens" that hold throughout a speech community. . . . *This system resists change:* social and technological development will yield rapid expansions, but the basic structure of a linguistic system (which Sapir described as being self-contained) changes very slowly. It thus permits a body of conventional and customary forms to be carried from one generation to another.

'So to Whorf, a linguistic system is not a simple reproducing instrument but is itself the shaper of ideas, the program and guide for the individual's mental activity, for his analysis of impressions, for his synthesis of his mental stock in trade. . . . To speak a language is to follow the system of organization and classification of data which the language itself decrees. No member of a speech community is, therefore, free to describe nature as he pleases since he is constrained by the modes of interpretation impressed upon him by the language he uses' (Landau 1965: 4; italics added).

It seems to me that a very important implication of these remarks is that the communication of political messages across the sorts of linguistic (and thereby cultural) boundaries which exist in most developing countries is precarious indeed. Ideology, whether generated within the nation or imported from abroad, must pass through many filters indeed, both those which reflect different status positions within any particular country and those which are generated by different language and thought systems.

In a study of language and nation-building in Africa, Pierre Alexandre explores the problems of 'compound misunderstandings' – 'vertical' between the originators of the modern institutions and the ordinary citizen, 'horizontal' between citizens of different tribes – then discusses results obtained when French, English, or Arabic terms are incorporated in indigenous African languages in conjunction with transfer of institutional or procedural concepts, and designations of government or administrative offices or officers. He shows that the adapted, most likely corrupted, forms tend to convey associations and meanings which may prove to be quite dysfunctional and which are certainly different from those intended originally. To cite but one of his illustrations, concerning parliamentary and political party functions: '. . . the use of Swahili *chama* (association, group) for "party" certainly does not connote the same picture of an M.P.'s role as Bulu *nsamba*, originally "raiding party, armed trade caravan" ' (Alexandre 1968: 124–125).

Alexandre grants that borrowed or adopted terms, given sufficient time, may prove entirely sufficient (Alexandre 1968: 124–125). But, he argues, 'this kind of naturalization' may require more time than is available given the pressures of present-day state formation. According to Alexandre, coining a term like *nda ya minloman,* literally 'house of the sent-out-persons', a Fang device to capture the meaning of *chambre des députés,* may prove more misleading than may be desirable in the interest of successful statecraft (Alexandre 1968: 124).

POLITICAL BEHAVIOR, INFLUENCE, AND CONTROL: THE INDIVIDUAL LEVEL

We know that language is a means used by man to conceal as well as to reveal. It is often a means of deception, partly to assure survival. As the octopus has his inky substance, so do we have, in language, a means of obscuring our traces, our intellectual traces as it were. If we accept that survival – either physical or social or economic – is at the core of politics and that much of political behavior is verbal, then language must be accorded a high priority in political, especially behaviorally oriented, research.

Several of the chapters in this volume deal with judicial processes, certainly a vital aspect of political life insofar as it governs access to wealth, privilege, power, or defense against encroachment by others. When defenses against charges of violation of law or of custom must be argued in 'foreign' languages, as they must so often be in each of the three countries considered in this volume, facility in the legal language may become a critical factor in deciding the outcome of court cases.

The recent concern with scientism in political science contains the risk of losing sight of the basic fact that politics is an art and a delicate one at that. We may also lose sight of the place of emotion in politics, the creative component of the art, and of deep personal commitment to the political act. Most children are introduced into this world and have the world interpreted to them through a single language, their mother tongue. Personality is formed to a considerable extent, if not altogether in all critical respects, under that influence. When acquisition of a second language is socially compelling, as a result of conquest, or economic pressure, an experience common to a majority of mankind in their adult lives, new and substantially different ways of viewing and describing the world are introduced. Words spoken to a child in his mother tongue evoke certain emotions, memories, and thoughts. Do words spoken in a secondary language, an alien one, produce the same or even similar results? Or is the product of speech in one language quite unlike the product of speech in the other? This is important since a second language is – for most of the developing areas of the world – the language of politics at the highest levels, frequently at intermediate levels as well. Since critical decisions, of greatest survival interest to most, are made at such levels, knowledge or facility in that language are of the essencc. Mastery of that language may well be *the* key to success.

POLITICAL BEHAVIOR, INFLUENCE, AND CONTROL: THE GROUP LEVEL AND BEYOND

When one moves from the individual to the group, to larger aggregations ending up eventually at the national level and beyond, the sheer numbers of language communities increase and the potential for distortion and misunderstanding in these multilingual, multicultural environments rises. At this level, something near total information loss may result where a European language is employed to direct messages at a mass audience speaking one or more different languages, none of which bears much relation to the European tongue.

If we consider further the known tendency of political leaders everywhere to employ language to conceal their intents and purposes rather than reveal them, to obfuscate rather than educate, and if we consider, furthermore, the ever more pressing requirement for obfuscation in light of inability to deliver on promises, a special form of political translation or interpretation may have to be developed (Bretton 1973: 117–118, 307).

A comment on political propaganda in Africa by P. Alexandre is pertinent here. He notes that typically doctrines, ideological propositions, and even political programs are formulated and discussed at higher levels of government either in English or in French; at the same time, propaganda directed at the masses reflects these discussions and formulations only vaguely. More likely, the resemblence is superficial and the messages confined to 'larger issues' only. Comparing European and African political party propaganda methods, Alexandre suggests that in Europe the difference between political expressions at the top and at base is in some way 'quantitative' whereas in Africa it is 'qualitative' marked by 'total change in conceptual and expressive usage'. He argues that there is indeed a discontinuation of facts, if not intent (Alexandre 1961: 4, 21).

GOVERNMENT, LAW, ADMINISTRATION, AND TECHNOLOGICAL DEVELOPMENT

Entire social and legal orders may have been subverted and new forms maintained and defended by shifts in the meaning of key words which alter substantially the original purposes and intents. To an extent, language revolts in the former colonial territories are a reaction to that particular aspect of foreign domination and control, accomplished through imposition of ideological systems, and the enforcement of those, first through the educational system – by tests and examinations and the punishment and reward structure in the schools throughout – then through the legal-constitutional system, by literacy tests, for example. Legal codes of necessity define forbidden, authorized, or required human actions in verbal terms. Politics and law are inseparable, one being the arm of the other. The following passage from Bram cannot be improved upon as a reminder of what the impact of language is on the combined product of law and politics:

'[Verbal definition of legal norms] is based on the hope that diverse as lawless behavior may be, every specific deviation will fall under some "line and verse" of the code, enabling punishment to be meted out in accordance with the tables of misdeeds and penalties. In practice it soon becomes apparent, on the one hand, that every human act can be described in a number of ways and, on the other, that every written law lends itself to a variety of interpretations. Consequently, the ultimate task of the courts and of men of law takes the form of laborious elucidation of the relationship between legal texts and human deeds[5]' (Bram 1955: 45).

Legal codes, constitutions, and other legal-pointed or legal-administrative documents are thus political commandments handed down by those who rule the verbal manufacturing process. In other words, manipulation of language is an integral part of the process of government and administration, and we must plum the depth of language to appreciate its governmental, administrative, legal, and technical potentialities and implications (Harries 1968: 423–425).

Insofar as legal and administrative processes govern social behavior – somewhat like canals directing the flow of water – 'language provides a vehicle for the transmission of technical inventions as well as social conventions' (Bram 1955: 23). Imposition of French upon the customs and conventions in the Ivory Coast, for example, aided by the simultaneous imposition of a Paris-created legal constitutional and administrative grid, and further aided by the penetration of all phases of public and private life by French personnel, certainly furthered the development of certain technical-administrative inventions. Eventually, the resultant reference-expert power relationship – indigenous thought is shaped by reference to French expertise – becomes a source of social conventions as well. This is as true of the government-administrative department as it is of the engineering office. The process is one of built-in cultural alienation and conflict.

Here, as in other respects, a wide gap separates the wish from fulfillment. For example, eager as Tanzanian leaders may be to replace English fully with Swahili, the costs involved in the technical elaboration and development of Swahili for the special needs of government, education, and the like may be too expensive given the country's present needs and resources available to help satisfy them. Meanwhile, Alexandre's warning is pertinent: 'The best laid plans of experts and ministers are apt to fail when explained in kiBongo-Bongo to the waPongo-Pongo, and this may have serious political consequences' (1968: 123).

LANGUAGE AS A POLITICAL ISSUE

This is probably the best covered aspect of the language and politics relationship from the point of view of political science. Literature on nationalism, ethnicity, and related topics has for more than half a century reflected a deep awareness of the political sensitivity of language preference, imposition, and promotion. It is clear why blood is drawn over language in certain situations: language is the key, or the set of keys, needed to unlock the gates of access to survival kits – employment, advancement, social security, physical security. We have discussed some of the dimensions of this above.

Much of the tension, and certainly the panic, generated over language disputes are a matter of threat perception. Fear of being barred from access to sources of wealth, or from employment, fear of having one's children barred from the more prestigious – hence more rewarding – sources of income, has propelled masses of youth and their parents into sometimes bloody confrontations around the world. In much of Africa, typified by polyethnic societies, prevalence of illiteracy creates special opportunities for education: the abrupt introduction of a school system may be perceived as a void into which demand for education rushes. Under such conditions the decision on which language to elevate to the principal one in a given area, possibly to the exclusion of others, unleashes survival fears and panic on the part of those who perceive themselves as being disadvantaged permanently by the decision.

More than the courts, the educational system attracts the attention of what might be called language-politicians, because education goes to the roots of subsistence, security, and survival interests. Control of school eventually assures control of courtroom language; but defeat in the battle of education may foreclose direct access to the language in which punishment as well as rewards are meted out. Loss in that battle will move the users of the defeated language to the periphery of social power, insofar as it is administered through the courts, and no translation or interpretation will help. But it should be clear that since wealth can buy court judgment in many of the less developed countries and in all probability in the more developed ones as well, in the absence of that most potent of all languages – the language of money – inability to follow the legal proceedings, the quick, even rapid-fire repartee of attorneys, prosecutor, and judge, in effect, cuts the accused out of the process, leaving him almost entirely at the mercy of the interpreter.

The unreliability of poorly trained and poorly paid translators and interpreters cannot be too strongly emphasized in this connection. Lang's analysis in Chapter 16 amply illustrates the problem in one particular court in rural New Guinea; yet his findings ring all too true for other multilingual nations. Given the prominence of the courts in many areas where land reform is underway, with the unavoidable litigation over property rights, generated by ancient and often nebulous claims, the inability of litigants to penetrate the language barrier – made even more impenetrable by introduction of technical jargon and concepts of foreign origin – undoubtedly contributes to moving the language issue to the center of the political stage.

Here it must be recognized that to the individual dependent on one language alone, any other language is a foreign one, even though it may be one of the languages spoken within a few miles, in the same national territory. This of course is one of the reasons why European languages are preferred in education and government in many parts of the world, in certain parts of Africa and South India for instance; though foreign, they may seem less alien, and less threatening, than the indigenous language next door.

Language means security to the highly educated and the well-to-do as to the uneducated and the poor. Language, rule, caste, and class are part of a chain which secures positions of power and influence for some and excludes others. Language has become a political issue where it has been used by certain groups, in the bureaucratic system for instance, as a code of confidentiality, as a device to exclude competing groups.

Discussing work by Renzo Sereno on the social fortunes of the Castilian-speaking bureaucracy in Puerto Rico, Bram reports: 'When Puerto Rico passed from Spanish to American sovereignty the loss of power by the Castilian-speaking elites spelled the doom of their language' (Bram 1955: 31). The resultant upheavals – peasants speaking the island-dialect pouring out of the mountains, growth of urban slums along the coast – are being replicated today on Madagascar, and elsewhere in Latin America, Africa, and Asia. In such situations, defense of the elite language becomes the central political issue.

Not directly related to individual survival fears, but a major political issue nevertheless, is the dilemma posed by (a) the need for a national unifying symbol, or means of unification, and (b) the requirement of ever greater contact with technologically advanced areas of the world, the issue of inner- versus outer-directed language orientation. Noah Webster, thinking of the then young United States of America, recommended that: '. . . our honor requires us to have a system of our own, in language as well as government. Great Britain whose children we are, and whose language we speak, should no longer be our standard; for the taste of her writers is already corrupted and her language on the decline . . .' (quoted in Bram 1955: 56). The outcome of that story is well known.

Part is this issue is the technological proficiency of a language. And here we return to the beginning of our discussion. Language is the product of culture, reflecting basic human needs. It is structured to fulfill certain purposes; it takes on the coloring of the social setting within which it develops. To Whorf, language 'is itself the shaper of ideas, the program and guide for the individual's mental activity, for his analysis of impressions, for his synthesis of his mental stock in trade' (Landau 1965: 4). While language can be adjusted to limitless varieties of needs and situations, its proficiency and efficiency will not be the same under all conditions, in all cases. When under the Hitler regime, German nationalist-linguists attempted to substitute the word *Bernzieh* for electrical locomotive – in an anti-Latin, anti-Greek campaign – they surely did not thereby improve German technological capacity. Piecing together an indigenous German word not really applying to what it was intended to convey – electric energy – and a word for pull, the end product was clearly not locomotive as understood by railway engineers. African attempts to stretch indigenous languages by similar patchwork methods to cope with technological advance are likely to have the same end-effect as had the German experiment. The latter was abandoned under the pressures of more urgent industrial and eventually military requirements. But the issue will remain. Regardless of its value as an instrument of communication, like numerous other extensions of our existence, language is converted inexorably into a social symbol, soon to generate its own social myth. These same qualities convert language into sources of political divergence, cleavage, antagonism, and tension. Or it turns it into a catalyst of unification or preservation of cultural identity. As such, it serves beleaguered minorities, the Poles for instance in their struggle to survive Russian and Germanic pressures.

In East Africa especially, language became a highly charged political issue because it served as a vehicle for three major political forces, basically incompatible and on a collision course: colonial administrative (first German, then British), missionary, and educational. While colonial-administrative interests favored Swahili for administrative convenience and educational interests favored English, the Christian churches identified Swahili as a spearhead of Islam and promoted 'local languages' instead.

John Paden (1968) offers the best analysis of the role and function of Hausa in modern Nigeria. There Hausa came to be identified as a symbol of political intent, or as a prime political issue, by detrimentally opposed groups, each seeing in that language substantially different qualities or values. The traditional rulers of the Northern region saw in Hausa a means of preserving their own cultural and political position relative to other competing groups in the South in an ethno-linguistically pluralist country undergoing rapid and dramatic changes. On the other hand, the other language groups, or cultures, principally Yoruba and Ibo, saw in Hausa the spearhead of a hostile pressure, a wedge driven into their midst by elements they deemed inferior, largely because they indentified the North with opposition to progress.

Language then may indeed be the most explosive issue universally and over time. This mainly because language alone, unlike all other concerns associated with nationalism and ethnocentrism – with the possible exception of sex-related issues where those are relevant – is so closely tied to the individual self. Fear of being deprived of communicative skills seem to raise political passion to a fever pitch.

It should be obvious from the preceding discussion that our research priorities are almost boundless. Yet resources available for research are limited and some priorities may therefore have to be identified. I have tried in this brief essay to highlight a number of problems which are found throughout the three cases considered in this volume but which are deserving of much more attention from political scientists in their future studies.

NOTES:

1. Deutsch: 'In the main, these pages offer notions, propositions, and models derived from the philosophy of science, and specifically from the theory of communication and control – often called by Norbert Wiener's term "cybernetics". . .' (1963: viii). Wiener: 'Naturally, no theory of communication can avoid the discussion of language. Language, in fact, is in one sense another name for communication itself, as well as a word used to describe the codes through which communication takes place' (1954: 74).
2. Ethel Albert, reporting speech situations in Burundi, writes: 'There are many women who in fact make the decisions presented publicly by their husbands, or who become politically or economically powerful through skillful, if discreet and private, use of rhetoric. Except at the extreme top and bottom of the social scale, each individual learns verbal formulas and styles appropriate to a variety of roles, some those of a social superior, some those of an inferior' (1964: 38).
3. Second language may be a misnomer. In parts of Africa, Swahili or Hausa may be the first, English or French, the second, and another indigenous language third. Or it may be the other way around. What is actually meant by second language is alternate secondary means of expression; the ranking is a function of the patterns of usage and familiarity of the particular languages spoken in the country and their patterns of knowledge.
4. The difficulties in translation of the passage are no doubt related to the young man's level of education. The fact of the matter is, however, that all civil servants have not achieved high levels of formal education and this sort of difficulty may not be uncommon. An educationally accomplished and linguistically experienced Ghanaian friend of mine, Michael Dei-Anang, when asked by me to translate the same passage without preparation, on the spur of the moment, came up with a more comprehensive, hence more accurate Twi version which translates back into English as follows: 'The elders of the community who are responsible for the nation of Nigeria have passed a law prohibiting individuals from trade negotiations with South Africa until the South African nation had made it possible for black and white people in that country to live on terms of equality.' He agreed that a person less educated and less experienced would most likely 'make a mash of it'.
5. Pity the poor Congolese who had to appear before a Belgian judge speaking Flemish, then one of the two official languages of the Colony (Bram 1955: 45).

ARNOLD H. LEIBOWITZ

Language and the Law: The Exercise of Political Power through Official Designation of Language

In this chapter, I intend to demonstrate the sorts of concerns in language and politics which are most relevant to the law. I will do this, not so much by a review of specific issues raised by the case studies in this volume, but by a review of some of the ways in which the official designation of language has been used by those in control of the decision-making machinery as a means of political manipulation and control. The materials on which my argument is based are drawn exclusively from a single country, the United States of America. The processes, however, are general and serve well as a background for viewing similar problems in Tanzania, India, New Guinea, and elsewhere.

The thesis to be presented here is simple: language is primarily a means of control. I believe this proposition is generally true, as true as 'language is a means of communication' or 'language is a means of social intercourse' or the host of other definitions which come to the fore when language is discussed. I believe that not only is the definition true but when viewed that way it may be of considerable significance. Since its proof as a general proposition would involve us in a lengthy debate, far removed from the immediate concern, I wish to treat here only a specific but important aspect of this general proposition: the case when the government acts in an official way and designates a specific language requirement as a condition of participating in a given activity. We will not be concerned here – although it is relevant – with actual language usage but rather only language designation by the official authorities. In that case, when politics and language relate most openly, we can see more clearly the use of language as a means of expressing power, as a way of controlling and manipulating people in society.

I shall discuss this latter thesis by relating examples from the political and legal practice of the United States. We shall look at language designation in three general areas: (a) the school system, (b) citizenship and voting, and (c) the economic life of the country. The significant point to be noted is that language designation in all three areas followed a marked, similar pattern so that it is reasonably clear that one was responding not to the problems specifically related to that area (i.e. job requirements in the economic sphere) but to broader problems in the society to which language was but one response. Language designation was almost always coupled with restrictions on the use of other languages; it was also coupled with discriminatory legislation and practices in other fields, including private indignities of various kinds which make it clear that the issue was a broader one. We shall show that the pattern was as follows: (a) from 1789 to 1880, the implicit designation of English as the official language but with great tolerance for the use of other languages; (b) from 1880 until World War II, the blatant use of English language requirements to exclude and discriminate against various minorities and immigrant groups; and (c) since World War II, and especially in the last decade, the relaxation of these requirements and even the encouragement of the use of other languages.

THE OFFICIAL LANGUAGE OF THE SCHOOL SYSTEM

Let me begin by discussing the case where a government embarks on what is conceded to be one of its functions: the education of its people. One can hardly argue with the proposition that a population should be uplifted via education and, if illiterate, should be provided the means to read and write. But note that the governmental actions can be carried out in a linguistically neutral manner. Education requires funds for school buildings, teachers, and text books. Nothing need be said *officially* about the language in which the instruction is to take place. And in the early days of American history this was the case. At that time all schools were financed by private funds. The German schools of the 1700s were sectarian ones in which ministers were commonly the teachers. School instruction in parts of Pennsylvania, Maryland, Virginia, and the Carolinas was given in German, often to the exclusion of English (Faust 1909: 203). As the number of German immigrants increased greatly during the 1817–1835 period, the pattern continued and German instruction became more prevalent.

Most immigrants to America were concentrated in those districts where the land was most readily available and cheap: the western frontier states of Indiana, Illinois, Ohio, Wisconsin, Minnesota, Michigan, Iowa, and Missouri. In these farming districts, the Germans initially had no teachers at their disposal who were familiar with English and, in any event, there was little need for a command of English during those early settlement years. Thus, most of the earliest school laws made no mention of the language to be employed in the public schools (Kloss 1970: 200).[1]

In 1837, in response to the German demand, the Ohio legislature passed a law authorizing the teaching of the German language in the public schools in those districts where a large German population resided. During this initial state of tolerance, Pennsylvania also passed a law permitting German schools to be founded on an equal basis with English ones (Faust 1909: 151–152). Germans were practically the sole immigrants of any significant number during the first half of the nineteenth century, hence to focus on their experience in this early period is appropriate.

Increased interest in English as the language of instruction began in the late 1880s and continued through World War I and was related to the religious and economic fears engendered by the increased immigration and the wartime xenophobia during these years. This increased migration and the first world war brought about a much greater emphasis on 'Americanization' (Rider 1920; Hartmann 1948) and the need for English as the instruction medium to effect this. Thus, in the decade 1913–1923, partly in response to the urging of the federal government, states passed as many statutes requiring English to be the language of instruction in the public and private schools as had been passed in all the years previously. In 1903, fourteen states had such a statutory requirement; in 1913, the number had increased to seventeen; and in 1923, the number was thirty-four (Flanders 1925: 18–19), the same number found today.[2]

These statutes were usually coupled with others relating to the

Americanization movement: the requirement of the pledge of allegiance, the teaching of American history and government, and the restriction of the teaching of foreign languages. The constitutionality of these latter were called into question in a series of cases arising after World War I. The leading case, *Meyer* v. *Nebraska,* made clear that the prohibition or undue inhibition of the use or teaching of a foreign language is a violation of due process and unconstitutional (Hartman 1948: 252).[3] However, it also explicilty assumed that a state statutory requirement of English instruction in the public and private schools was sanctioned by the Constitution.

In a series of cases on school regulation in the 1920s the Supreme Court stated its view that (a) requiring the language of instruction be English in a state or territory of the United States was constitutional, but (b) held that restriction of complementary or supplementary secondary language efforts by various ethnic groups was unconstitutional. The Court did not eliminate the possibility of some regulation of foreign language instruction but indicated its general disfavor with this type of state restriction.

Although we have focused on the Germans for the sake of continuity similar restrictive legislation concerning the language of instruction took place during this period against the Indians (Adams 1946), Japanese (Ichihashi 1932; Daniels 1969), the Puerto Ricans (Osuna 1949), and the Mexicans (Manuel 1965; U.S. Commission on Civil Rights 1971). To cite one example, English-language instruction in the Indian schools was first mentioned in the 1868 report of the Indian Peace Commission and in 1879 the first off-reservation boarding school – the institution which was to dominate Indian education for the next fifty years – was established at Carlisle, Pennsylvania. The purpose of this school became clear in the succeeding decades: to separate the Indian child from his reservation and family, strip him of his tribal lore and mores, emphasize industrial arts, and prepare him in such a way that he would never return to his people. Language became a critical element in this policy. English-language instruction and abandonment of the native language became complementary means to the end.

Generally, the legislative and executive branches, at both the state and federal level (the latter in its treatment of territories and Indians),[4] took a consistent line in favor of English until the passage of

Title VII of the Elementary and Secondary Education Amendments of 1968,[5] the 'Bilingual Education Act'. The significance of this act is that it marks the first time the federal government has taken cognizance of the special educational problems of children who are the products of 'environments where the dominant language is other than English' and not only permitted but encouraged instruction in a language other than English.[6] By 1968, when the federal government for the first time by its passage of the Bilingual Education Act, suggested the permissibility – even the desirability – of instruction in the native language, the political and moral context had substantially changed. The executive and legislative branches had both come out rather strongly for civil rights and focused on the deprivations suffered by various minority groups. The wave of ethnic nationalism which accompanied the civil rights movement and social changes in the 1960s no longer reguired Spanish-speaking parents to remain mute or to soften their desire that the Spanish language be given a more meaningful role in their children's education.

Educational support for the bilingual program was couched in terms of the need to change the existing system; most importantly, the drop-out rate for Mexican-Americans was high and many Spanish-speaking children failed to attend school at all. Although a list of schools where bilingual education was in effect was submitted to the Congress during the hearings on the Bilingual Education Act, the statistical data to measure the educational advantages or disadvantages of these innovations were not available. The question of what beneficial effects instruction in the native tongue would have on the dropout rate or other educational desiderata could not be answered.

Some educators urged that instruction be in the language of the home so that the valuable resources of foreign-speaking peoples be maintained. Other educators placed greater stress on the fact that the best way to teach any subject to children from homes where English was not the native tongue was via their first language. For these educators, the emphasis was on teaching a particular subject and the most effective method for doing that, rather than on the preservation of a cultural heritage. Educators who approached the problem as one of retention of native language resources did not have to meet the issue of the effect on general information or to compare bilingual education with teaching in English only. But what they did emphasize was that bilingualism or multilingualism meant pluralistic cultural patterns as well.

The response from the state governments so far has been relatively good. California, New Mexico, Arizona, and Texas in the past five years all passed statutes authorizing bilingual education. The effect of the passage of the Bilingual Education Act on the climate of federal opinion may be seen in the case of *Lau* v. *Nichols.*[7] In that case non-English-speaking Chinese students petitioned the court to require the San Francisco School District to provide compensatory Chinese language instruction to permit them to obtain an adequate public education. The United States Government filed a brief as a friend of the court in favor of the petitioners. The United States relied on Title VI of the Civil Rights Act of 1964 which provides that 'no person in the United States shall, on the ground of . . . national origin . . . be denied the benefits of . . . any program or activity receiving Federal financial assistance.' The Court reasoned that the language distinction and the racial discrimination was too closely linked to be permitted without violating Title VI of the Civil Rights Act of 1964. For, as the state officials have recognized, the distinction which triggers, the inequality is one which ineluctably originates from the group's nationality: language.

Although the remedy is unclear (the U.S. Government in *Lau* v. *Nichols* requested the school board to put forth a plan), the changed tone is important to an understanding of language and politics issues.

POLITICAL ACCESS

The same pattern of implict recognition (1780–1880), active support of languagae qualifications in order to discriminate (1880–1920 and continuing to a lesser degree through World War II), then an active questioning and reversal to permit greater tolerance of language differences as part of a changing political framework is to be seen in the political arena.

Voting qualifications. The first language cases to reach the Supreme Court primarily involved the role of English as the exclusive language of the school system. The statutes requiring English literacy as a condition of voting, although slower to reach the court, had a longer history and their discriminatory aspect was more deeply felt. Therefore, when, after World War II, the language issue was again to reach the Supreme Court in a series of voting cases, the matter was not to be resolved without great debate and federal legislation. For the issue of the right to vote portended major changes in the political structure of the country.

The Supreme Court cases arose out of the efforts of various southern states to disenfranchise eligible black voters by English literacy statutes which on their face or by hostile administration limited the suffrage. The initial 'model statutes' for these laws were in Connecticut (1855) and Massachusetts (1857) and were directed against the Irish at the instigation of the Native American (Know Nothing) Party which had captured the Massachusetts State Legislature and was highly influential in Connecticut (Bromage 1930; Billington 1938: 412–415). The increased immigration from 1890–1920 threatened to change the political balance in many states. This fact, coupled with the nationalistic fervor created by World War I, contributed to the repression of ethnic identity and the distinction between the 'new' immigrants and the 'old' immigrants became fashionable.

The specific reason behind the passage of English literacy test suffrage in each state is difficult to reconstruct, but whenever litigants have questioned these tests their discriminatory origins have been disclosed. The anti-Negro basis of the Southern literacy test suffrage laws has been well established; the Connecticut and Massachusetts anti-Irish bias is also thoroughly documented. Thus, in California, in addition to the general anti-foreigner bias, the literacy test was aimed at the Oriental and the Mexican.[8] In Alaska, the test sought to restrict Indian suffrage.[9] There is evidence that in Wyoming the focus was on the Finnish coal miners.[10] In the state of Washington, the legislative history of the literacy statement also indicates an intent to prevent the Oriental from participating in the political process. Chinese laborers were brought into Washington in the 1860s and 1870s as cheap labor to work in the gold mines and in the 1880s to work on the railroads. Anti-Chinese sentiment led to violent race riots in 1885–86. Bills were introduced in the Territorial

Legislature, beginning in 1885, to prohibit Chinese from owning land, from operating laundries, and from being hired – all designed to harass the Chinese population and encourage them to leave. During the Constitutional Convention of 1889 in Washington, both literacy and Chinese-exclusion proposals were made in connection with voting qualifications. And on the same day in 1895 that the literacy amendment was introduced, bills penalizing persons 'who wear a queue' were also introduced.[11] Thus, one can conclude that the legislative setting of all of these statutes was as tainted as those Southern statutes found later invalid by the Court and overruled by the Congress in the Voting Rights Act of 1965.

In 1959, in *Lassiter* v. *Northhampton Election Board,* the Supreme Court for the first time met the language issue squarely and upheld a North Carolina statute requiring the prospective voter to 'be able to read and write any section of the Constitution of North Carolina in the English language'. The reasoning of Justice Douglas, who wrote the opinion for a unanimous Court, was that 'the ability to read and write . . . has some relation to standards designed to promote intelligent use of the ballot . . . [and is] neutral on race, creed, color, and sex'.[12] The opinion cited the fact that nineteen states had some kind of literacy test as a precondition to voting. (Presumably, if that many states did it, it followed that it must be reasonable.) The Court cautioned it would strike down the English literacy test if it was employed to perpetuate discrimination; but, since no such charge was before the Court, it sustained the statute on its face. The Court did not discuss any of the earlier language cases of the 1920s nor the 'legislative setting' of the North Carolina requirement.

The problem with the opinion was that it postulated a totally unreal situation: a neutral English literacy test. In actual fact, English literacy tests were passed with the very purpose of discriminating against a particular group clearly identified by race, religion, or country of origin. The Supreme Court in the cases following *Lassiter* was to discover the racial character of English literacy suffrage requirements which proliferated throughout the South beginning in the 1890s. What it did not see, and is the thesis here, was that these English literacy restrictions were part of a more extensive discriminatory pattern developed at that same time throughout the nation of using English literacy requirements to restrict various religious and racial groups from participating in and contributing fully to the life of the country.[13]

United States v. *Mississippi*[14] and *Louisiana* v. *United States*[15] brought the Southern legislative pattern officially to the Court's attention.[16] Both of these states had passed legislation in the 1890s requiring English literacy as a prerequisite to voting which they coupled in later years with the requirement of 'interpreting' and 'understanding' the state constitution.[17] The Supreme Court this time, as it had not done in *Lassiter,* examined the origin of these educational requirements at some length before holding that the legislation 'as written and as applied was part of a successful plan to deprive Louisiana Negroes of their right to vote'.

The Supreme Court did not explore the question of whether a more objectively designed test, such as had been sustained in *Lassiter,* passed with the motive and effect of discriminating against the Negro, would have been valid. The Mississippi provision as originally passed in 1890 (which served as the model for the other English literacy statutes in the South) raised exactly such a question since the Mississippi constitutional delegates were aware that 60 percent of the Negroes, but only 10 percent of the whites, could not read English.[18]

The Voting Rights Act of 1965 was passed to meet this pattern of Southern anti-Negro suffrage legislation which the courts had been struggling with on a case-by-case basis. The Act suspended literacy tests and other educational prerequisites to voting in any state where they were in force and less than 50 percent of the eligible voters had registered or voted in the 1964 Presidential elections. The extensive hearings on the Act were limited to the problem of discrimination in the administration of these tests in the South and it was expected that the force of the Act would be to permit 'millions of non-white Americans . . . to participate for the first time on an equal basis in the government under which they live',[19] although technically the Act applied to some Northern states as well.[20] In *South Carolina* v. *Katzenbach*[21] the Supreme Court upheld the key portions of the Voting Rights Act of 1965, permitting the suspension of literacy tests where past performance indicated discriminatory administration of the test.

These Southern cases were relatively easy since the intent of the original legislation was so clear, but they laid the groundwork for the expansion into other areas of the country and the questioning of the validity of English literacy as distinguished from literacy in any language, as a condition of voting. Thus, Section 4(e) of the Voting Rights Act of 1965, provided that:

'no person who had successfully completed the sixth grade in a public or private school in the United States, its territories, the District of Columbia, or the Commonwealth of Puerto Rico in which the predominant classroom language was other than English, shall be denied the right to vote in any . . . election because of his inability to read or write . . . English.'

Since Puerto Rico is the only area 'in the United States . . . in which the predominant classroom language was other than English', the statute was clearly directed to the Puerto Rican migrant to the United States who, in many cases, could not vote because of the 1922 New York State amendment to its Constitution which provided that no person could vote unless he was able 'to read and write English'.[22] The Court has ruled that federal action modifying the literacy test was constitutional.[23]

Thus, although the constitutionality of the literacy test is still unclear,[24] the trend is away from the use of the tests.[25] Since 1965, two states, Hawaii and Maine, have repealed them and the New York State Constitutional Convention also suggested repeal. In addition, in other states the law was – even prior to the 1970 law – enforced in only about nine of the states outside the South.[26] A number of groups, the American Civil Liberties Union, the Civil Rights Commission, and a recent Presidential Commission, have urged the elimination of the tests.[27] If the discriminatory purpose as the baisis for the original passage of the statutes is clear, we may note that their discriminatory effect is still present. In the South, the Negro continues to be affected: the race legislated against originally. In the North and West, the racial victim's situation has changed partly because of assimilation and changes in immigration patterns and partly because of changes in state voting laws requiring U.S. citizenship as a condition to voting.

Many states at one time or another permitted aliens who had declared their intention of becoming citizens to vote. At present, since 1926, all states require citizenship as a precondition to voting (Aylsworth 1931: 114). This fact, combined with the change in the naturalization statute so that since 1950 English literacy is required, narrows the focus of any state English literacy statute as a precondition to voting to native-born citizens: the Negro, the migrant from Puerto Rico (since persons born in Puerto Rico are natural-born citizens), the Mexican-American of the Southwest, and the Indian. This means that the English literacy burden here, and in other areas as well, at present, falls – as never before – on non-immigrant groups who are, generally, distinguishable by color.

Naturalization requirements. Prior to 1906, there was no requirement in the naturalization laws that an alien either speak or be lirerate in English. Indeed, the only relevant provision was that a would-be United States citizen had to demonstrate an attachment to the principles of the constitution.[28]

Some Federal courts imposed an English literacy gloss on this language of the naturalization statute on the grounds that the applicant could not be attached to a document he could not read.[29] But the cases were not unanimous in this regard. Further, Congressional practice prior to 1906 belied any linguistic prerequisite to citizenship since Congress had, on several occasions, collectively naturalized large numbers of non-English speaking persons.[30]

The relationship between naturalization and language might have remained loose and somewhat ambigious had not voting frauds forced a discussion of the problem. The courts, often corrupt, would engage in wholesale naturalizations on the eves of election and many voters were bought and sold. These abuses in the naturalization administration and its effects on the franchise were recognized and became the subject of a President's Report to Congress in 1905. The Report called for regularized naturalization laws, restriction of the franchise, and, as a not wholly required corollary of the latter, the need for aliens wishing to become citizens to speak English. Thus, in the Nationality Act of 1906 it first became law that an alien had to *speak English* to become naturalized and this requirement was codified in the Nationality Act of 1940. The requirement that one wishing to become a citizen must show an ability *to read and write English* was adden ten years later in the Internal Security Act of 1950.[31]

The constitutionality of the literacy requirement as a condition of citizenship was upheld in the lower courts.[32] The legal reasoning was that citizenship is a privilege which Congress may condition before bestowing, and these conditions may be quite different from conduct required of native-born citizens.[33] The stated policy basis for the statute – that being able to read the Constitution in the original language assures the seriousness of purpose and adherence to its principles which the oath of citizenship demands[34] – is questionable since there is little reason to believe that the Constitution and its principles can no longer be understood if read in a foreign tongue. Nor is there any reason to believe that ability to comprehend constitutional niceties in any way relates to good citizenship.[35]

One practical basis for the English literacy requirement is the fact that if the naturalized citizen can read, write, and speak the English language, his acclimatization to American life and the adjustment of his children is much smoother. Natural-born citizens, even those born abroad, are likely to be English speaking and the only concern, therefore, need be with the naturalized citizen. The exceptions in the naturalization statute are very minor so that for practical purposes citizens by law must know English. This argument may indeed reflect the fact of the matter; but it is doubtful that the legal sanction is of major significance. The other rationale behind the English literacy test qualification for citizenship is less substantive and more symbolic. The purpose of designating a language, frequently, is to act as a unifying symbol and to emphasize the continuity of a given cultural tradition quite apart from any specific operative effects. It establishes the fact that the United States has an English cultural tradition and that its citizens will have to learn English in order to participate fully in it. It establishes the 'official' character of the language.

ECONOMIC ACCESS

Qualifications for obtaining employment and operating a business. The same citizen groups primarily affected by the English literacy suffrage requirements are also the ones most concerned with English literacy requirements affecting access to other areas: public service and business. Prior to the 1880s exclusion of foreigners from various occupations was relatively uncommon. The Pacific States had excluded the Chinese from several occupations, and California had passed an exclusionary tax on foreign miners. But most of the statutory English literacy restrictions in the economic sphere arose during the critical period noted earlier, 1890–1920. The most significant of these related to entrance examinations – conducted in English – for occupations ranging from the professions to barbering. These statutes were part of the anti-foreigner legislation common in the United States at that time.[36] The economic activities of foreigners came under particular scrutiny during this period because of the increased role the alien played in the United States labor force. In 1909, it was estimated that alien labor composed one third of the labor of the principal industries in the country (Vagts 1961). This economic competition was exacerbated by the depression of 1913–1914.

All states handled the matter directly: by passing statutes limiting governmental service and private business operations to citizens or those who had declared their intention to become citizens. This extensive restriction of the alien's right to work, both in public and private employment, was the subject of considerable litigation. The initial rationale for sustaining legislation preventing aliens from obtaining public employment proceeded from the idea of a common ownership or interest which citizens had in the government and which they could decide they wished to distribute only to themselves. This theory also advanced and sustained legislation restricting the operations (issuances of licenses) of aliens in areas where public resources were involved (e.g. hunting). The most recent Supreme Court case, decided right after World War II, seemed to limit this extension of the theory and required rather that there be a reasonable relationship between the classification being adopted, and the business regulated or resource being pressured.[37] The need to know English in order to practice the profession safely (i.e. a railroad trainman or a driver of a truck carrying explosives having to know English in order to read certain signs) is within the criterion of reasonableness. But not all such requirements are so clearly based on need. Many appear to bear little relationship to the task to be performed (i.e. prison helpers and miners having to know English).

It should be noted that the statutory requirements are only a small part of the English literacy requirements imposed on individuals. Municipal ordinances and administrative regulations multiply these statutory requirements manyfold. Most important, however, is the nonlegal, practical necessity of knowing English in a variety of situations. For example, almost all states require examinations before permitting an individual to practice certain professions. To my knowledge, all of these are conducted in English, although as noted above this is the result of a direct statutory mandate in only five states. While these few tests are administered in English because of legal regulations, many more such language entrance requirements arise by custom as a reflection of the actual linguistic background of the people administering the test.

The importance of these non-statutory English literacy impediments should not be underestimated. The practical and legal consequences that flow from the ability to handle the paper economy, the language of which is English, are enormous. Although, as we have seen, the courts have generally been hostile to statutory impositions of English, this has not been true in common law situations where the courts, in the few decisions that have discussed the issue, usually have reinforced the practical need for a knowledge of English. Thus, the general rule is that illiteracy will not rebut the presumption that a bank depositor has knowledge of the rules printed in his passbook, and posting railroad signs in English has been held to fulfill the notice requirements imposed on a railroad company by state statute – even though the statute did not mention language and the injured plaintiff could not read English. A more recent example of the pressure exerted by the combined legal and practical consequences of English literacy is the selective service examinations, which are given only in English. These practical compulsions undercut the rationale behind many of the statutes, some of which are justified as a legal impetus to the assimilative process.

CONCLUSION

To a people language brings into play an entire range of experience and an attitude toward life which can be either immensely satisfying and comforting or, if imposed from without, threatening and forbidding. From a central government's standpoint, a common language forges a similarlity of attitude and values which can have important unifying aspects, while different languages tend to divide and make direction from the center more difficult. Every federal government – and the United States is no exception – has been concerned with balancing the role that a non-national mother tongue plays for its citizenry: on the one hand the annealing, productive, and harmonizing effect resulting from the comfort obtained in the course of its use by members somewhat alien to the culture of the dominant society, and on the other the divisive potential brought on by its retention and strengthening.

I have tried to show the political pattern behind the imposition of English literacy requirements and their subsequent relaxation. The decisions to impose English reflected the popular attitudes toward the particular ethnic group and the degree of hostility evidenced toward that group's natural development. If the group is in some way (usually because of race, color, or religion) viewed as irreconcilably alien to the prevailing concept of American culture, the United States has imposed harsh restrictions on its language practices; if not so viewed, use of the foreign tongue language has gone largely unquestioned or was even encouraged. As might be expected, language restriction was only one limitation to be imposed. These language restrictions were always coupled with other discriminatory legislation and practices in other fields.[38] To the minority group affected, the significance of the language requirement was very great; and, therefore, it was the act of imposition itself which created the reaction by the minority group rather than the substantive effects of the policy.

NOTES

1. For example, Missouri in 1817; Illinois in 1825; Michigan in 1835; and Iowa in 1841.
2. A bill was introduced in the Senate which would have required English as the 'language of instruction in all schools, public and private'. Sec. 10 of Sen. Bill 1017 introduced May 28, 1919.
3. 262 U.S. 390 (1923). The statute is question was Nebraska Laws 1919, c. 249. Similar legislation prohibiting teaching in foreign languages was passed

in 1919 by 14 other states: Alabama, Arkansas, Colorado, Delaware, Illinois, Idaho, Iowa, Kansas, Michigan, Minnesota, Nevada, New Hampshire, Oklahoma, and Oregon.

4. A review of English language school policy in the territories and states with respect to Indians, Puerto Ricans, Mexican-Americans, Japanese-Americans, and German-Americans is found in Leibowitz (1971).
5. P. L. 90–247, Jan. 2, 1968; 81 Stat. 783, especially Sec. 704. A history of the Act is given in Leibowitz (1971: 105–121).
6. Under this Act, funds were provided to (a) develop special instructional materials for use in bilingual educational programs, (b) provide in-service training to prepare teachers, teachers' aides, and counselors to participate in bilingual programs, and (c) establish, maintain, and operate special programs for children of limited English-speaking ability.
7. *Lau* v. *Nichols*, Cir. No. C-70 627 LHB (D.C.N.D. Calif., May 26, 1970). The case is now on appeal (9th Cir. No. 26155).
8. *Oakland Morning Times*, June 2, 1892, p. 4; *San Jose Daily Herald*, Oct. 17, 1892, p. 2.
9. *The Seward Gateway*, Sept. 25, 1926, p. 5, col. 3; Oct. 12, 1926, p. 1; See also *Seward Gateway*, Oct. 11, 1926, p. 1.
10. *Rassmussen* v. *Baker*, 7 Wyo. 117, 50, p. 819 (1897).
11. See petitioner's brief before the Supreme Court in the case of *Jimenez* v. *Naff*, 400 U. S. 986 (1970), vacating *Mexican-American Federation-Washington State* v. *Naff*, 299 F. Supp. 587 (E. D. Wash. 1969).
12. 360 U.S. 45 (1959).
13. A thorough analysis and review of all state statutes and territorial legislation dealing with language is to be found in Leibowitz (1969). The relation between Southern anti-Negro legislation and state legislation affecting other religious and racial groups in discussed in Higham (1955: 166 ff.).
14. 380 U.S. 128 (1965) reversing 229 F. Supp. 925 (S.D. Miss. 1964).
15. 380 U.S. 145 (1965) affirming 225 F. Supp. 353 (E.D. La. 1964).
16. The most thorough exploration of Southern anti-Negro suffrage legislation was in the United States Commission on Civil Rights Report, *Voting* (1961). Unfortunately, this report, like the hearings on the subsequent Voting Rights Act of 1965, confined itself to problems of Negro suffrage in the South. House of Rep., *Voting Rights, Hearing before Subcommittee No. 5 of the Committee on the Judiciary on H.R. 6400* (89th Cong., 1st Sess., 1965); U.S. Sen., *Voting Rights, Hearings before the Committee on the Judiciary on S. 1564* (89th Cong., 1st Sess., 1965).
17. The Mississippi Constitution in 1890 introduced the English literacy condition as a prerequisite to the exercise of suffrage. In later years this was coupled with the requirement of 'interpreting' are 'understanding' the state constitution. *United States v. Mississippi*, 380 U.S. 128, pp. 132–133 (1965).
18. United States Commission on Civil Rights, *Voting in Mississippi* (1965) pp. 4–5. The Supreme Court was to note this fact and give it considerable

prominence in sustaining Federal legislation. *South Carolina* v. *Katzenbach*, 338 U.S. 301, 311 (1965). The lower court opinion in *Louisiana*, which had painstakingly examined the legislative history of the Louisiana voting requirements, had been careful to distinguish the Louisiana statute from simply the ability to read and write which had been held valid on its face in *Lassiter*. *Louisiana* v. *United States*, 225 F. Supp. 353, 356. 385–6 (E.D. La. 1964).

19. *South Carolina* v. *Katzenbach*, 383 U.S. 301, 337 (1965).
20. Alaska, three counties in Arizona, and one county in Hawaii and Idaho were covered by the Act. Consent judgments (agreed to by the Attorney General) excluding these jurisdictions were obtained under 4(a) of the Act on the grounds that the tests have not been used to discriminate on the basis of race or color during the five years preceding the filing of the action. The Navajo tribe objected without avail to the Attorney General's consent. In Alabama, Georgia, Louisiana, Mississippi, South Carolina, Virginia, and 40 counties in North Carolina the Act went into effect and the tests were suspended. The Attorney General refused a consent judgment to permit North Carolina to remove itself from coverage of the Act (U.S. Commission on Civil Rights 1968: 11).
21. 383 U.S. 301 (1966).
22. The history of the New York provision is by no means as clear as that presented in the South but there was substantital evidence that its prime effect and original intention was to prevent 1,000,000 Jews from voting in New York in order to preserve Republican government in the City. *New York Times*, July 1, 1915, p. 5, col. 2; Aug. 25, 1915, p. 5, col. 2; Aug. 26, 1915, p. 5, col. 1; Oct. 23, 1921, Sec. 7, p. 2, col. 1; Nov. 10, 1921, p. 1, col. 1.
23. *Katzenbach* v. *Morgan*, 384 U. S. 641 (1966). See also *United States* v. *Monroe County Board of Elections*, 248 F. Supp. 316 (W.D.N.Y. 1965), *Castro* v. *State of California*, 466 P. 2d 244 (Calif. Sup. Ct. 1970), *Jimenez* v. *Naff*, 400 U.S. 986 (1970), vacating *Mexican-American Federation-Washington State* v. *Naff*, 299 F. Supp. 587 (E.D. Wash. 1969).
24. *Oregon* v. *Mitchell*, 400 U. S. 112 (1970).
25. In *Gaston County, North Carolina* v. *U. S.*, 395 U. S. 285 (1969), the Supreme Court made a link between educational discrimination and political discrimination which is important to the thesis of this essay in addition to indicating the constitutional weakness of the English literacy test as a condition of voting. In that case the court held the test discriminatory because of past inequalities in the school system.
26. *Voting Rights Act Extension*, U. S. Cong., Hearings before Subcommittee No. 5 of the Committee of the Judiciary (91st Cong., 1st Sess.) May 14, 15; June 19, 26; July 1, 1969.
27. Minnesota specifically requires assistance for voters who cannot speak English. The Texas Code which does not have a literacy requirement as a condition of voting provided as follows: '. . . no voter shall be entitled to

any assistance in the marking of his ballot on the ground of illiteracy'. The provision was challenged on the ground of illegal discrimination since exceptions were permitted for the physically handicapped. The court agreed. An illiterate voter could visually perceive and manipulate, but could not mentally identify the alternatives.

28. 2 Stat. L., 153, enacted April 14, 1802.
29. Petition of Katz, 21 F. 2d 867 (E.D. Mich. 1927). But see the exact opposite reasoning applied in *In re Rodriguez,* 81 F. Supp. 337 (W.D. Tex. 1897).
30. Treaty with French Republic, April 30, 1803, Art. III, 8 Stat. 202 (1846), T. S. No. 86 (effective October 21, 1803). Treaty of Amity, Settlement and Limits, with his Catholic Majesty, Feb. 22, 1819, Art. VI, 8 Stat. 256 (1846), T. S. No. 327, (effective Feb. 22, 1821). Treaty of Peace, Friendship, Limits, and Settlement with the Republic of Mexico, Feb. 2, 1848, Art. VIII, 9 Stat. 929 (1851) T. S. No. 206 (effective July 4, 1848).
31. 64 Stat. 1018, enacted Sept. 23, 1950, ch. 1024; 8 U.S.C.A. 1423 (1).
32. *In re Swenson,* 61 F. Supp. 376 (D.C. Ore. 1945); *Martinez* v. *Mitchell* (C.A. 70–2767–cc) (D.C. Calif. C.D. March 16, 1971).
33. *United States* v. *Bergmann,* 47 F. Supp. 765 (S.D. Calif. 1942); *Schneider* v. *Rusk,* 377 U.S. 193 (1964) limited the distinction between naturalized and native-born citizens with respect to expatriation but as yet no such limitation has been suggested with respect to the original grant of citizenship.
34. *Petition of Katz, supra* at 868.
35. *In re Rodriguez, supra* at 355.
36. The Federal government to try to exclude aliens from public works employment – the bill passed the House but failed in the Senate – and similar measures were passed in the several states.
37. *Takashashi* v. *Fish and Game Commission,* 334 U.S. 410, 418–419 (1948); NOTE, *Constitutionality of Restrictions on the Alien's Right to Work,* 57 Colum L. Rev. 1012 (1957); NOTE, *National Power to Control State Discrimination Against Foreign Goods and Persons: A Study in Federalism,* 12 Stan. L. Rev. 355, 364–69 (1960).
38. The most obvious instance of this was school segregation under the cover of linguistic need. U.S. Comm. on Civil Rights, *Ethnic Isolation of Mexican-Americans in the Public Schools of the Southwest* Mex.-Am. Education Study Rep. 1 1970); *Gonzalez* v. *Sheely,* 96 F. Supp. 1004 (D. Ariz. 1951); *Mendez* v. *Westminster School District,* 64 F. Supp. 544 (S. D. Calif. 1946) aff'd.; *Westminster School District* v. *Mendez* 161 F. 2d 774 (9th Cir. 1947).

Bibliography

Abdulaziz, M. H. (1971), 'Tanzania's national language policy and the rise of Swahili political culture', in Wilfred H. Whiteley (ed.), *Language Use and Social Change* (London: Oxford University Press for the International African Institute), 160–178.

Adams, Evelyn C. (1946), *American Indian Education* (New York: King's Crown Press).

Albert, Ethel M. (1964), ' "Rhetoric", "logic", and "poetics" in Burundi: culture patterning of speech behavior" ', *American Anthropologist* 66 (6, Part 2), 35-54.

Alderson, H. W. (n.d.), *The Khonds.* Manuscript.

Alexandre, Pierre (1961), 'Sur les possibilités expressives des langues africaines en matière de terminologie politique', *L'Afrique et L'Asie* 56 (4), 13–28.

– (1968), 'Some linguistic problems of nation-building in Negro Africa', in Joshua A. Fishman, Charles A. Ferguson and Jyotirindra Das Gupta (eds.), *Language Problems of Developing Nations* (New York: John Wiley and Sons), 119–127.

Almond, Gabriel A., and James Coleman (1960), *The Politics of Developing Areas* (Princeton: Princeton University Press).

Anderson, James L. (1970), *Cannibal: A Photographic Audacity* (Sydney: Reid).

Apte, Mahadev L. (1970), 'Some sociolinguistic aspects of interlingual communication in India', *Anthropological Linguistics* 12 (3), 63–82.

Ardener, Edwin (1971a), 'Introductory essay: social anthropology and language', in Edwin Ardener (ed.), *Social Anthropology and Language* (London: Tavistock Publications, ASA Monographs No. 10), ix – cii.

Ardener, Edwin, ed. (1971b), *Social Anthropology and Language* (London: Tavistock Publications, ASA Monographs No. 10).

Arens, W. (1972), 'The *Waswahili:* an emerging ethnic group'. Paper presented to the American Anthropological Association, Toronto.

Austen, Ralph (1968), *Northwest Tanzania Under German and British Rule* (New Haven: Yale University Press).

Austin, John L. (1965), *How to Do Things with Words* (New York: Oxford University Press).

Aylsworth, Leon E. (1931), 'The passing of alien suffrage', *American Political Science Review* 25 (1), 114–116.

Bailey, F. G. (1957), *Caste and the Economic Frontier* (Manchester: Manchester University Press).
– (1960), *Tribe, Caste and Nation* (Manchester: Manchester University Press).
– (1963), *Politics and Social Change: Orissa in 1959* (Berkeley: University of California Press).
– (1964), 'Two villages in Orissa', in Max Gluckman (ed.), *Closed Systems and Open Minds* (Edinburgh: Oliver & Boyd), 52–82.
– (1965), 'Decisions by consensus in councils and committees', in *Political Systems and the Distribution of Power* (London: Tavistock Publications, ASA Monographs No. 2), 1–20.
– (1968), 'Parapolitical systems', in Marc Swartz (ed.), *Local-Level Politics* (Chicago: Aldine), 281–294.
– (1969), *Stratagems and Spoils* (Oxford: Blackwell).
– (1972a), 'Conceptual systems in the study of politics,' in Richard Antoun and Iliya Harik (eds.), *Rural Politics and Social Change in the Middle East* (Bloomington: Indiana University Press), 21–44.
– (1972b), 'Tertius gaudens aut tertium numen'. Paper prepared for Wenner-Gren Symposium No. 55.
Barnett, T. E. (1969), 'The local court magistrate and the settlement of disputes', in B. P. Brown (ed.), *Fashion of Law in New Guinea* (Sydney: Butterworths), 159–179.
Barth, Fredrik (1959), *Political Leadership among Swat Pathans* (London: Athlone Press).
– (1966), *Models of Social Organization.* Occasional Paper No. 23, Royal Anthropological Institute of Great Britain and Ireland.
– (1969), *Ethnic Groups and Their Boundaries* (Boston: Little, Brown).
Basham, A. L. (1959), *The Wonder That Was India* (New York: Grove Press).
Bates, Margaret L. (1962), 'Tanganyika', in Gwendolen Carter (ed.), *African One-Party States* (Ithaca: Cornell University Press), 395–484.
Bay, Christian (1965), 'Politics and pseudopolitics: a critical evaluation of some bahavioral literature', *The American Political Science Review* 59 (1), 39–51.
Becker, Howard S. (1963), *Outsiders: Studies in the Sociology of Deviance* (New York: Free Press).
Berlin, Brent (1972), 'Speculations on the growth of ethnobotanical nomenclature', *Language in Society* 1, 51–86.
Berlin, Brent, and Paul Kay (1969), *Basic Color Terms: Their Universality and Evolution* (Berkeley and Los Angeles: University of California Press).
Berry, Jack (1970), 'Language system and literature', in Edward Soja and John Paden (eds.), *The African Experience,* Volume I (Evanston, Ill.: Northwestern University Press), 80–98.
Bettison, D., C. Hughes, and P. van der Veur, eds. (1965), *The Papua New*

Guinea Elections, 1964 (Canberra: Australian National University Press).

Bienen, Henry (1967), *Tanzania: Party Tranformation and Economic Development* (Princeton: Princeton University Press).

– (1970), *Tanzania: Party Transformation and Economic Development* (Princeton: Princeton University Press). Expanded Edition.

Billington, Ray Allen (1938), *The Protestant Crusade: 1800–1860* (New York: The Macmillan Company).

Blumberg, Abraham (1967), *Criminal Justice* (Chicago: Quadrangle).

Bram, Joseph (1955), *Language and Society* (Garden City, N. Y.: Doubleday).

Brash, E. (1971), 'Tok pilai, tok piksa na tok bokis', *Kivung* 4, 1–20.

Brass, Paul R. (1966), *Factional Politics in an Indian State: The Congress Party in Uttar Pradesh* (Berkeley: University of California Press).

Brennan, Paul W. (1970), 'Enga referential symbolism: verbal and visual', in Paul W. Brennan (ed.), *Exploring Enga Culture: Studies in Missionary Anthropology* (Wapenamanda, New Guinea: Kristen Press), 17–50.

Brennan, Paul W., ed. (1970), *Exploring Enga Culture: Studies in Missionary Anthropology.* Second Anthropological Conference of the New Guinea Lutheran Mission (Wapenemanda, New Guinea: Kristen Press).

Bretton, Henry L. (1973), *Power and Politics in Africa* (Chicago: Aldine).

Bromage, Arthur W. (1930), 'Literacy and the electorate', *American Political Science Review* 24 (4), 946–962.

Bromley, Myron (1967), 'The linguistic relationships of Grand Valley Dani: a lexico-statistical classification', *Oceania* 37, 286–308.

Brown, B. J. (1969), 'Justice and the edge of law: towards a "Peoples" Court', in B. J. Brown (ed.), *Fashion of Law in New Guinea* (Sydney: Butterworths), 181–215.

Brown, B. J., ed. (1969), *Fashion of Law in New Guinea: Being an Account of the Past, Present and Developing System of Laws in Papua and New Guinea* (Sydney: Butterworths).

Brown, Paula (1963), 'From anarchy to satrapy', *American Antropologist* 65, 1–15.

– (1967), 'The Chimbu political system', *Anthropological Forum* 2 (1), 36–52.

Brown, Roger and A. Gilman (1960), 'The pronouns of power and solidarity', in T. A. Sebeok (ed.), *Style in Language* (Cambridge: MIT Press), 253–276.

Bruner, Jerome S. (1966), 'An overview', in Jerome S. Bruner *et al., Studies in Cognitive Growth* (New York: Wiley and Sons), 319–326.

Bruner, Jerome S., *et al.* (1966), *Studies in Cognitive Growth* (New York: Wiley and Sons).

Burger, Angela S. (1969), *Opposition in a Dominant Party System* (Berkeley: University of California Press).

Burridge, Kenelm (1965–66), 'Tangu political relations', *Anthropological Forum* 1 (3–4), 393–411.

Cameron, Donald (1939), *My Tanganyika Service and Some Nigeria* (London: Allen and Unwin).

Capell, A. (1971), 'The Austronesian languages of Australian New Guinea', in T. A. Sebeok (ed.), *Current Trends in Linguistics* 8 (The Hague: Mouton), 240–340.

Cedergren, Henrietta (1972), 'Interplay of social and linguistic factors in Panama'. Unpublished Ph. D. dissertation, Cornell University.

Chagla, M. C. (1967), *Chagla on Language and Unity* (Bombay: Popular Prakashan).

Chidzero, B. T. G. (1961), *Tanganyika and International Trusteeship* (London: Oxford University Press).

Chomsky, Noam (1965), *Aspects of a Theory of Syntax* (Boston: MIT Press).

Chowning, Ann, *et. al.* (1971), 'Under the volcano', in A. L. Epstein, R. S. Parker and Marie Reay (eds.), *The Politics of Dependence: Papua-New Guinea 1968* (Canberra: Australian National University Press), 49–90.

Cloward, Richard A., and Lloyd E. Ohlin (1961), *Delinquency and Opportunity* (Glencoe: Free Press).

Cole, J. S. R. and W. N. Denison (1964), *Tanganyika: The Development of Its Laws and Constitution* (London: Stevens & Sons).

Colebatch, Hal K. (1968), 'Educational policy and political development in Australian New Guinea', in R. J. Selleck (ed.), *Melbourne Studies in Education* (Carlton, Victoria: Melbourne University Press), 102–147.

Colebatch, H. K., *et al.* (1971), 'Free elections in a guided democracy', in A. L. Epstein, R. S. Parker and Marie Reay (eds.), *The Politics of Dependence: Papua-New Guinea 1968* (Canberra: Australian National University Press), 218–274.

Commonwealth of Australia (1954–55), *Parliamentary Debates*, Twenty-First Parliament, Volume 8 (Canberra: Commonwealth Government Printer).

– (1972), *Report to the General Assembly of the United Nations: Administration of Papua New Guinea 1 July 1970 – 30 June 1971* (Canberra: Australian Government Publishing Service).

Contractor, M. K. (n.d.), *Our Language Problem and Unity of India: An Approach* (Surat, India: M. K. Contractor).

Coupland, R. (1944), *The Indian Problem* (New York: Oxford University Press).

Crick, Bernard (1962), *In Defence of Politics* (London: Penguin Books).

Criper, Clive (1965), 'The Chimbu open electorate', in D. Bettison, C. Hughes, and P. van der Veur (eds.), *The Papua–New Guinea Elections, 1964* (Canberra: Australian National University Press), 120–146.

Crocombe, Ron (1968), 'That five year plan', *New Guinea* 3 (4), 57–70.

Daniels, Roger (1969), *The Politics of Prejudice: The Anti-Japanese Movement in California and the Struggle for Japanese Exclusion* (Berkely: University of California Press).

Das Gupta, Jyotirindra (1969), 'Official language problems and policies in South Asia', in T. A. Sebeok (ed.), *Current Trends in Linguistics* 5 (The Hague: Mouton), 578–596.

– (1970), *Language Conflict and National Development* (Berkeley and Los

Angeles: University of California Press).

– (1973), 'Language planning and public policy: an analytical outline of the policy process related to language planning in India', in Roger W. Shuy (ed.), *Sociolinguistics: Current Trends and Prospects, Report of the 23rd Annual Roundtable Meeting on Linguistics and Language Studies* (Washington: Georgetown University Press), 157–165.

Das Gupta, Jyotirindra, and John J. Gumperz (1968), 'Language communication and control in North India', in Joshua A. Fishman, Charles A. Ferguson, and Jyotirindra Das Gupta (eds.), *Language Problems of Developing Nations* (New York: John Wiley and Sons), 151–166.

DeCamp, David (1971), 'Toward a generative analysis of a post-creole speech continuum', in Dell Hymes (ed.), *Pidginization and Creolization of Languages* (New York and Cambridge: Cambridge University Press), 349–370.

Desai, M. P. (1956), *Our Language Problem* (Ahmedabad: Navajivan).

– (1964), *The Problem of English* (Ahmedabad: Navajivan).

Deutsch, Karl W. (1953), *Nationalism and Social Communication: An Inquiry into the Foundations of Nationality* (New York: John Wiley and Sons).

– (1963), *The Nerves of Government* (New York: The Free Press).

Doob, Leonard (1961), *Communications in Africa: A Search for Boundaries* (New Haven: Yale University Press).

Downs, Ian (1972), *The Stolen Land* (Melbourne: Wren).

DuBow, Fredric (1973), 'Justice for people: law and politics in the lower courts of Tanzania'. Unpublished Ph. D. dissertation, University of California, Berkeley.

Dundes, Alan, Jerry W. Leach, and Bora Özkök (1972), 'The strategy of Turkish boys' verbal dueling rhymes', in John J. Gumperz and Dell Hymes (eds.) *Directions in Sociolinguistics: The Ethnography of Communication* (New York: Holt, Rinehart and Winston), 130–160.

Eastman, Carol (1971), 'Who are the Waswahili?', *Africa* 41, 228–236.

Edelman, Murray (1964), *The Symbolic Uses of Politics* (Urbana: University of Illinois Press).

Edwardes, S. M., and H. L. O. Garrett (1956), *Mughal Rule in India* (Dehli: S. Chand and Co.).

Elias, T. O. (1956), *The Nature of African Customary Law* (Manchester: Manchester University Press).

Emeneau, M. B. (1956), 'India as a linguistic area', *Language* 32, 3–16.

Enloe, Cynthia H. (1973), *Ethnic Conflict and Political Development* (Boston: Little Brown and Company).

Epstein, A. L. (1970), 'Autonomy and identity: aspects of political development on the Gazelle Peninsula', *Anthropological Forum* 2 (4), 427–443.

Epstein, A. L., R. S. Parker, and Marie Reay, eds. (1971), *The Politics of Dependence: Papua New Guinea 1968* (Canberra: Australian National University Press).

Fanon, Frantz (1961), *Les damnés de la terre* (Paris: François Maspero).

Faust, Albert B. (1909), *The German Element in the United States* (Boston: Houghton Mifflin Company).

Ferguson, Charles A. (1959), 'Diglossia', *Word* 15, 325–340.

– (1971), 'Absence of copula and the notion of simplicity: a study of normal speech, baby talk, foreigner talk, and pidgins', in Dell Hymes (ed.), *Pidginization and Creolization of Languages* (New York and Cambridge: Cambridge University Press), 141–150.

Freguson, Charles A., and John J. Gumperz, eds. (1960), *Linguistic Diversity in South Asia* (Bloomington, Indiana: Research Center in Anthropology, Folklore and Linguistics).

Fink; Ruth A., (1965), 'The Esa'ala-Losuia open electorate', in D. Bettison, C. Hughes, and P. van der Veur (eds.), *The Papua-New Guinea Elections, 1964* (Canberra: Australian National University Press), 280–317.

Fishman, Joshua A. (1968), 'Sociolinguistics and language problems of the developing countries', in Joshua A. Fishman, Charles A. Ferguson, and Jyotirindra Das Gupta (eds.), *Language Problems of Developing Nations* (New York: John Wiley and Sons), 3–16.

– (1972), *Language and Nationalism* (Rowley, Massachusetts: Newbury House).

– (1973), 'Language modernization and planning in comparison with other types of national modernization and planning'. *Language in Society* 2 (1), 23–43.

Fishman, Joshua A., Charles A. Ferguson, and Jyotirindra Das Gupta, eds. (1968), *Language Problems of Developing Nations* (New York: John Wiley and Sons).

Fisk, Edward K. (1966), 'The economic structure', in Edward K. Fisk (ed.), *New Guinea on the Threshold* (Canberra: Australian National University Press), 23–43.

Fisk, Edward K., ed. (1966), *New Guinea on the Threshold* (Canberra: Australian National University Press).

Flanders, Jesse K. (1925), *Legislative Control of the Elementary Curriculum* (New York: Teachers College, Columbia University).

Fortes, Meyer, and E. E. Evans-Pritchard, eds. (1940), *African Political Systems* (London: Oxford University Press).

Fortune, R. F. (1963), *Sorcerers of Dobu* (New York: Dutton). Revised edition. (First published 1932.)

Frank, Jerome (1949), *Courts on Trial* (Princeton, N. J.: Princeton University Press).

Fried, Morton (1967), *The Evolution of Political Society* (New York: Random House).

Friedland, William H. (n.d.), *The Evolution of Tanganyika's Political System* (Syracuse University Program of Eastern African Studies, Occasional Paper No. 10).

Friedrich, Paul (1962), 'Language and politics in India', *Daedalus* 91, 543–559.

Galanter, Marc (1967), 'The uses of law in Indian studies', in *Languages and Areas: Studies Presented to George V. Bobrinskoy* (Chicago: University of Chicago Press), 37–44.

Gandhi. M. K. (1956), *Thoughts on National Language* (Ahmedabad: Navajivan).

Garfinkel, Harold (1967), *Studies in Ethnomethodology* (Englewood Cliffs, N. J.: Prentice-Hall).

Glasse, Robert M. (1968), *Huli of Papua: A Cognatic Descent System* (The Hague – Paris: Mouton).

Gluckman, Max (1965), *The Ideas in Barotse Jurisprudence* (New Haven: Yale University Press).

Goffman, Erving (1961), *Encounters* (Indianapolis: Bobbs-Merrill).

– (1972), *Relations in Public* (New York: Harper and Row).

Gokak, V. K. (1964), *English in India* (Bombay: Asia Publishing House).

Goody, Jack, ed. (1968), *Literacy in Traditional Societies* (Cambridge: Cambridge University Press).

Gopal, Ram (1966), *Linguistic Affairs of India* (New York: Asia Publishing House).

Gostin, Olga *et al.* (1971), 'Personalities versus politics', in A. L. Epstein, R. S. Parker and Marie Reay (eds.), *The Politics of Dependence: Papua-New Guinea 1968* (Canberra: Australian National University Press), 91–131.

Government of Ghana (1965), *Parliamentary Debates* (Accra: Government Printer).

Government of India (1928), *Report of the Nehru Committee, All Parties Conference* (Allahabad: All-India Congress Committee).

– (1948), *Report of the Linguistic Provinces Committee* (New Delhi: Government of India Press).

– (1952–1960), *Parliamentary Debates* (New Delhi: Government of India Press).

– (1953–1954), *Report of the States Reorganization Commission* (New Delhi: Government of India Press).

– (1954), *Census of India, 1951: Languages – 1951 Census,* Paper No. 1 (New Delhi: Government of India Press).

– (1957), *Report of the Official Language Commission* (New Delhi: Government of India Press).

– (1957–1968), *Commissioner for Linguistic Minorities, Reports* (New Delhi: Government of India Press).

– (1961), *Census of India, 1961: India Languages Tables,* Vol. I, Part II-C (ii), (New Delhi: Government of India Press).

– (1969), *Propagation and Development of Hindi, 1952–1967* (New Delhi: Ministry of Education).

Government of Orissa (1957), *Rules of Procedures and Conduct of Business in the Orissa Legislative Assembly* (Cuttack: Orissa Government Press).

– (1958), *Statistical Outline of Orissa 1957* (Cuttack: Goswami Press).

Government of Papua New Guinea (1972–1973), *House of Assembly Debates, Third House, Sixth Meeting of the First Session* (Port Moresby: Government Printer).

Greenberg, Joseph (1959), 'Africa as a linguistic area', in William R. Bascom and Melville J. Herskovits (eds.), *Continuity and Change in African Cultures* (Chicago: Phoenix Books), 15–27.

Grierson, G. A. (1886–1928), *Linguistic Survey of India,* Volumes I-XI (Calcutta: Government of India Central Publication Branch).

Gulliver, Phillip H. (1963), *Social Control in an African Society* (London: Routlege & Kegan Paul).

– (1969), 'The conservative commitment in northern Tanzania', in Phillip H. Gulliver (ed.), *Tradition and Transition in Eastern Africa: Studies of the Tribal Element in the Modern Era* (London: Routledge & Kegan Paul), 222–242.

Gumperz, John J. (1957), 'Some remarks on regional and social language differences in India', in Milton Singer (ed.), *Introducing India in Liberal Education* (Chicago: University of Chicago Press), 69–79.

–(1961), 'Speech variation and the study of Indian civilization', *American Anthropologist* 63, 976–988.

– (1969), 'Communication in multilingual societies', in Stephen A. Tyler (ed.), *Cognitive Anthropology* (New York: Holt, Rinehart and Winston), 435–449.

–(1970), 'Sociolinguistics and communication in small groups', Working Paper No. 33, Language Behavior Research Laboratory, Berkeley.

Gumperz, J. J, and E. Hernández (1969), 'Cognitive aspects of bilingual communication', Working Paper No. 28, Language Behavior Research Laboratory, Berkeley.

Gumperz, J. J. and R. Wilson (1971), 'Convergence and creolization: a case from the Indo-Aryan/Dravidian border', in Dell Hymes (ed.), *Pidginization and Creolization of Languages* (New York and Cambridge: Cambridge University Press), 151–167.

Hall, Robert A., Jr. (1943), *Melanesian Pidgin English: Grammar, Texts, Vocabulary* (Baltimore: Linguistic Society of America).

Hardgrave, Robert L., Jr. (1970), *India: Government and Politics in a Developing Nation* (New York: Harcourt, Brace and World, Inc.).

Harding, Thomas G. (1965), 'The Rai Coast open electorate', in D. Bettison, C. Hughes, and P. van der Veur (eds.), *The Papua-New Guinea Elections, 1964* (Canberra: Australian National University Press), 194–211.

– (1967), *Voyagers of the Vitiaz Strait: A Study of a New Guinea Trade System* (Seattle: University of Washington Press).

Harries, Lyndon (1966), 'Language and law in Tanzania', *Journal of African Law* 10, 164–167.

– (1968), 'Swahili in modern East Africa', in Joshua A. Fishman, Charles A. Ferguson, and Jyotirindra Das Gupta (eds.), *Language Problems of Developing Nations* (New York: John Wiley and Sons), 415–429.

– (1969), 'Language policy in Tanzania', *Africa* 39, 275–280.

Harrison, Selig S. (1960), *The Most Dangerous Decades: An Introduction to*

Comparative Study of Language Policy in Multilingual States (Princeton: Princeton University Press).

Hartmann, Edward G. (1948), *The Movement to Americanize the Immigrant* (New York: Columbia University Press).

Hasluck, Paul (1956), *Australia's Task in Papua and New Guinea* (Melbourne: Australian Institute of International Affairs).

–(1958), 'Present tasks and policies', in John Wilkes (ed.), *New Guinea and Australia* (Sydney: Angus & Robertson), 75–117.

Hastings, Peter (1968), *New Guinea: Future Prospects* (Sydney: Cheshire Publishers).

Haudricourt, A. G. (1961), 'Richesse en phonèmes et richesse en locuteurs', *L'Homme* 1, 5–10.

Henle, Paul, ed. (1958), *Language, Thought and Culture* (Ann Arbor: University of Michigan Press).

Henson, Hilary (1971), 'Early British anthropologists and language', in Edwin Ardener (ed.), *Social Anthropology and Language*, ASA Monographs No. 10 (London: Tavistock Publications), 3–32.

Hertzler, Joyce O. (1965), *A Sociology of Language* (New York: Random House).

Higgins, Benjamin, Robert A. Dahl, and Vladimir I. Kollontai (1971), 'Political dimensions and planning', in Peter Lengyel (ed.), *Approaches to the Science of Socio-economic Development* (Paris: UNESCO), 319–378.

Higham, John (1955), *Strangers in the Land: Patterns of American Nativism, 1860–1925* (New Brunswick, N. J.: Rutgers University Press).

Hogbin, I. H. (1947), 'Native trade around the Huon Gulf, northeastern New Guinea', *Journal of the Polynesian Society* 56, 242–255.

Hollyman, K. J. (1962), 'The lizard and the axe: a study of the effects of European contact on the indigenous languages of Polynesia and Island Melanesia', *Journal of the Polynesian Society* 71, 310–327.

Hooley, B., and K. A. McElhanon (1970), 'Languages of the Morobe District, New Guinea', *Pacific Linguistics*, Series C (No. 13), 1065–1094.

Hopkins, Raymond F. (1971), *Political Roles in a New State: Tanzania's First Decade* (New Haven: Yale University Press).

Howlett, Diana R. (1967), *A Geography of Papua-New Guinea* (Sydney: Thomas Nelson Limited).

Hughes, Colin A., and Paul W. van der Veur (1965), 'The elections: an overview', in D. Bettison, C. Hughes, and P. van der Veur (eds.), *The Papua-New Guinea Elections, 1964* (Canberra: Australian National University Press), 388–429.

Hydén, Göran, and Colin Leys (1972), 'Elections and politics in single-party systems: the case of Kenya and Tanzania', *British Journal of Political Science* 2, 389–420.

Hymes, Dell (1961), 'Functions of speech: an evolutionary approach', in F. C. Gruber (ed.), *Anthropology and Education* (Philadelphia: University of Pennsylvania Press), 55–83.

– (1966), 'Two types of linguistic relativity', in William Bright (ed.), *Sociolinguistics* (The Hague: Mouton), 114–165.

– (1971), 'Introduction to part III', in Dell Hymes (ed.), *Pidginization and Creolization of Languages* (New York and Cambridge: Cambridge University Press), 65–90.

– (1972), 'On the origin and foundation of inequality among speakers'. Unpublished manuscript.

Ichihashi, Yamato (1932), *Japanese in the United States* (Stanford: Stanford University Press).

Iliffe, John (1969), *Tanganyika Under German Rule 1905–12* (Cambridge: Cambridge University Press).

Jackson, Jean (1972), 'Marriage and linguistic identity among the Bará Indians of the Vaupés, Colombia'. Unpublished Ph. D. dissertation, Stanford University.

Jernudd, Björn H., and Jyotirindra Das Gupta (1971), 'Towards a theory of language planning', in Joan Rubin and Björn H. Jernudd (eds.), *Can Language Be Planned?* (Honolulu: University Press of Hawaii), 195–215.

Jewell, Malcolm E. (forthcoming), 'Legislative representation and national integration', in Albert F. Eldridge (ed.), *Legislatures in Plural Societies* (Beverly Hills, California: Sage Publications).

Jewell, Malcolm E., and Samuel C. Patterson (1973), *The Legislative Process in the United States* (New York: Random House).

John, K. K. (n.d.), *The Only Solution to India's Language Problem* (Madras, India: K. K. John).

Johnson, Frederick (1935), *A Standard Swahili-English Dictionary* (London: Oxford University Press).

Johnson, S. H. (1969), 'Criminal law and punishment', in B. J. Brown (ed.), *Fashion of Law in New Guinea* (Sydney: Butterworths), 83–104.

Kaberry, Phyllis M. (1965–66), 'Political organization among the Northern Abelam', *Anthropological Forum* 1(3–4), 334–372.

Kaplan, A. (1973), 'On the strategy of social planning', *Policy Sciences* 4 (1), 41–61.

Kay, Paul (1971), 'Language evolution and speech style', Paper read at the 70th Annual Meetings of the American Anthropological Association, New York City. To appear in M. Sanches and B. Blount (eds.), *Ritual, Reality and Innovation in Language Use* (New York: Seminar Press).

Kay, Paul, and Gillian Sankoff (1972), 'A language-universals approach to pidgins and creoles'. Paper read at the 23rd Georgetown Roundtable on Languages and Linguistics, Washington, D.C.

Keesing, Felix M., and Marie M. Keesing (1956), *Elite Communication in Samoa: A Study of Leadership* (Stanford: Stanford University Press).

Kelly, Gerald (1966), 'The status of Hindi as a lingua franca', in William Bright (ed.), *Sociolinguistics* (The Hague: Mouton), 299–305.

Kelman, Herbert C. (1971), 'Language as an aid and barrier to involvement in the national system', in Joan Rubin and Björn H. Jernudd (eds.), *Can Language Be Planned?* (Honolulu: University Press of Hawaii), 21–51.

Kidder, Robert L. (1971), 'The dynamics of litigation: a study of civil litigation in South Indian courts'. Unpublished Ph. D. dissertation, Northwestern University.

– (1973), 'Courts and conflict in an Indian city: a study in legal impact', *Journal of Commonwealth Political Studies* 2(2), 121–139.

– (1974), 'Litigation as a strategy for mobility: the case of urban caste association leaders', *Journal of Asian Studies* 33 (2), 177–191.

Kloss, Heinz (1970), *The Bilingual Tradition in the United States* (Rowley, Mass.: Newbury House Publishers).

Knappert, Jan (1968), 'Language in a political situation', *Linguistics* 39, 59–67.

Kornai, J. (1970), 'A general descriptive model of planning processes', *Economics of Planning* 10 (1–2), 1–19.

Kothari, R. (1970), *Politics in India* (Boston: Little, Brown).

Kumaramangalam, S. Mohan (1965), *India's Language Crisis* (Madras, India: New Century Book House).

Laberge, Suzanne, and Michelle Chaisson-Lavoie (1971), 'Attitudes face au Français parlé à Montréal et degrès de conscience de variables linguistiques', in R. Darnell (ed.), *Linguistic Diversity in Canadian Society* (Edmonton: Linguistic Research Inc.), 89–126.

Labov, William (1965), 'On the mechanism of linguistic change', in Charles W. Kreider (ed.), *Report of the Sixteenth Annual Round-Table Meeting on Linguistics and Language Studies* (Washington, D.C.: Georgetown University Press), 512–538.

– (1966a), *The Social Stratification of English in New York City* (Washington: Center for Applied Linguistics).

– (1966b), 'Hypercorrection by the lower middle class as a factor in linguistic change', in William Bright (ed.), *Sociolinguistics* (The Hague: Mouton), 84–113.

– (1972), 'Rules for ritual insults', in David Sudnow (ed.), *Studies in Social Interaction* (New York: The Free Press), 120–169.

Landau, Martin (1965), 'Due process in inquiry', *American Behavioral Scientist* 9 (2), 3–19.

Lang, Adrianne (1971), 'Nouns and classificatory verbs in Enga (New Guinea): a semantic study'. Unpublished Ph. D. dissertation, The Australian National University.

Lang, Ranier (1970), 'Enga questions: structural and semantic studies'. Unpublished Ph. D. dissertation, The Australian National University.

Langness, L. L. (1968), 'Bena Bena political organization', *Anthropological Forum* 2 (2), 180–198.

Larson, James E. (1970), 'The dynamics of Enga persuasive speech', in Paul W.

Brennan (ed.), *Exploring Enga Culture: Studies in Missionary Anthropology* (Wapenamanda, New Guinea: Kristen Press), 1–16.

Lawrence, Peter (1964), *Road Belong Cargo* (Manchester: The University Press).

– (1965–66), 'The Garia of the Madang District', *Anthropological Forum* 1 (3–4), 373–392.

Laycock, D. C. (1966), 'Papuans and pidgin: aspects of bilingualism in New Guinea', *Te Reo* 9, 44–51.

– (1970a), 'Materials in New Guinea pidgin', *Pacific Linguistics,* Series D, No. 5.

– (1970b), 'Pidgin English in New Guinea', in W. S. Ransom (ed.), *English Transported* (Canberra: Australian National University Press), 102–122.

Leach, E. R. (1954), *Political Systems of Highland Burma* (London: London School of Economics and Political Science)

Legge, J. D. (1956), *Australian Colonial Policy* (Sydney: Angus & Robertson).

Leibowitz, Arnold H. (1969), 'English literacy: legal sanction for discrimination', *Notre Dame Lawyer* 45, 7–67.

– (1970), 'English literacy: legal sanction for discrimination', *Revista Jurídica de la Universidad de Puerto Rico* 39 (3), 313–400.

– (1971), *Educational Policy and Political Acceptance: The Imposition of English as the Language of Instruction in American Schools* (Washington, D.C.: Center for Applied Linguistics).

Listowel, Judith (1968), *The Making of Tanganyika* (London: Chatto & Windus). Second Edition.

Lobenthal, Joseph S. (1970), *Power and Put-On:Law in America* (New York: Outerbridge & Dienstfrey).

Lok Sabha Secretariat (1967), *Lok Sabha Handbook for Members* (New Delhi: Lok Sabha Secretariat). Fourth Edition.

Lowman-Vayda, Cherry (1968), 'Maring big men', *Anthropological Forum* 2 (2), 199–243.

Lowy, Michael J. (1971), 'The ethnography of law in a changing Ghanian town'. Unpublished Ph. D. dissertation, University of California, Berkeley.

Lunt, Horace (1959), 'The creation of Standard Macedonian: some facts and attitudes', *Anthropological Linguistics* 1 (5), 19–26.

Mair, Lucy B. (1970), *Australia in New Guinea* (Melbourne: Melbourne University Press). Second Edition.

Malinowski, B. (1935), *Coral Gardens and Their Magic,* Vol. II (London: Allen & Unwin).

Mannheim, Karl (1951), *Freedom, Power and Democratic Planning* (London: Routledge).

Manuel, Herschel T. (1965), *Spanish-Speaking Children of the Southwest* (Austin: University of Texas Press).

Marwick, Max G. (1965), *Sorcery in its Social Setting* (Manchester: Manchester University Press).

Mason, Philip, ed. (1967) *India and Ceylon: Unity and Diversity* (London: Oxford University Press).

Mazrui, Ali (1967), 'Language and politics in East Africa', *Africa Report* 12 (6), 59–62.

McAuslan, J. P. W. B., and Yash P. Ghai (1966), 'Constitutional innovation and political stability in Tanzania: a preliminary assessment', *Journal of Modern African Studies* 4 (4), 479–515.

McDavid, Raven I., Jr. (1948), 'Postvocalic -r in South Carolina: a social analysis', *American Speech* 23, 194–203.

McKaughan, Howard (1964), 'A study of divergence in four New Guinea languages', *American Anthropologist* 66 (6, Part 2), 98–120.

McKaughan, Howard, ed. (1971), *The Languages of the Eastern Family of the East New Guinea Highland Stock* (Seattle: University of Washington Press).

Meggitt, M. J. (1965), *The Lineage System of the Mae-Enga of New Guinea* (Edinburgh: Oliver & Boyd).

– (1967), 'Uses of literacy in New Guinea and Melanesia' *Bijdragen Tot de Taal-, Land- en Volkenkunde* 73, 71–82.

Middleton, John, and David Tait, eds. (1958), *Tribes Without Rulers* (London: Routledge and Paul).

Mihalic, F. (1957), *Grammar and Dictionary of Neo-Melanesian* (Port Moresby: The Mission Press).

– (1971), *The Jacaranda Dictionary and Grammar of Melanesian Pidgin* (Milton, Queensland: The Jacaranda Press).

Miller, G. A. (1956), 'The magical number seven plus or minus two: some limits on our capacity for processing information', *Psychological Review* 63, 81–97.

Minogue, J. P. (1969), 'The law of evidence', in B. J. Brown (ed.), *Fashion of Law in New Guinea* (Sydney: Butterworths), 105–115.

Mitchell-Kernan, Claudia (1972), 'Signifying and marking: two Afro-American speech acts', in John J. Gumperz and Dell Hymes (eds.), *Directions in Sociolinguistics: The Ethnography of Communication* (New York: Holt, Rinehart and Winston), 161–179.

Morris-Jones, W. H. (1957), *Parliament in India* (Philadelphia: University of Pennsylvania Press).

– (1967), 'Language and region within the Indian union', in Philip Mason (ed.), *India and Ceylon: Unity and Diversity* (London: Oxford University Press), 51–66.

Nayar, Baldev Raj (1969), *National Communication and Language Policy in India* (New York: Frederick A. Praeger).

Nicholas, R. (1968), 'Rules, resources, and political activity', in Marc Swartz (ed.), *Local-Level Politics* (Chicago: Aldine), 295–321.

Nyerere, Julius K. (1968a), *Freedom and Socialism* (Dar es Salaam: Oxford University Press).

– (1968b), *Ujamaa: Essays on Socialism* (New York: Oxford University Press).

– (1972), *Decentralisation* (Dar es Salaam: Government Printer).

O'Barr, William M. (1971), 'Mutilingualism in a rural Tanzanian village', *Anthropological Linguistics* 13, 289–300.

Osuna, Juan José (1949), *A History of Education in Puerto Rico* (Rio Piedras, Puerto Rico: Editorial de la Universidad de Puerto Rico). Sceond Edition.

Paden, John N. (1968), 'Language problems of national integration in Nigeria: the special position of Hausa', in Joshua A. Fishman, Charles A. Ferguson, and Jyotirindra Das Gupta (eds.), *Language Problems of Developing Nations* (New York: John Wiley and Sons), 199–213.

Parker, Gary (1969), 'Comparative Quechua phonology and grammar I: classification', University of Hawaii, Department of Linguistics, *Working Papers in Linguistics* 1 (1), 65–87.

– (1973), 'Notes on the linguistic situation and language planning in Peru', in Joan Rubin and Roger Shuy (eds.), *Language Planning: Current Issues and Research* (Washington, D. C.: Georgetown University Press), 67–71.

Parker, Robert S. (1966), 'The growth of territory administration', in Edward K. Fisk (ed.), *New Guinea on the Threshold* (Canberra: Australian National University Press), 187–221.

Pilley, A. T. (1962), 'The multi-lingual parliaments of Asia', *Babel* 8, 19–22.

– (1971), 'Report on the recruitment and training of simultaneous interpreters in Hong Kong'. Multilith.

Poddar, Arabinda, ed. (1961), *Language and Society in India* (Simla: Indian Institute of Advanced Study).

Pye, Lucien W. (1966), *Aspects of Political Development* (Boston: Little, Brown and Company).

Pye, Lucien W., ed. (1963), *Communications and Political Development* (Princeton: Princeton University Press).

Radin, Max (1933), 'Courts', *Encyclopedia of the Social Sciences* (New York: MacMillan Co.), 4, 515–529.

Read, K. E. (1965), *The High Valley* (New York: Charles Scribner's Sons).

Reay, Marie (1959), *The Kuma: Freedom and Conformity in the New Guinea Highlands* (Melbourne: Melbourne University Press for the Australian National University).

– (1964), 'Present-day politics in the New Guinea highlands', *American Anthropologist* 66 (4, Part 2), 240–256.

– (1965), 'The Minj open electorate', in D. Bettison, C. Hughes, and P. van der Veur (eds.), *The Papua New Guinea Elections, 1964* (Canberra: Australian National University Press), 147–180.

Richards, Audrey (1971), 'Introduction' in Audrey Richards and Adam Kuper (eds.), *Councils in Action* (Cambridge: Cambridge Papers in Social Anthropology No. 6), 1–12.

Rider, Harry (1920), 'Americanization', *American Political Science Review* 14 (1), 110–115.

Robins, R. H. (1911), 'Malinowski, Firth and the "context of situation" ', in

Edwin Ardener (ed.), *Social Anthropology and Language,* ASA Mongraphs No. 10 (London: Tavistock Publications), 33–46.

Rogers, Everett M., with Lynne Svenning (1969), *Modernization Among Peasants: The Impact of Communication* (New York: Holt, Rinehart and Winston).

Rose, Richard (1973), 'Comparing public policy', *European Journal of Political Research* 1, 67–94.

Ross, Alan S. C. (1954), 'Linguistic class indicators in present-day English', *Neuphilolgische Mitteulungen* 55, 20–56.

Ross, H. Lawrence (1970), *Settled Out of Court* (Chicago: Aldine).

Rowley, C. D. (1958), *The Australians in German New Guinea 1914–21* (Melbourne: Melbourne University Press).

Roy, Archélas (1960), 'La grammaire', *Cahiers de l'Académie Canadienne-Française* 5, 107–120.

Roy, N. C. (1962), *Federalism and Linguistic States* (Calcutta: Firma K. L. Mukhopadhyay).

Rubin, Joan (1968), *National Bilingualism in Paraguay* (The Hague: Mouton).

Rubin, Joan, and Björn H. Jernudd, eds. (1971), *Can Language Be Planned? Sociolinguistic Theory and Practice for Developing Nations* (Honolulu: University Press of Hawaii).

Sacks, Harvey, Emanuel A. Schegloff, and Gail Jefferson (1974), 'A simplest systematics for the organization of turn-taking for conversation', *Language* 50(4), 696–735.

Sackschewsky, Marvin (1970), 'The clan meeting in Enga society', in Paul W. Brennan (ed.), *Exploring Enga Culture: Studies in Missionary Anthropology* (Wapenamanda, New Guinea: Kristen Press), 51–101.

Sadock, Jerrold M. (1969), 'Hypersentences', *Papers in Linguistics* 1, 283–371.

Salisbury, Richard F. (1962), 'Notes on bilingualism and linguistic change in New Guinea', *Anthropological Linguistics* 4 (7), 1–13.

– (1964), 'Despotism and Australian administration in the New Guinea highlands', *American Anthropologist* 66 (4, Part 2), 225–239.

– (1966), 'Politics and shell-money among the Tolai', in Marc Swartz, Victor Turner, and Arthur Tuden (eds.), *Political Anthropology* (Chicago: Aldine), 113–128.

– (1967), 'Pidgin's respectable past', *New Guinea* 2 (2), 44–48.

– (1969), *Vunamami: Economic Transformation in a Traditional Society* (Berkeley: University of California Press).

– (1971), *Problems of the Gazelle Peninsula, August 1971* (Port Moresby: Government Printer).

– (1973), 'The anthropologist as societal ombudsman'. Paper presented to the Congress of Anthropological and Ethnological Sciences, Chicago.

Sankoff, Gillian (1968), 'Social aspects of multilingualism in New Guinea'. Unpublished Ph. D. dissertation, McGill University.

– (1969), 'Mutual intelligibility, bilingualism and linguistic boundaries', in

International Days of Sociolinguistics (Rome: Luigi Sturzo Institute), 839–848.

– (1972), 'Language use in multilingual societies: some alternative approaches', in J. Pride and J. Holmes (eds.), *Sociolinguistics* (Harmondsworth, Middlesex: Penguin), 33–51.

– (1973), 'Wanpela lain manmeri ibin kisim Tok Pisin ikamap olosem tok ples bilong ol: yumi ken bihainim gutpela Tok Pisin bilong ol'. Paper read at the Conference on Pidgin, University of Papua New Guinea, September, 1973.

Sankoff, Gillian, and Henrietta Cedergren (1971), 'Some results of a sociolinguistic study of Montreal French', in R. Darnell (ed.), *Linguistic Diversity in Canadian Society* (Edmonton: Linguistic Research Inc.), 61–87.

Schaffer, Bernard B. (1971), 'Political change in New Guinea', *Communication Series* No. 37 (Sussex, England: Institute of Development Studies, University of Sussex).

Schwartz, Theodore (1962), 'The Paliau movement in the Admiralty Islands, 1946–1954', *American Museum of Natural History Anthropological Papers* 49 (2), 206–421.

Selby, David (1963), *Itambu:* (Sydney: Currawong).

Service, Elman R. (1962), *Primitive Social Organization* (New York: Random House).

– (1971), *Cultural Evolutionism: Theory in Practice* (New York: Holt, Rinehart and Winston).

Shah, A. B., ed. (1968), *The Great Debate: Language Controversy and University Education* (Bombay: Lalvani Publishing House).

Shepard, W. J. (1933), 'Legislative assemblies: history and theory', *Encyclopedia of the Social Sciences* (New York: MacMillan Co.), 9, 355–361.

Shuy, Roger, and Ralph W. Fasold, eds. (1973), *Language Attitudes: Current Trends and Prospects* (Washington, D. C.: Georgetown University Press).

Smith, Vincent A., *et al.* (1961), *The Oxford History of India* (London: Oxford University Press). Third Edition.

Southworth, Franklin C. (1972), 'Linguistic masks for power: some relationships between semantic and social change'. Paper presented to the American Anthropological Association, Toronto.

Srivastava, Gopi Nath (1970), *The Language Controversy and the Minorities* (Delhi: Atma Ram and Sons).

Staats, Stephen (1970), 'Land and political violence in New Guinea', Reprint No. 2 (Melbourne: Papua-New Guinea Society).

– (1973), 'Australian post-war policy towards Papua-New Guinea, with specific reference to the promotion of political and economic development'. Paper presented to Joint Commonwealth Seminar, Center for Commonwealth Studies, Duke University, Durham, N. C.

Stanner, William E. (1953), *The South Seas in Transition* (Sydney: Australian Publishing Co.).

Steere, Edward (1964), *A Handbook of the Swahili Language* (London: The

Sheldon Press). Originally published 1870.

Steward, Julian H. (1955), *Theory of Culture Change* (Urbana: University of Illinois Press).

Strathern, Marilyn (1972a), *Official and Unofficial Courts: Legal Assumptions and Expectations in a Highlands Community*, New Guinea Research Bulletin 47 (Canberra: New Guinea Research Unit, Australian National University).

– (1972b) 'Absentee businessmen: the reaction at home to Hageners migrating to Port Moresby', *Oceania* 43, 19–39.

Sudnow, David, ed. (1972), *Studies in Social Interaction* (New York: Free Press).

Swartz, Marc (1965), 'Continuities in the Bena political system', *Southwestern Journal of Anthropology* 20, 241–253.

– (1966), 'Bases for compliance in Bena villages', in Marc Swartz, Victor Turner, and Arthur Tuden (eds.), *Political Anthropology* (Chicago: Aldine), 89–108.

Swartz, Marc, ed. (1968), *Local-Level Politics* (Chicago: Aldine).

Swartz, Marc, Victor Turner, and Arthur Tuden, eds. (1966), *Political Anthropology* (Chicago: Aldine).

Tambiah, S. J. (1967), 'The politics of language in India and Ceylon', *Modern Asian Studies* 1 (3), 215–240.

Tanner, R. E. S. (1970), 'The selective use of legal systems in East Africa', in R. E. S. Tanner, *Three Studies in East African Criminology* (Uppsala: Scandinavian Institute of African Studies), 35–49.

Taylor, Charles Lewis, and Michael C. Hudson (1972), *World Handbook of Political and Social Indicators* (New Haven: Yale University Press). Second Edition.

Taylor, J. Clagett (1963), *The Political Development of Tanganyika* (Stanford: Stanford University Press).

Temu, Peter (1966), *Uchumi Bora* (Nairobi: Oxford University Press).

Territory of Papua and New Guinea (1970), *Departmental Standing Instructions: General Field Administration*, Volume I (Port Moresby: Division of District Administration, Department of the Administrator).

Tessler, Mark A., William M. O'Barr, and David H. Spain (1973), *Tradition and Identity in Changing Africa* (New York: Harper & Row).

Tinker, Hugh (1968), *The Foundations of Local Self-Government in India, Pakistan and Burma* (New York: Frederick A. Praeger).

Tomasetti, W. E. (Forthcoming), 'Interpretation problems in district administration', in S. A. Wurm (ed.), *Current Trends in the Study of Study of New Guinea Area Languages* (The Hague: Mouton).

Topan, Farouk (1971), 'Swahili literature plays a social role', *Africa Report* 16, 28–30.

Tordoff, William (1967), *Government and Politics in Tanzania* (Nairobi: East Africa Publishing House).

Traugott, Elizabeth Closs (1973), 'Some thoughts on natural syntactic processes', in C.-J. N. Bailey and R. W. Shuy (eds.), *New Ways of Analyzing Variation in English* (Washington: Georgetown University Press), 313–322.

Treadgold, Michael L. (1971) 'Bougainville copper and the economic development of Papua–New Guinea', *Economic Record* 47 (118), 186–202.

Tudor, Judy, ed. (1969), *The Handbook of Papua New Guinea* (Sydney: Pacific Publications). Sixth Edition.

Turner, Victor W. (1957), *Schism and Continuity in an African Society* (Manchester: Manchester University Press).

United Nations Trusteeship Council (1963), *Report of the United Nations Visiting Mission to the Trust Territories of Nauru and New Guinea 1962* (New York: United Nations).

U. S. Commission on Civil Rights (1961), *Voting* (Washington, D. C.: Government Printing Office).

– (1965), *Voting in Mississippi* (Washington, D. C.: Government Printing Office).

– (1968), *Political Participation* (Washington, D. C.: Government Printing Office).

– (1971), *Mexican-American Education Study* (Washington, D. C.: Government Printing Office).

Vagts, Detlev (1961), 'The corporate alien: definitional questions in federal restraints on foreign enterprise', *Harvard Law Review* 74 (8), 1489–1551.

Van der Veur, Paul W. (1965), 'The first two meetings of the House of Assembly', in D. Bettison, C. Hughes, and P. van der Veur (eds.), *The Papua New Guinea Elections, 1964* (Canberra: Australian National University Press), 445–504.

Waddell, Eric (1972), *The Mound Builders: Agricultural Practices, Environment, and Society in the Central Highlands of New Guinea* (Seattle: University of Washington Press).

Wallace, Anthony F. C. (1961), *Culture and Personality* (New York: Random House).

Watson, James B. (1965), 'The Kainantu open and South Markham special electorates', in D. Bettison, C. Hughes, and P. van der Veur (eds.), *The Papua New Guinea Elections, 1964* (Canberra: Australian National University Press), 91–119.

Weiner, Myron (1967), *Party Building in a New Nation* (Chicago: University of Chicago Press).

Weinreich, U., William Labov, and M. Herzog (1968), 'Empirical foundations for a theory of language change', in W. P. Lehmann and G. Malkiel (eds.), *Directions for Historical Linguistics* (Austin: University of Texas Press), 97–195.

Weston, A. B. (1965), 'Law in Swahili: problems in developing a national language', *Swahili* 35 (2), 2–13.

– (1969), *Swahili Legal Terms* (Dar es Salaam: Government Printing Office).

Whiteley, Wilfred (1968), 'Ideal and reality in national language policy: a case study from Tanzania', in Joshua A. Fishman, Charles A. Ferguson, and Jyotirindra Das Gupta (eds.), *Language Problems of Developing Nations* (New York: John Wiley and Sons), 327–344.

– (1969), *Swahili: The Rise of a National Language* (London: Methuen and Company).

– (1971a), 'Some factors influencing language policies in eastern Africa', in Joan Rubin and Björn H. Jernudd (eds.), *Can Language Be Planned?* (Honolulu: University Press of Hawaii), 141–158.

– (1971b), *Language Use and Social Change* (London: Oxford University Press).

Wiener, Norbert (1954), *The Human Use of Human Beings: Cybernetics and Society* (Garden City, N. Y.: Doubleday). Second Edition.

Wolfers, Edward P. (1967), 'Death of a politician'. Letter to the executive director, Institute of Current World Affairs, May 15, 1967.

– (1968), 'The 1968 elections – iv: the candidates'. Letter to the executive director, Institute of Current Wolrd Affairs, December 9, 1968.

Wolff, Hans (1959), 'Intelligibility and inter-ethnic attitudes', *Anthropological Linguistics* 1 (3), 34–49.

Wurm, S. A. (1960), 'The changing linguistic picture of New Guinea', *Oceania* 31, 121–136.

– (1966), 'Language and literacy', in E. K. Fisk (ed.), *New Guinea on the Threshold* (Canberra: Australian National University Press), 135–148.

– (1971a), 'The Papuan linguistic situation', in T. A. Sebeok (ed.), *Current Trends in Linguistics* 8 (The Hague: Mouton), 514–657

– (1971b), 'New Guinea highlands pidgin', *Pacific Linguistics*, Series D, No. 3.

Wurm, S. A., and D. Laycock (1961), 'The question of language and dialect in New Guinea', *Oceania* 32, 128–143.

Yadav, R. K. (1966), *The Indian Language Problem* (Delhi: National Publishing House).

Biographical Notes

Mahadev L. APTE teaches anthropology at Duke University. Born in India, he received his doctorate from the University of Wisconsin in 1962. His reasearch in India has included studies of linguistic acculturation and pidginization processes in Bombay (1959, 1964–65), and Tamilnad (1971–72). In addition to several articles based on this research, he edited, with Franklin Southworth, a special issue of the *International Journal of Dravidian Linguistics* (January, 1974) devoted to contact and convergence in South Asian languages. Current research interests also include ethnography of humor, anthropology through literature, and ethnicity.

F. G. BAILEY teaches anthropology at the University of California at San Diego. He received his Ph. D. from the University of Manchester in 1954. During the 1950s, he conducted extensive anthropological research in Orissa, India (1952–56, 1959) where he focused on the topics of politics and social change; more recently he has been studying social change in Cuneo, Italy (1968). His many publications include *Caste and the Economic Frontier* (1957), *Tribe, Caste, and Nation* (1960), *Politics and Social Change* (1963), *Strategems and Spoils* (1969), as well as two collections which he edited, *Gifts and Poisons* (1971) and *Debate and Compromise* (1973).

Henry L. BRETTON is distinguished professor of political science at the State University of New York at Brockport. After receiving his Ph. D. from the University of Michigan in 1951, he studied party politics and elections in West Germany (1953–57). Since 1956 his interests in African politics have taken him to Ghana, Nigeria, Ivory

Coast, Senegal, and East Africa where his research has focused on political thought, power and influence, and power and stability. In addition to several articles, he has published *Stresemann and the Revision of Versailles* (1953), *Power and Stability in Nigeria* (1962), *The Rise and Fall of Kwame Nkrumah* (1967), and most recently *Power and Politics in Africa* (1973). He has taught at the Universities of Ghana and Nairobi.

Eugene A. CONTI is a Ph. D. candidate in anthropology at Duke University. In addition to language and politics in developing countries, his interests include the economics of subsistence in the Appalachian region of the United States.

Jyotirindra DAS GUPTA teaches political science at the University of California at Berkeley. Born in India, he received his doctorate at Berkeley in 1966. His research has focused primarily upon language conflicts, ethnic politics, and the politics of planning in India. Since 1964, he has made several research trips to India. From 1969–72, he was engaged in an international language planning project in collaboration with Charles A. Ferguson, Joshua A. Fishman, Joan Rubin, and Björn Jernudd. In addition to a number of articles and contributions to symposia, he has published a major work on language politics in India: *Language Conflict and National Development* (1970).

Frederick DUBOW teaches sociology at Northwestern University. He received his Ph. D. from the University of California at Berkeley in 1973. In 1969–70, he studied local courts and law and politics in Tanzania and, since 1973, has been engaged in the study of community security in chicago. In addition to several papers based on his Tanzanian research, he edited, with Amatai Etzioni, *Theory and Method: An Introduction to the Comparative Method* (1970).

Barbara W. FLYNN teaches history at Union College. She is a Ph. D. candidate in Indian history at Duke University. Research for her dissertation, *The Communalization of Politics: Indian Political Activity 1926–1929,* was conducted in London and New Delhi in 1971–72.

John M. FLYNN is a Ph. D. candidate in political science at Duke University. He is completing his dissertation on administrative reform in the Indian civil service for which he conducted research in London and New Delhi in 1971–72.

Malcolm E. JEWELL teaches political science at the University of Kentucky. He received his doctorate from Pennsylvania State University in 1958. He served as editor of the *Midwest Journal of Political Science.* His extensive research on legislatures has resulted in the publication of numerous articles and symposia contributions as well as *Legislative Representation in the Contemporary South* (1967) and, with Samuel C. Patterson, *The Legislative Process in the United States* (1966).

Robert L. KIDDER teaches sociology at Temple University. He received his Ph. D. from Northwestern in 1971. In 1969–70, he studied social process and litigation in the urban courts of Bangalore, South India. Since 1973, he has been conducting a study of crime rates in Philadelphia. He is a member of the Committee on Asian Law of the Association for Asian Studies in the United States. He has published several papers based on his Indian research.

Ranier LANG teaches anthropology and linguistics at the Australian National University where he is a member of the New Guinea Research Unit. He received his Ph. D. from the Australian National University in 1971. In addition to extensive linguistic and anthropological research in Papua New Guinea since 1967, he has also studied Northern Paiute peoples of Walker River Reservation, Nevada (1965). He is the author of several papers.

Arnold H. LEIBOWITZ is an attorney in Washington, D. C. and is President of the Institute of International Law and Economic Development. He teaches in the Graduate School of Business and Public Administration at Howard University. In addition to his long-term interest in United States legislation involving language, he has studied jurisprudence at the University of Heidelberg (1956–57). He has published several papers related to language policies and language and the legal process in the United States.

Jean F. O'BARR teaches political science at Duke University, where she is also director of the programs of continuing education and career development. She received her Ph. D. from Northwestern in 1970. In the late 1960s, she spent eighteen months studying local party organization and political participation in rural Tanzania. She is planning a study of women in politics. Her publications include several papers on local-level politics in Tanzania, and, with Joel Samoff, she has edited *Cell Leaders in Tanzania,* to be published by East African Publishing House.

William M. O'BARR teaches anthropology at Duke University. He received his Ph. D. from Northwestern in 1969. His African research concentrated on the ethnography of the Pare peoples of Tanzania (1967–68, 1972). He is now studying language variation in American trial courtrooms. His publications include *Tradition and Identity in Changing Africa* (1973), with Mark Tessler and David Spain, and *Survey Research in Africa* (1973) of which he was a co-editor. In collaboration with Gerald Hartwig, he prepared *The Student Africanist's Handbook* (forthcoming) and is currently preparing a volume for the *Ethnographic Survey of Africa.*

Joan RUBIN teaches sociolinguistics at Georgetown University. She received her Ph. D. from Yale University in 1963. She has done extensive research in linguistics, including problems of machine translation, bilingualism, and language planning. She has worked in Paraguay (1960–61, 1965, 1967), Hawaii (1968–69), Indonesia (1969–72), and the continental United States (1956–60). Her publications include several papers on problems of development and language planning, a study of national bilingualism in Paraguay (1968), as well as *Can Language Be Planned?* (1971), edited with Björn Jernudd, and *Language Planning: Current Issues and Research* (1973), edited with Roger Shuy.

Richard F. SALISBURY teaches anthropology at McGill University. He received his Ph. D. from the Australian National University in 1957. His extensive research in economic development has included field studies in New Guinea (1952–53, 1961, 1967, 1971), Guyana (1964–66), and the Canadian North (1971–73). In addition to many articles and books in the anthropology of development, he has published several papers on sociolinguistics in New Guinea.

Gillian SANKOFF teaches anthropology at Université de Montréal. She received her Ph. D. from McGill University in 1968. Her research has included studies of Buang language and ethnography (1966–67), multilingualism (1968), Tok Pisin in Papua New Guinea (1971), and of spoken French in Montreal (1971–73). She has published several papers on Tok Pisin and on sociolinguistic topics.

Steven STAATS is a Ph. D. candidate in the Department of Political Economy at the University of Toronto. After receiving an M. A. degree in Political Science from Duke University in 1973, he became a Canadian Commonwealth Fellow at the University of Toronto. He plans doctoral research in the German Democratic Republic.

Marc J. SWARTZ teaches anthropology at the University of California at San Diego. Prior to receiving his Ph. D. from Harvard in 1958, he conducted field research on Romonum Truk Atoll in the East Caroline Islands (1955–56). In 1962–63 and 1965, he worked among the Bena of the Southern Tanzanian Highlands. He edited *Political Anthropology* (1966), with V. W. Turner and A. Tuden, and *Local-Level Politics* (1968). He is the author of several papers on political anthropological topics.

[illegible] articles and books on the anthropology of development. He has published several papers on [illegible] in New Guinea.

[illegible] teaches anthropology at University of [illegible]. She received her Ph.D. from McGill University in [illegible]. [illegible] and [illegible] (1989). [illegible] she has published several papers on [illegible] anthropology and [illegible] topics.

[illegible] is [illegible] in the Department of [illegible] at the University of [illegible]. [illegible] Political Science from [illegible] 1973 [illegible] Research Fellow [illegible]. He [illegible] in the [illegible] public.

[illegible] anthropology at the University of [illegible]. [illegible] of the Southern [illegible] Highlands [illegible] [illegible] and [illegible] on [illegible] and [illegible].

Index of Names

Index of Subjects